Britain Can Take It

D1386597

For Arthur Marwick

FCH LIBRARY
Swindon Road, Cheltenham
Gloucestershire GL50 4AZ
Telephone: 01242 714600

UNIVERSITY OF
GLOUCESTERSHIRE
at Cheltenham and Gloucester

WEEK LOAN

3464 11/2012

© Anthony Aldgate and Jeffrey Richards 1986, 1994

First edition published in hardback 1986 (by Basil Blackwell)
Second edition published in paperback 1994

Edinburgh University Press Ltd
22 George Square, Edinburgh

British Library Cataloguing in Publication Data

Aldgate, Anthony
Britain can take it: the British cinema in the
Second World War.
1. World War, 1939—1945 — Propaganda   2. Radio
in propaganda   3. Moving-pictures in propaganda
I. Title   II. Richards, Jeffrey
940.54'88   D810.P6

ISBN 0 7486 0508 5

Library of Congress Cataloging in Publication Data

Aldgate, Anthony.
Britain can take it.
Filmography: p.
Includes index.
1. World War, 1939—1945 — Motion pictures and
the war.   2. Moving pictures — Great Britain — History —
20th Century.   I. Richards, Jeffrey.   II. Title.
D743.23.A43   1985   1994   791.43'09'09358   85—15679

Typeset by Pioneer, Perthshire
Printed in Great Britain by
Bell and Bain Ltd, Glasgow

Contents

Acknowledgements

Chapters 1, 2, 4, 6, 8, 11 and 13 of this book were the work of Anthony Aldgate and chapters 3, 5, 7, 9, 10, 12 and 14 were the work of Jeffrey Richards. The authors would like to thank the following for advice, assistance and information: Jane and Hannah Aldgate, Michael Balfour, Roy Boulting, Elaine Burrows, Sidney Cole, Stephen Constantine, Thorold Dickinson, Julian Fox, Philip French, Sidney Gilliat, John Gilman, Ronald Howard, John Illingworth, Michael Jubb, Herbert Marshall, John Marshall, Robert Murphy, Gerald Pollinger, Vincent Porter, James C. Robertson, Wendy Simpson, Michelle Snapes, Jeff Walden, Victoria Wegg-Prosser and Linda Wood. Thanks are also due to the staff of the Public Record Office, Kew; BBC Written Archives, Caversham; Newspaper Library, Colindale; British Museum Reading Room; the Stills and Viewing Departments of the National Film Archive; the British Film Institute Library; Birmingham Reference Library; London Library; Lancaster University Inter-Library Loans Department; the Open University Library; the Imperial War Museum. The British Academy generously provided a grant to facilitate research, as did the Arts Faculty of the Open University. The poem 'For Johnny', from John Pudney's *Collected Poems*, published by G. B. Putnam, is quoted by permission of David Higham Associates. Film stills appear by courtesy of the Stills Division of the National Film Archive and the British Film Institute.

Preface to the Paperback Edition

For this paperback edition of *Britain Can Take It* we are reprinting the original text as it stands since we have found no reason to alter our interpretations of the individual films or our perspective on British cinema in the Second World War. But we are adding two new chapters at the end which round out the original book. Chapter 13 by Anthony Aldgate is devoted to *Tunisian Victory* and explores the tensions between British and American documentary-makers and chapter 14 by Jeffrey Richards reassesses *Ships With Wings* in the light of the post-war rewriting of British wartime cinema history. Both chapters originally appeared as articles in the *Historical Journal of Film, Radio and Television* to which we are grateful for permission to reprint. Stills from *Tunisian Victory* appear by courtesy of the Trustees of the Imperial War Museum.

Since the book first appeared, several excellent studies have been published which can usefully be read in conjunction with this book. Among them are: Antonia Lant, *Blackout: Reinventing Women for Wartime British Cinema* (Princeton University Press); Philip M. Taylor (ed.), *Britain and the Cinema in the Second World War* (Macmillan Press); Clive Coultass, *Images for Battle* (Associated University Presses); Robert F. Moss, *The Films of Carol Reed* (Macmillan Press); Jeffrey Richards, *Thorold Dickinson: the man and his films* (Croom Helm); Robert Murphy, *Realism and Tinsel: cinema and society in Britain 1939–1948* (Routledge); Geoffrey Macnab, *J. Arthur Rank and the British Film Industry* (Routledge) and Jeffrey Richards and Dorothy Sheridan (eds), *Mass-Observation at the Movies* (Routledge).

1

The British Cinema
during the Second World War

The Second World War began on an inauspicious note for the British cinema. With the outbreak of war on 3 September 1939, all cinemas in Britain, along with other such venues as theatres and sports arenas, were closed. The fear of mass slaughter in crowded places and wholesale destruction by enemy bombers accounted for an Order in Council which brought about their forcible closure. But as the air raids failed to materialize and no German bombers appeared immediately on the horizon, the government relented in the face of commercial and public pressure, and proceeded to give local authorities the freedom to exercise their own discretion in the matter.

Most places of entertainment and recreation began to reopen after a while. On 11 September, cinemas outside of the urban districts were reopened and from 15 September, the cinemas in city areas were allowed to open, until 10 pm, with the exception of those in the West End of London which were to shut at 6 pm. On 4 October, they too were allowed to remain open in the evening, albeit on a weekly rota basis, but by 4 November, all cinemas were permitted to remain open until 11 pm.[1]

Inevitably, however, as the war progressed the exhibitors had to contend with more than just government restrictions, as indeed did the distribution and production sectors of the industry. Bomb damage, the shortage of equipment, the call up of key staff to the services or their loss to employment on vital war work, the need to maintain adequate air raid precautions, combined with an embargo on cinema construction or even the completion of unfinished cinemas, all conspired to make life exceedingly difficult for the exhibitors. A growing shortage of film supply exacerbated by the wartime conditions was the biggest problem to confront the distributors, who estimated that they needed 600 long films a year for the British cinemas to operate successfully.

The production arm of the industry was presented with similar difficulties: shortage of materials, loss of personnel, and, last but not least, the requisitioning by government of vast amounts of studio space for war purposes such as storage or shadow factory accommodation. Two-thirds of film technicians were called up, in time, and between 1939 and 1942 the number of studios in operation as such diminished from 22 (using 65 sound stages) to 9 (with 30 sound stages). Pinewood, Elstree, Sound City and Amalgamated — with 7 stages each and a total floor space of 444,000 square feet at their disposal — were among the studios lost to feature film production. And, finally, all realms of the film industry were to suffer the effects of increased taxation in the form of an Excess Profits Tax and an Entertainments Tax, which was raised three times during the war and by 1945 amounted to 36 per cent of gross receipts. Seat prices also rose as a consequence.[2]

Yet despite all these problems, the period of the Second World War was, as one commentator has observed, 'a time of relative prosperity for the British film industry',[3] and the reasons why that proved to be so are not difficult to fathom. There were approximately 4,800 cinemas in existence at the outbreak of war and though a number of them were forced to close over the next six years, it has been estimated that 'the maximum number closed at any one stage of the war was probably never more than 10 per cent of the total'.[4] To combat the shortfall in the supply of films (there was undoubtedly a considerable decline in the number of long films being registered, with 638 registered in the year immediately before the war but only 480 on average for each of the war years), the distributors suggested that the amount of programme changes be reduced, and more use was made of such simple expedients as the re-issuing of old films and giving some of the new films an extended run. The variety of films on offer in cinema programmes was thereby much reduced but by such means the overall effect was that 'there was practically no falling-off in the actual gross footage of film exhibited throughout the country'.[5]

Of course film production in Britain itself was particularly badly hit. Some 103 long films were registered as being of British origin for 1939 (and that was when domestic film production was still suffering the after-effects of the 1937 slump in the industry, 228 films had been registered in the year before). But during the ensuing war years domestic film production averaged just 69 films per year, with 108 films being registered as British in the best year, 1940, and 46 in the worst, 1942. The exigencies of war took their toll, but even though the production sector was inevitably forced to contract in those years, the point has been well made that 'what remained of it was healthy', and, significantly, 'British films enjoyed unprecedented popularity and both the critics and the trade acknowledged a great improvement in quality'.[6]

The war was definitely to prove 'a golden age' as far as domestic films were concerned. In short, British films continued to play an important and necessary part in ensuring that cinemagoing in Britain remained, as it had been throughout the 1930s, an 'essential social habit'.[7]

Indeed, if anything, the appeal of the cinema was enhanced overall during the war years as people found that other sorts of amusement were either denied them or severely curtailed, and that there was generally a scarcity of things upon which they might spend their money. It provided an easy, convenient and vital form of relaxation, in part, and it became, as one notable historian of the era, Angus Calder, has put it, 'far and away the most popular entertainment'.[8] Despite the increases in seat prices, the average weekly attendance rose from an estimated 19 million in 1939 to over 30 million in 1945, and gross box office receipts nearly trebled in that time.

Doubtless this massive rise in what were already large weekly audiences must be partly attributed to the fact that a good many people were going to the cinema who might not otherwise have been inclined to do so. It attracted some people who had never been before. But, as the Wartime Social Survey of 1943 confirmed, the actual composition of the cinemagoing audience changed very little, in all, and, once again, it remained substantially the same as it was during the 1930s. In large measure, the period of the war served only to accentuate the prevailing trends in cinemagoing habits.[9]

The Wartime Social Survey, entitled *The Cinema Audience*, was based on a small sample of the civilian population and it was conducted during the months of June and July, which were traditionally held to be 'quiet' months by the film trade and when it was expected that potential customers would prefer to be outside enjoying the good weather rather than indoors. Despite its obvious limitations, it was quite a sophisticated survey for its day and apart from spotlighting general trends it proceeded to isolate and to analyse cinemagoers by economic group, by education, by occupation and by location. Essentially, it found that 70 per cent of adults claimed they sometimes went to the cinema and 32 per cent overall, went at least once a week. Younger adults attended more often than older people and, not surprisingly, children more frequently than adults.

The lower income groups (who were classified as earning a wage rate of £5 or less per week) and those with only an elementary education (with no secondary, technical or university education) frequented the cinema most often. And relatively high proportions of factory workers, clerical and distributive workers went to the cinema more than once a week whereas managerial and professional workers went less often. As was to be expected, town dwellers went to the cinema more than people living in the country, due in no small part to the problems of access and availability of cinemas. More people went to the cinema in the North, North West, the Midlands and Scotland than did so in the South East, the South West and East Anglia.

Finally, the survey compared the average cinema attendances per month with those people among the sample who saw a morning newspaper, bought a weekly or monthly magazine, or read a book. Here it found that the cinema reached appreciably more people than did those other media of visual communication, particularly among the lower income groups. 'In general', it concluded, 'it may be said that the larger groups of the population are relatively better represented in the cinema audience than they are in the publics reached by other visual publicity media such as newspapers and books'.[10]

Of course little of this would have been unknown to members of the film trade and few of the Wartime Social Survey's findings regarding the cinema audience would have taken them by surprise. They would probably have argued that it merely confirmed what they knew already from experience, but then it was not intended for the industry. The survey was undertaken for the Ministry of Information and its purpose was solely to provide the Ministry with further information, so that it might learn more about 'what sort of people go to the cinema and how often they go' and be better acquainted overall with the nature, composition and habits of the undoubtedly vast cinemagoing audience. The MoI also recognized full well that 'The cinema is an important publicity medium', not least in wartime, and this survey was yet another sign of the extent to which the cinema figured prominently in its thinking and planning. In addition, as we shall see, Mass-Observation regularly briefed the MoI on the subject as indeed, on occasions, did the Home Intelligence Division.[11]

The story of the British cinema in the Second World War is inextricably linked with that of the Ministry of Information. It was the Ministry's function, after all, to 'present the national case to the public at home and abroad', and to this end it was responsible for 'the preparation and issue of National Propaganda', as well as for 'the issue of "news" and for such control of information issued to the public as may be demanded by the needs of security'.[12] Given that task, clearly the cinema was always going to be of considerable use in furthering the national cause generally and, on the home front especially, it was ideally suited to help in sustaining civilian morale. The MoI appreciated as much, even if some historians seem subsequently to have ignored that fact, and the papers and minutes of its Policy Committee (whose job was 'to formulate and to approve departmental policy over the whole range of the Ministry's domestic and overseas functions'), its Planning Committee (which was designated 'to work out means for carrying out domestic policy and to recommend courses of action to sustain civilian morale'), and, inevitably, its Films

Division, all provide evidence of the way in which the cinema was enlisted to serve the cause of national propaganda.[13]

The Ministry of Information has usually been condemned for taking an inordinate amount of time to get into its stride. And certainly there is much to support the charge that 'in the early stages' of the war, as the historian Arthur Marwick recounts, the Ministry was 'often dilatory, hesitant and downright contradictory in its policies'.[14] The frequent changes in the administration and the fact that there were four ministers in the initial two years of the department's existence did not exactly help in formulating a consistent propaganda policy. Lord Macmillan was in charge from September 1939 to January 1940, Sir John Reith until May 1940, Duff Cooper until July 1941, and Brendan Bracken took over thereafter (and was to survive in the post until May 1945). But whatever the strengths and weaknesses of the various personalities involved, the changes were generally more the effect than the cause of the problem. There was also inefficiency, mistakes and blunders were committed, and the Ministry was rightly found guilty of being an occasional source of irritation rather than reassurance to the public. It earned the nickname 'Ministry of Dis-information' during this early period and the press roundly attacked it over such matters as the 'Cooper's Snoopers' affair, when a survey team was criticized for prying into people's private lives and upsetting the public. It was some time before a more positive and sensible attitude was adopted by the MoI and only gradually did it assume an authoritative position and establish good working relationships with the media and the public alike.

Similar charges were laid at the door of the Films Division in the opening years of the war, though with less reason. Once again there were changes at the top — Sir Joseph Ball was in charge until the end of 1939, Sir Kenneth Clark took over until April 1940 and, subsequently, Jack Beddington was in command until 1946. The Films Division was necessarily affected by the malaise which permeated the whole of the Ministry in the first year or so of the war, but it is not strictly accurate to suggest that 'its activities until the spring of 1940 were largely without purpose and effect'.[15] Plans were made and laid in that time, a good deal was attempted, more so perhaps than in many other sections of the MoI, and the respective directors were pretty clear about their intentions for the Films Division, even if their priorities did not always accord with what certain interested parties in the film industry would have liked to see adopted.

Sir Joseph Ball, for instance, clearly favoured what he described as the 'leaders' of the British film industry, by which he specifically meant the newsreel companies and some key producers like Alexander Korda.[16] Even before the onset of war he had gone out of his way to cultivate relations with the heads of the newsreel companies, in particular. And the result was an invitation to the Newsreel Association of Great Britain to join the discussions with the Home Secretary 'in regard to the setting up of a skeleton Ministry of Information which would become effective immediately in the event of an outbreak of war'. The newsreels were considered to be 'of no little importance' and their advice was sought on matters 'such as availability of film stock, requirements as to the importation of celluloid, methods of transport and distribution in wartime, and any other particulars that the newsreel companies thought would be useful'.[17]

Once installed as head of the Films Division, Ball continued to afford his favourites preferential treatment. Korda was given considerable help by way of 'technical facilities' on *The Lion Has Wings*, the first feature-length film of the war. The film was not officially commissioned but it was officially sanctioned and the MoI proceeded to pocket some of the profits for the assistance it had provided. The newsreels received a variety of commissions and undoubtedly enjoyed one of their most influential periods of the war. Ball, though, obviously had little time for the work of Britain's documentary film movement, which had earned a considerable reputation in some quarters during the 1930s. Its mentor, John Grierson, was in Canada from the outset of the war but a good many of its members and film-makers were around, active and keen to contribute to the national effort. Ball was not interested in what they had to offer and this, together with his party political affiliations (he had been engaged at Conservative Central Office as Director of Publicity from 1927 to 1929, and Director of the Research Department from 1929 to 1939, as well as being Deputy Director of the National Publicity Bureau from 1934 to 1939), was enough to damn him in their eyes.[18]

Much more was expected on the documentary front from his successor, Sir Kenneth Clark, although the new-found *Documentary News Letter*, in its first edition for January 1940, was emphatic that his arrival should be 'welcomed by everyone save the less imaginative of Wardour Street'.[19] Clark was indeed soon circulating within the Ministry a wide-ranging and imaginative 'Programme for film propaganda', which envisaged using all three kinds of films — feature films, documentaries and newsreels — as part of a concerted effort to put across 'The principles underlying British wartime propaganda'. Commissions were forthcoming for documentary production and, during his time at the Films Division, arrangements were set in motion to embark upon the first feature film of the war, *49th Parallel*, to be directly financed by the MoI.

However, Clark was not in the post of director long enough to see his plans come to fruition: he was promoted after just four months. In truth, a lot of them did not do so. Many of the documentaries failed to materialise and *49th Parallel* only saw the light of day after considerable setbacks.

But, if nothing else, Clark opened the doors of the Films Division to more than just the elite that Ball had fostered. He created a healthy atmosphere which prompted film-makers to approach the division with ideas and some of them subsequently acknowledged the impetus he provided to their work.[20] Furthermore, after his promotion, he continued to show an interest, and a good deal of sense, in the Ministry's discussions on the film industry. At Policy Committee meetings in June 1940, when the question of the 'Compulsory exhibition of films' was raised, the point was made that Defence Regulation 55 might be appropriate, if necessary, to enforce the exhibition in the cinemas of films which the Ministry deemed essential viewing. Sir Kenneth Clark argued against the proposal, preferring instead that a deal be made with the Cinematograph Exhibitors' Association whereby they would agree to set aside, voluntarily, something like 10 minutes in each programme for 'such films as we required'. To invite cooperation rather than to induce co-option was the best move, and the CEA duly obliged.[21]

Fortunately, cooperation was also the hallmark of Jack Beddington's term as director and under his supervision the Films Division made great advances. He undoubtedly benefited from the spirit of openness which Clark had brought to the section and from the fact that he was in the job long enough to see plans and projects through to completion. But he was also very much his own man and he had considerable professional experience of publicity and public relations — he was previously assistant general manager and director of publicity of Shell Mex and BP Ltd. He, too, was well received within the documentary ranks. The *Documentary News Letter* commented that 'He will bring to his new post both taste and a sense of need — two qualities only too rarely associated with commercial ability'.[22] For the most part, they were not to be disappointed.

At Beddington's instigation, in June 1940, the programme of 'theatrical distribution' (for films to be shown in commercial cinemas) and 'non-theatrical distribution' (films to be shown by 16 mm mobile units outside the normal cinema circuits, in church halls, factory canteens, and the like), was reorganized and expanded. He brought in Ian Dalrymple to head production at the GPO Film Unit, on Alberto Cavalcanti's departure to Ealing Studios, and in August 1940 it was resuscitated, renamed the Crown Film Unit, and thereafter given a more significant part to play in the propaganda process. And when, subsequently, the Select Committee on National Expenditure threatened the whole documentary programme (as well as the Ministry's interest in feature films), and the Treasury worried about the spiralling costs of individual films such as *Western Approaches*, it was Beddington who came to the rescue. He was instrumental in devising the means whereby Select Committee and Treasury strictures could either be neatly circumvented or fruitfully confronted, by documentarists and feature film producers alike.

Yet for all that he was an ally to the documentary film-makers and sympathetic to their ideas, he was by no means a total convert to their cause and he kept them firmly in their place. Beddington certainly provided them with a considerable amount of work. It has been estimated that 74 per cent of all the films produced or commissioned by the Films Division for British distribution between August 1940 and the end of the war, were 'either written, directed or produced (or all three) by members of the documentary film movement'.[23] But as one of their number, Paul Rotha, subsequently pointed out, the more politically committed members among their ranks, 'the makers of what we may call the social and informational documentaries', were largely confined to producing films for the non-theatrical field where audiences were comparatively small and where, in effect, they could do no harm.[24] They were, in short, marginalized and Beddington reserved his greatest effort and interest for those large, prestigious feature-length documentaries like *Target for Tonight*, *Desert Victory* and *Western Approaches*, more obviously inspirational and celebratory productions which received a wide commercial distribution in the everyday cinemas.

By the same token, another documentary film-maker, Harry Watt (who also moved on to do feature work at Ealing, with Cavalcanti), has complained that Beddington was just as eager as any director of the Films Division to be 'in with the newsreels'. When the newsreel companies expressed an interest in some of the material he had shot for inclusion in *Dover Front Line*, in 1940, Beddington handed it over to them on the spot arguing that 'the newsreels were very important for propaganda and so on'. Watt had little say in the matter and was left without the climax he had intended for his film.[25]

The documentary film movement did indeed have a lot to offer the wartime cinema and it was finally used to great effect. But the Films Division, for one, extracted from it what could most fruitfully be employed in the propaganda effort and showed scant interest in the rest. When some documentarists pressed for more of a part to play, for instance, they were curtly rejected. Paul Addison has put the matter in that regard most succinctly:

> The leaders of the documentary film movement, notably Basil Wright, challenged the Films Division of the Ministry of Information to adopt a propaganda policy, by which they meant a set of war aims in line with their own left-wing inclinations: not surprisingly, no such policy was adopted.[26]

The Films Division was quite prepared to engage politically motivated film-makers. In fact, it was suggested in some quarters of the MoI that 'The greater proportion of persons likely to be of use to the Ministry in a creative capacity would be of a left-wing tendency'. But the willingness to recruit left-wingers was invariably tempered by reminders that 'it was necessary to pay some attention to public opinion', especially when the Ministry received occasional 'complaints of left-wing bias'.[27] Consequently, the role assigned to the documentarists was very much the role that the MoI wanted them to play.

Similarly, the commercial cinema in general assimilated as much of the documentary influence as served its own best interests. There can be no doubt that once again it made an impact, not least on such as Ealing Studios, where imported directors like Cavalcanti and Watt had a considerable effect upon the content and style of the films which were made during the war. But, as Charles Barr has elaborated, 'There was no special political or aesthetic *rigour* in the documentary tradition which created a barrier to its easy assimilation by a commercial studio'; and, 'Perhaps the main influence was in the areas of: location shooting, editing techniques, *sober* narratives'.[28]

Of course there was more to film propaganda than just documentary films. And nobody appreciated that fact better than Beddington. Indeed, when he attended the first of many meetings he had with the British Film Producers Association, Beddington went out of his way to stress that 'The Ministry held the opinion that any good British production could be regarded as "propaganda" even though the subject matter of the film could not in some cases be so described'. Such a statement begged as many questions as it answered — what, then, did the MoI construe as 'propaganda' and what constituted a 'good' film? Those questions would only be answered in the fullness of time, at subsequent meetings. But for all Beddington's apparent woolliness on this occasion, the commitment 'to give all possible aid' to every realm of British film production was evident none the less.[29]

The ways in which this was achieved have been described by various people who participated in the process. Sidney Bernstein, who was an honorary adviser to the Films Division, recalls the more practical features:

> The Ministry both advised the producers on the suitability of subjects which they had suggested, and proposed subjects which we thought would do good overseas. Whenever the Ministry had approved a subject we gave every help to the producer in obtaining facilities to make the film. For instance, we helped them get artists out of the services, we aided them to secure raw-stock, travel priorities and so on.[30]

Others have laid emphasis upon the importance of the MoI input at the level of ideas, not least in the formation of the Ideas Committee, which Paul Rotha has described in the following impressionistic terms:

> This consisted of a number of writers and directors from feature films and a

number of directors and others from documentary, who met round a table over beer and rather lousy sandwiches, once every fortnight. He [Beddington] started this about 1942, and it went on throughout the war. We would talk backwards and forwards across the table for about a couple of hours, and then we'd go down to the theatre and see some films, and this was a very healthy and excellent thing.[31]

When so described, the committee sounds like something of a hit-and-miss affair, and given the changes in film rank personnel which inevitably occurred (it included, at various times, Michael Balcon, Michael Powell, Sidney Gilliat, Rodney Ackland, Leslie Howard, Charles Frend and Anthony Asquith, among others), the wonder is that anything worth while emerged from it at all. But the procedure proved invaluable for it meant, as Vincent Porter has recently and rightly observed, that 'Here subjects and themes were discussed and checked against the MoI's information and propaganda policy'. In effect, it amounted to an 'informal pre-censorship of projects' and, in fact, 'the Ideas Committee was the fount of feature film production ideology'.[32]

By such means, the MoI was able to exert a measure of content control, in addition to that already exerted by such bodies as the British Board of Film Censors, sufficient to ensure that British film production in general, and not just the 'official' films, followed precisely the line that the Ministry wished it to follow in mobilising support for the war effort and in constructing the essential wartime ideology of popular national unity. Those, at least in the first instance, were the primary objectives.

The system suffered occasional setbacks, however, and it would not do to paint too harmonious a picture of the working relations between the MoI and the film industry. 'At one stage', Monja Danischewsky recounts, the producer Michael Balcon, 'fulminating against what he considered lack of Government policy and guidance, impatient of delays and eager to get on with what he felt to be an important job, publicly announced that he would no longer work with the MoI and that Ealing Studios would make their own propaganda films, short and long'.[33] And the producers Michael Powell and Emeric Pressburger caused an anxious moment or two in some quarters (not least for Winston Churchill), and a considerable amount of press publicity, over their intentions with regard to the production of *The Life and Death of Colonel Blimp*.[34]

But despite his criticisms, Balcon remained in the fold and his Ealing Studios more than most contributed significantly to the stock of propaganda films, both official and otherwise (the 1943 production of *San Demetrio London*, for example, which was dedicated 'To the officers and men of the British Merchant Navy', was based upon F. Tennyson Jesse's factual narrative for the MoI of the events it depicted). And for all Churchill and the War Office's fears, the film of *Blimp* did no harm to either the image or the standing of the British Army, as both Bracken and Beddington sensibly realised for their part. They were quite prepared to work with Powell and Pressburger once again and subsequently inspired them to make a film about Anglo-American relations, resulting in the 1946 production of *A Matter of Life and Death*. The system could stand the strain of these occasional differences because 'the fact was', as Arthur Marwick has concluded, almost all the film-makers were 'only too happy to follow the patriotic line'.[35] It was their country, after all, that was engaged in total war and a fight for survival.

In addition, though, the system worked because the film-makers found that the MoI did respond, in large measure, to their requests for help and assistance. In July 1942, for instance, C. M. Woolf used the occasion of his re-election as president at the annual general meeting of the British Film Producers Association to issue a call for 'fewer war films'. 'The public', he felt, 'was already getting tired of this type of picture and was asking for films which took their minds off the tragedy now taking place in the world'. And he concluded: 'They wanted some relaxation and entertainment from the stress of events and were entitled to have it'. In particular, Woolf pointed out that the MoI had been helpful in securing the release of artists from the services but usually only for war films of an obvious patriotic nature. Now he wanted to see them being released to participate in films with more of an 'entertainment' function to them.[36]

The MoI was not unaware of the value of that sort of 'entertainment' but, once again, it clearly had to be 'entertainment with a purpose'. Two years before Woolf made his speech, Sir Kenneth Clark had argued at a Policy Committee meeting that 'If we renounced interest in entertainment as such, we might be deprived of a valuable weapon for getting across our propaganda'.[37] Much the same thinking was in evidence in response to Woolf's speech, with a few important embellishments. The public's desire for 'entertainment' should be indulged and film producers helped accordingly. But as far as the MoI was concerned, the 'entertainment' so provided could still be utilized for propaganda purposes, it should also be uplifting, and it should be invested with 'quality' and thereby further increase the overall standard of British film production. The MoI was especially keen on enhancing the 'quality' of British cinema and providing what Beddington referred to as 'good' films, and it claimed some credit on this front. Ernest Thurtle, the Parliamentary secretary to the MoI, reported to the House of Commons in July 1942 that 'British film production has necessarily fallen in quantity during the war but I think it can be fairly claimed it has risen in quality'.[38] Subsequently, experienced observers like Thorold Dickinson, who worked for both the MoI and the commercial cinema, have argued that this success must be partly attributed to the procedure whereby 'The Films Division was given control of all negative film which was made available to producers only after approval of each script'. 'This veto, intelligently applied', he adds, 'raised the quality of the British product without removing the element of competition'.[39]

At the end of July 1942, the Films Division replied to the concern expressed by the BFPA about the prevalence of war films and it proceeded to spell out the conditions for providing help of the sort that had been requested. It expressed a 'willingness to support all types of pictures, including entertainment of a dramatic and comedy kind' but it insisted that they should be of 'the highest quality and neither maudlin, morbid nor nostalgic for the old ways and old days'. It recognized, furthermore, that 'A balance between war and non-war propaganda is desirable' but, in case anyone should fail to understand what was intended by its use of the term 'non-war propaganda', it stated that 'emphasis should be given to the positive virtues of British national characteristics and the democratic way of life'. It stressed that 'Realistic films about everyday life dealing with matters not directly about the war but featuring events in various phases of life in the factory, the mines and on the land etc., are advocated' and it promised, finally, that 'Special support will be given to the production of such films'.[40] As always, the Films Division was determined to exact a reward for its continued support. If the film producers were no longer so keen on the idea of making war films, because their audiences no longer welcomed them, the Films Division for its part was still intent on fostering a specific 'projection of Britain', because that was its function after all.

In the event, however, the cinema was more than 'simply a vehicle for the downward transmission of ideologies which uniformly supported official needs'.[41] Had that not been the case, then it would probably never have achieved the 'genuine rapport between film-makers and their audiences' which, commentators agree, so conspicuously distinguished the British cinema during the Second World War.[42] The cinema was a popular medium and it reflected the changing experiences of the population, evoked the currents of opinion in the country at large, and helped visibly to manifest a good many of the concerns that captured the public's thoughts and imagination in the years between 1939 and 1945.

Historians still argue about the question of the Second World War as a catalysis for change and about the extent to which it did in fact alter society. And they continue to engage in fruitful debate over how profound the changes were and how far the war was responsible for them. Some contend that 'The effect of the war was not to sweep society on to a new course, but to hasten its progress along the old grooves'.[43] Arthur Marwick, one of the proponents, indeed an architect, of the view that war effects change, has repeatedly outlined what he sees as the social consequences of the war for Britain: the war caused 'destruction and disruption', it brought damage, dislocation and upheaval but it also had a 'reconstructive' effect and led to a desire to rebuild better than before; the war was a 'test', it challenged society, imposed new stresses and strains, induced the collapse of some institutions and the transformation of others; the war invoked the 'participation' of underprivileged groups in the national effort and brought consequent social gains; and, finally, the war had a 'psychological' effect, it provided a great emotional experience, reinforced 'in-group' feelings and generally rendered change acceptable.[44]

Similarly, Paul Addison has charted the significance of the war in effecting political change. After the fall of France and the setback at Dunkirk, especially, there was a distinct swing to what might loosely be called 'the left' in Britain. This tide of popular feeling was not necessarily of a political character, nor indeed was it always channelled along Labour Party or Socialist lines, though clearly Labour was to be an immediate beneficiary in 1945. But it was 'directed against the Conservative Party' in so far as this represented, despite Chamberlain's departure and his replacement by Churchill, 'the so-called "Men of Munich", "the old gang", "Colonel Blimp" and similar diehard types'. It manifested itself, furthermore, in a feeling of revulsion against 'vested interests' and 'privilege', and in a general agreement that 'things are going to be different after the war'.

In addition to the movement in popular opinion, there was a change in thinking at the top. 'A massive new middle ground had arisen in politics', Addison continues, and a new political consensus evolved which was quite unlike the species of consensus that had existed before the war, when Baldwin and MacDonald adopted 'safety first' policies and resolved 'to prevent anything unusual from happening'. 'The new consensus of the war years was positive and purposeful' and there was a convergence of opinion in favour of 'pragmatic' economic reform and social amelioration. Beveridge and Keynes inspired those 'socially concerned professional people' who lent their weight to the reform programme, and though little was actually achieved during the war in the way of new laws, except on family allowances and education, with such as Butler's 1944 Education Act, nevertheless much of the ground was prepared by the time the Labour Party came to power in 1945.[45]

As one might expect, the evidence proffered by the British cinema does not provide an easy or obvious answer to the overarching question of war and change, any more than does the other evidence put forward by those eminent historians engaged in the debate. But it does bear eloquent witness to the fact that many people thought profound changes were afoot in society, born largely of the country's wartime experiences, and that these changes could be beneficial. It also provides evidence in abundance of the desire and commitment to build 'a better world' once the war had been won. Finally, it is clear that the cinema played a positive and purposeful role in its own right in generating adherence to the new found consensus of the war years.

This did not come about overnight, of course. Films such as *Ships with*

Wings and *The Demi-Paradise*, in 1941 and 1943 respectively, continued throughout the war to purvey the conventional image of gallant officers doing heroic deeds or to project the traditional image of the nation as a class-bound, hierarchically structured society. But there was also increasing emphasis on the idea of 'the people's war' and the contribution made by 'ordinary' people to the war effort in films like *The Foreman Went to France* (1942), and working class figures were given a fuller and more rounded characterization in such as *Millions Like Us* (1943). Gradually, 'the image of a progression towards greater democracy and "class unity"' became more evident.[46]

Subjects were broached in the cinema that had been barely touched upon before. Director John Baxter could contemplate making a film of Walter Greenwood's 1933 novel *Love on the Dole*. This had not been possible in the 1930s because the British Board of Film Censors had informed would-be producers that they felt it could only show 'too much of the tragic and sordid side of poverty'. Significantly, no such objections were made in 1941 and John Baxter turned the novel into a serious and moving film.[47] Its message for a Britain at war was enhanced by a postscript caption at the film's end, which was signed by A. V. Alexander, the Labour MP and First Lord of the Admiralty, that read:

> Our working men and women have responded magnificently to any and every call made upon them. Their reward must be a New Britain. Never again must the unemployed become forgotten men of peace.

John Baxter's next film, *The Common Touch* (made in 1941 and with a title lifted from a verse of Kipling's poem 'If' which is heard over the soundtrack in an early part of the film), also evoked the new consensus. This time, he began with a caption that proclaimed:

> This picture is dedicated to the humble people of our great cities whose courage and endurance have gained for us all the admiration and support of the free countries of the world.

Thereafter, Baxter treated the audiences to a whimsical social fantasy in which a young toff experiences life in a doss house as well as at the top of the firm he has just inherited. His adventures teach him a lot about human nature and the values of life. He leaves the doss house 'better fitted to start on the work of rebuilding', and the film ends with an exchange of dialogue between two of the doss house characters:

> *Tich*:   All this talk about better things, homes and all that. Do you suppose they really meant it or will they forget?
>
> *Ben*:   No, I think they really mean it this time, Tich.

Tich: Blimey, it'll be like heaven on earth.
Ben: And why not?

Such sentiments were neither uncommon nor incidental. For his part, Baxter reiterated them endlessly in his later films like *Let the People Sing* (1942, based upon J. B. Priestley's novel) and *The Shipbuilders* (1943, from George Blake's novel), and they were as much in evidence in the work of other film-makers, everything from the short film of *The Dawn Guard* (1941), which Roy and John Boulting made for the MoI, to the hugely schematic Ealing Studios' adaptation of J. B. Priestley's play, *They Came to a City* (1944). All these films were imbued with the same vision of a 'brave new world' arising from the ruins of the old and of the war as the 'midwife of social progress'. It was a message that was peculiarly suited to Britain's wartime circumstances. As C. G. H. Ayres, who wrote the original story upon which the screenplay of *The Common Touch* was based, simply but effectively put it in 1942 when broaching with John Baxter some ideas for their next project together, 'The political outlook for our type of stuff was never more promising'.[48]

There was among these film-makers something of a 'mild revolution', to borrow Michael Balcon's phrase, and his subsequent elaboration aptly serves to outline its nature: 'We were middle class people brought up with middle class backgrounds and rather conventional educations. Though we were radical in our points of view, we did not want to tear down institutions . . . We were people of an immediate post-war generation, and we voted Labour for the first time after the war; this was our mild revolution'.[49] The consensus which they represented was put at its most explicit, in filmic terms, in the opening scenes of Powell and Pressburger's *A Matter of Life and Death* (1946), where the airman, played by David Niven, in danger of imminent death, describes himself to an off-stage radio operator and adds, 'Politics . . . Conservative by nature, Labour by experience'. The words put into the character's mouth at that point are surely Powell and Pressburger's comment upon Britain by the end of the Second World War, a Britain 'whose life and imagination have been violently shaped by war', to use a phrase from the introduction to their film. 'Conservative by nature, Labour by experience', accurately describes the nature of the wartime and immediate post-war consensus in Britain.

To understand fully the British cinema during the Second World War, then, one must see it in its historical context, and that is the overriding purpose of this book. With each of the films we have chosen for scrutiny our aim has been, on the one hand, to analyse what the film said, who said it and why, and, on the other, to place each film firmly in the context of the social and political situation which helped to produce it. Thereafter, we have sought to ascertain how the film was received and what the audience reactions were. With these aims in mind, we have drawn upon an extensive and varied amount of documentation, including, for example, the papers housed in the Public Record Office relating to the activities of the Ministry of Information and the Army Film Unit, the minutes of the Newsreel Association of Great Britain and the British Board of Film Censors scenario reports, all of which proved useful and illuminating.

Mass-Observation and Home Intelligence reports also helped considerably, though, of course, these had to be treated with caution. The information they provided was often born of random sampling and unsystematic techniques. But for all their limitations, these reports remain indispensable. They are, as Paul Addison comments, 'a source for which there is no parallel or substitute in understanding wartime Britain', and, as Angus Calder concurs, 'probably the richest source of material available to the social historian of the period'.[50] In addition, the traditional array of supporting literature generated by the film industry itself proved invaluable — scripts, the trade press, box office returns (when available) and the papers lodged with the British Film Institute by individual film-makers — as did newspaper reviews. Newspaper reviews are all too often ignored, but Winifred Holmes, writing on cinemagoers' habits in 1936, felt that 'Newspaper reviews of films are read with interest and play a large part in influencing people of all classes in an appreciation of the films shown'.[51] By 1941, Mass-Observation thought that little had changed in this regard: 'The advance press analysis of films has an important influence in conditioning the approach of the audience to the film. Favourable reviews exert social sanction, disposing people favourably towards the film before they have ever seen it'.[52] We have chosen to include them among our sources.

The films themselves were chosen according to several criteria: for the light they shed on some of the issues at stake in the war, because they were popular and because they represent examples of good films emanating from directors of note in what was a particularly successful era for the British cinema. It was not possible to cover everything, of course, and inevitably there are omissions, sometimes significant omissions, and lacunae. This was partly due to the fact that certain subjects have been comprehensively dealt with elsewhere. Consequently, we have spent little time in this volume on such matters as the depiction of the army or women in the wartime cinema, on the work of Ealing Studios (with two notable exceptions), or, indeed, on American films and the larger question of the American dominance of the British film industry.[53] American films were certainly popular; that cannot be denied. *Gone With the Wind* was the box office phenomenon of the war years and, for all that some commentators have derided them, *Mrs Miniver* and *Random Harvest* were the biggest attractions in 1942 and 1943 respectively (though they were closely followed by *The First of the Few* and *In Which We Serve*). However, we have decided to concentrate our efforts here on British films. Finally, we had no wish to replicate what had already been covered in our previous book together, *Best of British*, where we looked at two other important wartime films — *The Life and Death of Colonel Blimp* and *A Canterbury Tale*.[54]

Of the films we did select, Powell and Pressburger's *49th Parallel* was the top moneymaker at the British box office for 1941. It was financed by the MoI, and it conscientiously sought to explain 'what we are fighting for'. *Pimpernel Smith*, another considerable box office success, was the work of that most quintessential of Englishmen, Leslie Howard, and it played upon that theme to great advantage. The George Formby vehicle, *Let George Do It*, exemplifies the realm of popular comedy, a much neglected genre in most standard histories of the British cinema. Thorold Dickinson's *The Next of Kin* and Alberto Cavalcanti's *Went the Day Well?* show how long-standing MoI campaigns were taken up by the cinema to warn against dangerous gossip and to allay fears of an impending German invasion.

History was subtly put to work by Carol Reed in *The Young Mr Pitt* while the more recent past provided the inspiration for Roy Boulting's diatribe against the 'Guilty Men' in *Thunder Rock*. Noël Coward paid homage to the Royal Navy and his good friend, Lord Louis Mountbatten, with *In Which We Serve*, yet another box office winner but a film which for all its credentials was made in the face of opposition from the MoI and Beaverbrook's *Daily Express*. And the work of the documentary film movement is represented by Humphrey Jennings's *Fires Were Started* and Pat Jackson's *Western Approaches*, two Crown Film Unit productions paying tribute to the fire services and the merchant marine, respectively. Finally, there is Anthony Asquith's *The Way to the Stars*, with its celebration of both the RAF and Anglo-American relations.

In short, this is a necessarily limited but we hope representative selection of films. Apart from being intrinsically and historically interesting, in their own right, they serve to show the immense richness of the British cinema during the Second World War, in what was undoubtedly one of its most fruitful and creative periods.

NOTES

1   Mass-Observation File Report No. 24, 'The cinema in the first three months of the war', January 1940, pp. 11–12.
2   Political and Economic Planning, *The British Film Industry*, London, 1952, pp. 80–5.
3   Margaret Dickinson, 'The State and the Consolidation of Monopoly', in James Curran and Vincent Porter (eds), *British Cinema History*, London, 1983, p. 74.

4   PEP, *British Film Industry*, pp. 80—1.
5   PEP, *British Film Industry*, p. 82. There were, for example, some 41.646 million feet of long films shown in 1938—9 and 41,084 million feet exhibited in 1942—3: 419 British long films were registered during the war years.
6   Dickinson, 'Consolidation of Monopoly', pp. 74—5.
7   A. J. P. Taylor, *English History 1914—1945*, London, 1965, p. 313.
8   Angus Calder, *The People's War. Britain 1939—1945*, London, 1971, p. 423.
9   For the 1930s see, in particular, S. Rowson, 'A Statistical Survey of the Cinema Industry in Great Britain', *Journal of the Royal Statistical Society*, 99, 1936, pp. 67—129.
10   Wartime Social Survey, *The Cinema Audience* (An inquiry made by the Wartime Social Survey for the Ministry of Information by Louis Moss and Kathleen Box), New Series, No. 37b, June—July 1943, p. 2.
11   See Ian McLaine, *Ministry of Morale*, London, 1979, pp. 7—9, and 52—3, for the roles played by Mass-Observation and Home Intelligence and their relationships with the MoI. On Mass-Observation, especially, see Angus Calder and Dorothy Sheridan, *Speak for Yourself*, London, 1984, and Tom Harrisson, 'Films and the Home Front', in Nicholas Pronay and D. W. Spring (eds), *Propaganda, Politics and Film, 1918—45*, London, 1982, pp. 234—48.
12   Quoted in McLaine, *Ministry of Morale*, p. 12.
13   Despite the mass of invaluable documentation assembled by McLaine, *Ministry of Morale*, and Michael Balfour, *Propaganda in War 1939—1945*, London, 1979, neither author deals adequately with the question of films and the cinema. Marion Yass, *This Is Your War*, London, 1983, goes some way towards rectifying this fault but still only covers the ground fleetingly.
14   Arthur Marwick, *The Home Front*, London, 1976, p. 105.
15   The Arts Enquiry, *The Factual Film*, London, 1947, p. 63.
16   T. J. Hollins, 'The conservative party and film propaganda between the wars', *The English Historical Review*, 96, 1981, p. 368.
17   Minute 209, Meeting of the Principal Representatives of the Council of the Newsreel Association of Great Britain and Ireland Ltd, 4 July 1939 (British Movietonews, Denham).
18   Frances Thorpe and Nicholas Pronay with Clive Coultass, *British Official Films in the Second World War*, Oxford, 1980, pp. 31—4.
19   *Documentary News Letter*, 1, January 1940, p. 4.
20   Michael Powell, for example, felt Clark to be a 'good appointment'. See David Badder, 'Powell and Pressburger: The War Years', *Sight and Sound*, 48, Winter 1978/79, p. 9. But for a less sanguine opinion, see Nicholas Pronay, '"The Land of Promise": the Projection of Peace Aims in Britain', in K. R. M. Short (ed.), *Film and Radio Propaganda in World War II*, London, 1983, p. 57.
21   Policy Committee minutes, 11 June 1940 and 14 June 1940, INF 1/849.
22   *Documentary News Letter*, 1, May 1940, p. 1.
23   Pronay, 'The Land of Promise', p. 59.
24   Paul Rotha, *Rotha on the Film*, London, 1958, p. 229.
25   Quoted in Elizabeth Sussex, *The Rise and Fall of British Documentary*, Berkeley, 1975, pp. 122—3.

26   Paul Addison, *The Road to 1945. British Politics and the Second World War*, London, 1977, p. 144.
27   Policy Committee minutes, 10th meeting, 15 March 1940, INF 1/848.
28   Charles Barr, 'Projecting Britain and the British Character', *Screen*, 15, Spring 1974, p. 97.
29   Quoted in Paul Morley Titmuss, *Commercial Feature Film Production and the Ministry of Information*, unpublished MA Thesis, Polytechnic of Central London, 1982, p. 50.
30   Quoted in Robert Murphy, 'British Film Production, 1939 to 1945', in Geoff Hurd (ed.), *National Fictions. World War II in British Films and Television*, London, 1984, p. 15.
31   See Sussex, *The Rise and Fall of British Documentary*, pp. 140—1.
32   Vincent Porter and Chaim Litewski, '*The Way Ahead*: Case History of a Propaganda Film', *Sight and Sound*, 50, Spring 1981, p. 110.
33   Monja Danischewsky (ed.), *Michael Balcon's 25 Years in Film*, London, 1947, p. 24.
34   See Jeffrey Richards and Anthony Aldgate, *Best of British. Cinema and Society 1930— 1970*, Oxford, 1983, pp. 61—74. Also, Nicholas Pronay and Jeremy Croft, 'British Film Censorship and Propaganda Policy During the Second World War' in Curran and Porter (eds), *British Cinema History*, pp. 155—63.
35   Marwick, *The Home Front*, p. 105. The MoI was also instrumental in promoting the production of many other films, such as *The Demi-Paradise* and *Henry V*, as Sir Laurence Olivier recalls in *Confessions of an Actor*, London, 1984, pp. 130—1.
36   *Kinematograph Weekly*, 2 July 1942.
37   Policy Committee minutes, 26 July 1940, INF 1/849. For all its acknowledgement of the value of 'entertainment', however, the MoI showed little immediate awareness of the importance of broad comedy and humour.
38   *House of Commons Debates*, vol. 381, c.656—7, 7 July 1942.
39   Thorold Dickinson, *A Discovery of Cinema*, Oxford, 1971, p. 77. Dickinson was to enjoy 'official' support once again when he embarked upon the production of *Men of Two Worlds*. See Jeffrey Richards, *Thorold Dickinson*, (forthcoming).
40   *Kinematograph Weekly*, 30 July 1942.
41   Geoff Hurd, 'Notes on Hegemony, the War and the Cinema', in Hurd (ed.), *National Fictions*, p. 18.
42   Murphy, 'British Film Production, 1939 to 1945', in Hurd (ed.), *National Fictions*, p. 17.
43   Calder, *The People's War*, p. 20. For a useful summary of the debate see John Stevenson, *British Society 1914—45*, Harmondsworth, Middlesex, 1984, p. 460.
44   Arthur Marwick's thesis has been argued extensively in *Britain in the Century of Total War*, London, 1968, and, *War and Social Change in the Twentieth Century*, London, 1975.
45   Paul Addison, *The Road to 1945*, pp. 14—15, 162—5, and, 276—7.
46   Arthur Marwick, *Class: Image and Reality in Britain, France and the USA since 1930*, London, 1981, p. 227.

47   Jeffrey Richards, *The Age of the Dream Palace. Cinema and Society in Britain 1930—1939*, London, 1984, pp. 119—20. The matter of censorship during the war years in particular is well covered in James C. Robertson, *The British Board of Film Censors: Film Censorship in Britain, 1896—1950*, London, 1985, pp. 109—44.

48   Letter from C. G. H. Ayres to John Baxter, 2 March 1942, Item 13, Box II, Ayres Special Collection at the British Film Institute, London. Before *The Common Touch* was made in 1941, Ayres' story had already provided the inspiration for two other Baxter films — *Doss House* in 1933 and *Hearts of Humanity* in 1936 — and it was to be reworked yet again by Baxter for his 1952 production of *Judgement Deferred.*

49   Quoted in John Ellis, 'Made in Ealing', *Screen*, 16, Spring 1975, p. 119.

50   Paul Addison, 'Introduction', *The British People and World War II: Home Intelligence Reports on Opinion and Morale, 1940—1944*, Brighton, Sussex, 1983, Reel 1, p. 8 (microfilm collection); and, Angus Calder, *The People's War*, p. 14. The Mass-Observation File Reports are now also available on microfiche.

51   *World Film News*, 1, December 1936, p. 4.

52   Mass-Observation File Report No. 967, '*Ships with Wings*', November 1941, p. 9. It should be pointed out, however, that there was not always a direct correlation between critical approval and success. Some films which received a generally favourable press, like *Thunder Rock*, were not greatly successful at the box office. The Gainsborough melodramas, universally execrated by the press, were box office hits.

53   For the depiction of the Army during the war see Porter and Litewski, '*The Way Ahead*'; for the debate on women in the war see Marwick, *Britain in the Century of Total War* and *War and Social Change in the Twentieth Century*, and, for a more recent opinion, Penny Summerfield, *Women Workers in the Second World War*, London, 1984. The depiction of women in the cinema is dealt with by Sue Aspinall, 'Women, Realism and Reality in British Films, 1943—53', in *British Cinema History*, and in Hurd (ed.), *National Fictions*. Charles Barr's *Ealing Studios*, London, 1977, provides an invaluable guide to that studio's output during the war. And the matter of American films is dealt with by Colin Shindler, *Hollywood Goes to War*, London, 1980, with regard to their content, and by Margaret Dickinson and Sarah Street, *Cinema and State*, London, 1985, in the context of the American dominance of the British cinema.

54   Richards and Aldgate, *Best of British*, pp. 61—74, and 43—60.

2

Why We Fight

49th Parallel

With the advent of war, the film-makers inevitably felt it their duty to play a part in the patriotic cause. None moved more quickly than the film producer Alexander Korda. He was responsible for the first feature-length film of the war that was made entirely for propaganda purposes. Indeed, *The Lion Has Wings* was well on its way into production by the time war was declared. As the associate producer on the film, Ian Dalrymple, recalls:

> A few days before 3 September, some of us working at the Denham Studios — a fortuitous gaggle of directors and writers of various ages and origins, all of sadly unbellicose aspect — were summoned to Alex's office. He told us that we were to make a film to reassure the public of the power of the Royal Air Force, and that a liaison officer from the Air Ministry was on his way to assist us. Almost immediately the door opened and a fair young god in sky-blue with the rank of squadron leader appeared. There was an odd happening. All of us rose to our feet as one, in dramatic salute to this representative of our potential guardian angels. The squadron leader, named appropriately H. M. S. Wright, was quite taken aback.[1]

As Dalrymple's account implies, the film was to be marked by two features above all else — it was made at great speed, and it was to prove grandiloquently patriotic. On 2 September, the day after Poland had been invaded, Korda announced that work would begin on 'an urgent propaganda film about the Air Force and the country's preparation for war', and immediately thereafter three units were assigned to the job.

Michael Powell was dispatched to Mildenhall to film preparations for the first bomber raid of the war, on the Kiel canal, and to Hornchurch to cover fighter operations. Brian Desmond Hurst was given the task of filming dramatized scenes between Ralph Richardson and Merle Oberon,

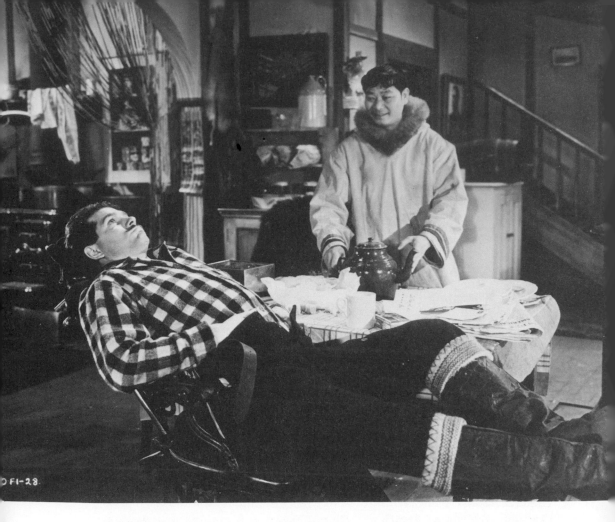

49th Parallel, *the first feature film of the war to be directly financed by the MoI, pitted democratic ideals against the Nazi New Order in a series of ideological confrontations. Johnnie Barras (Laurence Olivier), a French Canadian trapper, relaxes at the trading post after a year spent hunting in the wilderness.*

occasionally abetted by Korda himself, and of covering civilian observer posts, and Adrian Brunel dealt with the build up to the crisis over Poland. In addition, actuality material was bought in from the GPO Film Unit and from the newsreel companies, and Dalrymple put together an opening sequence denigrating Nazism.[2]

Location shooting took three weeks, with some of it completed before a final script was ready, and editing started immediately film was processed and forthcoming from the laboratories, under the supervision of an American, William Hornbeck, with the assistance of Henry Cornelius and Charles Frend. Further library footage was sought from feature film sources, not least from *Fire Over England* (1937). Two distinguished newsreel commentators were engaged to provide a narration throughout

— E. V. H. Emmett, from Gaumont British, for the domestic version of the film, and Lowell Thomas, from Movietonews, for the American version. Richard Addinsell added a score.

The film was completed within record time. A show print was ready within three weeks of the last shot being taken and in all the production process took somewhere in the region of five to six weeks, from start to finish. The film was shown to the Ministry of Information, given a trade show on 17 October, and put on general release from 3 November.

To the last, *The Lion Has Wings* was afforded the same measure of urgency and importance which had accompanied its production throughout. The film was distributed without 'bars' and the distributors decided that they would not seek to invoke or to enforce their virtual 'closed shop' agreement, whereby a film was rented to just one cinema in a given locality. As a result, some 200 copies of the film were made instead of the usual 70. The film was shown by the Gaumont, Granada, Odeon and County circuits, and most of the independents, with only the ABC circuit declining to take it. To add to the film's prestige, furthermore, it was the first film to be seen by the King and Queen after the outbreak of war.

In some respects, *The Lion Has Wings* was indeed a remarkable achievement, but its success was easily exaggerated. Though the film attracted large audiences and much effusive critical acclaim, considerable reservations were expressed about both its style and content, and its resort to blatant jingoism. Mass-Observation reported that cinemagoers complained about there being 'too much propaganda' and Tom Harrisson came to the conclusion that 'it was a powerful contribution towards Chamberlainish complacency', and some critics thought it 'a hotch potch'.[3] One of the most damning reviews appeared in the pages of the *Documentary News Letter*:

> This film was made to reassure us at home and to instruct neutral countries in the justice of our cause and our ability to win the war. Newsreel clips, documentary cuts, material shot, scenes from *Fire Over England*, fictitious scenes and reconstructions of events are linked by Emmett. Effective are the impressionistic 'Lilliput' sequences on Britain and Nazi Germany, the Kiel Raid reconstruction and the repulse of an air attack on Britain . . . Puerile it is that all the successes should be on our side, that the Nazi pilots are cowardly morons (remember — 'Kaiser, The Beast of Berlin'?), that the Nazi air command is ignorant of the balloon barrage. Finally, Merle Oberon sums up for the women of England. She starts talking to Ralph Richardson beneath a Denham tree. The camera moves up until, as she gulps 'and — kindliness', she is in full close-up. Sadly she turns from the audience to Richardson — her audience. He is asleep, a smile of forbearance lingering on his face. This may be 'realism' but it is poor understanding of the psychology of film propaganda.[4]

The Lion Has Wings may not have been universally accepted, then, as a good example of film propaganda, but it was the first effort from the mainstream cinema of the day. Moreover, as a result of at least committing himself to the fray and of being the first in the field, Korda's intervention did prove to be particularly significant. By virtue of rushing into production, as he did, Korda had been compelled to strike up an immediate working relationship with the new-found Ministry of Information, and in so doing, he provided a considerable impetus to the Ministry's thoughts on how to best use the medium of film in its propaganda armoury, and on how the relationship between itself and the commercial film-makers might fruitfully evolve.

The MoI had been involved with *The Lion Has Wings* from the outset. The exact terms of the relationship are not clear, though doubtless it would have helped in the provision of a liaison officer from the Air Ministry. Ian Dalrymple has gone down on record as saying that Korda 'had no financial help from the government' in making the film,[5] and that comment is to some extent borne out by a memorandum from Sir Kenneth Clark written several months after the film had opened, on 27 February 1940, in which he stated that 'So far the Ministry has not paid for or contributed to the production of a long feature film'. (Though significantly, in the light of what was shortly to ensue over *49th Parallel*, he went on to add that 'We should probably do so in the near future'.[6])

However, that is by no means the whole story, for all that the MoI may not have contributed directly to the funding for the production of the film, strictly speaking, there were other indirect ways in which it was of immense help. Some of these entailed practical assistance and some of them a financial outlay, but overall they certainly resulted in the MoI having a financial stake in the film's progress.

For one thing, the MoI provided 'technical facilities' in the production of the film and a deal was struck whereby it was accordingly afforded a share of the profits. Figures as high as '50 per cent of the profits' were quoted by some sources and were 'the cause of a great deal of discontent in the industry'.[7] Whatever the exact sum, however, the MoI did not do badly out of *The Lion Has Wings*. It was able to pass on to the Exchequer £25,140 from the film,[8] and that was a straight profit, after it had covered whatever costs had accrued and after it had paid out £3,000, late in November 1939, 'to secure the distribution of dubbed or sub-titled prints abroad'.[9] The film was dubbed into French for exhibition in France, Belgium and Switzerland, and sub-titled for Holland, Portugal, Spain and the Scandinavian countries. The English-language version, though with Lowell Thomas's commentary of course, served for America, where it was heavily promoted. The MoI's links with the commercial film industry were well and truly forged over *The Lion Has Wings*.

The MoI was not, incidentally, the only body that Korda dealt with over the film, for he had also used a considerable amount of newsreel footage in his production and the reaction of the newsreel companies to the film's success proved nothing if not awkward for a while as far as the industry was concerned. The Newsreel Association met on 30 October and debated the matter. As the minutes of the meeting show, they were not exactly pleased:

> It was felt that here was an instance of a feature picture, undoubtedly of considerable value for national publicity purposes, for which the credit was given to the feature producer, whereas an important part of it was in fact the work of the newsreel companies who had only been paid a small sum for the considerable length of footage purchased, and were not entitled to participate in any profits that might be earned.
>
> After discussion it was resolved that members of the Association would not in future supply material from their libraries to any feature producer or to any shorts producer unless such producers were associates of one or other of the newsreel companies.[10]

The loss of access to the immense libraries held by the newsreel companies made life potentially very difficult for many film producers, of feature films and documentaries alike. Associated Talking Pictures, for instance, were immediately caught by the ban. They had already started production on their latest George Formby vehicle, *Let George Do It*, and had intended to insert actuality film of a Nazi rally in the midst of it. Confidently expecting to get it as they had done in the past, they applied for newsreel footage. Since their application was in the pipeline when the ban was effected, however, the newsreel companies relented on this occasion while making it very clear that this was to be seen as 'an exception only'.[11] Several other producers were not so lucky.

The newsreel companies stuck firmly to their guns and only after many representations and considerable pressure (including, it seems, from the MoI), did they relent further. On 22 January 1940, the Newsreel Association agreed to write to the British Film Producers Association informing them that they were still 'not disposed' to alter their previous decision, but that 'in future they would be prepared to give careful consideration to any individual application brought forward whereby the film concerned involved *national* interest'.[12]

The newsreel vision of the 'national interest' meant, as it always had, something very specific.[13] The newsreel companies were inclined to grant permission for their material to be used by Ealing Studios in *Convoy* (1940),[14] and when it came to considering the application from Ortus Films for newsreel footage to be included in *49th Parallel* (1941), then once again 'it was decided to supply the material required for this film in the usual way'.[15] Two Cities Films also got what they wanted, finally, for *In Which We Serve* (1942).[16]

But when it came to considering an application from British National Films for the release of newsreel material that they hoped to see included in their production of *Love on the Dole* (1941) — a banned subject during the 1930s, of course, as far as the British Board of Film Censors was concerned — then the Newsreel Association wanted to know more about the matter. Significantly, they consulted neither British National Films nor the BFPA, but the MoI. On 5 February 1940, the principals of the council of the Newsreel Association requested the secretary 'to write to the MoI asking on what grounds they consider this subject to be of propaganda value'.[17] Whatever reply they received evidently did not convince them, for the minutes of a subsequent meeting, held on 24 February, record that in the case of the request for film for *Love on the Dole:*

> It was decided not to supply this material under the arrangement made with the MoI re. recommending assistance, and that the Secretary should write to the Ministry mentioning that the members' libraries were, under that arrangement, open only for propaganda films in the national interest.[18]

British National went ahead with their production regardless. John Baxter directed the film and this time there were to be no problems over censorship. With the advent of war and a Ministry which sought to exercise several of its functions, the BBFC proved malleable and changed its attitude somewhat to meet the times. In truth, it had no choice but to accommodate for the presence of the MoI. The newsreel companies were less inclined to do so: they proved more intractable. This was to be by no means the only occasion when the Newsreel Association was to find itself at odds with the MoI during the war.[19]

After its experiences with Korda over *The Lion Has Wings*, the MoI for its part soon got down to formulating some more specific ideas with regard to film and its value as part of the propaganda programme. Taking its cue also from a Policy Committee Paper, written by the Minister himself, Lord Macmillan, in which he outlined 'The principles underlying British wartime propaganda',[20] the Films Division circulated a definite plan, a 'Programme for film propaganda'.[21] It stressed 'the importance of films as a medium of propaganda' in putting across the themes that Macmillan had suggested: what Britain is fighting for; how Britain fights; and the need for sacrifices if the fight is to be won. All three realms of film — feature films, documentaries and newsreels — could be fruitfully employed, but the feature film was singled out as being especially useful to convey *British life and character* ('showing our independence, toughness of fibre, sympathy with the under-dog'), *British ideas and institutions* ('ideals such as freedom, and institutions such as parliamentary government . . .'), *German ideals and institutions in recent history* ('. . . Pan-German ideas from Bismarck onwards . . . the activities of the Gestapo stressing, as more easily credible, the sinister rather than the sadistic aspect, but the Germans should also be shown as making absurd errors of judgement'). *Goodbye Mr Chips* (1939) and *The Lady Vanishes* (1938) were cited as good examples of the sort of film that should be made, but *The Lion Has Wings* was criticized for being 'three documentaries strung together to attain feature length'.

It was, for the most part, a reasonable and rational film programme though it was noticeably lacking in suggestions for comedy and good humour. Fears that certain things might be interpreted on the Continent 'as evidence of slackness and stupidity' obviously meant there was little room for light relief and induced the extraordinary injunction that 'Shots of our soldiers laughing or playing football must be cut out of all newsreels and documentaries sent to France'. However, it ranged far and wide, advocating that films be made on the Indian war effort, the Dominions, railways, roads, ports and canals, and, most of all, it appeared to appreciate

The peace is rudely shattered with the arrival of a band of escaping German submariners (Raymond Lovell and Eric Portman), and Johnnie is subsequently killed.

certain salient features about the nature of film and its value to the propagandist with comments such as 'A film which induces boredom antagonises the audience to the cause which it advocates', and, 'film propaganda will be most effective when it is least recognizable as such'.

By the beginning of 1940, then, under the guidance of Sir Kenneth Clark, the Films Division had what it construed as a viable blueprint for success even if the rest of the MoI was still struggling to find its feet. Of course, to have a plan is one thing, to see it realised is another, but the Films Division had ideas in abundance and, moreover, it had finance at its disposal. It was now in the market place for suggestions to see its plans brought to some kind of fruition. The means whereby it hoped to achieve its ambitions were still very much in the making, and until the Select Committee on National Expenditure produced its Thirteenth Report, in August 1940, the Films Division had free rein. Thereafter, its activities were to be severely curtailed; but, as the evidence indicates, in those six months the Films Division was to enjoy one of its most fruitful and productive periods of the war, at least as far as the instigation of projects was concerned.

By the time that Clark came to compile his notes for inclusion in a general report to the Cabinet, in February 1940, he was able to record that within a month or so, the Films Division had commissioned 32 films, all documentaries, showing 'various aspects of our part in the war'. Some were designed to reassure, others to prevent apathy and a number were intended primarily for foreign or Empire distribution. Furthermore, 'as a result of active cooperation the selection and quality of newsreel material has improved', and, after negotiation with the British and American feature film companies, he had persuaded 'nearly all of them to produce films which present our war aims and effort in a favourable light'.[22]

Specialist sources, not least in America, provided adequate testimony that 'films are always welcome'. *The Lion Has Wings* had enjoyed 'considerable popularity' there, in particular, and *South Riding* (1938) 'with its pure statement of some of the finest British ideals was very valuable indeed'.[23] Other sources provide further evidence of the extent to which the word was out and about that the Films Division was touting for suggestions. Michael Powell, for example, remembers:

> About February, John Sutro, who was a great friend of Korda's and one of his directors on the board, came to me and said the government definitely wants to back films, they will even put government money into it if we can't raise the money elsewhere. I went with him to see Kenneth Clark, who had been appointed head of the Films Division of the Ministry of Information. This was the first smell of any organization to do with films, and since Kenneth Clark was director of the National Gallery and presumably knew about pictures, he was put in charge of the Films Division. Fortunately, it was a very good appointment . . .[24]

The meeting was to prove especially fruitful. In the first instance, Clark wanted Powell to do a film about minesweepers for which some plans were already in existence. But Powell had ideas of his own and offered instead the bare outline of a story 'dealing with Canada's entry into the war', which he had worked up with Emeric Pressburger.

However rough and ready, the proposal was by no means unwelcome. It was passed on to the Empire Division and the Dominions Office, but Clark must have known full well it would accord quite neatly with ideas which were circulating on that front. He was receiving all the papers on the subject of 'Publicity about the British Empire', and very early on in 1940 it had been agreed that there was room for 'a first class feature film developing as an exciting story the history of the growth of freedom, referring to the American parallel and stimulus in order to give it appeal to US audiences'.[25] Furthermore, the proposed plans of the Empire Division for the months of April to September, 1940, contemplated making at least two full-length feature films, 'one for Canada on the NW Mounted Police and one for South Africa on the life of General Botha'. The budget for these films would be met 'from the Films subhead of the Ministry's vote, amounting to £500,000 in 1940 and need not be estimated separately'. But, luckily for Powell, none of the feature film proposals 'has yet reached the stage at which accurate costing is possible'.[26]

In short, if Powell and Sutro moved quickly enough, as Clark doubtless intimated, then the odds were in their favour that money could be found and the proposal given the go-ahead. They moved quickly all right. A scheme was proposed whereby a team comprising Powell, Pressburger and three others would go to Canada to plan the film and, indeed, to come up with a full scale story line. The Treasury provided somewhere in the region of £3,000 to £5,000 for the purpose. Vincent Massey, the High Commissioner for Canada, gave the project a sympathetic nod of approval, and, as Powell recalls, 'in a week or two we were off'.[27]

On the voyage out, Pressburger evolved the basic idea for the plot of *49th Parallel*: 'I think we wreck a German submarine somewhere in Canada and then follow the survivors all across Canada and that way we shall see Canada, and we've got a good suspense story'. After six weeks reconnoitring the principal cities and other locations, they returned better prepared to give both a detailed account of what the film might entail and how much it would cost. Subsequently, promises were exacted from Laurence Olivier, Elizabeth Bergner, Leslie Howard and Anton Walbrook that they would be willing to appear in the various episodes of the film.

On their return, however, Powell and Pressburger also wondered whether the circumstances were still as favourable for their venture as they had been at the outset. The 'Phoney War' had come to an end and there was justifiable concern at the push to the west by the German forces. Sir Kenneth Clark had been promoted and Jack Beddington had

The German sailors then proceed to disrupt the tranquillity of a Hutterite settlement, of which the refugee Anna (Glynis Johns) is a member.

replaced him as head of the Films Division. There was even a new Minister of Information, Duff Cooper. Changes were afoot and questions were increasingly being asked, not least by the Select Committee on National Expenditure, whether the Ministry should be involving itself so much with feature film production. Luckily, Powell and Pressburger had little cause to worry. Beddington proved sympathetic and Duff Cooper turned out to be particularly helpful. Indeed, Duff Cooper took a considerable interest in the project, evidently thinking that if anything the circumstances warranted an increase in the propaganda effort (an attitude that was also reflected in the personal support he extended to the play of 'Thunder Rock', as we shall see), and he succeeded in inducing the Treasury to release money for the film of *49th Parallel* to go into production.

Powell's production crew was already on location and shooting in Canada by the time the 13th Select Committee produced the results of its inquiry into the affairs of the MoI and the Films Division, in August. The film was too far advanced, though, for the committee's strictures regarding the difficulties of employing feature film 'as an instrument of propaganda' to have much immediate effect. But the Films Division certainly had its hands full, for it had to contend with a report which essentially sought to undermine a lot of the work it had done, in the preceding months, in the promotion of both feature films and of documentaries. The report recommended that henceforth the emphasis should be put upon the newsreels since the Select Committee considered they were 'the most important for propaganda purposes of the three principal kinds of films'. The newsreels, then, should be the recipients of extensive help from the Ministry and it was they who should be afforded whatever support was available. Furthermore, the report suggested that the production of documentaries should be virtually abandoned and, with a sly gibe at the arguments which had been marshalled in defence of 49th Parallel, it advocated that 'no more feature films should be undertaken even if the film now being made should be as successful as it had hoped to be'.[28]

In effect, the Select Committee's report attacked the basis of the Films Division's list of priorities for film propaganda. Fortunately, after considerable internal wrangling, a compromise of sorts was achieved. Documentary production could continue though with a reduced programme of activities, and while the Films Division agreed not to spend money on feature film production, it was allowed to instigate and develop projects which might then be sold and taken up by commercial producers, and to help with the provision of production facilities. The arguments did not stop there but at least the Films Division was able to retain a measure of interest and influence in both the feature film and documentary camps and, by virtue of playing its cards very carefully thereafter, it managed to do just that and more besides.[29]

Meanwhile, production continued unabated on 49th Parallel, though clearly there was now increased expectation that it would indeed turn out to be the success that many people had predicted. The location shooting in Canada did not pose too many problems, as Michael Powell recalls:

Almost immediately after we landed my chief of construction, Sid Streeter, started to build the submarine in Halifax while I was already shooting; I think we started in the mid-west. We'd roughed the whole script out and then Emeric started to write the actual script with dialogue with Rodney Ackland . . . They started on the first episode while I went off to shoot the rest of the stuff off-the-cuff. We had to: we had to catch the harvest for the Hutterite sequence, then I had to shoot the stuff in the Rockies and then go up to Hudson Bay and round the Labrador coast to get the submarine scenes and the landing at the Hudson Bay post. All before it was too late, because if you're too late in the Hudson Bay the ice can be early. It was all working against time, but as we had complete control ourselves, nobody to argue with, we brought it all off. When we came back to England the Blitz was on. We had shot Raymond Massey's sequence with Eric Portman in a little documentary studio in Montreal because he was already in the Forces and couldn't come over.[30]

And it was really only on returning to Britain, with the location shooting complete, that the production began to experience difficulties. The word soon got out and as the *Documentary News Letter* recounted in December 1940:

> The press lately has been full of the *49th Parallel*, a feature film on Canada, partly financed by the Films Division of the MoI. This film has gone wrong, largely because the star, Austrian born Elizabeth Bergner, refuses to return to London from Hollywood to complete the studio scenes. Among the general sensation-mongering, two points have been overlooked: the idea of the original script was and remains a good one; in spite of Miss Bergner's absence, there is, as yet, no reason to suppose, either that the film will not be finished, or that it will not be a success.[31]

Hopes were still high, then, in some quarters at least, that the film would be completed, but clearly that would necessitate a replacement actress, the likely reshooting of certain sequences, more time, and, of course, more money.

Most of the problems were solved. Glynis Johns was engaged to replace Elizabeth Bergner for the studio work. David Lean, the editor, cleverly managed to retain some of the location material done with Bergner — the long shots in which her features could not be clearly discerned — and J. Arthur Rank was cajoled into putting up £60,000 to match the £60,000 that the MoI had invested in the production. But the whole process did take an inordinate amount of time. As a result the film was not completed and ready until well over a year and a half after that initial meeting with Clark. The premiere was held at the Odeon, Leicester Square, on 8 October 1941 and the film was put on general release in Britain from 24 November.

Not surprisingly, the film visually enshrined many of the principles which formed the basis of the MoI's 'Programme for film propaganda' and consciously so. In particular, it harped upon the theme of 'why we fight' and 'what we are fighting for'. But the scope of the film was as wide as its geographical canvas. Its credentials are evident from the outset in a caption, which reads:

> This film is dedicated to Canada and to Canadians all over the Dominion who helped us to make it; to the Governments of the USA, of the Dominion of Canada, and of the United Kingdom, who made it possible, and to the actors who believed in our story and came from all parts of the world to make it possible.

The film's title is explained with a short voice-over narration which stresses freedom, and amity between Canada and America, against a visual backdrop of expansive vistas of mountains, fields, cities and lakes, to the accompaniment of a highly evocative and stirring score from Ralph Vaughan Williams — a prelude that may well have been planned from early on but which was clearly intended for American consumption, most of all, by the time the film was released. It states:

> I see a long straight line athwart a continent. No chain of forts, or deep-flowing river, or mountain range, but a line drawn by men upon a map nearly a century ago, accepted with a handshake and kept ever since. A boundary which divides two nations yet marks their friendly meeting ground, the 49th Parallel, the only undefended frontier in the world.

Then, we are into the film proper. The German submarine, U37, is marauding off the Gulf of St Lawrence and sinks a merchant ship. 'The curtain rises on Canada', says the submarine's commander, and his first officer, Lieutenant Hirth (Eric Portman), deals harshly if efficiently with the survivors in his attempt to interrogate them about their cargo. The merchant seamen are kicked away from the submarine, however, when it crash dives to escape oncoming Canadian aircraft, and the submarine is compelled to seek refuge in the Hudson Straits.

A place of safety is required, a haven in which they can rest up and take on further provisions. Hirth and a party of five men are dispatched ashore to reconnoitre. After they land, their submarine is spotted by Royal Canadian Air Force planes and bombed to pieces. Hirth's little band is left alone to fend for itself and to make its own way to freedom, if possible. The odds are against the six men but they are determined to try, and Hirth, a fanatical Nazi party member, is adamant that they can do it.

They arrive, first of all, at the Hudson's Bay Company post of Wolstenholme and there follows the first set piece encounter between Nazi ideology and democratic ideals. It is carefully constructed. The French Canadian trapper, Johnnie Barras (Laurence Olivier), has returned to the post after a year in the wilderness. He is out of touch with affairs in Europe and the Scottish factor (Finlay Currie) brings him up to date. There is a war on, he says, the Germans 'wiped out Warsaw and machine gunned down the refugees, the poor women and children who tried to get away'. 'The Germans are ordinary men, same as you and me', retorts Johnnie, 'I wouldn't do a thing like that . . . That's all newspaper talk'. He is sceptical and for the sake of peace and quiet, they both decide to drop the conversation. 'What does it mean to us?', they agree, after all, the war 'won't bother us out here'.

But they are rudely awakened when the party of German submariners break in, and they are soon alerted to Nazi intentions. Johnnie's Eskimo helper has his skull smashed in and Hirth declares 'Eskimos are racially as low as Negroes . . . Negroes are semi-apes, only one degree above the Jews. Those are the Fuhrer's own words from *Mein Kampf.*' For his part Johnnie boasts that 'My father gave you a good licking the last time and we do it again', and he taunts the German sailors, mocking the goose-step. He is not convinced by Hirth's promises of freedom for the 'oppressed minority', the French in Canada. 'I am free', he replies, 'We French Canadians have always had our own schools, our own church, and the right to speak as we want'. But he too is mortally wounded when he attempts to alert the outside world, over the radio, to their plight. One of the German sailors looks kindly upon Johnnie on his death bed and gives him his rosary beads, before he proceeds to tear down the picture of 'Le roi and la reine', that Johnnie pinned up, and carves out in its stead a Nazi swastika with his bayonet.

The Germans effect their escape when they gun down in cold blood the pilots sent out to answer the post's emergency call. One of their number is shot down by the Eskimos, in return, but the rest manage to get away in the captured airplane. 'Germans should also be shown as making absurd errors of judgement', said the MoI 'Programme for film propaganda', and that is precisely what ensues when the band take to the air and optimistically plan their route to safety in neutral America.

The point had already been made when a sailor thoughtlessly smashed the radio, and inner dissension surfaced when Hirth and the second in command, Lieutenant Kuhnecke (Raymond Lovell), engaged in petty argument about seniority. Now, stupidity, rivalry and deep seated divisions are shown increasingly and threaten to thwart the escape. Kuhnecke is piloting the plane but forgot to check the fuel tank level. The plane crashes, a long way short of their objective, and Kuhnecke is killed. Hirth is unforgiving. Vogel (Niall MacGinnis), the same man who took pity upon Johnnie, instinctively crosses himself and thereby reveals his religious feelings. The matter does not go unnoticed by Hirth.

The next set piece encounter and conflict of ideologies occurs when the four remaining Germans happen upon a religious Hutterite settlement. Since the Hutterite community is largely of German origin, Hirth expects that they will be favourably received. They are, indeed, well looked after and given food and lodging. But they are bemused when they cannot distinguish the Hutterite 'leader' Peter (Anton Walbrook) among the crowd and when there is no agreed 'salute' with which to greet or address him. Vogel settles down instantly, he is reminded of home in 'the old days', and he happily takes on the role of baker for the community. He also befriends the young Anna (Glynis Johns), who lost her mother on the voyage to America when the boat in which they were travelling was torpedoed by a German submarine. Vogel laments 'The ships we sank, the Eskimos at the post, the unarmed men we shot in the back', and adds, 'We were good at that'. But he is sternly rebuked and put in his place by Hirth, who embarks on a significant speech which is redolent, once again, of the MoI's informal dictates regarding film propaganda.

> You forget, Vogel, we are at war. You can't expect to win without the methods of total warfare. Men, women and children — they are all our enemies and must be treated as such. Do you remember what Bismarck said? Leave them only their eyes to weep with.

Subsequently, Hirth also gets a chance to address the Hutterite community. In an impassioned speech he tells them of 'a new wind blowing in the east' and of 'the greatest idea in history, the supremacy of the Nordic race, of the German people'. 'It is a question of blood, the deepest of racial instincts', he continues, as he invites them to join the

The intellectual Philip Armstrong Scott (Leslie Howard) is also made aware of Nazi intentions when Lohrmann (John Chandos) and Hirth (Eric Portman) burn his books and paintings.

OFI-110.

Nazi cause. But his pleas are rejected. In a restrained but increasingly forceful reply, Peter states that 'Our Germany is dead' and he emphasizes that 'We are not your brothers'. Many of the Hutterites left Germany, he points out, precisely because it was no longer possible to practice their faith in that country without fear of persecution. 'We hate the power of evil which is spreading over the world' and in Canada, by contrast, 'we all have found security, peace, tolerance and understanding'.

Vogel is convinced by Peter's arguments that he should leave the company of such 'gangsters'. He is captivated by the Hutterite philosophy, enjoys their life style and determines to stay, but he is brought before a makeshift courtmartial by Hirth, sentenced to death as a traitor and executed. The three remaining Germans — Hirth, Kranz (Peter Moore) and Lohrmann (John Chandos) — make for Winnipeg and plan to cross Canada to Vancouver, where they hope to be able to escape by stowing away on a ship.

Thereafter, the chase is on and it provides an admirable opportunity for shots of some glorious scenery and locations as the fugitives board the Canadian Pacific railway on its journey across the Rockies. Kranz is captured in Banff, during the exotic Indian Day celebrations, with the help of the crowd and the Mounties. His nerve broke. Hirth and Lohrmann take to the hills where, once more, they are befriended, this time by Philip Armstrong Scott (Leslie Howard).

Yet again, we are treated to an overt clash of ideologies. Scott epitomises, in a very obvious way, the cultured intellectual aesthete. But he is not meant to be construed as an ivory tower academic: he is an expert and writer on Indians, and lives in an Indian teepee, for all that it is littered with books, papers and paintings — everything from Hemingway's latest, Thomas Mann's *The Magic Mountain*, his notes on 'Blackfoot tribal customs', to his paintings by Picasso and Matisse. But he is self-critical, self-aware, acutely conscious of the quaint image he must present to an outsider, and, most of all, he is capable of being stirred into action if the occasion or situation demands it.

Hirth and Lohrmann, of course, scorn everything Scott stands for and they see him as being 'rotten to the core, soft and degenerate . . . not a man at all'. They overpower him and burn his books, his paintings and his papers. They behave 'like spiteful little schoolboys', as Scott puts it, but the historical allusion is plain for all to see. Once freed, Scott shows his courage and determination when he corners Lohrmann in a cave, advances in the face of gunfire, and beats him into subjection. 'That's for Thomas Mann . . . that's for Matisse . . . that's for Picasso . . . and that's for me', we hear from the cave, as the blows fall. And Scott emerges triumphant to declare: 'He had a fair chance. One armed superman against one unarmed decadent democrat'.

Now alone and hotly pursued, Hirth heads for the American border. German radio broadcasts make much of his exploits and he is awarded the Iron Cross, first class, in absentia. He seems set to effect his escape when, finally, he hides away in the freight car of a train destined for the frontier. There he encounters Andy Brook (Raymond Massey), a Canadian soldier who has gone absent without leave.

Brock is everyman to Scott's aesthete, and, to the last, the film hammers out its message when Brock complains about life in the army. Brock's complaints are superficial, hardly deep-seated — 'I can grouse about anything I like . . . We own the right to be fed up with anything we damned please and say so out loud when we feel like it . . . You can't even begin to understand democracy'. All he really wants to do is to get into the fighting, in earnest, and his first opportunity arrives when they are transported across the border at Niagara Falls. For Hirth this means freedom, as he planned, but for Brock it spells desertion, not what he intended at all. Hirth insists that the American customs officials grant him entry since America is a neutral country and not at war with Germany, and he demands to be conducted safely to the German consul. The Americans are not happy with the idea, since they have heard about the trail of death and destruction left in the wake of the submariners' trek across Canada.

Brock ingeniously suggests that they should refuse entry on the grounds that he and Hirth are both 'unlisted items . . . not in the manifest'. The Americans are only too pleased to be persuaded by such an argument and agree to return the freight car, with Hirth and Brock inside it, to Canada. 'Thanks a million', says Brock. 'We've all got to do our duty, soldier', says one American. And when Hirth protests that they should not do such a thing, the same American customs official retorts, 'Sonny boy, I've done it'. As the train backs down the railway track, over the Niagara Falls and into Canada, Brock dons his army cap, beckons to Hirth to defend himself, and, like Scott before him, he proceeds to exact his own personal and particular kind of retribution. At which point, the film ends.[32]

The film of *49th Parallel*, then, was nothing if not a thoroughly schematic and heavily programmed attempt to fulfil all the criteria of excellence for film propaganda laid down by the Films Division of the MoI. It addressed the larger question of 'what we are fighting for' and in so doing very carefully and conscientiously set out the advantages of adhering to democratic ideals and of following the democratic system of government, when compared with the hardships to be endured from espousing Nazi ideology and of living under the Nazi new order. Apart from depicting the conflict of ideas and issues at stake, it also managed to bring in the important matter of the part played by the Dominions in the war and incidentally, though not insignificantly, it sought to allude to the American

Andy Brock (Raymond Massey) corners Hirth at the last and puts an end to his ideas of triumphant escape back to Germany.

position as well and to the potential contribution that might be forthcoming from that quarter. In short, the film did everything that might have been expected of it. How, though, was it received?

The trade press was nothing if not wholeheartedly enthusiastic. Noting that 'The general interest taken in this Ortus production since its conception has been unusually keen', *Today's Cinema* commented:

> *49th Parallel* is not only a document of historical importance but an entertainment to rejoice the heart of the exhibitor in no small measure. We predict for it a success that is without parallel in the history of British showmen not only on the grounds of its magnificent cast and advance publicity but on its sheer entertainment merit. *49th Parallel* is an event in British production history, a remarkable achievement in many ways, an entertainment feast for all audiences and a natural box office record beater.[33]

And, indeed, such sentiments were echoed throughout the trade press where all agreed that the film was the 'best British effort since the war began'. Even the American trade press felt compelled to acknowledge that with *49th Parallel* (retitled *The Invaders* for the American market) 'Michael Powell consolidates his place as one of the minute band of directors in England whose work is equal to the best in Hollywood'.[34]

However, reservations were expressed in some quarters about the depiction of the enemy. William Whitebait, in the *New Statesmen*, noted:

49th Parallel is an adventure story, and a bit more. The bit more interests me, because it makes and mars. Six survivors from the crew of a sunk Nazi submarine fighting their way across Canada towards the border and dropping out one by one — there's the story. Such tales of escape are not uncommon in wartime, when every hill in enemy territory becomes a Himalaya and every trout stream an unexplored Amazon; every day we are thrilled to read in the newspapers of French schoolboys crossing the Channel in a canoe, Polish soldiers who have struggled half across Europe to freedom.

Possibly we should be less thrilled by similar feats of the Nazis, but still our response would be to adventure and not to patriotism, the hero would be the pursued. The difficulty, then, of *49th Parallel* is that the natural heroes of its adventures are the campaigning Nazis. The further they get and the more hardships they have to undergo, the more inclined shall we be to sympathise.

Our sympathies are checked in a number of ways. Before the submarine is sunk, we are shown scenes of its last victim, a tanker crew left in an open boat to drown; and the brutalities of 'total warfare' accompany the overland trek of the escaping Nazis. They shoot their way through a happy looking outpost of Lapps, batter a French Canadian trapper to death, execute one of their own crew who tries to join a peaceful settlement of Hutterites, and even keep four bullets for Leslie Howard, writing about Indian customs and cherishing a Picasso in a tent in the Rockies.

With each new episode the argument between Hitlerism and Democracy turns another page; the innately peaceful countryside, splendidly photographed and extending over a thousand miles of cornland and mountain, is Democracy's trump card, and its half-dozen invaders are made to look like cobras in a Surrey garden. This, with Mr Howard's cool-card act and Mr Raymond Massey waiting in his short tails to knock out the last Nazi, carries the film successfully to its end. More or less successfully. *49th Parallel* doesn't go with a bang like *Pimpernel Smith*, and it isn't single-minded enough to be continuously exciting. However, if the case for Democracy, a thrilling adventure, a constellation of actors (Laurence Olivier and Eric Portman must be added to those mentioned), and a landscape album can all be crammed into one film, here it is.[35]

And the question of the sympathetic depiction of the enemy was raised, and rejected, in the course of a long *Documentary News Letter* review of the film, which read in part:

> Granted, however, that the film has strong entertainment value, there still remains the consideration of its value as propaganda. Views on this appear to differ. On the negative side it has been claimed (*a*) that we have been so conditioned by Hollywood to being on the side of the hunted rather than the hunters that there is bound to be some sympathy with the pursued Nazis; (*b*) that it's a pretty poor show if six Germans can be at large for so long in a hostile country; and (*c*) that an episode such as that in which an Englishman is presented as a dilettante is just playing into German hands, and that the toughness of the pay-off doesn't redress the negative effect.
>
> On the whole these accusations will probably turn out to be more academic than real. The film throughout shows signs of the most careful scripting from the propaganda point of view, and each episode may be said to be conceived as a positive answer to questions arising from insinuations regarding the democratic standpoint.
>
> As far as the pursuit goes, it must be remembered that the actions of the Nazis throughout the film include brutalities of various description, including cold-blooded murder. And if Eric Portman's brilliant performance as the Nazi commander gains a certain warmth at times, it is only in terms of that blind and fanatical loyalty which has so far been one of Hitler's major secrets of success. It is a loyalty which this film, step by step, reveals as a false faith. It just doesn't make the grade in the long run.
>
> Leslie Howard's portrayal of the dilettante is bound to cause a certain amount of heartburn over here, but there is a good deal of justification for this particular sequence as far as opinion in the New World is concerned. Whether we like it or not, a picture of the Englishman as soft and decadent has grown up over the past ten years, especially in the USA, and it is probably good propaganda to take the bull by the horns and put him on the screen. Here the trick is to give your audience a picture of someone whom they wrongly think is representative, and to turn the tables on them by revealing him as unexpectedly tough. Whatever opinion over here may be, it's a likely bet that Howard's knockout of the Nazi will be a good propaganda stroke in the USA.[36]

In the event, the film certainly appeared to repay the faith that was placed in it, for it turned out to be a huge popular and commercial success. The film was the top moneymaker at the British box office for 1941, and it won an Academy Award in 1942 for Emeric Pressburger's screenplay. It more than repaid the MoI's financial investment and, in time, the MoI was able to hand over to the Exchequer a clear profit of £132,331 on the film.[37] Adequate testimony of its effectiveness as propaganda in neutral countries was provided, again in 1942, when the Argentine government sought to bar it from their cinema screens, lest it 'Injure the cordial relations existing between Germany and Argentina'.[38]

In one respect, clearly, the film of *49th Parallel* did not accord fully with

MoI intentions by the time of its release. When the project was conceived, one line in MoI thinking was definitely of the opinion that it was still possible to make a distinction between the German people and its National Socialist leaders and that, in particular, 'The overthrow of National Socialism is the one hope for the future of the German people'.[39] In its occasionally sympathetic portrayal of the enemy, *49th Parallel* may be said to have manifested that feeling. In the spring of 1940, however, the tone and tenor of British propaganda underwent an abrupt change as the war was engaged in earnest, and for the rest of the war 'the new orthodoxy', as Ian McLaine describes it, was very much one which signalled that 'there can be no distinction between a German and a Nazi' and which held to the belief that 'Nazism is but the latest and most virulent manifestation of the inherent wickedness of the German race'.[40] This was especially true of the MoI's various Anger Campaigns.

49th Parallel exhibited few such tendencies, but then perhaps that was no bad thing: the MoI found it exceedingly difficult to sell the idea to the British public that all Germans should be tarred with the same Nazi brush. Perhaps, in the final analysis, *49th Parallel* was a success precisely because, for all its evident intentions, it did not resort to the simple propagandist expedient of painting the enemy universally black.

NOTES

1   Ian Dalrymple, 'The Crown Film Unit, 1940—43', in Nicholas Pronay and D. W. Spring (eds), *Propaganda, Politics and Film 1918—45*, London, 1982, pp. 209—10.
2   Michael Powell's brief account of the film's production was given in an interview with David Badder, 'Powell and Pressburger: The War Years', *Sight and Sound*, 48, Winter 1978/79, p. 8. But considerably more detail on the circumstances surrounding the film's production and reception can be found in Mass-Observation File Report No. 15, '*The Lion Has Wings*', December 1939.
3   See M-O File Report No. 15, pp. 19—22, and pp. 27—8. Also Tom Harrisson, 'Social Research and the Film', *Documentary News Letter*, 1, November 1940, p. 10.
4   *Documentary News Letter*, 1, January 1940, p. 8.
5   Dalrymple, 'The Crown Film Unit', p. 210.
6   Memorandum by Sir Kenneth Clark to Regional Information Officers, 27 February 1940, INF 1/196.
7   See the letter by Christopher Brunel, dated 2 December 1939, in M-O File Report No. 15, pp. 33—4.
8   'Receipts from commercial distribution of films, summary of statement 18 prepared for evidence for the Public Accounts Committee in May 1944', INF 1/199.

9   Co-ordinating Committee minutes, 19th meeting, 23 November 1939, INF 1/867.
10 Minute 252, 25th meeting of the Newsreel Association of Great Britain and Ireland Ltd, 30 October 1939 (British Movietonews, Denham.)
11 Minute 260, 26th NRA Council Meeting, 20 November 1939.
12 Minute 303, 29th NRA Council Meeting, 22 January 1940.
13 See Anthony Aldgate, *Cinema and History. British Newsreels and the Spanish Civil War*, London, 1979, for the newsreels throughout the 1930s.
14 Minute 317, 30th NRA Council Meeting, 8 February 1940; minute 344, 31st NRA Council Meeting, 14 March 1940; and minute 360, 32nd NRA Council Meeting, 11 April 1940.
15 Minute 679, 45th NRA Council Meeting, 15 May 1941.
16 Minute 812 of the Resumed Emergency NRA Council Meeting, 20 October 1941; and minute 1006, NRA Council Meeting, 9 April 1942.
17 Minute 588 of the Emergency NRA Council Meeting, 5 February 1941.
18 Minute 604 of the Emergency NRA Council Meeting, 24 February 1941.
19 See Nicholas Pronay, 'The News Media at War', *Propaganda, Politics and Film*, pp. 173–208. The minutes of the NRA Council Meetings also bear eloquent and unexplored testimony to the many rifts.
20 Policy Committee Paper No. 4, 'The principles underlying British War Time Propaganda', INF 1/848.
21 Co-ordinating Committee Paper No. 1, 'Programme for film propaganda', INF 1/867.
22 Quoted in Marion Yass, *This Is Your War*, London, 1983, p. 16. Of course by no means all the projects came to fruition and some were scrapped along the way.
23 Policy Committee Paper No. 33, 26 March 1940, p. 4, INF 1/848.
24 In Badder, 'Powell and Pressburger: The War Years', pp. 8–9.
25 Policy Committee minutes, 'Publicity about the British Empire (Empire Publicity Division)', 22 January 1944, INF 1/848.
26 Policy Committee Paper No. 35, 'Proposed plans and budget of the Empire Division, April–September 1940: Propaganda about the Empire', INF 1/848.
27 See Kevin Gough-Yates, *Michael Powell: in Collaboration with Emeric Pressburger*, London, 1971, p. 7, and the notes on 'How *49th Parallel* was born' on the microfiche for the film held at the British Film Institute Library, London.
28 *13th Report from the Select Committee on National Expenditure*, August 1940, p. 5, INF 1/59. Two commentators have recently concluded that even before it handed down its recommendations, the Select Committee had already been 'misled' on at least two counts: the actual audience figures for non-theatrical film showings, and the costs involved in the production of *49th Parallel*. For the first matter see Nicholas Pronay, 'The News Media at War', p. 187, and for the latter, see Paul Morley Titmuss, *Commercial Feature Film Production and the Ministry of Information*, unpublished MA Thesis, Polytechnic of Central London, 1982, p. 29.
29 For the advances on the feature film front see Vincent Porter and Chaim Litewski, '*The Way Ahead*. Case history of a propaganda film', *Sight and

Sound, 50, Spring 1981, pp. 110—16. For the documentary film, see Nicholas Pronay, '"The Land of Promise": the Projection of Peace Aims in Britain', in K. R. M. Short (ed.), *Film and Radio Propaganda in World War II*, London, 1983, pp. 51—77.

30   In Badder, 'Powell and Pressburger: The War Years', pp. 9—10.

31   *Documentary News Letter*, 1, December 1940, p. 2.

32   Rodney Ackland did not like Emeric Pressburger's script for the film's end at all since he felt that Brock's attack on Hirth only served to undermine the anti-Nazi message of the film. See Rodney Ackland and Elspeth Grant, *The Celluloid Mistress*, London, 1954, pp. 93—103, for Ackland's account of the production of the film.

33   *Today's Cinema*, 10 October 1941, p. 7.

34   *Motion Picture Herald*, 8 November 1941, p. 349. It also commented: 'The partial financial interest of the British Ministry of Information might be noted by the cautious showman'.

35   *New Statesman*, 18 October 1941.

36   *Documentary News Letter*, 2, November 1941, p. 215.

37   The film made £116,432 up to May 1944 and another £15,899 in the months thereafter up to September 1944. See 'Receipts from commercial distribution of films . . .', INF 1/199. Powell believes that Columbia 'made a fortune out of it' in America, see Kevin Gough-Yates, *in Collaboration with . . .* , p. 7. Certainly, Rank should have been happy with his share since 'In the end the film earned a good return'. See Alan Wood, *Mr Rank*, London, 1952, p. 153.

38   *The Times*, 10 August 1942.

39   Ian McLaine, *Ministry of Morale*, London, 1979, p. 140.

40   McLaine, *Ministry of Morale*, p. 146.

3

The Englishman's Englishman

Pimpernel Smith

The publication in 1981 of Ronald Howard's graceful and illuminating account of the last years of his father's life once again turned attention on the mystery surrounding his death.[1] Leslie Howard died on 1 June 1943, when the civil aircraft in which he was travelling back to England from a lecture tour of Spain and Portugal was shot down over the Bay of Biscay by German fighter planes. Two principal views exist, neither of them conclusively provable, as to why the Germans should have singled out this particular plane for attack. One view is that they believed that Winston Churchill was aboard, a view Churchill himself accepted and which was argued by Ian Colvin in a book about the tragedy, published in 1957.[2] The other view, advanced by the Howard family and developed at length by Ronald Howard, is that the Germans were actually after Leslie. Why? Ronald Howard says it was because his father was 'Britain's most powerful and effective propagandist.' The impressive and varied body of Leslie's propaganda work, the gloating prominence accorded to news of his death in Nazi newspapers, the threats made against him on the air by 'Lord Haw-Haw' ('We will make this pompous British actor repent his words'), and the known fact that he was under close enemy observation from the day he landed in Lisbon in April 1943 all suggest that the Germans regarded him as being of especial significance.[3]

Contemporary British newspapers were in no doubt of Leslie's propaganda importance. Hannen Swaffer wrote of him in the *Daily Herald*:

> Leslie Howard died as he would have wished it — serving his country. Really good actor though he was, film star though he became, he was proudest of the propaganda work he did in the war, on screen, on the platform and on the air. His broadcasts to the States and Canada were admirable. They had in them not only eloquence but deep sincerity.[4]

Ernest Betts declared in the *Daily Express*:

> Howard used the screen as the voice of England speaking to the world. Since the war he had become one of the BBC's foremost commentators on the thoughts and ideals of England. His fans will mourn him as a personal friend, and British films as one of the most brilliant of leading men.[5]

The *Star* proclaimed him:

> undoubtedly one of the most effective propaganda agents that England has employed during the war, and the sincerity and force in all he said arose from an ardent patriotism.[6]

The *Sydney Morning Herald* said:

> If historians ever compile a list of Englishmen who helped to save their country from going under when the full force of Hitler's might weighed down upon her, they surely will include in it the name of Leslie Howard — actor, writer and patriot.[7]

This view was confirmed in immediate post-war assessments of the wartime propaganda effort. The *British Film Yearbook for 1945* recorded:

> Leslie Howard, whose presence in England, as a producer, director and actor, constituted in itself one of the most valuable facets of British propaganda, was responsible for many fine British productions. This kindly, intelligent and cultured Englishman did much in his screen appearances to present to the rest of the world the embodiment of the finest qualities of the British people. His dignity, charm and tolerance, as apparent on the screen as off it, were indeed invaluable propaganda assets. He was representative of the finest type of Englishman and his loss . . . was one of the tragedies of the war.[8]

In the filmgoer's diary she contributed to *Red Roses Every Night* (1948), the *Observer*'s film critic C. A. Lejeune, wrote:

> The death of Leslie Howard was a tragic loss to the British cinema: for Leslie Howard, both as actor and director, was something of a symbol to the British people. He came home from America to help us when times were bad; his *Pimpernel Smith* and *The First of the Few* were the right films at the right moment. The public liked and trusted his quiet voice and whimsical judgement; he had, and always will have, a very special place in his country's affections.[9]

It was perhaps because he was in a very real sense seen both at home and abroad as the Englishman's Englishman, the ideal and epitome of all that was best, noblest and most civilized in the embattled island race, that he was the object of so much affection on the one hand and of such Nazi animosity on the other.

In its obituary of him, the *Manchester Guardian* specifically located his appeal in his Englishness:

> A frank, intensely English quality in Howard's voice, face and bearing must be taken as part explanation of his sustained popularity in New York. It was this same intensely English quality which made him popular everywhere in intensely English film parts like Sir Percy Blakeney, his modern contemporary Pimpernel Smith and the professor of phonetics in *Pygmalion*.[10]

The war brought into sharp focus the meaning of England and Englishness. There is in wartime a heightening of the emotions, a quickening of the pulse. It is a time for poetry and brave words. Sentiments can be uttered and felt and believed which in prosaic peace time seem inflated, exaggerated, unreal. Feelings come bubbling to the surface in people who face every day the prospect of death, feelings which in ordinary times are buried so deep that they may not even be known to exist, for there is a need to articulate why we fight and for what.

The result of that need was a spate of books analysing and investigating England and the English; books with titles like *The English People, The Character of England* and *God's Englishman.* There were also anthologies of poetry and prose which sought to project an image of England. Over and over again in these works one finds recurring the ideas that together make up the concept 'England' — a love of tradition, balance and order; a belief in tolerance and humanity; and above all, perhaps, a sense of humour, that redoubtable bulwark against tyranny.

It is these values and virtues which were powerfully expressed and embodied by the two men who come first to mind as speaking for England in the darkest days of the war. It was Winston Churchill who, in the words of President Kennedy, 'mobilized the English language and sent it into battle'. It was Churchill who was the official voice of Britain, speaking with a deep consciousness of the weight of history, his language deliberately archaic and therefore timeless. When he said after Alamein 'a bright gleam has caught the helmets of our soldiers' he might have been talking of Caesar's army or that of Richard the Lionheart. The golden rhetoric, delivered in those distinctive rolling cadences, drew on the majestic imagery and language of a heroic past, of Shakespeare and Milton, of Tennyson and Kipling. When he said 'Hitler and his Nazi gang have sown the wind, let them reap the whirlwind,' he awoke memories of the King James' version of the Bible in all its majesty and splendour, while from the classic war commentaries of the Ancient World like Caesar and Thucydides came sentences like 'Even if the Nazi legions stood triumphant

Pimpernel Smith celebrates the Englishman as committed idealist and romantic adventurer. Leslie Howard perfectly incarnated these qualities. His absent-minded professor conceals a courageous anti-Fascist (Howard with Hugh McDermott).

on the Black Sea, or indeed upon the Caspian, and if Hitler was at the gates of India, it would profit him nothing.' He compared the young pilots of the RAF to the knights of the Round Table and the Crusaders, the Battle of Britain to the struggle against the Spanish Armada, Hitler's invasion plans to those of Napoleon, and talked of the danger of us sinking into the 'abyss of a new Dark Age'. He saw and depicted the war on an epic scale — the conflict of the forces of light against the forces of darkness, the sea-girt islands of Britain as the last bastion of freedom against the hordes of 'ferocious pagan barbarians', the Huns, as he liked to call them. He saw the question 'Why we fight' on the broad canvas. He saw a nation walking with destiny.

Like the man himself, it was an awe-inspiring vision, patriotic, passionate, romantic, huge. Yet with all this, it was still shot through with that Puckish humour which enabled him to call his arch-enemy 'Corporal Hitler', to produce classic one-liners like the joke about England having its neck wrung like a chicken — 'Some chicken, some neck' — and the deliberate mispronunciation of words like Nazi and Luftwaffe, done with all the glee of a mischievous overgrown schoolboy.

From the start, his broadcasts struck the right chords. Mass-Observation recorded of October 1939:

> October came with everyone still waiting for something to happen. There were months of waiting still ahead, but they were not to know that. All that happened for a time was a series of speeches. The first of these, Winston Churchill's broadcast on October 1, was different from anything that had come from our Government so far. People as they listened felt once again that this country really was at war; instead of uncertainty and bewilderment, here was plain speaking that anyone could understand. The effect was registered by the diaries:
> 'Churchill gave us a good fruity speech this evening.'
> 'Winston's wonderful talk.'
> 'Hear Winston's speech. Very good. Think he ought to be Prime Minister . . . Thought his definition of what we are fighting for was put plainer than we had had it before.'

Mass-Observation also recorded a conversation between two Bolton millworkers:

> A: Ah bet tha' heard Churchill.
> B: Aye, I did.
> A: He doesn't half give it them. I corn't go to sleep when he's on. He's best talker we have.
> B: He tells 'em straight. Everybody listens to him. We were talking about him at work today. He's the only gradely man we have.[11]

At the other end of the social scale, the broadcasts by Churchill helped to confirm doubters about his capacity to lead the nation at war. On 11 May 1940 the weekly magazine *Time and Tide* were declaring their unequivocal support for Lord Halifax 'as the man who at this moment stands out amongst all the possibilities as the one most fitted to be Prime Minister. He has that rare quality, absolute integrity.'[12] But by May 25, they were writing:

> Mr Churchill's broadcast last Sunday definitely registered a lift-up in the national morale. The nation, worried rather than dismayed, recognized in that speech, not a man reading from a departmentally prepared script, but its true national leader . . . He spoke from his heart and the clarion call from Judas Maccabeus was a perfect ending to his moving words. In these dread

days England recognizes that she is governed by a great man whom the hour and opportunity are making greater still.[13]

By June 22, they were calling him 'the essential Englishman, the descendant of Marlborough, the shaggy lion that never admits defeat.'[14]

Another reaction to his broadcasts is recorded by the left-wing journalist Hamilton Fyfe in his wartime diary (9 February 1941):

> Churchill gave another of his really stirring radio talks this evening, stressing especially the probability of invasion. Richard Acland was right when he said in the House not long ago 'we literally love the Premier'. It is odd that one who is half-American — and that the better half — should so completely embody the John Bullishness which the English like to consider their main characteristic. Baldwin tried to act the part and failed. Churchill does it instinctively. When he calls Mussolini 'a crafty, cold-blooded, black-hearted Italian', and Hitler 'that wicked man whose crime-stained system is now at bay', the phrases come from his inmost being. When he tells how he gave Wavell the word 'Go' in the language of the Gospel according to St Matthew: 'Ask and it shall be given, seek and ye shall find, knock and it shall be opened unto you,' and then exclaims triumphantly: 'The Army of the Nile has asked and it was given. They sought and they have found. They knocked and it has been opened unto them', he hits exactly that mixture of piety and profanity which the English learn from their earliest years.[15]

The BBC recorded that when Churchill spoke on the radio, 70 per cent of the population listened.[16]

But Churchill's was not the only voice to galvanize the listening public. As Aneurin Bevan wrote of him in 1940: 'His ear is so sensitively attuned to the bugle note of history that he is deaf to the raucous clamour of contemporary life.'[17] At the same time as Churchill was speaking and broadcasting the 'official' message, setting the war in its historical context, another voice was focusing on the details of everyday life, the unofficial voice, the voice of Everyman as opposed to Superman — J. B. Priestley, who in 1940 and 1941 broadcast postscripts to the BBC's Sunday evening news bulletins.[18] Priestley's oft-repeated creed was that 'the true heroes and heroines of this war, whose courage, patience and good humour stand like a rock above the dark morass of treachery, cowardice and panic, are the ordinary British folk'.

In his warming Yorkshire accent, he spoke of 'the simple, kindly, humorous, brave . . . ordinary British folk . . . a good people, who deep in their hearts only wish to do what they feel is God's will.' He rejoiced in the sense of community and the qualities sustaining it, kindness, humour and courage, qualities which he saw projected from the ordinary folk on to the nation as a whole ('the kindness of England, of Britain, of the wide

Empire forever reaching out towards new expressions of freedom'). He proclaimed his faith in the Common Man at his greatest moment of truth:

> To oppose those men and their evil doctrine, we must not only summon our armed forces, wave our flags and sing our national anthem, but we must go deeper and, by an almost mystical act of will, hold to our faith and our hope. We have to fight this great battle not only with guns in daylight, but alone in the night, communing with our souls, strengthening our faith that in common men everywhere there is a spring of innocent aspiration and good will that shall not be sealed.[19]

He spoke to his audience of things they could relate directly to — of spring in his garden, of seaside holidays and family reunions, of the factory canteen and Home Guard duty, and they responded. As he was to say many years later:

> To this day middle-aged and elderly men shake my hand and tell me what a ten-minute talk about ducks on a pond or a pie in a shop window meant to them, as if I had given them *King Lear* or the Eroica.[20]

But it was the tangible realities of the duckpond and the pieshop for which Britain was fighting as much as for the abstract concepts of freedom and democracy.

Nothing perhaps encapsulates the difference of style between Churchill and Priestley so much as their response to Dunkirk. Where Churchill spoke in ringing heroic terms of the abstract qualities it demonstrated — 'valour, perseverance, perfect discipline, faultless service, resource, skill and unconquerable fidelity' — Priestley eulogized the little seaside pleasure steamers pressed into service for the evacuation and evoking the world they represented, the world of 'pierrots and piers, ham and egg teas, palmists, automatic machines and crowded, sweating promenades.'

Even more significantly, a difference emerged about the ultimate aim of the war. For Churchill it was simple: 'We have to gain the victory. That is our task'; and beyond the victory, the vague generalized statement that the world would move forward into 'broad sunlit uplands'. But for Priestley it was what came after the war that was vitally important. We were fighting, he said, 'not so that we can go back to anything. There's nothing that really worked that we can go back to'. So our aim must be 'new and better homes, real homes, a decent chance at last — new life.' He had detected the radical shift in the national mood which the war had triggered:

> The war because it demands a huge collective effort, is compelling us to change not only our ordinary, social and economic habits but also our habits of thought. We've actually changed over from the property view to the sense

of community, which simply means that we realize we're all in the same boat.[21]

Mass-Observation reported in November 1940: 'In the last few months it has been hard to find, even among women, many who do not unconsciously regard this war as in some way revolutionary and radical.'[22] Foreign observers noted the shift in popular attitudes. Ralph Ingersoll, editor of the New York paper *P.M.*, wrote in his *Report on England* (1941): 'In direct answer to the questions Do you believe there is a social revolution in England? And if so, in which direction? I would have no hesitancy in answering: Yes, to the left'.[23]

A new consensus was forming around the demand for full employment, social security, a national health service, forward planning and educational reform. The rapturous reception of the Beveridge Report in 1942, which according to Home Intelligence many regarded as 'the ark of the Covenant', signalled the emotional and intellectual victory of this new consensus.[24]

Priestley's postscripts were one of the harbingers of the new consensus. *Time and Tide* talked of their impact and how they reflected the new spirit of Britain in October 1940:

> A significant mark of our awakening spirit is the way in which the Priestley broadcasts have been received, the sudden fame and immense popularity of these short Sunday evening postscripts. Somehow J. B. Priestley has succeeded in evoking for us — for almost all of us — the very spirit of the age we want to live in. A world of kindness, equality, justice, simplicity and fellowship. There are, of course, still a few people who mistrust the spirit of the Priestley broadcasts, people who have no wish whatever to listen to forecasts of a more just and equal society where their privileges will mean nothing and their chances be the same as those of their fellows. . . . Over the country as a whole the Priestley broadcasts have been accepted by the vast majority of the well-to-do, as well as by the vast majority of the less well-to-do and the badly-to-do, as the expression of their own desire for a new order of a very different stamp from the old order . . . The foundations of the new England must be laid to provide for immense improvements in such directions as housing, health and education.[25]

The BBC credited Priestley with 'the biggest regular listening audience in the war' — 30 per cent of the regular listeners, an unprecedentedly large figure for talks.[26]

But a third name needs to be added to those of Churchill and Priestley, that of Leslie Howard. C. A. Lejeune wrote of him that he had 'a passion for England and the English idea that was almost Shakespearean'.[27] He had returned to England as the war loomed, burning with a desire to contribute to the war effort. His activities were prodigious. He broadcast regularly, particularly to the United States and the Empire. He joined the ideas committee of the Ministry of Information. He acted in the MoI's first full-length feature film *49th Parallel* (1941), playing an aesthete roused to action when fugitive Nazi submariners destroy his books and pictures, and in the documentary short *From the Four Corners* (1941), in which he showed three Commonwealth soldiers round London and talked about the ideals they were all fighting for. He spoke the final epilogue for Noël Coward's tribute to the Navy *In Which We Serve* (1942) and spoke the commentary for *The White Eagle* (1941), a documentary about exiled Poles in Britain striving to preserve their culture. He produced a film about nurses, *The Lamp Still Burns* (1943) and directed and narrated a memorable film tribute to the ATS, *The Gentle Sex* (1943). He made his final public appearance as Nelson on the steps of St Paul's reciting the last prayer before Trafalgar. C. A. Lejeune recalled it when writing his obituary:

The public really loved him. I shall never forget the electric thrill that ran

Pimpernel Smith send up the humourless Nazis (Howard with Francis L. Sullivan and Raymond Huntley).

through the crowd outside St Paul's Cathedral when he appeared as Nelson in the pageant of the *Cathedral Steps*. That brief moment stopped the show.[28]

But above all, he directed and starred in two of the finest British wartime films, *Pimpernel Smith* (1941) and *The First of the Few* (1942). Their humanity and their humour, their sensitivity and idealism, and above all their quiet and abiding Englishness make them masterworks of the British cinema.

It is in these films that we see that aspect of Englishness that Leslie Howard particularly incarnated. He had always been unique in the galaxy of film stars. For while the other star types — tough guy, 'honest Joe', 'Latin lover' — had many exponents, there had only ever been one intellectual star, Leslie Howard, the thinking man as hero. He managed to sidestep the deep rooted mistrust of intellectuals, the idea that they are all 'too clever by half', by romanticizing and humanizing them. He made acceptable, even attractive to the general public, the man of brains rather than brawn. It was partly his looks and partly his manner. 'Frankly and intensely English' they may have been, despite the fact that his father was a Hungarian Jew, but the sensitive features and blond good looks, the cultured speaking voice, the slightly absent-minded air, offset by the dry, donnish wit, all combined to give the appearance of the 'absent minded professor'. He returned again and again to the role of the intellectual humanized, brought down from the heights of academe to discover personal commitment and the real world — in *The Petrified Forest, Stand-In* and most notably as Henry Higgins in *Pygmalion*. His wartime roles were similarly intellectual and it is worth noting in this context that it was a war in which Oxbridge dons became codebreakers, history lecturers turned into experts in black propaganda and the affectionate term 'boffin' was invented for scientists working with the forces. Scientists and intellectuals were never to occupy the same place in public esteem again.[29]

But there was another dimension to the Howard persona and it is perhaps in this that his appeal truly lay. It was that dreamy, other-worldly air which enabled him to play some of the most memorable roles of his film career. In *Outward Bound*, he was a drunken intellectual on a ship of dead souls drifting towards their last judgement. In *Smilin' Through*, he was the old baronet communing with the spirit of his dead sweetheart and eventually joining her on 'the other side'. In *Berkeley Square* he was a young American, obsessed with the past, who is transported back to the 18th century and there falls in love with a woman whom he knows he can never have. All three films were subsequently remade but no one ever equalled the understanding and subtlety that Howard brought to the roles.

In the light of this, it seems reasonable to assume that what he represented to wartime audiences was that visionary aspect of Englishness, that fey, mystical quality, that striving after the secrets of the eternal, that crops out periodically in English writing and English thought. It is there in the music of Elgar and Vaughan Williams, in the writings of Kipling and Haggard, in the poetry of Henry Newbolt and Rupert Brooke. It has a peculiarly potent linkage with war, and it can be seen in the lifestyle and ideas of a remarkable succession of soldier-mystics, who sought out deserts and high places in order to commune with the Almighty — Lawrence of Arabia, Gordon of Khartoum, Younghusband of Tibet, Orde Wingate of the Chindits. It runs parallel with a visionary Imperialism which emerged at the end of the 19th century, transcending mere national origin and compounded of the ideas of destiny, duty and the British as the elect whose God-given mission it was to bring peace, order and good government to the world.

As Kipling put it:

Came the whisper, came the vision, came the power with the need,
Till the soul that is not Man's soul was lent us to lead.

It is curious to observe in a whole gallery of Victorian and Edwardian worthies almost a double life. There is the surface image of the bluff and hearty clubman and public servant, the pipe smoke and the tweeds, the bracing early morning walks and the rigours of the full English breakfast. But behind this, there is a powerful inner spirit — beliefs in reincarnation and communication across the void, the desire to peer through 'the gap in the curtain', to make contact with 'the people of the mist'. It is no coincidence that it should revive powerfully in wartime, when nation and empire were as one, when the old Imperialist Winston Churchill was at the helm and when death was all around.

Leslie Howard reflected this blend of nation, empire, mysticism and war in his very first broadcast to the United States, when he said:

I can't explain the mystery of the call that comes to people from the land of their birth — I don't have to explain it to you anyway. The call of Britain seems particularly potent, doesn't it — look at the way they've come hurrying in response from the four corners of the earth, especially as that call comes at what must be the most critical moment of our whole long history. Most of you, I'm sure, will know what I mean when I speak of the curious elation which comes from sharing in a high and mysterious destiny. The destiny of Britain we cannot know for certain, but we can guess at it and pray for it and work towards it as we find ourselves singled out of all the nations in the world for the rare honour of fighting alone against the huge and ruthless forces of tyranny.[30]

It caught a particular mood in people, a mood also expressed in the last verse of Rupert Brooke's *The Soldier*, which enjoyed renewed popularity during the Second World War. He talks of a fallen combatant buried in 'some corner of a foreign field that is forever England' and ends:

> And think, this heart, all evil shed away,
> A pulse in the eternal mind, no less
> Gives somewhere back the thoughts by England given;
> Her sights and sounds; dreams happy as her day;
> And laughter learnt of friends; and gentleness
> In hearts at peace, under an English heaven

That this is not just poetic fancy is confirmed by this passage from the last letter of a Fleet Air Arm officer to his parents:

> My life has been given and taken in company with so many others for the preservation of things by nature spiritual. I believe in these things for which I have joined the fight. I believe in them with all my being. They are so much bigger, so infinitely more important, so much worthier than I am. But those spiritual things are a part of me and I a part, minute though it may be, of them.[31]

In Leslie Howard's two great wartime films this sense of spirituality was added to the other ingredients, the Englishness, the sense of humour — gentle, ironic, understated and witty — and the sense of proportion — the restraint, compassion and sensitivity. In that sense the war was his apotheosis.

Howard had already been planning to move from acting into writing and directing. In spite of his success as an actor, he had always secretly desired to be a writer. He wrote prodigiously and continuously but almost wholly unsuccessfully. He had several thriller stories accepted by boys' papers when a teenager. He wrote articles for the *New Yorker* and *Vanity Fair*. Of the plays he wrote, only two were produced (*Murray Hill* and *Alias Mrs Jones*) and both flopped. But as a director he found a role in which all his talents could be blended together. He could contribute to screenplays, shape film projects, play the leading roles and create the visual realization of his ideas himself. Adrian Brunel, who worked with him on several wartime projects, left this record of working with Howard:

> Leslie had a first class brain and, in spite of his inclination to roam, he had great concentrative ability. Before he began to direct a scene, we would usually discuss its shape; he would outline his plan, using me as a sounding board and getting my technical reactions. Then he would either go from his dressing room where our discussions often took place or he would break away from our huddle in a corner of the studio, and take charge on the floor. Finally he would go over his own lines, if it was a scene in which he

appeared, and by a tremendous power of concentration, would speak the lines without fault. When he came to photograph a scene, the lines came from him with such apparent naturalness and effortlessness, with such clarity, sincerity and mastery of meaning that it was a revelation. He was a really great artist.[32]

He liked a relaxed atmosphere in which to work, rarely did much before 10.30am, improvised freely within the bounds of narrative development and brought to his films that creative enthusiasm which made them so much his own. Harold Nicolson experienced this enthusiasm when he dined on 2 April 1940 with Kenneth Clark, then director of the Films Division of the MoI and Leslie Howard was among the guests:

> We have an agreeable dinner and talk mostly about films. Leslie Howard is doing a big propaganda film and is frightfully keen about it . . . I come back with Leslie Howard and he continues to talk excitedly about his new film. He seems to enter into such things with the zest of a schoolboy and that is part of his charm.[33]

Howard had been steadily gathering experience in the late thirties. He had co-directed *Pygmalion* with Anthony Asquith and had acted as associate producer on *Intermezzo*, part of the deal by which producer David O. Selznick persuaded him to take the role of Ashley Wilkes, which he hated, in *Gone With the Wind*. He had taken a skiing holiday in Austria shortly before the Anschluss in 1938 and his discussions with Austrians, including the painter Alfons Walde, about the hated and feared prospect of a Nazi takeover made an indelible impression on him. He began to develop the idea of a film story based on the rescue of a famous painter from Nazi-occupied Austria. Early in 1940, he worked with the refugee writer Wolfgang Wilhelm developing a treatment for a feature film 'in which the cause of freedom and Britain's part in it would be clearly defined'. The work was interrupted by a trip to Paris in April 1940 to make arrangements for an Anglo-French propaganda film to star himself and Danielle Darrieux and to be directed by René Clair, but the fall of France put a stop to that.[34]

Howard enlisted the novelist A. G. Macdonell, author of *England, their England*, to help turn his treatment into a scenario. It was Macdonell who suggested making the hero a modern Pimpernel figure and he came up with the idea of an archaeology professor with a secret life as adventurer and freedom-fighter. They envisaged the role as a combination of Henry Higgins and Raffles, but Howard did not want his hero to be an aristocrat and deliberately chose the surname Smith to suggest his oneness with the people.

Macdonell was not a professional scriptwriter and so to turn the scenario into a shooting script, Howard brought in the prolific screenwriter Anatole

Smith managed, even in extreme situations, to outwit the Nazis.

de Grunwald. It was de Grunwald who suggested switching the university from Oxford to Cambridge, his own *alma mater*, and Howard fell in with this as it allowed him to quote from Rupert Brooke's *Grantchester*. In all Howard worked for eight months on the script, finally recruiting Roland Pertwee to do a polishing job, reshaping some scenes, adding others and supplying additional dialogue. Howard's habit of making script changes just before shooting kept Pertwee busy throughout the filming and he was present on the set, not only rewriting but also playing the small role of Professor Smith's diplomat brother.

Howard had from the first planned the film as a commercially backed project, but he found difficulty in getting a backer. Eventually Lewis Jackson of British National agreed to finance it and contracts were signed on 31 October 1940. The film was shot at Denham Studios between January and April 1941. The editing of *Pimpernel Smith* was supervised by Sidney Cole, whom Howard insisted should be present throughout the filming. Interviewed in 1985, Cole recalled: 'He wanted me on the floor, so that if there was anything I spotted as an editor about any shot I wanted, or any comment like that, I could say at the time instead of waiting for the rushes.' Cole thought Howard 'a very good director. He had a great sense of style, which came from his acting, and I found that the rhythm of his acting which then went over into his directing . . . was a guideline for the way I edited the film so as to preserve that very smooth, elegant flow of the picture.' The finished film was released in July 1941.

The film declares itself 'a fantasy but . . . based on the exploits of a number of courageous men who were and still are risking their lives daily to help those unfortunate people of many nationalities who are being persecuted and exterminated by the Nazis'. The picture is dedicated to them. They are epitomized by Pimpernel Smith, the committed intellectual, the dreamer with a cause.

The twin facets of his character are established at the outset. In Berlin in the spring of 1939 the anti-Nazi research scientist Dr Benckendorff is rescued within minutes of the Gestapo arriving to arrest him. His rescuer is a mysterious figure known as 'The Shadow', who sends the doctor a message to alert him — 'the mind of man is bounded only by the universe.' The familiar silhouette of Leslie Howard on the wall, a few whispered words, the tune 'there is a tavern in the town' whistled, and they are away. The Propaganda Ministry hasten to deny the activities of the rescuer: 'In Nazi Germany no one can hope to be saved by anybody.' The film then cuts to the Museum of Antiquities in Cambridge, where vague, absent-minded, bespectacled Professor Horatio Smith is complaining about the dust on his favourite statue of Aphrodite. He delivers an impromptu lecture on the goddess to an astonished crocodile of schoolgirls and then is reminded that he is half an hour late for his lecture. Arriving to deliver it, he drives out the female students by making disparaging remarks about the presence of women in the university and then announces his intention of taking a small party of students with him to Germany to investigate the question of whether or not there was an ancient Aryan civilization in Germany. After this, he dashes off for tea and crumpets, reciting Lewis Carroll as he strides through the college cloisters.

He departs for Germany with his student party, putting up at an inn near the Swiss frontier, from where, unknown to his students, he makes forays to rescue the artists and intellectuals he is pledged to save. On one such expedition, he disguises as a scarecrow and is shot in the arm. Next day, travelling by train to Berlin, the students read an account of the 'Shadow's' latest exploit, including the arm wound. They see that Smith is similarly wounded, put two and two together and insist on joining his rescue mission.

Meanwhile General von Graum heads the search for the 'Shadow'. His investigations lead him to a reception at the British Embassy but he makes no headway. He blackmails a Polish girl, Ludmilla Koslowski, into helping him trap the 'Shadow' by offering her the life of her imprisoned editor father, Sidimir Koslowski. She discovers that Smith is the 'Shadow' and enlists his aid to save her father. Smith and his student assistants rescue Koslowski and four others from a concentration camp and get them across the frontier. Smith himself goes back for Ludmilla with whom he has fallen in love, and gets her safely across the border. But he is himself trapped by von Graum at the frontier station. Nevertheless Smith outwits him and slips across the frontier to safety.

The keynote of the film's attitude to Germany is set by a shot of a poster of a buxom German wench, saying 'Come to Romantic Germany', accompanied on the soundtrack by the sound of Hitler ranting, jackboots crunching and gunfire. Thereafter the film proceeds to ridicule the Germans as uncultured, humourless, ungentlemanly and uncivilized. There is a succession of very funny, beautifully constructed scenes in which this is done. General von Graum, the Gestapo chief, investigates the English secret weapon — their sense of humour. He ploughs through P. G. Wodehouse, Edward Lear, Lewis Carroll and *Punch*, reading extracts to his bemused assistants, without raising a laugh and concludes that the English sense of humour is a myth. But the point of this sequence is in a sense the justification of the film. The film demonstrates unequivocally that a sense of humour is the English secret weapon: it is the essential quality which separates a civilized society from an uncivilized one. It is also one of the best means of transmitting propaganda and maintaining morale, something the Germans in reality never understood. But the fact that George Formby was, according to the *Motion Picture Herald*, the top British box office star from 1939 to 1943, demonstrates the importance of humour to the British in the darkest days of the war.

Equally funny are the scenes in which acrimonious high level discussions are held with a string quartet to try to identify the tune which the 'Shadow' whistles. It is eventually identified correctly as 'There is a tavern in the town' by a minor, music-hating clerk called Wagner. Smith himself mercilessly sends up von Graum at the Embassy reception, particularly when von Graum insists that Shakespeare is a German. Later Smith does a hilarious impersonation of a hectoring Nazi official in pinstriped suit, with rolled umbrella, constantly threatening to telephone Dr Goebbels.

But the humour was solidly underpinned by an exposition of Leslie Howard's philosophy, which he had already developed in his radio broadcasts. First, there is the glowing love of England. It had been his suggestion to add John of Gaunt's 'This England' speech from Shakespeare's *Richard II* to the finale of *The Scarlet Pimpernel* (1935). In *Pimpernel Smith*, sitting in a railway carriage with Ludmilla and heading for the border, he recites lines from Rupert Brooke's *Grantchester*:

> God, I will pack and take a train,
> And get me to England once again,
> For England is one land I know
> Where men with splendid hearts may go.

There is the hatred of violence and war, and even stronger, the detestation of those responsible for such horrors. He had declared in one broadcast:

> Most civilized people are . . . by nature pacific. Good men have always dreaded the horror of war, and, since the dawn of human intelligence, have tried to devise ways of preventing it . . . a nation which thinks only of war and aggression, which plots and plans to achieve its ends and its destiny by brute force, is exhibiting the symptoms of retrogression and uncivilization, and has become a criminal member of the society of nations.[35]

But he coupled this with a need to fight for these beliefs, for peace, freedom and democracy. Praising President Roosevelt for his brave, outward-looking concept of American democracy, he had said on the wireless:

> Democracy, to survive at all, must be as militant as autocracy, and what the world is desperately in need of now is not the gentle, philosophic democracy of Jefferson, but the outspoken, militant and ringing democracy of Roosevelt, representing the righteous anger of the free people of the world aroused against the cynical arrogance of the totalitarian feudalists.[36]

This righteous wrath suffuses the climactic sequence of *Pimpernel Smith*. In an early scene Smith tells Benckendorff: 'I hate violence. It seems such a paradox to kill a man before you can persuade him what's right. So uncivilized.' His philosophy comes into direct confrontation with von Graum's in the station on the frontier. Smith tells von Graum he despises violence, the new German god. Von Graum replies: 'Violence means power and power crushes opposition. The epoch of the council chamber is over. I tell you that power and strength and violence will rule the world.' Tomorrow, he goes on, the Nazis invade Poland and will go on to make a German Empire of the world. As the camera slowly tracks in to close-up and his eyes begin to glow with wrath, Horatio Smith tells him:

> You will never rule the world because you are doomed, all of you who have demoralized and corrupted a nation are doomed. Tonight you will take the first step along a dark road from which there is no turning back. You will have to go on from one madness to another, leaving behind you a wilderness of misery and hatred, and still you will have to go on because you will find no horizon and see no dawn until at last you are lost and destroyed. You are doomed, captain of murderers, and one day sooner or later, you will remember my words.

Von Graum takes Smith on to the platform, intending to shoot him 'while trying to escape'. Smith lights a last cigarette and stands wreathed in smoke beneath a lamp, a strange, ethereal figure, more spirit than substance. Smith continues to taunt von Graum until the German drops the vase he is holding, the proof that no ancient Aryan civilization existed in Germany. Von Graum's aides rush forward and in the confusion, Smith vanishes across the frontier, his voice mockingly echoing from the shadows: 'Don't worry, I'll be back. We'll all be back.' For all the humour of the preceding passages, the final sequence makes clear that while violence brings its own inevitable destruction, the battle against it will be long and hard, the necessary counterpart to an exposure of the uncivilized and humourless nature of the Hun.

It has been suggested that Smith's concentration on the rescue of artists, intellectuals and scientists is elitist, but it is central to Howard's interpretation of the war that it is a struggle for civilization, a word that recurs constantly in his films and his broadcasts. The Huns herald the new dark age of barbarism and ignorance, but Howard, like Professor Smith, clearly believes that 'progress and civilization depend in every age upon the hands and brains of a few exceptional spirits.' The preservation of those exceptional spirits ensures the survival of civilization after the war and that is surely one of the war's objectives. This stance was also in line with official policy, as embodied in an MoI policy committee memorandum, which noted that it was important for British propaganda to stress the difference between the first and second World Wars, 'pointing out how in the last war all the best elements of German culture and science were still in Germany and were supporting the German cause, whereas now they were outside Germany and are supporting us'.[37] *Pimpernel Smith* demonstrated just that.

As a director, Howard showed to the full his very English sense of humour and of restraint, telling his story with economy, sensitivity and skill. A notable instance is the scarecrow scene. A group of prisoners working on a road find a note left for them by the 'Shadow' in a heap of rubble. A brutal German guard breaks up their discussion and moves on. Howard cuts to the head of the scarecrow near the road turning to follow him. To give the prisoners a lesson about the talking, the German jocularly fires his rifle at the scarecrow, telling the prisoners they will be next if they are not careful. Cut to close-up of the scarecrow's hand with blood dripping down it. As an actor, Howard's performance is brilliant. He combines the decisiveness, quick-wittedness and self-possession of the adventurer, with the professorial appearance of vague, shambling, pipe-smoking, bespectacled absent-mindedness, as in the sequence of his ambling apparently aimlessly round the embassy reception in an ill-fitting dinner jacket, hands in pockets and cigarette dangling from between lips, constantly seeking to engage the increasingly irritated von Graum in conversation. To this the third and essential element which so endeared Howard to his public is added, the humanization and romanticization of the intellectual. A misogynist, whose love has been hitherto reserved for a statue of Aphrodite, his ideal of perfect womanhood, he falls in love with the courageous Ludmilla and in a telling moment of wordless declaration he shows her his ideal woman in a photograph of Aphrodite and then tears it up.

The film also brought excellent supporting performances from Francis L. Sullivan, the fat, chocolate-guzzling, bombastic but cunning Gestapo chief, clearly modelled on Goering; from Raymond Huntley, as his sneering, acidulous assistant, significantly called Marx; and from Mary Morris as the Polish patriot's daughter who charms Professor Smith. It is worth noting too that one of Howard's student assistants is a brash American, David Maxwell, who after initial reluctance joins the expedition and

Professor Smith is established at the outset of the film as a donnish misogynist (Howard with Joan Kemp-Welch).

becomes a key member, a timely reminder of the identity of interest between Britain and the USA.

The Swedish scholars Furhammer and Isaksson suggest that part of the appeal of *Pimpernel Smith* lies in the fact that it draws on fundamental mythic sources, consciously or unconsciously. Firstly and most obviously, it recalls Howard's earlier film success, *The Scarlet Pimpernel* (1935), in which he had played the English gentleman who risks all to spirit doomed French aristocrats from the grip of 'the Terror' in revolutionary France. Indeed the plot outline of *Pimpernel Smith* follows that of *The Scarlet Pimpernel* with remarkable fidelity. Baroness Orczy's novel sequence reached back for its inspiration to Dickens' *A Tale of Two Cities* and according to Furhammer and Isaksson, back even beyond that to the primal myth of the hero and the monster, St George and the dragon, Perseus and Andromeda.

But even more resonant is the interpretation of the film as Christian allegory:

> *Pimpernel Smith* is a saviour in the literal sense, who has arrived in an evil world where his origins seem very mysterious and the authorities go all out to destroy him. No one else has his ability to pass from this evil world to the ideal one. He is a teacher, surrounded by a small group of disciples who first do not understand his greatness and his mission — even if they are unconsciously speaking of him when they talk about 'the greatest man in the universe'. They are not convinced of his identity until, at a later stage, they see his 'pierced' hands. These wounds have been explained, with perfect consistency, in a scene in which Smith, disguised as a scarecrow, erected in a concentration camp, is on a cross, hanging with arms outstretched and head falling forward as if in a Passion painting, his hand is gorily pierced by a guard. The film ends with Smith announcing that he will soon be back.[38]

It may be that both these aspects of the character are what appealed to the Swedish diplomat Raoul Wallenberg, who, after seeing the film at the British Embassy in Stockholm, told his half-sister that he would like to do the same thing.[39] He subsequently saved the lives of thousands of Hungarian Jews before being arrested by the Russians in 1945 and disappearing from history.

The critics liked the film. The *Daily Express* called it 'war entertainment of the finest possible calibre' and the *New Statesman* declared 'the mingling of excitement and the battle for freedom has been done with admirable tact . . . *Pimpernel Smith* is a success all round.'[40] The *Monthly Film Bulletin* thought it 'a most attractive and exciting production even though the propaganda is laid on with a somewhat heavy hand'.[41] *The Times* expressed its appreciation of Howard both as actor and director:

> Mr Leslie Howard as a director has several qualities in common with Mr

Leslie Howard the actor. He believes, that is, in the oblique rather than the direct approach, in the value of understatement and in the charm of the casual. He is also adept at the art of appearing to flick sentiment and feeling away from him at the same time as he is cunningly arranging them in his buttonhole. In *Pimpernel Smith* he is happy in both his choice of hero and in his method of directing.[42]

The trade paper *Kinematograph Weekly* enthused:

Exciting, fascinating, human and humorous story, neat twists, effective undercurrent of suspense, smooth dialogue, brilliant performance by Leslie Howard, first-rate supporting team, topicality, strong feminine angle, great title values and greater star.

It proclaimed the film 'excellent general booking for all classes, both sexes and all ages'.[43]

The box office returns confirmed this judgement. The film broke all box office records at the Granada Group's London cinemas and went on to be one of the top box office successes of the year.[44] It was narrowly beaten only by *49th Parallel* (in which Howard also starred) and *The Great Dictator* as a money-earner in British cinemas.[45]

Howard followed *Pimpernel Smith* by directing and starring in *The First of the Few* (1942). The film drew on some potent propaganda sources: inspiring passages from Churchill's speeches, a montage sequence of the building of the Spitfire to William Walton's heroic music, and a framing sequence of the Battle of Britain. But Leslie was less concerned with the Few than with R. J. Mitchell, the first of the Few, the man who designed the Spitfire and died in 1936. His story is told in flashback to the Battle of Britain pilots now flying his plane. The film is a deeply felt, loving portrait of a man with whom Howard seems to have felt an instinctive rapport — the solitary visionary battling against government indifference, commercial pressure and ill-health to produce the plane that will be his country's salvation.

The mood is set when the film dissolves from the tumult of the Battle of Britain to the quintessentially peaceful scene of Mitchell lying on his back on top of the cliffs, looking through his binoculars at the sea birds wheeling gracefully in the sky and determining to design a plane that will fly like them. It establishes him at once as the dedicated dreamer, whose life is planes and plane-making. He seeks to win the Schneider Trophy for Britain and when he does, he regards his work as completed. But all this is changed by a trip to Germany, when he learns the nature of German plans for rearmament and world domination. He returns to England, determined to build 'the fastest and deadliest fighter in the world' so that his country can defend itself. Although warned by a specialist of the consequences if he does not rest, he works on and finally dies after learning that the government has accepted his plane — the Spitfire.

It is hard to make a successful film about a lone pioneer devoted to research and animated by pure love of his subject, but Leslie Howard succeeded brilliantly and he did so for several reasons. First, he himself was perfectly cast as R. J. Mitchell, the sort of part he had been born to play — the shy, absent-minded, pipesmoking visionary. He captivates us with the sincerity of the pioneer as he explains with bubbling enthusiasm the plans for his new plane. He moves us with the serene self-confidence of the martyr when the government tell him: 'You've got a year to produce the plans. It's all the time we can give you' and, recalling the specialist's advice, he replies: 'You can have them in eight months. It's all the time I can give you.' Noël Coward called his performance 'Acting that transcended acting'.[46]

Secondly, there is a full measure of humour, much of it handled in his inimitable style by a cheerfully insouciant David Niven as the test pilot, Geoffrey Crisp. The enemy, of course, come in for plenty of satire. The Italians are personified by the self-important Mayor (played by film producer Filippo del Giudice) at the Schneider Trophy races. He is constantly announcing: 'Silencio! A telegram from Il Duce' and proceeding to read out a bombastic message from Mussolini. The Germans are portrayed as loud, humourless, arrogant, fanatical and infinitely dangerous. The essential difference between them and the English is brought out in a scene in which Mitchell and some German aviators watch gliders. 'Efficiency' say the Germans, 'Poetry' responds Mitchell. 'Ach, you English, you sentimentalize everything' is the German reply.

Finally, there is Leslie Howard's special talent as a director. As one would expect, he handles the actors very well, but he also reveals an instinctive grasp of mood and nuance, imbuing his films with a quality of controlled gentleness and evoking the maximum emotional response from the audience by a characteristically English and wholly effective technique of underplaying. This mastery of mood can be seen, for instance, in the chilling scene in Germany at a party which is initially played for comedy with a drunken David Niven insulting the Hun but in which the mood gradually darkens, as from their urbane insinuations and fanatical rantings Mitchell realizes that the Germans are planning to rearm. The technique of underplaying is perfectly demonstrated in Mitchell's scenes with his wife, understandingly played by Rosamund John. There is the scene where he tells her of his illness, she reads out a letter from their son at school and he agrees to take a holiday but then catches sight of the newspaper headline 'German bombers destroy Spanish town'. No more needs to be said. We know and he knows that he must go on with his work. Finally when news arrives that the government have accepted the Spitfire, Mitchell is lying on a couch in the garden, worn out by his exertions. He says he will sleep for a while and his wife goes towards the house. Suddenly she stops and shudders and a shadow passes over Mitchell's face. On the soundtrack we hear the screech of a sea-bird — Mitchell's soul departing.

The First of the Few, along with *Pimpernel Smith*, became Leslie Howard's cinematic testament. They gave him roles in which he could demonstrate to perfection the qualities which had made him a unique screen star. They showed him possessed of a blossoming directorial talent which the film industry could ill-afford to lose. But above all they captured something of the spirit of the nation at war — and the nation responded. They made *The First of the Few* the top British moneymaker of 1942 and they made Leslie Howard one of the most popular of British stars. According to the *Motion Picture Herald*'s rankings of box office popularity, Leslie Howard rose from 19th most popular British star in 1940 to second in 1942. *Kinematograph Weekly* made him the most popular British star in 1941 and 1942. At the time of his death he was planning a film version of *Hamlet* to star himself. It was to be set in the present day and to evoke parallels with the war, depicting Claudius as a Quisling and Hamlet as a Danish resistance leader.

He was never one to under-estimate his audience, either in film-making or in broadcasting. Speaking about his appearances on the popular *Brains Trust* series, he said:

> I am a tremendous believer in the power of broadcasting . . . I don't believe anything is too good for the public . . . In my own experience I have proved that the cinema public is as ready to patronize the work of Bernard Shaw, the music of William Walton and film technique at its most subtle.[47]

He believed that the regular listening audience of 10—12 million attracted by the *Brains Trust* confirmed his view of the high level of intelligent appreciation in British audiences.

What is perhaps forgotten today is that Leslie Howard was almost as important for his wartime broadcasting as he was for his films. Many of his obituaries stressed this aspect of his work. A BBC spokesman declared: 'His calm, steady confidence and quiet patriotism did much to keep our people overseas in good heart. The services he rendered the Empire and indeed the world cannot be too highly assessed.'[48] This was not mere rhetoric: writing of his overseas broadcasts in July 1940, the *Daily Mail* proclaimed him the 'Number 2 public speaker to J. B. Priestley in the overseas service'.[49] The *Manchester Daily Despatch* recalled in 1943:

> BBC 'feature tests' showed that Howard was one of the most successful of the overseas speakers. His 'fan mail' from all parts of the British Empire and outside it showed that he had struck chords that had wide appeal. This was especially so in the dark days which Dunkirk ushered in.[50]

Smith's misogynism is transformed into love by his encounter with a Polish heroine (Howard with Mary Morris).

His importance in this area is confirmed by an internal BBC memorandum, dated 5 November 1940:

> Leslie Howard has been having a great success in the American Transmission. We are anxious that he should continue, and it would seem particularly important that he should in view of Priestley's absence for the time being. I hear the Home Programmes are also trying to make use of him. The trouble is that he is uncertain as to how much he can do and he has already been saying that with the film that he is engaged on he may have to give up the talk for us. So far we have persuaded him not to, but it would be rather sad if he chose between the Home Programme and the North American Transmission in favour of the Home Programme.[51]

Apart from his *Brains Trust* appearances and two radio plays (*The Petrified Forest* and *Nelson*), Howard delivered several talks on the Home

Service and one postscript (10 November 1940) in the slot which Priestley had made so much his own. BBC Audience Research reported that general reaction was favourable, though much less than for Priestley. There was enthusiasm for his voice and general approval for his topic (*Creatures of Habit*), though 'great enthusiasm seemed almost entirely absent'.[52] A sample of 135 people was questioned about whether he should have a regular postscript slot: 84 said yes, 43 no and 8 gave no reply. Approval of him was significantly higher among the working class respondents than among the middle-class ones, suggesting perhaps a degree of intellectual snobbery about film stars appearing in 'serious talks' slots.

But it was his influence in America and Canada that was most highly valued. Between 16 July 1940 and 7 August 1941 he delivered some 22 talks in the North American Service in a regular Monday evening slot.[53] Thereafter, between 26 October 1941 and 14 February 1943, he made 9 appearances on the *Answering You* programme, 3 as compere. This was a programme in which questions from transatlantic listeners were answered by a resident panel. He narrated the 13 shows in the *Britain to America* series, a star-studded series of impressions of life in wartime Britain. The co-editor of the series, D. G. Bridson, recalled Leslie Howard as 'not merely a gifted actor and sincere narrator, but also quite one of the most likeable people I ever met'. The series provoked a 'deluge of ecstatic cables . . . from New York'.[53] Howard was also chosen to host the BBC's birthday tribute to President Roosevelt on 30 January 1943.[54]

It is interesting to observe that Howard fulfilled almost exactly the criteria laid down by Professor F. C. Bartlett in 1940 for the ideal qualifications and the ideal material for broadcasting to neutral countries, like the United States, and to the Commonwealth. Bartlett said that the BBC should use people representative of the wider national culture rather than the more narrow and immediate areas of politics or diplomacy. He declared that the basis of all good democratic propaganda was news and news delivered in the idiom of the people to whom you are speaking. He said that neutral countries should be treated as friends, with a community of interest aside from the war. As far as the Commonwealth was concerned:

> The primary aim is to keep alive and vital faith and friendship for the home country and for its policy, and at the same time to leave each member of the Commonwealth unimpaired freedom of decision . . . In distant communities there will always be an army of people who are most moved to friendship when they can see or hear how the common life is going on at home.[55]

In his regular Monday talks, Howard declared his aim to be 'to give you a contemporary picture of this island fortress of England and some of the people both civil and military who are taking part in our defence'. He explained to his overseas listeners that he realized on returning to Britain that he was a dual personality — an Englishman and an American:

> I am an Englishman because I was born and raised one, and an American because I have lived the greater part of my adult life in the United States, during which time I lived among Americans, earned my living from them and came into close contact with great masses of them in private and public . . . I believe that I understand thoroughly the American way of life and attitude of mind; in fact, to a large extent, I have made them my own.[56]

He stressed the community of interest between Britain and the United States:

> You are very much in our minds nowadays, probably more than you have ever been since the Declaration of Independence aroused the conscience and admiration of all liberal Englishmen. Though more than 40 million free people in this island are again involved in the eternal fight against European continental domination, their eyes are towards the West, their thoughts and instincts follow the sun as their forefathers followed it upon the sea for many centuries. For there, across thousands of miles of dangerous waters, there on your great continent, lives the biggest group of democratic peoples in the world today. And although we and you have many superficial differences, when the world goes mad the English-speaking peoples come very close together. So much so that there are many Americans serving with the British forces today — more than is realized.[57]

He provided news but always with a human interest angle. He interviewed a US soldier, serving with the British forces, and a serving British seaman, his son, Ronald. He visited Portsmouth and described the effects of and the heroic resistance to the Blitz. He recounted his meetings with a Free French soldier and other foreign nationals. He visited an airfield and described the work of the pilots, taking time to give a reasoned defence of the British estimates of enemy losses in the Battle of Britain. He described the vital but unsung work of the Observer Corps. He painted a picture of 'business as usual' in war-torn London.

He was particularly good at taking on contentious issues and discussing them freely, humorously but always effectively: for instance, to what extent were his talks propaganda. He described how the English were shy of and bad at propaganda, and when compelled by war to take it up, they did so 'to a degree which has been the despair of their friends and the astonishment of their foes, cautiously, politely and with a painstaking rectitude.' By contrast, the German propaganda machine had overdone it. Americans, he thought, have:

> A deep and instinctive understanding of the state of the world and of the supreme danger in which human freedom stands. It was indeed German

propaganda that largely brought this about and the virtual non-existence of British propaganda was thereby justified.[58]

His own talks were not propaganda, for he was just saying what he felt without calculation, simply chatting to friends as if on the transatlantic telephone.

One of the things he 'chatted' about regularly and was concerned to correct was negative American perceptions of Britain and the British. He had discovered in America 'a fundamental distrust of the democratic character of the British constitution.' He sought to play this down:

> I was confronted with solid republican objections to our whole system of titles, privileges and the ruling class. First of all we were a monarchy, then we had too many lords (who were regarded as either comic or sinister), too much Harrow and Eton, and Oxford and Cambridge, too much class distinction, no real equality. I interposed the usual arguments about class distinction in the United States and the autocracy of the dollar, but that didn't prove British democracy. I defy anyone to prove it in words, for it is a paradox and our constitution is not a document like that of the United States, it is simply an instinct in the minds of the English, an instinct which governs their laws, their institutions and their behaviour. But I soon began to understand and be understood by my American friends and to discover how much we had in common.[59]

He also carefully set up a description of the archetypal upper class English youth now serving in the RAF and quoted the views on such men of the padre, a self-styled 'fighting Irishman' with a Dublin accent:

> Decadence, we used to hear a lot about the decadence of modern English youths. They were supposed to be precious, high-brow, artistic, didn't believe in fighting; they said the universities were full of them . . . I used to wonder myself, but then I am Irish, I know now. They never made them so tough, with such powers of resistance. 16 hours a day means nothing to them. I've never seen such a case of nerves, they haven't got any nerves. With cubs like these, the Lion is invincible. That's what I say — and I am an Irishman.[60]

In explaining the English to the Americans, Howard characteristically highlights their idealism. He notes the qualities which have emerged during the war:

> qualities which seem to me to represent the best there is in human nature; the qualities of courage, devotion to duty, kindliness, humour, cool-headedness, balance, common sense, singleness of purpose. But there is a master quality which motivates and shines through all these — that of idealism. Mind you, you have to be smart to spot it. The English do their best

to conceal it and they succeed pretty well. They are awfully afraid of idealism, very shy of it, almost ashamed of it, and they go to great lengths to conceal and deny it, for they believe it becomes them very ill. Only in rare cases are foreigners able to spot it at all. In my case it is the Englishman in me that is able to unearth it and the American in me that is able to stand off and marvel at it.[61]

What are the ideals that inspire British resistance? These are illustrated in Howard's account of a visit to the House of Commons, still in session despite the war, 'the living expression of human liberty, of Common Man's social and political progress, the natural foe of oppression, the eternal guardian of individual freedom'. It is, he reminds his listeners, 'a vital part of the newest and most progressive concept that the human race has been able to evolve for the management of its affairs — a government of the people, by the people, for the people.'[62] This apposite deployment of the words of President Lincoln to describe the British democratic system was followed up in a later talk by a ringing declaration in a shared belief in the principles underlying the very foundation of the United States. He talked feelingly about British interest in the American Presidential elections and the enormous popularity in Britain of President Roosevelt:

There is something in the foundations of American liberty and in the birth of the American nation, to which every British soul must by its very nature respond.

He quoted the words of the Declaration of Independence:

I make no apology for repeating them, for, if the world needed them in 1776, it needs them infinitely more today. They should be heralded far and wide, for they are the simple creed of Democracy and contain the germs of the only collective happiness possible to mankind. They were written for the oppressed. Let the oppressed take comfort in them, and particularly let the oppressors take heed of them. Listen, Hitler, listen to these words — 'We hold these truths to be self-evident, that all men are created equal, that they are endowed by their creator with certain inalienable rights, that among these rights are life, liberty and the pursuit of happiness.' Today more than ever they belong to the whole world of free men and those who hope for freedom.[63]

He had words of praise too for Canada ('In sending your sons you have given the ultimate and perfect evidence of your faith in our great unity'). He sees Canada as living proof of the democratic and tolerant traditions of the Commonwealth and also as a valuable bridge between Britain and the United States. He devoted one of his talks to discussing the making of his documentary film *From the Four Corners*, in which he shows three

Commonwealth soldiers, from Australia, New Zealand and Canada, the sights of London, which symbolize a shared heritage, culminating in Westminster, the mother of parliaments, where in the 18th century Englishmen cheered the victories of the American colonists over the German troops of George III, where equal rights were conceded to the Maoris in New Zealand, the Boers in South Africa and the French in Canada. Once again, he quotes the Declaration of Independence as summarizing the ideals they are fighting for:

> Those words and that spirit were born and nourished here and your fathers carried them to the four corners of the earth. They are our inheritance from the past, our legacy for the future.[64]

His final summation of what Britain was fighting for, what the Commonwealth was fighting for and what the United States would in due course join the fight for, came in a talk where he contrasted the Nazi New Order with the achievements of the English-speaking peoples. They had peopled five continents, spread the English language, spread the Roman idea of codified law and the Greek ideal of democracy, accepted the French idea of the family unit as the basis of settled society, and preserved the Christian ethic inherited from Judaism:

> One thing we have contributed to the civilization of the world which was new and our own; something of which the Germans have never known the meaning; something called tolerance. All the English-speaking nations have planted that flower of civilization wherever they have taken up their governments. It is one form of that freedom for which the Greeks fought at Marathon, and Bruce's Scots at Bannockburn, and Elizabeth's English in the Channel and the French at Valmy, and the American colonists at Saratoga. That the worship of God shall be free; that speech and writing shall be free; that national assemblies may contain oppositions; that racial or political minorities shall live in peace; that neither creed nor colour nor class shall bar a man from the privileges of a citizen; we believe all these things to be good and right and just. That faith we English-speaking peoples will maintain as long as we are free nations; and to teach that faith to the world has been, above all, our destiny.[65]

This resounding declaration encapsulates all that Leslie Howard stood for in his films and his broadcasts — a mystical belief in the spiritual values, the ideals, the civilization of the English-speaking peoples. Where Winston Churchill, orator, warlord, historian, looked to the past to evoke the epic and historic nature of Britain's struggle, and where J. B. Priestley, the bluff, common-sense, plain-speaking Yorkshireman, talked of the heroism of ordinary folk and their hopes for the future, Leslie Howard spoke for another England, an inner England, an England of the soul, the spirit of a quiet, thoughtful, tolerant, humorous, idealistic nation, roused to action by an evil more monstrous than any the world had yet known. It was a mystic England, but it was one for which, in the end, he gave his life.

NOTES

1   Ronald Howard, *In Search of My Father*, London, 1981. On Leslie Howard's life and career, see also Leslie Ruth Howard, *A Quite Remarkable Father*, London, 1960.
2   Ian Colvin, *Flight 777*, London, 1957. For Churchill's view see Winston Churchill, *The Second World War*, 4, London, 1951, p. 742, where he notes with regret the loss of 'the well known British actor Leslie Howard, whose grace and gifts are still preserved for us by the records of the many delightful films in which he took part.'
3   The quote from Lord Haw-Haw was reported in *The Star*, June 3, 1943.
4   *Daily Herald*, 3 June 1943.
5   *Daily Express*, 3 June 1943.
6   *Star*, 3 June 1943.
7   *Sydney Morning Herald*, 5 June 1943.
8   Peter Noble (ed.), *British Film Yearbook for 1945*, London, 1945, p. 74.
9   Guy Morgan, *Red Roses Every Night*, London, 1948, pp. 73−4.
10 *Manchester Guardian*, 4 June 1943.
11 Tom Harrisson and Charles Madge (ed.), *War Begins at Home*, London, 1940, pp. 157−8.
12 *Time and Tide*, 11 May 1940.
13 *Time and Tide*, 25 May 1940.
14 *Time and Tide*, 22 June 1940.
15 Hamilton Fyfe, *Britain's Wartime Revolution*, London, 1944, p. 131.
16 R. J. E. Silvey, 'Some recent trends in listening', *BBC Year Book*, 1946, pp. 28−9.
17 Paul Addison, *The Road to 1945*, London, 1977, p. 126.
18 These are collected in J. B. Priestley, *All England Listened*, New York, 1967, and in J. B. Priestley, *Postscripts*, London, 1940.
19 Priestley, *All England Listened*, p. 73.
20 J. B. Priestley, *Margin Released*, London, 1962, pp. 220−1.
21 Priestley, *All England Listened*, p. 57.
22 Mass-Observation Report 496, quoted by Angus Calder, *The People's War*, London, 1971, p. 160.
23 Ralph Ingersoll, *Report on England*, London, 1941, pp. 231−2.
24 This process is fully described in Addison, *Road to 1945*.
25 *Time and Tide*, 12 October 1940.
26 Silvey, 'Some recent trends in listening', pp. 28−9.
27 C. A. Lejeune, *Chestnuts in her Lap*, London, 1947, p. 97.
28 Lejeune, *Chestnuts in her Lap*, p. 96.
29 On Howard's film persona see Jeffrey Richards, 'Leslie Howard: the thinking man as hero', *Focus on Film* 25, Summer-Autumn, 1976, pp. 37−50, and

for his career in the 1930s, see Jeffrey Richards, *Age of the Dream Palace*, London, 1984, pp. 225−41.

30   Quoted in Colvin, *Flight 777*, p. 46.

31   Collie Knox (ed.), *For Ever England*, London, 1943, p. 240.

32   Adrian Brunel, *Nice Work*, London, 1949, pp. 190−1.

33   Harold Nicolson, *Diaries and Letters 1930−1964* (ed. Stanley Olson), London, 1980, p. 176.

34   The production history of the film is recounted in Leslie Ruth Howard, *A Quite Remarkable Father*, pp. 249−55 and Ronald Howard, *In Search of My Father*, pp. 61−103.

35   A number of Leslie Howard's wartime broadcasts are reprinted in Leslie Howard, *Trivial Fond Records* (ed. Ronald Howard), London, 1982. This one, entitled *The Female of the Species*, is on p. 165.

36   Howard, *Trivial Fond Records*, p. 175.

37   Memorandum by Sir Kenneth Clark, MoI Policy Committee, 23 January 1941, INF 1/849. It also fulfils the call in MoI Policy Committee Paper 5 (INF 1/848) that British propaganda should depict the Germans as morally damnable by personal attacks on their leaders, by the revelation of their atrocities and the exposure of the 'inquisitorial methods of the Gestapo (which) represent the overthrow of the rights of man and of that belief in the supreme value of the individual which is the ethical basis of Western civilization.'

38   Leif Furhammer and Folke Isaksson, *Politics and Film*, translated by Kersti French, London, 1971, p. 232.

39   John Bierman, *Righteous Gentile*, Harmondsworth, 1982, p. 29.

40   *New Statesman*, 12 July 1941; *Daily Express* 5 July 1941.

41   *Monthly Film Bulletin*, 8, 1941, p. 81.

42   *The Times*, 2 July 1941.

43   *Kinematograph Weekly*, 26 June 1941.

44   Morgan, *Red Roses Every Night*, p. 89.

45   *Kinematograph Weekly*, 8 January 1942. It was released in the USA as *Mister V* (presumably for the 'V for Victory' campaign), when the *New York Times* (13 February 1942) said: 'It is all absurd derring-do, of course . . . But "Mister V" becomes a tense excursion because of Mr Howard's casual direction and even more because of the consummate ease and the quiet irony of his performance. Although the Nazi terror has burst the boundaries of 1938, "Mister V" is still a gallant figure to capture the imagination and stir the blood'.

46   Ronald Howard, *In Search of My Father*, p. 122.

47   *North-Eastern Gazette*, 21 October 1942.

48   *Manchester Daily Despatch*, 4 June 1943.

49   *Daily Mail*, 31 July 1940.

50   Manchester Daily Despatch, 4 June 1943.

51   Leslie Howard Talks File 1937−43, BBC Written Archives, Caversham.

52   BBC Audience Research Reports, Sound: Talks and Postscripts 1941−42, BBC Written Archives, Caversham.

53   Five of Howard's American broadcasts and his Home Service postscript are reprinted in Leslie Howard, *Trivial Fond Records*, pp. 150−76. The

remainder of the American broadcasts are preserved at the BBC Written Archives, Caversham, Script Library, Talks Script Microfilm 234.

54 D. G. Bridson, *Prospero and Ariel*, London, 1971, pp. 92−3.
55 F. C. Bartlett, *Political Propaganda*, Cambridge, 1940, p. 150.
56 Leslie Howard, 'Shopkeepers and Poets', broadcast 14/15 October 1940.
57 Howard, 'Radio Beam', 12/13 August 1940.
58 Howard, 'The Unspeakable Word', 16/17 December 1940.
59 Howard, 'Radio Beam'.
60 Howard, 'Tails Up', 26/27 August 1940.
61 Howard, 'Shopkeepers and poets'.
62 Howard, 'Tree of Liberty', 30 September 1940.
63 Howard, 'Life, liberty and the pursuit of happiness', 11/12 November 1940.
64 Howard, 'Three Soldiers', 30 December 1940.
65 Howard, 'New Order in Europe', 23/24 December 1940.

4

Raise a Laugh

Let George Do It

Large bureaucratic organizations are rarely credited with possessing or displaying a sense of humour. Britain's Ministry of Information during World War II was little different. In formulating its early plans for film propaganda the point was well made that, 'The film being a popular medium must be good entertainment if it is to be good propaganda'.[1] But it took a while before it was fully appreciated that humour and comedy formed a part of the cinema's staple diet of entertainment.

Of the MoI's first wave of 'short' films — some 17 'official' films in all, intended for distribution in late 1939 and early 1940 — it was reported that, 'The lack of humour has been a striking feature of many of the films; only four have made any real attempt to exploit humour, and in two of them mass taste has been considerably misjudged'.[2] All too often, according to Mass-Observation who compiled such reports, these films had evoked laughter where none was intended, and people were laughing at rather than with the films. The GPO's *Do It Now* (1939), for instance, made the necessity for adequate air raid precautions seem 'only foolish', and engendered 'disbelief and lack of sympathy' among spectators. By contrast, the same film unit scored something of a success with *The First Days* (1939), an impressionistic account of the opening days of the war, in large part because it invested 'recognizable situations with a humorous twist'. The film displayed a fair amount of 'good humour', not least in its depiction of little things 'such as the expression on a painter's face as a bus runs over his white lines'.[3]

It was a simple joke, but effective none the less, and in time, the MoI made more use of such evocative comic ingredients. In addition, the MoI injected humour into its propaganda by the simple expedient of 'buying in' professional expertise, from the commercial film companies, scriptwriters, and well known British comedians. Sydney Howard ignored the blackout regulations, to his cost, in *Mr Proudfoot Shows a Light* (1941), made by

20th Century — Fox, with the experienced Herbert Mason as director and a script commissioned from Sidney Gilliat by John Betjeman, when script editor at the MoI's Films Division. Tommy Trinder savoured the delights to be found in British restaurants in *Eating out with Tommy Trinder* (1941), made for Strand by Desmond Dickinson. Gainsborough's team of producer Edward Black and director Val Guest used Arthur Askey to warn of the working days lost through the spreading of 'coughs and sneezes', in *The Nose Has It* (1942), and Michael Balcon at Ealing Studios engaged the veteran director, Walter Forde, to demonstrate the right and wrong ways to tackle incendiary bombs, through Will Hay's bumbling efforts, in *Go to Blazes* (1942). Even the celebrated newsreel satire, *Germany Calling* (1941), in which Charles Ridley cleverly re-edited actuality film of goose-stepping Nazi soldiers at Hitler rallies (taken from Leni Riefenstahl's 1934 *Triumph of the Will*) to the popular British tune of 'Lambeth Walk' to hilarious and ridiculous effect, was effectively 'bought in' from Spectator Films and subsequently released through the Newsreel Association.

In short, when it came to humour and comedy, in particular, the commercial cinema had the edge. It was, quite simply, so much more experienced and accomplished at it. The MoI sensibly recognized that fact, in time, but it did take time and, doubtless, the repeated prompting and insistence by Mass-Observation, born of its many surveys, that humour was an essential prerequisite of the propagandist's armoury in waging total war. From the outset of the war, Mass-Observation demonstrated the need for a sustained measure of comic relief among the population at large, in order to offset the periodic bouts of depression which inevitably ensued, not least in moments of grave crisis, and, generally, to engender and maintain a level of morale beneficial to the national cause. Much of what it had to say seems now, in retrospect, to amount to nothing more than common sense, but, at the time, the MoI was in need of a good dose of common sense, almost as much as it required a health-giving injection of laughter into its otherwise humourless system.

The Mass-Observation work on humour drew upon many sources and appeared in various guises, but it was usually collated and compiled into edited reports by Len England, who was obviously given the responsibility of looking after all the subjects which fell into the general areas of leisure and the popular media of entertainment. He was eventually called up into the forces, but between 1939 and 1942 he produced an impressive collection of 'file reports'.[4] Humour was the paramount concern of an extensive survey entitled 'Joke report' (June 1940, with follow-up reports in November 1941 and August 1942), which contained material based upon interviews with comedians and writers from radio, films and the variety theatre, and some analysis of their jokes. It also figured prominently in reports upon music halls (February and June, 1940), on pantomime (March 1940), on MoI films (January and October, 1940, July 1941, and

March 1942), and the realm of feature films (March, April, and September, 1940, and March 1942).

The newsreels were monitored throughout, in part for the use they made of humorous stories, and an occasional eye was cast upon the results of newspaper competitions which might prove useful, such as the 'film joke' competition run by the *Sunday Dispatch*, to find the funniest situation in any film the readers had seen (June 1940). In addition, special studies were made of particular film comedies and audience reactions to them. *Let George Do It* was singled out for individual and exhaustive attention in the first instance (September 1940), and this was followed with *The Great Dictator* (June 1941). There was often considerable repetition in the questions asked from one survey to another, despite the seemingly disparate aims, and sometimes the findings were pretty obvious, but in general the material amassed did provide a sufficiently detailed body of work with which to assess British reactions to humour in the opening years of the war.

Let George Do It *brought the ever-popular George Formby to the screen in the first comedy from the Ealing Studios with a topical wartime setting.*

GEORGE FORMBY
IN
"Let George do it" (U)
PRODUCED BY MICHAEL BALCON   DIRECTED BY MARCEL VARNEL
EALING   DISTRIBUTION

Not surprisingly, there was a notable increase in the demand for humour immediately after the onset of war. In the cinema, for instance, where spy films appeared to predominate throughout most of 1939 — there was a plethora of them including *Q Planes*, *Spies of the Air*, *The Four Just Men*, *An Englishman's Home*, *Traitor Spy*, with Michael Powell's *The Spy in Black* proving especially popular — it was found that audiences were soon expressing a marked preference for more in the way of comic relief. *The Frozen Limits*, a vehicle for the many talents of the Crazy Gang under the direction of Marcel Varnel, turned out to be a box office hit in the early months of 1940, and in particular, as Mass-Observation noted, the best received films were those which were concerned with depicting 'the lighter side of life in the services'.[5] Suddenly, comic films about the services were in vogue, and responding to demand, as always, the film industry produced them in abundance. Tommy Trinder proceeded to *Laugh It Off* for director John Baxter in a story about a new recruit who enjoys life in the Army except for the perennially bothersome presence of the sergeant-major. Sandy Powell accidentally joined the Navy and suffered the consequences of being *All at Sea*; and even Arthur Lucan was inveigled into joining the ATS to prove that *Old Mother Riley Joins Up*. 'Joining up' films were almost obligatory for comedians of note and the trend lasted well into 1941.

In part, of course, these films were successful simply because they were topical, and since British comedies could be notoriously quick and easy to produce, it was possible for them to be released and out in time to capitalise upon the more topical elements, not least their themes and jokes. Thus, *The Frozen Limits*, which did not have a wartime setting, reportedly achieved some of its biggest laughs for a joke at Neville Chamberlain's expense. As the destitute Crazy Gang eye a report in their fish and chips paper relating news of a gold find in Alaska, one of them wonders what the date of the paper is. It is missing, torn off. But another member spots a story in an adjacent column recounting that Mr Chamberlain says, 'We must be prepared . . . England must be strong'. It must be a recent paper, the Crazy Gang quip, 'He's only talked like that lately'. 'This invariably aroused a tremendous laugh from the whole belly of the audience', Mass-Observation found.[6] Though the Crazy Gang find that in the event it was a very old newspaper indeed, reporting upon a speech made by Joseph Chamberlain.

Topical references did go down well, then, provided they were pertinent, and the jokes were funny. But they quickly became outdated, of course, as the circumstances which produced them changed. Much the same applied to jokes specifically related to the war itself. War jokes might be successful when the war was going well, or at least not badly, for the country at large, but they slumped when things fared ill. At Christmas 1939, for example, Mass-Observation noted that 'war jokes were wildly popular' across all the media of entertainment, and they constituted a third of the total number of jokes tabulated in their music hall and pantomime surveys. By August 1940, they were 'less popular' though their number was still around the 30 per cent mark.[7] By the end of October 1941, however, war jokes made up less than 10 per cent of all jokes spotted. The new recruit was still very much a figure of fun and the cookhouse and the sergeant-major had to some extent supplanted the kitchen and the mother-in-law, respectively, as subjects for laughter, but there was considerably less use made of the war as a source of humour in variety and the cinema.[8] Even the more successful jokes, such as comedian George Bolton's ditty implicitly lamenting the need to carry a torch almost everywhere, apparently lost something in the telling — though in this case it is implied that he might also have suffered from the fact that he repeated it endlessly, not least at the height of summer.[9]

The jokes that went down consistently well, however, invariably harped upon well-worn themes such as ill health, sex, and domestic affairs. These were the three big categories that appeared over and over again in Mass-Observation surveys of humour. Some subjects, like the war, might come and go, their popularity rising and falling according to the extraneous dictates of fortune. Some subjects varied in appearance anyway from one medium of entertainment to another — 'lavatory' humour was found more frequently in music halls than the cinema, in part because of the stricter codes applied by the British Board of Film Censors to thwart 'vulgarity'.[10] Other topics like food, money and alcohol were ever-present, though they proved less evocative overall. But ill health, sex and domestic affairs were tried, tested and true, so Mass-Observation argued, in large measure because they gave audiences something with which they might most readily identify. They struck the right note, as often as not, because they bore out the obvious maxim that to be successful, 'humour must concern events of everyday life'.[11]

George Formby, of course, hardly needed to be told much about humour. He had been purveying it for years and had proved particularly successful at it, not least in the cinema. Indeed, he turned out to be the top British box office attraction in the years from 1938 to 1943, inclusive, and in 1946 he was awarded the OBE for his wartime efforts on the morale front.[12] His screen popularity was doubtless enhanced by the fact that in the early years of the war, especially, there was little or no competition from his two greatest rivals, Gracie Fields and Will Hay. Will Hay broke up his successful team of many years' standing — actors Graham Moffatt and Moore Marriott and scriptwriters Val Guest, Marriott Edgar and J. O. C. Orton — after the 1939 hit, *Where's That Fire?*, in an attempt to make it as a solo star once more. He did not return until 1941 with *The Ghost of St Michael's*, the first of a series of comedies he made for Ealing Studios.[13] Gracie Fields for her part did not make any films between 1939

*George unintentionally becomes a British agent and lands up in Bergen where he
encounters the alluring Iris (Coral Browne).*

and 1942. In addition, her popularity suffered somewhat after her ill-fated
decision to leave the country in 1940, albeit on a tour of Canada for the
Navy League, in order partly to prevent her Italian born husband, the film
director Monty Banks, from being interned. (Banks was, ironically, the
director of Formby's first two films for the Ealing Studios, *No Limit* in
1935, and *Keep Your Seats Please* in 1936.)

The vitriolic and exaggerated press campaign which accompanied Gracie
Fields' departure, though grossly unfair, did much to harm her standing in
the eyes of many people. It caused such a furore, in fact, that Home
Intelligence at the MoI felt compelled to investigate the matter. It found
that 'At the beginning of the press publicity (which not only recorded
questions in the House but gave editorial and news comment), public
opinion was favourable to Gracie'. Initially, the public 'refused to think ill
of her and attributed any possible evil to her Italian husband', and this
tallied with BBC Listener Research findings to the effect that 'she has

become highly thought of as an individual as well as an artiste'. But the sheer weight and persistence of unfavourable press notices inevitably took its toll and although not strongly antagonistic to her personally, public opinion was increasingly found to be 'much more critical than it was'.[14] Gracie Fields returned in 1941 and rightly re-established herself after a string of variety tours both at home and abroad, where she entertained the troops for ENSA. However, as a result of the bad press she received over the one incident, 'she never became the national symbol during the war years that she had been during the Thirties'.[15]

George Formby remained a national symbol throughout and his film output was prolific, with nine films completed between the onset of war and its close. *Let George Do It* was the first of them, and it was also the first comedy emanating from the Ealing Studios to deal directly with the war. The original screenplay was written by Angus MacPhail, Basil Dearden, John Dighton and Austin Melford. It was something of a new team, since Anthony Kimmins, one of the regular contributors to Formby scripts, as well as being the director of five of his films between 1937 and 1939, had been called up into the forces.[16] With Kimmins' departure, a new director was required, so producer Michael Balcon borrowed the services of Marcel Varnel from Gainsborough. Varnel, like Kimmins and Banks before him, was ideally suited for Formby's purposes. Though a Frenchman by birth, he had developed during the 1930s into an accomplished director of British film comedy with a number of box office hits to his credit, largely for Will Hay and the Crazy Gang.

Let George Do It (which was retitled *To Hell With Hitler* for its New York release) opens with a caption announcing 'The greater part of this story takes place in Norway, before the war spread'. It is Bergen, a hotel, and the resident band, under its leader Mark Mendez (Garry Marsh), are playing their signature tune 'Oh, Don't the Wind Blow Cold' when the ukulele player is shot dead in their midst. Back in England this causes consternation in Intelligence circles. The dead man was a British agent, hot on the trail of a German spy who is passing on shipping information to the U-boats. Another trusted man must be sent and with the aid of a theatrical agency a new ukulele player is engaged, also a secret service agent, to take his place in the Mendez band. It is arranged that final instructions shall be given him at Dover before embarking that night.

But the theatrical agency also engages the Dinkie Doo concert party, for which George Hepplewhite (Formby) is the ukulele player, to play in Blackpool, and they too must travel by boat and leave from Dover 'because the railways have all been commandeered by the Ministry of Information'.

At Dover, confusion ensues. The blackout is the excuse for innumerable gags and routines and incidental comment regarding the difficulties of finding one's way around by torchlight alone. The man sent to contact the Dinky Doos asks a porter 'Where are the Dinky Doos?', and receives the almost inevitable reply, 'First door on the left, sir'. He then asks a woman, 'Are you a Dinky Doo', to which her husband retorts, 'She is not. She is a respectable married woman'. And in an attempt to escape the blackout, George mistakenly takes the hand of the same woman, much to her husband's increasing fury — the beginnings of a long battle between George and the couple, the Neilsons (Bernard Lee and Helena Pickard), and a running joke throughout the film — before escaping a fight and making his way finally to the comparative safety of the station bar. He meets up with the Dinky Doos and celebrates the prospect of their next engagement in Blackpool with a lively rendition to all and sundry of one of his mildly risqué songs, 'My Grandad's Flannelette Nightshirt'.

But George never makes it to Blackpool. He is mistaken, of course, for the secret service agent and dispatched on the boat to Bergen. The interlude at sea draws heavily on a traditional array of comic escapades. Suffering badly from seasickness, George mis-reads the number of his berth ticket as 9 instead of 6 and inadvertently spends the night in the top bunk of Mrs Neilson's cabin. She snores in unison with George's moaning. The next morning he realizes the extent of his predicament. He is in a foreign country, he has an angry Mr Neilson on his hands, once again, and he is shortly in trouble too with the customs officer, who looks suspiciously upon the bag of stage tricks that George has brought with him and proves far from happy when he turns out to be the butt of its many hidden jokes. He is rescued, however, by a henchman of Mendez, Slim (Romney Brent), and whisked off to the hotel for an audition. He tries to explain what has happened, but Mendez wants a ukulele player, George is a ukulele player, and 'Mr Wu's a Window Cleaner Now' is sufficient to secure him the job.

Subsequently, the spy plot is brought very much to the foreground. It turns out that the hotel receptionist, Mary (Phyllis Calvert) is yet another British agent and she suspects Mendez of passing on coded messages to the enemy, by means of the musical broadcasts he makes over the radio from the hotel ballroom. But what is the code? She makes contact with George, confidently expecting the help of a fellow agent. Though quickly appraised of his true credentials, or lack of them, she tries to cajole him into working for the British Intelligence Service. 'But I'm not intelligent', he pleads in his defence. It is a telling point. But even George can imagine the glory that might come his way if he proves successful, and he is won over to the idea.

In a scene replete with all the trappings of mock suspense — George eludes discovery in Mendez' bedroom, he hides in a wardrobe, he hides under the bed, Mendez drops a coin under the bed and attempts to retrieve it, George proffers one of his own, Mendez wanders off to his bath muttering 'funny' — George happens upon the code hidden in the bandleader's baton. He photographs it but is then compelled to effect a speedy escape. His subsequent antics turn into broad farce as he drops the

With the aid of the attractive Mary (Phyllis Calvert), George soon breaks the German code.

camera into a bakery. In his attempts to retrieve it, George is covered in flour, lands in a vat, is churned up and almost baked. Still, he wins the day, and he and Mary pass on the code to British Intelligence. It is transmitted over the airwaves, nevertheless, in the course of the next broadcast by Mendez and his orchestra — it was an ingenious idea, the message being passed on to the waiting submarines by means of musical morse code during the breaks from different sections of the band as they play 'Count Your Blessings' — but this time the British fleet is waiting as well, and the U-boats are sunk. George and Mary are triumphant.

For most films, this would have been sufficient. The villains have been vanquished, the heroes are victorious, and a lot of good fun has been had in the midst of a slick, fast-paced comic espionage thriller, but that was clearly not enough for a George Formby vehicle. The film relentlessly pursues its goal, and there follows a set piece comic finale in which fantasy truly comes to the fore.

Mendez determines to find out who was responsible for his failure and to get revenge. He corners George and administers a truth drug; George tells all and is left in a stupor.[17] Whereupon, he dreams that single-handed he sees off the threat from Mendez and Slim, and then seeks a marriage with Mary that is 'made in Heaven'. On arriving at the Pearly Gates, however, he is told that he has yet to come up with the 'ace of knaves' — Adolf Hitler. So, off he goes to Berlin, with the aid of a barrage balloon. The Fuhrer is seen below, ranting away at a Nazi rally. George shins down a rope, claims Hitler as his 'last territorial demand in Europe', and punches him, to the evident delight of the surrounding stormtroopers who go wild with joy.

On waking up after that, 'reality' is as nothing to George. Mary manages to get away to sea on the *SS Macaulay*. George has a performance to do with the band, which Mendez intends will be his last, but George thwarts the attempt to shoot him. All his avenues of escape from the ballroom are blocked but the chandeliers will suffice. The place is reduced to a shambles and Mrs Neilson is brought to tears — 'Oscar, it's that man again'.

George finally hides away on a motor boat. It is, of course, the boat that Mendez uses to make his getaway to a waiting submarine. Disguised as a sailor, George boards the submarine, overpowers the wireless operator, and warns the *Macaulay* that it is about to be torpedoed. A British destroyer soon puts pay to that idea, however, and depth charges (along with a few more subversive antics from George which send everybody into a spin) force the submarine to the surface. The crew and spies are taken prisoner, but in a last desperate act, Mendez fires the torpedo tube in which, little known to him, George has sought refuge. George flies through the air shouting 'Moother'. His luck is in to the last. He falls harmlessly on the *Macaulay*, lands up in Mary's arms and utters his catchphrase, 'Turned out nice again, hasn't it?'.

Let George Do It was shown to the film trade on 6 March 1940. The trade press greeted it enthusiastically and with an obvious, if not unexpected, eye on its business potential. All agreed that success was virtually assured. *Kinematograph Weekly* claimed it was Formby's 'best performance to date', felt confident it was 'a box office certainty', and concluded, 'All told, the film is easily the star's best and that, need we add, is good enough to guarantee record receipts'.[18] *The Cinema* concurred, noting that 'The sure fire hilarities of George Formby are shrewdly interwoven here with a topical tale of U-boat nastiness. With such a combination no British showman can go wrong and the film will inevitably clean up a packet at the box office'.[19]

In the event, however, no immediate release date was fixed for the film. In part, of course, this can be put down to the fact that there was invariably something of a gap between a film being shown to the trade and being put on general release. In addition, the previous Formby film, *Come on George*, was still doing the rounds of the tail end cinemas that would have got the film towards the close of its first run and doubtless this would have added to the delay in releasing a follow up. But in the case of *Let George Do It*, one might also reasonably assume that the film was to some extent a victim of its own attempted topicality. For on 8 April the Germans marched unopposed into Denmark and invaded Norway, seizing every important port from Oslo to Narvik. 'The British had imagined, mistakenly, that they controlled the North Sea', A. J. P. Taylor comments, 'Now their sea power was openly defied'.[20] Not surprisingly, the MoI found that 'public morale was at a low ebb'.[21]

The Ealing Studios must have thought that their press release stressing the 'topical wartime background' to the latest Formby comedy now had a hollow ring to it, not to mention the fact that references to 'neutral Norway' were clearly wrong. Undaunted, however, they wrote into the plot synopsis a phrase to the effect that 'The action takes place before the Nazi invasion of Norway', added that caption to the opening of the film itself stating that the story '. . . takes place in Norway, before the war spread', and, after a suitable delay, put the film into a showcase venue, the Empire, Leicester Square, from 12 July, at the beginning of its general release.[22]

The film was the box office hit of August 1940 and the trade press reported that as far as cinema takings for that month were concerned, it was 'out on its own'.[23] Thereafter, Mass-Observation sought to analyse the film's reception in more detail. Interestingly, it found that for once the film was almost as successful with the critics as it was with the cinemagoing public, though not for the same reasons. Traditionally, Formby films were anathema to many of the critics, especially those on the prestige papers, but this time there was considerable praise for Formby and his morale boosting efforts.[24] The popular press loved it, of course, and the critic for the *Sunday Chronicle* stated, 'I can sit through the film again and again just watching his artistry', while the *Sunday Express* proclaimed, 'It's cheerful, tonic, topical, and British made'. But even the *Spectator* was prompted to remark: 'Never mind the plot, but don your lowest and most receptive brow, cast your inhibitions to the winds, and enjoy fully a manifestation of that social quality which in no small measure represents what we are fighting to defend'. There was a division of opinion regarding the dream sequence, with the *Sunday Dispatch*, for instance, finding it 'inspired', while the *Observer* felt that, 'Few of us today really think of Hitler as a funny man', and concluded, 'It leaves a sour taste in what is otherwise a tonic picture'. And just as there were arguments over the film's occasional lapses into 'bad taste', so indeed there were conflicting opinions as to whether the film constituted 'good' propaganda or not, with some believing that the Norwegian spy plot was inappropriate given that 'the audience knows that the German fifth column at Bergen was first class'.[25]

For their part, cinemagoers claimed not to have seen much propaganda

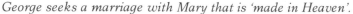

George seeks a marriage with Mary that is 'made in Heaven'.

intent in the film at all, though it was subsequently asserted that it gave 'rise to persistent and sometimes hysterical rumours that broadcasters, ranging from Vic Oliver and Charlie Kunz to Edward Ward and C. B. Cochran, have been arrested (interned, shot, hanged) for sending out coded messages over the radio'.[26] The dream sequence was enjoyed, at least in part and despite what some critics had felt, because of the simple fun to be had from seeing Hitler receive his come-uppance, in however outrageous a fashion, and because his followers were depicted as enjoying it hugely as well. The reasons for the difference in response between the critics and the public were not difficult to fathom. As Mass-Observation noted:

> The variation between the press and the public is explained by the fact that the attitude of the press is distinctly that of the West End picturegoer. Even the film critics in the popular press select as the funniest scenes those that were well received at the Empire and the Ritz and ignore those jokes that caused much laughter in Fulham and the Elephant and Castle.[27]

And as one got further afield from London, so indeed the film was increasingly enjoyed for its broad comic effect more than anything else. The spoken jokes might go down well in the West End, but it was the visual slapstick and the farcical elements that carried the day in the suburbs and the provinces. Whatever the variation in the public response, however, most cinemagoers agreed that on this occasion the film's success was hardly attributable to its much touted topical features, an unsurprising opinion given that its topical elements had been somewhat overtaken by events. No, the success of *Let George Do It* lay in the fact that it provided enough of the basic comic ingredients, enough in the way of light relief, in short, for audiences to flock to it in their droves.

Of course, one of the biggest problems confronting film comedy was the need to sustain an adequate input of new material. It was a problem at the best of times, comedy being such an evanescent and voracious medium. But the problem was exacerbated in wartime when the suppliers, key personnel such as the writers and the comedians, were likely to be called into the services, and when the demand for it continued unabated and was, if anything, enhanced. The British cinema had traditionally drawn upon certain realms for its comic inspiration — the variety theatre, the West End stage and regional comedians — and these sources remained productive throughout the war years with, for example, six out of the top ten British box office draws by 1941 being provided by comedy acts.[28]

The old guard — Formby, Fields, Hay, the Crazy Gang, Arthur Lucan and Kitty McShane — were joined by newcomers such as Tommy Trinder. Regular stage and screen farceurs, like Robertson Hare, merely continued along the same lines, as with the 1941 film of Ben Travers' *Banana Ridge*, or came up with similar material which was adapted ever so slightly to accommodate wartime settings and situations, as in the 1942 production of Vernon Sylvaine's play, *Women Aren't Angels*. Well worn West End hits were revived on film — *Charley's (Big Hearted) Aunt* in 1940, a broad reworking of the Brandon Thomas farce which first appeared in 1892, *The Middle Watch* in 1940, based upon Ian Hay and Stephen King-Hall's 1929 comedy that had already been filmed in 1930, and *The Ghost Train* in 1941, from Arnold Ridley's 1925 play which had already been made into a film twice over, in 1925 and 1931. Regional comedians like Max Miller and Frank Randle catered for their audiences in the south and the north respectively — Miller with *Hoots Mon* in 1939 and *Asking for Trouble* in 1943, Randle with a string of low budget slapsticks for Mancunian Films and Butchers, of which there were five in all between 1939 and 1945 (*Somewhere in England*, 1940, *Somewhere in Camp* and *Somewhere on Leave*, both 1942, *Somewhere in Civvies*, 1943, and, *Home Sweet Home*, in 1945).

Yet for all that its usual sources served it well, the comedy cinema was always in need of further inspiration, and in its constant quest for new blood, the cinema turned ironically to one of its greatest rivals, radio. In some respects, there was nothing new about this move. The cinema had already lifted a number of radio programmes and transposed them successfully to the screen. The *Inspector Hornleigh* series, for example, highly popular on the radio, was turned into a vehicle for the talents of Gordon Harker and Alastair Sim, resulting in three films between 1939 and 1941. But that was a crime series; rarely, before the war, had the transposition been attempted or achieved with comedy, in large part because the format of radio comedy as it had evolved — a compendium format with individual acts, discrete routines and an overall lack of continuity — hardly lent itself to easy transposition to the screen, where some measure of continuity and a distinct story line were considered essentials.

After the onset of war, however, there was something of a transformation in the style of presentation and the format of radio comedy, as indeed there were changes afoot in many realms of radio altogether. It was a gradual change, it was brought about as a result of the desire, increasingly evident in some quarters of the BBC at least, to popularise its programme output to meet the new found needs of a Britain at war, and it owed a little to the influence of American broadcasting.[29] But in the case of radio comedy, in particular, it resulted in a good deal more in the way of such features as slicker, faster presentation, added continuity, the use of a regular setting as the setting for a whole programme, and the use of a familiar band of comic characters. The old compendium format was never abandoned, but increasing reliance was placed upon the comedy

Victorious at the end, it all appears to have 'turned out nice again'.

programme with coherence, the situation comedy, and this in turn made radio comedy so much more accessible to the cinema.

Hi Gang, with Ben Lyon, Bebe Daniels and Vic Oliver, showed some of the signs of this new style in radio comedy, though it remained essentially rooted in the variety format. *Band Waggon*, with Arthur Askey and Richard Murdoch, showed considerably more and is credited with providing a stylistic bridge between the old format and the new. Both these shows began life, in fact, before the outbreak of war but they continued to enjoy considerable success after its onset. But it was really *ITMA*, with Tommy Handley, that brought it to fruition. It too was launched pre-war, on 12 July 1939, but it reached its peak of achievement and its largest audiences during the war. By the time the fourth *ITMA* series started, in autumn 1942, more than 16 million people were listening to the show in any one week and it 'proceeded to stamp itself indelibly on the life of the war years'.[30]

All three shows were snapped up by the cinema, as indeed were a number of other radio comedies and artists. Elsie and Doris Waters, who had made the characters of Gert and Daisy into a nationwide hit in the spring of 1940 with a series of short broadcasts on behalf of the Ministry of Food, turned up in *Gert and Daisy's Weekend* (1941), and *Gert and Daisy Clean Up* (1942).[31] The Harry Korris series *Happidrome* was made into a film of that name in 1943, and the comic duo of Charters and Caldicott, alias Basil Radford and Naunton Wayne, went through the incestuous process of being launched briefly, if successfully, in the cinema (in Alfred Hitchcock's 1938 production of *The Lady Vanishes*), finding greater acclaim in two six-part radio series devoted exclusively to them (with scripts provided by their creators, Frank Launder and Sidney Gilliat), and then having the radio series lifted wholesale as the basis for John Baxter's 1940 film *Crooks' Tour*, so called after the first of those series. (They further reappeared in supporting roles, but with due acknowledgement to Launder and Gilliat this time, in *Night Train to Munich*, also in 1940, and *Millions Like Us*, in 1943.)

Not all the comedy shows proved as successful on the screen as they had been on the radio. Despite the efforts of director Marcel Varnel and scriptwriters Val Guest and Marriott Edgar, who worked on both films for Gainsborough, *Hi Gang* (1941) was a flop and *Band Waggon* (1940) did only moderate business. However, the latter film did herald Arthur Askey's arrival as a film comic of note. Subsequent appearances in *Charley's (Big Hearted) Aunt* and *The Ghost Train* made him the fifth biggest draw among British artists by 1941, and later films such as *I Thank You* (1941) and *King Arthur Was a Gentleman* (1942), all for essentially the same Gainsborough team, with Walter Forde directing the first two and Varnel the others, did much to consolidate Askey's position as a box office winner during the war years.

Gainsborough and Walter Forde were also responsible for transposing
It's That Man Again and Tommy Handley to the screen late in 1942.
Forde later said that he personally thought it 'a very poor film'.[32]
Nevertheless, it did well, not least because it had a large ready made
audience and because it did evoke so much of what had made the radio
show a success. That had been described in May 1942, by Tom Harrisson
of Mass-Observation, in the following occasionally far-fetched terms:

> Few programmes have ever maintained such a high standard of technical
> proficiency and downright clean fun as *ITMA*, now ended for the time being,
> but nicely rounded off by a grand *ITMA* concert on Tuesday. Handley is the
> crazy Mayor of Foaming at the Mouth, the quintessence of local authority
> gone loco. The one thing at which the Mayor is efficient is talking quickly,
> opening most of his remarks with exclamations of amazement — 'Slap me
> down with a sausage rinser', and other meaningless masochist expressions,
> spoken with the vitality and verve which brings Handley through the air into
> every home.
>   Analyse the words and they don't mean much, often nothing. Many of the
> jokes are highly intellectual, and the whole construction of the programme is
> the nearest thing that the BBC has ever done to surrealism. Strange
> characters from the Freudian form book bob up and down without any
> direct relation to the programme. Mrs Mopp, the wheezy charlady,
> tremblingly asks every few minutes, 'Can I do you now, sir?'. At any
> moment you may hear a bubbling sound, a slight gurgle, and then just the
> four words, 'Don't forget the diver', followed by further bubbling as he
> presumably descends beneath the surface of the subconscious. Then there is
> the cheerful young man who rushes in, greets with 'Good morning, nice day',
> offers some sales line, is rudely refused by the Mayor and in a flash is away
> again with the same words. Every now and again the King of Cairo pedlars
> wanders across the air with that special pander voice of the Middle East,
> 'You gimme licence?'. Or there is the hoodlum boy who always arrives with,
> 'Hey, bawse — som'f'n terrible's happened'. All this, and more, bombard the
> Mayor, and to each he replies with an immediate wisecrack. While behind
> them all lurks the terrible unseen Funf, the Hitler figure, who keeps on
> ringing up Handley to threaten him with immediate destruction . . .
>   . . . I honestly believe that over these past difficult months, Tommy
> Handley has contributed more than any Cabinet Minister towards keeping
> up morale, without ever mentioning the war, yet without the sort of sloppy
> 'escapism' for which some programmes can be criticized by the purist.[33]

Whether surrealistic, escapist, or not, *ITMA* added to the store of good
humour and laughter which abounded in the British cinema during the
wartime years. It succeeded for the same reason that, in 1941, the Crazy
Gang succeeded with *Gasbags*, in which the Gang made something of
being incarcerated and confronted with a host of look-alike Hitlers, and
for the same reason that, in 1942, Will Hay succeeded with *The Goose*

Steps Out, in which he proceeded, among other things, to make great play out of as small a word as Slough. They succeeded, in all, because they brought a large measure of joy to a good many people in what was for the most part a pretty joyless world.

NOTES

1 Co-ordinating Committee Paper No. 1, 'Programme for film propaganda', INF 1/867.
2 Mass-Observation File Report No. 458, 'MoI Shorts', 25 October 1940, p. 1. See also Tom Harrisson, 'Films and the Home Front — the evaluation of their effectiveness by Mass-Observation' in Nicholas Pronay and D. W. Spring (eds), *Propaganda, Politics and Film 1918—1945*, London, 1982, p. 237.
3 M-O File Report No. 24, 'The cinema in the first three months of the war', January 1940, pp. 24—5, and 38. Both films were given a theatrical release, *Do It Now* in September 1939, and *The First Days* in November 1939. The latter did enjoy the immense advantage of being produced by Cavalcanti, and directed by Humphrey Jennings, Harry Watt and Pat Jackson.
4 Angus Calder and Dorothy Sheridan (eds), *Speak for Yourself: a Mass-Observation Anthology, 1937—1949*, London, 1984, pp. 88—9.
5 M-O File Report No. 57, 'Preferences for themes in films', March 1940, p. 10.
6 M-O File Report No. 24, pp. 32—3.
7 M-O File Report No. 435, '*Let George Do It*', September 1940, p. 6.
8 M-O File Report No. 943, 'War jokes. Comparisons between 1940 and 1941', November 1941, p. 1.
9 M-O File Report No. 943, 'War jokes.', pp. 1—2, and M-O File Report No. 177, 'War Jokes in Music Halls', 7 June 1940, pp. 2—3.
10 See James C. Robertson, *The British Board of Film Censors: Film Censorship in Britain, 1896—1950*, London, 1985, pp. 109—45. For the 1930s, in particular, see Jeffrey Richards, *The Age of the Dream Palace*, London, 1984, pp. 89—108.
11 M-O File Report No. 198, 'Film Joke Competition Report', June 1940, p. 3.
12 See Tony Aldgate, *The British Cinema in the 1930s*, Milton Keynes, 1981, pp. 21—5; see also the television programme on *Comedy* which was made to accompany this unit for the Open University course *Popular Culture* and which is broadcast on BBC TV each year throughout the life of the course.
13 Allen Eyles, 'Will Hay and Co.', *Focus on Film*, No. 34, December 1979, p. 15.
14 Home Intelligence Division, 'Daily report on Morale', No. 73, Monday 12 August 1940, p. 1, INF 1/264.
15 Richards, *The Age of the Dream Palace*, p. 203.
16 Anthony Kimmins re-joined the Royal Navy and subsequently became well known as a commentator for the BBC on naval operations. His services were

not entirely lost to the cinema during the war years, however, as the minutes of the Newsreel Association of Great Britain reveal. He sometimes acted as a liaison between the Admiralty and the NRA, not least on one occasion when Gaumont British were censured for showing film of an aircraft carrier, and he provided the newsreel companies with occasional amounts of film, shot by himself, of such as the Petsamo Raid and the Malta Convoys. He resumed his film career, of course, at the end of the war.

17   The script for *Let George Do It* held at the British Film Institute Library, London (dated 7 November 1939; S150), includes a scene at this point which does not appear in the film as released. George 'rises to his feet and adopts a Hitlerian stance'. He declares: 'Right. I'll tell you the truth, the whole truth and nothing but. I am the great white Nordic chief. Blood and soil. My people demand the return of Blackpool to the Reich. I must have living room. Bedroom won't do, I must have living room. I am determined on self-determination. I'll wipe the British Empire from the face of the earth — women and children first. Again and again I have pledged my word, my word I have. Bring me Winston Churchill's head on a charger. I'll fight this war to a finish if it takes me all night'. And then he slumps into a stupor and subsequent dream. Quite why the scene was not used is unclear, though it may well have been felt that George's tirade was not particularly funny and verged on the tasteless.

18   *Kinematograph Weekly*, 14 March 1940, p. 28.

19   *The Cinema*, 13 March 1940.

20   A. J. P. Taylor, *English History 1914—1945*, London, 1965, p. 470.

21   Ian McLaine, *Ministry of Morale*, London, 1979, p. 60.

22   See the microfiche on the film held at the BFI Library, London. The advertising campaign literature for the film still placed considerable emphasis on the fact that George was given 'a topical wartime background'.

23   *Kinematograph Weekly*, 9 January 1941, p. 26.

24   As Basil Dean recorded in *Mind's Eye*, London, 1973, p. 213, 'Superior persons may have affected to disregard George's naive comicalities. Certainly, none of his films did worth while business in the West End of London, but elsewhere it was a case of "all seats sold" most of the time'.

25   M-O File Report No. 435, pp. 1—4, 8, and 12.

26   Tom Harrisson, 'Social Research and the Film', *Documentary News Letter*, 1, November 1940, p. 10. See also M-O File Report No. 463, 'Summary of *Let George Do It* report', 21 October 1940, covering note to same.

27   M-O File Report No. 435, p. 4.

28   *Kinematograph Weekly*, 2 January 1941, p. 3. The top ten British box office draws comprised: 1, George Formby, 2, Robert Donat, 3, Gracie Fields, 4, Arthur Lucan and Kitty McShane, 5, Arthur Askey, 6, Charles Laughton, 7, Will Hay, 8, Conrad Veidt, 9, Gordon Harker, and 10, Anna Neagle.

29   See, in particular, David Cardiff and Paddy Scannell, *Radio in World War II*, Milton Keynes, 1981, pp. 67—9 and the audio cassettes related to the same.

30   Angus Calder, *The People's War*, London, 1971, p. 416.

31   Mass-Observation surveyed the public reaction to the nightly five-minute broadcasts by Gert and Daisy in April 1940 for its report on *Home Propaganda*, in *Change*, no. 2, 1941, pp. 29—30.

32   Quoted in Geoff Brown (ed.), *Walter Forde*, London, 1977, pp. 47—8.

33   M-O File Report No. 1252, 'Radio II', 11 May 1942, pp. 2—3. This is incorrectly entered under File Report No. 1952 for November 1943 in the *Mass-Observation Archive Guide to the File Reports*, University of Sussex, 1981.

5

'Careless Talk Costs Lives'

The Next of Kin

It was widely believed that the dramatic collapse of so many European nations before the Nazi *blitzkreig* was due to the activities of a 'fifth column' working within those countries. Warnings of similar danger in Britain were made almost at once. Churchill in his speech on Dunkirk talked darkly of 'this malignancy in our midst' and fifth columnists were said to be everywhere, in high places and low, spreading alarm and despondency, signalling to the enemy, wrecking communications, engaging in acts of sabotage, cooperating with enemy agents. As a Ministry of Information pamphlet declared in 1940:

> There is a fifth column in Britain. Anyone who thinks that there isn't, that it 'can't happen here', has simply fallen into the trap laid by the fifth column itself. For *the first job of the fifth column is to make people think that it does not exist.* In other countries the most respectable and neighbourly citizens turned out to be fifth columnists when the time came. The fifth column does not only consist of foreigners.[1]

Home Intelligence reported on 5 June 1940 that 'the fifth column hysteria is reaching dangerous proportions'. Aliens, many of them in fact anti-Nazi refugees, were rounded up, shipped to the Isle of Man and later dispersed to the Dominions. Sir Oswald Mosley and some of his Fascist followers were arrested and imprisoned. But in fact the fifth column hardly existed; the sorts of offences which brought prosecution included a man sentenced to seven years for smashing up telephone booths and a schoolmaster jailed for advancing 'defeatist theories' to his pupils — hardly the sort of offences likely to seriously impair the war effort.[2]

Actual German operations in Britain were not extensive. One historian has concluded that during the war 'the number of German agents in Britain was small, their information unreliable and most of their communications under observation.'[3] A number of German agents were smuggled into Britain but 18 of them were captured and hanged. Contact was established by the Abwehr with the IRA who perpetrated a number of bombing outrages on the mainland during war. But the chief success of the Abwehr was the recruitment of Tyler Kent, a Fascist fanatic on the American Embassy staff in London, who until his arrest in May 1940 handed over to the Germans microfilm of messages passed between London and Washington. However, the promotion of the idea of a vast secret army of German sympathisers; besides keeping people on their toes, did serve one useful function. It provided a convenient scapegoat for defeats and disasters, and discouraged people from concentrating on the military invincibility of the German forces, an idea strongly fostered by the success of *blitzkrieg*.[4]

Coupled with this fear of the fifth column was a fear of careless talk, furnishing vital information to the enemy. This was a recurrent theme of

The Next of Kin *warned against the dangers of careless talk, even between lovers (Nova Pilbeam and Geoffrey Hibbert).*

wartime propaganda, prompting a series of notable posters — 'Careless talk costs lives', 'Keep it under your hat', 'Keep Mum, she's not so dumb', 'Be like Dad; keep Mum'. One poster featured Hitler and Goering sitting behind two gossiping housewives on top of a bus. Yet here again the fears seem to have been out of proportion to the actual danger. Lord Swinton's Committee on National Security (1941) agreed that 'there was little evidence of careless talk and less evidence that it was put to good use by the enemy'. Nevertheless, a major anti-gossip campaign was ordered by Churchill in 1941.[5]

The twin themes of the fifth column and careless talk were combined in one of the most celebrated films to come out of World War Two, *The Next of Kin*, a film which started out as an Army instructional film but went on to become an enormous hit at the commercial box office, confirming the popularity of that new commitment to realism in character, theme and treatment that was one of the hallmarks of the best of British cinema in the war.

The fifth column had figured in films since the outset, appearing both in comedy and drama. *Traitor Spy* (1939), one of the earliest wartime features, centred on the unmasking of a worker at a vital armaments factory as a saboteur and spy. In *Went the Day Well?* (1942), the head of the local Home Guard turned out to be the chief fifth columnist. In the George Formby comedy *Spare a Copper* (1940) the fifth columnists included a prominent Merseyside businessman, a clerk and a funfair motor cyclist. In the Gordon Harker comedy *Inspector Hornleigh Goes to It* (1941), they included a public school headmaster, a dentist, a chatty barmaid and GPO sorters on the night mail. So *The Next of Kin* was in good company, but it was the first full-length film to be devoted to the dangers of careless talk, though Ealing had produced several 10 minute fictional shorts (*Dangerous Comment, Now You're Talking, All Hands*), featuring stars like John Mills, Frank Lawton and Sebastian Shaw.

At the outset of the war both Michael Balcon and Thorold Dickinson offered their services to the War Office but were told that their offer would be taken up 'when the war becomes real'. That time arrived in December 1940, when General John Hawkesworth, director of military training, contacted Balcon at Ealing Studios and asked him to produce a film on behalf of the War Office on the subject of security. Initially the War Office envisaged a 20 minute short, but the number of different things they wanted to get across made a feature film a more suitable format. Dickinson, who had just completed the shooting of *The Prime Minister* for Warner Bros., was asked to call on Balcon and discuss the film, and on 7 January 1941 he was formally invited to write and direct it. It was to take about three months and was to be done as cheaply as possible without sacrificing quality. The War Office was putting up £20,000, the maximum they could allocate. Ealing agreed to furnish the remainder of the finance, which eventually worked out at £50,000. It was agreed that the film would be commercially released in due course and that as soon as it started to earn a profit, Ealing would be repaid their investment plus a small percentage. The rest of the profits would go to the Crown.[6]

A story conference was held on 9 January, but it was clear the War Office had no ideas about what they wanted in the way of content. However, they promised full support, access to army records and the release of service personnel to work on the film. They secured Dickinson's release from Warner Bros., to whom he was under contract, and they assigned as liaison officer on the project Captain Sir Basil Bartlett Bart., who was himself a writer, and who agreed to help provide material for the screenplay.

Dickinson set to work on the screenplay at Ealing Studios with the Ealing story supervisor, Angus MacPhail. Bartlett suggested using the organization of security at a major seaport like Liverpool as the mainspring of the story. Dickinson and MacPhail then worked for three weeks constructing a story along these lines, with the threatened German invasion of Britain as the background. They spent three days in Liverpool itself as part of the research for this (20 — 23 January).

But when they presented their treatment to the War Office on 6 February, the War Office did not like it, vetoed the German invasion background and suggested instead a combined operations assault on the Continent as the background. Dickinson and MacPhail were furnished with a typical diary of the planning and execution of such an operation. A month later a new treatment along these lines was sent to the War Office, but at the script conference held on 13 March 1941, various elements of the schedule for this fictional operation were criticized and Dickinson decided to get an authoritative ruling from Lieutenant Colonel Ely of Combined Operations Department. He and Bartlett consulted Ely, assembled his criticisms of their treatment and, armed with these and further background information, prepared a third treatment, much wider in scope than originally intended. Finally on 22 April 1941 the War Office accepted the outline and since there was an urgent need to get on with it, John Dighton was drafted into the writing team to help prepare the shooting script from the detailed Dickinson—MacPhail treatment. The film was to go into production under the working title *Security*, but eventually Dickinson devised the title *The Next of Kin*, a reference to the familiar wartime radio announcement: 'The next of kin have been informed'. This was one of several films to take their titles from familiar wireless phrases (*Fires Were Started, One of our Aircraft is Missing*) and service phrases (*Target for Tonight, In Which We Serve*).

Interviewed in 1976, Dickinson remained intensely critical of the indecision and inaccurate guidance provided by the War Office. He had further cause for complaint when he was almost pulled out of the film. As

The Nazi agents and fifth columnists are shown as ruthless operators, quite capable of blackmail (Nova Pilbeam and Stephen Murray).

he was in the process of investigating Army records, it was discovered that he was technically a security risk. He had been classified as a 'premature anti-Fascist' because of his involvement in making a documentary in Spain in support of the Republicans during the Spanish Civil War. After some discussion, he was cleared to continue with his work.[7]

The shooting script was ready by May. Dickinson was anxious to avoid well-known faces in order to make the impact of the story greater, but Ealing seem to have favoured initially an all-star cast, such as that employed in a similar drama-documentary *The Big Blockade* (1942). A list of casting suggestions, dated 9 July 1941, includes John Clements as Richards, Clive Brook as the Brigadier, Jimmy Hanley as Durnford, Leslie Banks as the Colonel and Jessie Matthews as Clare. In the event, none of them appeared, but the list also includes Mervyn Johns, Stephen Murray, Basil Sydney, Frank Allenby and Torin Thatcher in the roles which they did eventually play. Peter Ustinov, cast as a German parachutist, was unavailable when shooting began. Although Lilli Palmer wanted to play the female lead, Beppie, that part went to Nova Pilbeam, partly to help take her mind off the death of her young film director husband Pen Tennyson in a flying accident.

In the end Dickinson settled for a blend of service personnel and character actors, handpicking them and avoiding star names. This had the additional advantage of keeping costs down, because the service personnel were given only their service pay. A disgruntled Second Lieutenant Jack Hawkins discovered that the civilian actors were getting £15 a day to his 11 shillings, so he and David Hutcheson went to see Michael Balcon to find out if something could be done to supplement their meagre pay. 'My dear boys, I have given my word to the War Office that you will only get your basic pay,' said Balcon and that was that.[8]

The film was shot between 26 July and 24 October 1941. The interiors, which took seven weeks, were completed on time, despite the fact that *The Next of Kin* had to compete with *The Foreman Went to France* for studio space and specialized equipment, and that Dickinson kept losing his cameramen through call-ups. Eventually 22 worked on the film. It was shot largely as written, though there were some cuts made in the script. A flashback framework was eliminated to give the story greater immediacy. Several scenes were also dropped in the interests of advancing the story: some conversations between soldiers, a flashback in the main story in which Richards tells about an incident involving Germans in British uniforms, and a comic little scene in which German spies are instructed in the pronunciation of English place names. It was too good an idea to lose permanently and duly turned up in the next Dighton—MacPhail collaboration, the Will Hay vehicle *The Goose Steps Out* (1942).

However, the studio began to complain when Dickinson overran the schedule for shooting the final battle scenes at Mevagissey by several weeks. This was due partly to bad weather and partly to the non-availability of essential items of naval and military equipment. The battle sequences had not been scripted in advance, apart from a general idea of the development of the action, so they were worked out exactly like a real combined operation by Dickinson, Bartlett, Cecil Dixon the production manager and officers of the Royal Worcestershire Regiment, which was providing the fighting forces. Six cameramen were used to get the maximum footage from the operation. Once the film was completed, William Walton provided a martial score for it and the film was ready for showing to service personnel by February 1942.

The film has neither a hero nor a conventional narrative thread. It is in fact a dramatization of a slogan 'Careless talk costs lives', a mosaic of stories and incidents constructed around that single central idea. In a film which switches so freely back and forth from an English to a German view of the proceedings, it is the slogan which gives the film its dramatic unity. Everything dovetails into it. Several obvious and directly propagandist devices are used to set out the message. At various points during the film the camera dollies into posters and notices, bearing the slogans: 'Keep it under your hat' etc. The message is amplified by security officers in lectures to their men ('You are the real security men'); but it also informs every aspect of the story.

The film falls essentially into three parts. The first part shows how leaks of information occur. When the Army decides on a raid on the French coast, the 10th Chilterns are transferred to Watercombe on the Cumberland coast for training and Major Richards is assigned as security officer. Two sources of leaks are developed and interwoven, embracing both officers and other ranks. Both involve emotional involvements, clearly seen as the greatest danger. A private, Johnny (Geoffrey Hibbert), gives away information at his meetings with his Dutch refugee girlfriend Beppie (Nova Pilbeam), and in his unauthorized letters to her, which he considers harmless. But this information is blackmailed out of Beppie by her employer, Ned Barratt, a Nazi agent (Stephen Murray). Lieutenant Cummings, a callow young officer (Philip Friend) is led on by dancer Clare, similarly revealing vital information about troop movements and plans. But Clare, a drug addict supplied by a Nazi agent (Mary Clare), passes the information on, enabling the Germans to build up a picture of the regiment's activities. The Nazi dupes almost all meet unhappy ends: Clare and her control are arrested and will hang; Beppie kills Barratt and is herself killed by agent Davis (Mervyn Johns); Cummings is killed in the final raid; the price of their witting or unwitting treachery. But the principal Nazi agent, Davis, survives with the important information that there are aerial photographs, which are the key to the British plan.

The second part of the film shows the Nazi espionage network swinging into action, detailing the sinister chain reaching from Berlin into the heart of England. A respectable dentist, a genial Irish sailor, the mild-mannered 'Welsh' evacuee Davis, a collection of spies and fifth columnists, each participate in the simple business of gaining the aerial photographs by switching briefcases with the careless Wing Commander, who is dining in a plush restaurant with a pretty girl, duplicating them, getting them out of England on a neutral ship to a neutral port and thence by plane to Berlin.

The third part of the film reveals the tragic consequences of this activity. The Germans identify Norville as the destination of the raid and move in extra troops. The British attack, and although they blow up vital installations, they suffer heavy losses, much heavier than they need have done, as a sombre narrator relates, because of the leaks of information — 'The next of kin have been informed.'

Dickinson deploys three weapons in putting over this story — casualness, lightness and realism, each of them making the message more grim. Apart from the monocled, heel-clicking stereotyped Hun in the Berlin headquarters scenes, Dickinson portrays his German spies for the most part as very ordinary, inoffensive, sympathetic figures, the least likely types to be involved in espionage and fifth column activities, and therefore the least likely to elicit suspicion. There is Barratt, the kindly, bespectacled, pipe-smoking, soft-spoken bookseller, who ruthlessly blackmails Beppie by threatening her family in Holland with concentration camp internment. There is Davis, the gentle, middle-aged Welsh evacuee, who murders Beppie and blows up an ammunition dump. There is Ma, the motherly, cheerful, cockney theatrical dresser, who forces the drug-addicted Clare to get information by threatening to withhold her 'coke ration'. When these figures have been established as spies, casual, apparently meaningless chatter in their hearing in pubs and at a dance takes on a sinister, and ultimately deadly, importance. This danger is the basis of an episode which takes place entirely on a train. Drunken soldiers chat in the railway buffet car, with a German spy in British army battle dress listening and pumping them. Another soldier becomes suspicious

The chief Nazi agent (Mervyn Johns) murders Beppie (Nova Pilbeam).

and reluctantly reports his suspicions to two officers, who equally reluctantly question the man, not wanting to make a fuss. Their suspicions aroused, they order him to strip, to see if he has the strap marks of a parachute on his shoulders. He attempts to bolt and is caught and arrested. The point of the episode is not only the ease with which information can be leaked, but the inbred reluctance of the British to make a fuss when they are suspicious, a reluctance which, the film suggests, must be overcome in the interests of national security. Even soldiers on duty are guilty of laxity in this regard, as Richards' arrival at the Watercombe HQ is made to demonstrate. En route, one soldier gives him directions to the camp without ascertaining his identity and another admits him without asking to see his pass. Both are reproved.

The simplicity and speed with which the Nazi spy chain gets the information to Berlin are conveyed by rapid cutting, movement and pace. But this is reinforced by a grim light-heartedness, which Dickinson found paid dividends. Several times Davis makes jokes about spies and at one point, in Barratt's shop, is found ostentatiously reading a book entitled 'I am a Nazi Agent'. The final gag ending of the film, not originally in the script, had Basil Radford and Naunton Wayne in a railway carriage, casually discussing secret plans. A man leans across to offer them a light and is revealed as Davis, still up to his nefarious activities. Similarly the switching of briefcases is done against a background of high key lighting, pretty girls and airy badinage between customers. Dickinson found that these were the scenes which frightened people most, reinforcing the impression of casualness and ease being fatal in wartime.

The absence of a central figure and the shifts in perspective that the film involves contribute to the overall concept of a 'paraphrase of reality', one of the descriptions Dickinson has applied to his work. Major Richards, the main candidate for the hero role, disappears from the action in the middle of the film and anyway, thanks to the quiet underplaying of Reginald Tate, never dominates the action at any stage. But this reticence lends a chilling force to his matter of fact answer to Cummings' question about what the authorities will do with Clare — 'try her in a court of law and hang her'. This sense of reality persists throughout the graphically shot and edited final battle scenes.

Dickinson employs a mobile camera, though much of his camera movement is unobtrusive, and he tracks frequently on movement, so as not to make audiences camera-conscious. Close-ups are used sparingly, generally for emphasis and notably at moments of high drama, such as the use of intercut close-ups in the scenes where Barratt blackmails Beppie and Clare wheedles information out of Cummings. There are long unbroken takes to get over essential information to the audience — in the discussion of the tactics of the Norville raid, in the questioning of the

German parachutist on the train and in the lectures and discussions on security.

But all is not straightforward realism. The opening sequence takes place in a church in Norville. The camera tracks in to two figures kneeling before the altar, exchanging information in whispers. They are a Free French officer spying for England and a local woman. A priest enters the frame and nods significantly to the two. Cut to the doorway where a German soldier stands threateningly. Then from behind the statue of the Virgin Mary there is a high-angle shot of the kneeling French patriots, the German oppressor in the doorway and behind him a statue of Christ suffering on the cross. The symbolism is quite clear. The camera tracks with the Frenchman as he leaves and then the shot dissolves to one of the Virgin Mary standing upright in a little boat, the seven symbolic stars of the sea forming a halo over her head. The composition of the scene and the visual symbols all contrive to invest the Allied cause with divine sanction and damn the Nazi regime as anti-Christian.

The result of Dickinson's efforts was a film that was not only a vivid illustration of the meaning of a wartime slogan but also a taut and exciting espionage thriller, with an extremely resourceful and gripping script, vividly staged action and a first-rate cast, with Mervyn Johns outstanding as the ubiquitous German agent.

The film had a number of interesting results. The War Office were so impressed by the film that they appointed Dickinson as head of production for the Army Kinematograph Film Unit with the rank of second lieutenant. He rapidly rose to the rank of major. The film created such a sensation that a sixty minute version of the script was broadcast on the radio. The film marked an advance in the liberalization of censorship, with its explicit mentions of drugs and drug addiction, something which had been taboo in the 1930s, and was thus part of a wider process of censorship liberalization initiated by the war. Looking back, Balcon was to call it 'One of the most important films made in the life of Ealing'.[9]

The Army regarded *The Next of Kin* as by far and away their most important cinematic production. In February 1942, Paul Kimberley, director of Army kinematography, reported to the War Office:

> The latest training film, entitled 'Next of Kin', dealing with the necessity for tightening up security measures in the services and graphically illustrating the fatal consequences of gossip, has been seen by the Army Council in the War Office cinema and by large representative audiences in the Curzon Cinema. Members of the Army Council unanimously expressed the view that the film should be seen by the troops immediately. An advance copy of the film has been sent to each command for screening to GOC's and their staffs, with a view to giving a stimulus to the general showing when a wide

The consequence of the careless talk was to be serious losses sustained by the British in a French coastal raid.

distribution of copies is made, as quickly as they become available from the laboratory. Every possible use will be made of civilian theatres now at our disposal for showing the film to HM Forces. There is a consensus of opinion, including that of the War Office Kinematograph Committee, who have viewed the film, that it should be made available for early distribution to the public. This question of the general release of the film to the public is now under consideration by the Army Council.

Subsequently, 26 screenings were given 'with great success' for War Office staff at Cheltenham. Some 4,000 personnel saw the film, which was shown five times daily for a week; 3,500 personnel from the Foreign Office also saw the film at special showings at the Curzon Cinema in London. It was then run for about 1,000 members of the Inter-Services Research Bureau and the general opinion expressed by them was that 'it had achieved more than one would hope to do in 12 months by talking, lectures etc.'[10]

But before it could be released to the public it encountered several obstacles, which demonstrate the pitfalls for film-makers in wartime. First of all, the film fell foul of the actual course of the war. As Dickinson himself recalled in 1976:

> The film went on at the Curzon (the armed forces cinema in London) in February — a few weeks before the St Nazaire Raid. Churchill heard about it and had a copy sent to Chequers and immediately said 'Take the film off' and I remember at the Curzon in the foyer talking to the MoI people, naval officers, army officers, and they were all saying 'What on earth can we do about this?' — because none of them knew about the St Nazaire Raid. Well, as soon as the St Nazaire Raid (on 28 March 1942) was a success, Churchill said: 'Now you can start showing it again, but I would like to see a few more dead Nazis and less dead British'. There was too much bloodshed. This man Hawkesworth demanded all the bloodshed — loved it. I nibbled these little bits out, totalling 20 feet, and Churchill's representative said, 'Yes, it's alright now' . . . It was entirely Churchill's own security work and sense of morale. If the St Nazaire Raid had been a flop, the film would have done more harm to the morale of the troops than good in warning them.

But the next problem was that the film fell foul of the Air Force. Dickinson recalled:

> With Basil Bartlett we worked the whole thing out as to how the enemy get the information about something that is going to happen. We found that the one thing that no ordinary man in the Army knows anything about is the time and place. That is a matter for officers of the rank of Lieutenant Colonel, Wing Commander or upwards. Below that rank, they don't know. So that if there's a bad giving of the show away, it really means that the top men are to blame. And we put this in the film, and we discovered an actual case with the briefcase. Everything was real. This infuriated the Air Force: why should the Army make this film and blame the Air Force?

The matter was discussed at the top level. The film was viewed and a report on it sent to Group Captain Sir Louis Greig, personal air secretary to the Secretary of State for Air, by R. Peck, presumably Air Vice-Marshal Richard Peck, assistant chief of the air staff:

> The film *Next of Kin* has a number of minor villains in it. The villain-in-chief, however, is without a doubt a Wing Commander whose carelessness is the main cause of the loss of life portrayed very graphically in the film. It could be held that, at a time when many people in the Army and among the public think that the Air Force lets the Army down, that it was unfortunate to portray the terrible example of it that this film does. On the other hand, cooperation by the Air Force in the actual attack is very well shown and it may well be that the general public would not be so sensitive to this inter-service aspect as we who are so close to it. On the whole, as the film is so

very good, I think we should be prepared to take the dose of medicine handed to us, and let the film go . . . It is a very fine film which will teach many useful lessons from which all could profit.[11]

But the men at the top insisted on a screening and Dickinson was ordered to attend:

I who was then a major in the Army was summoned to the Air Ministry and sat in a room with two projectors at the back, and the Air Minister and his wife and Lord Portal (then Air Chief Marshal Sir Charles Portal, chief of the air staff). I was sitting next to Portal, who was like a frozen General de Gaulle figure — never said a word. It was awful. I had to watch the whole bloody thing through again with them. The Air Minister was a little more civilized. Anyhow they had to stomach it. Churchill insisted on it going out again.

Release to the general public thus approved, the Ministry of Information took over the film from the War Office and by the terms of the rota on which the major companies worked with regard to films necessary for the war effort, United Artists undertook distribution. On 15 May 1942, the Army Council and representatives of the Cabinet attended the film's commercial premiere at the Carlton Cinema and on 2 June a special showing of the film was arranged at Badminton for Queen Mary ('The Queen Mother apparently thoroughly appreciated the film', reported Kimberley). The film went on general release in June. It won further plaudits from the Soviet Ambassador Maisky who pronounced it 'a good and necessary film'.[12]

The attempts to prevent the film's release provided admirable publicity. It was advertized as 'the most discussed film of the day.' The reviews were generally highly complimentary. *The Times* declared:

It is difficult to understand why there should ever have been any discussion as to whether or not *The Next of Kin* should be shown to the public. Certainly the sequences of a raid by our commandos are constructed with considerable realism, and the camera does not gloss over the fact that, in battle, men die violent and horrible deaths, but more gruesome shots have been seen in the newsreels, and the film, after all, is intended to jolt the public into awareness of the danger of careless talk.[13]

The popular press pulled out all the stops. 'You must see the film, because you are the people the film is about', said the *Sunday Graphic*. 'A film that was worth waiting for. Fine entertainment', said the *Sunday Express*. 'Every man and woman, either in or out of the services, must see *The Next of Kin*', said the *Empire News*. 'One of the finest pictures ever made', said the *Sunday Chronicle*.[14]

The quality press waxed more reflective, but shared the general enthusiasm. Dilys Powell in *The Sunday Times* wrote:

> If *The Next of Kin* is a fair sample of the kind of film made exclusively for the troops, the next few days should see a rush of film critics to join the Army. It is a most enjoyable, exciting, ingenious and salutary film: a topical film which is not forced, a warning which isn't a throwaway . . . A cautionary tale, in fact; but a tale told with authority and conviction, a caution which, however fantastic the possibilities presented, should seal our lips for the duration. The whole has been admirably directed by Thorold Dickinson, and the final sequences of the landing are rendered with an absence of heroics which is quite heartbreaking. The performances of Mervyn Johns and Stephen Murray as enemy agents come readily to the memory; but it is hardly just to single out players from a cast so uniformly good; a cast, by the way, in which many a name well known on the stage or the screen reappears with a service rank.[15]

C. A. Lejeune in the *Observer* concurred, calling it:

> meticulously done in every department of writing, direction and acting. So many individual credits are deserved that I shall not attempt to distribute them. With nobody's eye on the box office, everybody's mind has been on his work, and the result is a masterly team job, slick, unselfconscious, and about as dull as dynamite. I expect *Next of Kin*, which was not made for the box office, to be a box office hit up and down the country. The public who are almost as much interested in entertainment as they are in security, will find here the perfect spy story.[16]

William Whitebait in the *New Statesman* set the film in the broader context of the change coming over the British cinema:

> There was a time — not so very long ago — when English films flowed along opposite sides of a street. Reality and fiction, the documentary and the feature, every film kept to one side or the other, and disastrous was the occasional attempt to cross over. Some energy as well as imagination was needed to bring the two together. Audiences had their weakness for the sunny side, the villas and shop fronts of Filmlandia. There everything was posed and gaudy, and the sham fascinated. But with war exerting its pressure, the glamour of daydreams faded, naturalism came into its own. The film fixed in reality no longer had to carry a ridiculously unreal plot. *Next of Kin*, like *One of Our Aircraft is Missing*, is an admirable example of the new kind of English film, actual, thrilling and taking its tune from events. It compares well with the reconstructions of war incidents favoured by the Russians.[17]

The trade paper *Kinematograph Weekly* pronounced it 'excellent propaganda proposition, a box office certainty for all classes.'[18] Their prediction was fully borne out. United Artists reported in May 'that it is one of the best films they have handled from a box office point of view.' The trade press reported in June that 'following the terrific West End success at the London Pavilion and the Carlton, *The Next of Kin* has experienced a smashing general release, audiences packing theatres everywhere.' United Artists later reported that between 1 June and 14 July approximately three million people had seen the film in civilian cinemas and box office receipts totalled £47,000. It was estimated that the receipts would eventually reach £80,000. In fact, this estimate was exceeded. Cash receipts up to 19 December, 1942 had reached £89,000, of which 80 per cent went to the Treasury and the rest to Ealing. By 1944 the Ministry of Information had handed over £95,308 to the Treasury as profit from *The Next of Kin*.[19] Dickinson himself estimated that eventually United Artists handed over £120,000 to the Treasury, and this is quite likely.

What was the effect of the film on the people who saw it? It seems to have achieved its aim to alert the troops to the importance of security. Paul Kimberley reported in June 1942 that *The Next of Kin* had had such an effect on units in training camps in the Birmingham area that 'the boys won't even talk about the next day's training among themselves now'. General Alexander told Dickinson 'This film was worth a division of troops to the British Army.' But in at least one case the effect was far more dramatic than Dickinson intended. He recalled:

> It was then that I learned about the effect of film on the individual members of the audience, depending on the condition of the individual. The man running the Curzon — which was the armed forces cinema in London — there was an army officer managing it — after the first week he had to indent for a case of brandy for bringing back people who had fainted: it really knocked people out. This one woman — he phoned me to my office across the road in Curzon St House — he said: 'You've got to come over. I've got a case here I can't cope with.' Anybody with a security pass (civilians in the Civil Service) were all forced to go and see the film. Everybody was ordered to see it. This woman, who was a woman of about fifty-something, with two sons overseas in the war, she was working in the Civil Service. She didn't faint and she wasn't distraught, but her mind refused to believe the end of the film was fiction: to her it was fact; it had really happened. But when I said to her 'Well, how do you imagine we got out cameras on to the German side as well as on to the British', she said: 'I don't care about that. That's not important. What I saw on the screen has really happened.' We had to get a psychiatrist to her. Her brain had been lifted out of the normal intelligence into a state. She said: 'I shan't sleep again for the rest of the war. This thing will haunt me. It was a wicked, wicked thing to have done, to put this on the screen.'

As for the civilian audience, Mass-Observation did one of their spot checks on cinemagoers to assess the effect of the film, in this case interviewing about 90 people, just under half women, as they left cinemas in Central and North London.[20] Sixty-five per cent said they liked it very much, 25 per cent said they liked it, only 5 per cent said they disliked it. Approval and disapproval was equal amongst both men and women. The report noted that 80 per cent of those interviewed had got the message of the film, namely that it was a warning against 'careless talk' and many people actually mentioned the slogan. People were also asked what the film made them feel about the way the officers and men behaved in the film. The result was:

> there was a very definite feeling that the officers in the film were more to blame for what had happened than the men, and that the officers ought to have set a better example. People were much more indulgent where the men were concerned. There is very little sex difference in this attitude to men and officers but there is a feeling that the officers are more to blame than the men.

The raid on the French coast was actually shot at Mevagissey in Cornwall.

Of those questioned, 58 per cent thought the officers behaved badly, 38 per cent thought the men did. But as the comments recorded by the observer indicate, many thought the officers more at fault because it was they who had access to important information and not the men. The report concluded:

> Many people considered the film excellent propaganda and thought it would do good to show it as widely as possible. There was hardly any criticism and what there was came from the less intelligent. A few thought the film boring or too obvious, and a very few criticized some minor points in it. We have never in the writer's experience met with such a good response and such enthusiasm for any film.

The film had a less happy experience in America, however, In April 1942 the US Embassy in London was pressing for *The Next of Kin* to be shown in America. Colonel Darryl F. Zanuck, who was on leave of absence from 20th Century—Fox to supervise production of US Army training films, viewed the film on a trip to London and pronounced it 'a fine film'.[21] It was Zanuck's creed that 'a training film can teach everything a soldier needs to know.' In May 1942 the Embassy asked for facilities to show the film to all their military personnel in London and General Eisenhower ordered that it be shown to all US service personnel arriving in the United Kingdom. In November 1942 Paul Kimberley reported:

> My liaison officer with the US forces in this country has recently heard a number of favourable comments on *Next of Kin* from both officers and NCOs of the US Army . . . It is the opinion of US officers that *Next of Kin* has really brought home to American troops the importance of security and that the *Next of Kin* film may claim a share of the complete surprise achieved in the North African campaign.

Sidney Bernstein, who had been urging his MoI colleagues to adopt a more robust stance in the film propaganda sent to America and the emphasizing of the fact that Britons 'not only know how to die but how to win', despatched a print of *The Next of Kin* to David Selznick for an appraisal of its likely effect in the United States. Selznick viewed the film with director Ernst Lubitsch and screenwriter Nunnally Johnson and cabled his reply to Bernstein in four typed pages:

> Release in this country of the film in anything like its present version would be a dreadful error from the standpoint of British—American relations . . . All the English officers are portrayed as stupid, careless and derelict . . . Calculated to increase the fears of Americans and mothers especially that the British are simply muddling along, and that their sons will die because of British incompetence. This is aggravated by contrast with portrayal of

brilliance and complete efficiency of German intelligence . . . The latter point is felt so strongly that all here believe the film could be more profitably run in Germany for home consumption and for building German morale . . . Perhaps even worse is the portrayal of so many British civilians as informers and spies, giving the impression that England is overrun by traitors . . . So strong was the feeling that no attempt should be made even to salvage the film, that I had difficulty in forcing rational discussion.[22]

An attempt was, however, made to salvage the film. For its American release, 30 minutes was cut, leaving only the bare narrative skeleton and removing much of the textural detail so important to the film's effect. A foreword was added in which J. Edgar Hoover warned about the dangers of careless talk in the United States, and the film was distributed by Universal. The *New York Times* liked it:

> *Next of Kin* was put together to do something more important than entertain — a necessity which placed a rigid premium upon reality and credibility. Everyone connected with its production imported these virtues into it to an admirable degree. It is tightly and cleverly written, its incidents are dramatic yet always plausible. It was produced and directed expertly and is most impressively played.[23]

Dickinson, however, was appalled by the cutting, calling it 'a total numbing of a vital film'. This demonstrates very well the two-edged nature of the propaganda film and the wide gulf remaining in reaction to film between Britain and the United States, a reaction dictated by national circumstances, the wider propaganda context, national taste and character and the very different traditions of film-making that were emerging in response to the war.

NOTES

1   Ian McLaine, *Ministry of Morale*, London, 1979, p. 75.
2   Angus Calder, *The People's War*, London, 1971, pp. 150—7.
3   Ian Colvin, *Chief of Intelligence*, London, 1951, p. 75.
4   Louis de Jong, *The German Fifth Column in the Second World War*, New York, 1973.
5   McLaine, *Ministry of Morale*, pp. 224—5.
6   The precise reconstruction of the background to the making of the film was made possible by access to letters and memoranda in the possession of Thorold Dickinson, which I was permitted to examine. There are two production files on the film with the Thorold Dickinson Papers (items 34, 35), lodged with the British Film Institute. All quotations by Dickinson are

taken from a series of interviews with him conducted by the author in the spring of 1976. Sir Michael Balcon's account of the making of the film can be found in Michael Balcon, *Michael Balcon Presents . . . a Lifetime of Films*, London, 1969, pp. 134—7.

7   Balcon, *Michael Balcon Presents*, p. 136.

8   Jack Hawkins, *Anything for a Quiet Life*, London, 1975, pp. 84—5.

9   Balcon, *Michael Balcon Presents*, p. 134.

10 All information about the Army's use of the film and quotations from Paul Kimberley come from Kimberley's monthly reports to the War Office on the work of the Army Kinematography Department, WO 165/96, held in the PRO.

11 There is a copy of this letter, dated 9 March, 1943, in the Dickinson Papers, file 35.

12 Maisky's comment was reported by the *Daily Sketch*, 16 May 1942.

13 *The Times*, 14 May 1942.

14 These comments were reported in *Kinematograph Weekly*, 21 May 1942.

15 *The Sunday Times*, 17 May 1942.

16 *Observer*, 17 May 1942.

17 *New Statesman*, 23 May 1942.

18 *Kinematograph Weekly*, 21 May 1942.

19 The trade press and United Artists' statements are reported in Paul Kimberley's monthly reports, as are the receipts (WO 165/96). The MoI's financial total comes in INF 1/199.

20 Mass-Observation File Report 1342 (May 1942). Home Intelligence Report 88 (11 June 1942) also reported on reaction to *Next of Kin*. It was said to have made 'a very big impression' and to have earned 'a good deal of praise' (INF 1/292).

21 *Daily Sketch*, 16 May 1942.

22 Caroline Moorehead, *Sidney Bernstein*, London, 1984, pp. 147—8.

23 *New York Times*, 6 May 1943.

6

'If the Invader Comes'

Went the Day Well?

The film of *Went the Day Well?* is very carefully and consciously placed in time. It deals with events that overtake the fictional village of Bramley End during the Whitsun weekend of 1942, from Saturday 23 to Monday 25 May — hence the title given to the film on its American release of *48 Hours*. It owed a lot to the fears of invasion which the Home Intelligence Division of the MoI reported were keenly felt in Britain in the spring of 1942. But its origins can also be traced to a period some two years earlier, in the spring of 1940, when Graham Greene wrote a short story entitled *The Lieutenant Died Last*, upon which the film was subsequently, if loosely, based. The short story, too, was largely preoccupied with the threat of imminent invasion — as pronounced in 1940 as in 1942, if not perhaps more so — though there were other significant factors which contributed towards its genesis.

In April 1940, the MoI's Policy Committee was greatly exercised with thoughts and ideas on how best to project Britain's cause and case in America, an America still at peace. A Policy Committee paper highlighted the extent of its worries when noting that 'The United States, unlike many neutrals, has no fear of Germany . . . Its security, however, leads it to indulge in doubts about British determination and the reality of British democracy'. It continued, 'The Ministry counters this by arranging for unofficial British contributions to American papers and periodicals'.[1] Such efforts were by no means always rewarded, for within a month it was reported that 'The spreading of Allied propaganda in the USA is becoming increasingly difficult'.[2] But clearly there proved to be no problem in lodging a short story by the successful novelist Graham Greene within the pages of an American magazine, and *The Lieutenant Died Last* was published in *Collier's Weekly* for 29 June 1940. Just as clearly, the story was intended to allay those fears about 'British determination' and to provide incidental evidence of the realities of British democracy. It appeared under the jingoistic byline 'Dramatic information for the German High Command about the first parachute troops dropped in England'.[3] It told a domestic tale but its purpose was avowedly to woo American opinion. It conjured a stirring story of British bravery and fortitude in the face of adversity, but it was intended solely for American consumption, and it never appeared in print in Britain.

There was nothing new, of course, in the idea of enlisting the support of literary figures and eminent men of letters in the patriotic cause. It was an age-old and well-worn convention, especially in time of war. Much use had been made of them in the Great War by the MoI's predecessors and figures such as Hardy, Kipling, Bennett, Wells and Shaw had been employed to great effect on that occasion.[4] The same methods were utilized in the Second World War and a new generation of writers was engaged to bring its skills to bear in aid of the country's propagandists. Somerset Maugham was 'writing articles for the Ministry' by March 1940, and within a short while pamphlets were either in preparation or forthcoming from a host of writers, including E. M. Forster, Beverley Nichols, H. V. Morton, E. M. Delafield, Howard Spring and F. Brett Young.[5]

Unfortunately, Graham Greene's autobiography is of little use in outlining precisely how and when he was recruited into the ranks of the MoI. It is explicitly and emphatically impressionistic. He recounts that he was summoned to a draft board interview 'during the winter of 1939'. A major-general and two colonels expected he would want to join 'Intelligence', along with so many of his fellow reservists, and were clearly relieved when he opted for the infantry. So relieved, in fact, that they happily acceded to his request for postponement of his call-up for 'a few more months', in order that he might complete work on his latest novel, *The Power and the Glory*. He recalls that they gave him until June 1940. In the event, he missed out on the infantry — they 'were not to find themselves burdened with my inefficiency' — and ended up in intelligence after all — 'it had not proved so easy to escape in war the many-armed embrace of intelligence'.[6]

However, it is clear that his services were required by the MoI before that June 1940 deadline. A Policy Committee meeting of 5 April 1940 decided that a literary division be formed ('to be termed "literary publicity", under a director reporting to Sir Kenneth Clark'), and that one of its functions should be 'to commission and stimulate the writing of books and pamphlets, mostly by outside authors'.[7] But Greene, for his part, was not to be just another one of those outside writers. A Policy Committee meeting on 18 April 1940 minuted that 'Mr Graham Greene had assumed control of the present literary section', and, 'He was accordingly working under Mr Bevan'.[8] Subsequently, when a reorganization of the General Production Division was proposed, on 22 April 1940, R. A. Bevan was named as director, and Graham Greene was included as one of the two specialists in Branch II (Literature).[9]

Greene's experiences at the MoI during this period provided the inspiration for yet another short story, *Men at Work* (1940), in which he proceeded ironically to dissect the operations of the literary division and express considerable doubt about its worth and value.[10] But it was also obviously during these months that he set about providing the MoI with one of the things it urgently required, a short story extolling British virtues which might then be published by an American magazine. *The Lieutenant Died Last* was the result.

There is much in the story as it evolved that works intentionally against the propaganda grain, with little recourse to simple stereotyping, heightened emotion, or dramatic exposition. Greene consciously avoided resorting to the traditional array of images, of the cosy community, the seductive English village, leafy lanes, rose-strewn cottages and the like. Instead we are presented with a picture of normality and ordinariness, a somewhat drab setting, in fact, for the remote village of Potter, and a cast of characters notable only for their monotonous grumbles and grudges rather than any heroic features. A mundane and humdrum note is emphasized at the outset:

> You would hardly expect to find Potter the scene of the first invasion of England since French troops landed near Fishguard in the Napoleonic War. It is one of those tiny isolated villages you still find dumped down in deserted corners of what we call in England 'Metroland' — the district where commuters live in tidy villas within easy distances of the railway, on the edge of scrubby commons full of clay pits and gorse and rather withered trees. Walk for three miles in any direction from Potter and you will find cement sidewalks, nurses pushing prams, the evening paper boy, but Potter itself lies off the map — off the motoring map, that is to say. You have to take a turning marked No Through Road and bump heavily toward what looks like a farm gate stuck a mile or more over the shaggy common.
>
> Through the gate is nothing but Potter . . .

The village itself is made up of one public house, a shop cum post office, a small tin-roofed church, where services are held once a month, half a dozen cottages, and Lord Drew's mansion. It is hardly a romantic vision. The villagers are as uninspiring, none more so than Bill Purves, the local poacher, who repairs his cottage walls with petrol cans, is reputed to sleep on a bed of rags, and disappears three or four times a year into Lord Drew's grounds, armed with the rifle from his Boer War days and a bottle of whisky. The villagers grumble a lot, 'about rations, compulsory service, blackouts, all the usual things', but at least they enjoy that 'sense of security Englishmen normally feel, the security that allows them to grumble'.

It is this sense of security which is rudely shattered one spring day when a small band of German parachutists land in the vicinity, proceed to imprison most of the villagers in the inn, and set about their task of destroying the main railway line to Scotland and the north coast which lies just a mile and a half across the common from Potter. The villagers are surprised, for though the Germans were in uniform, their uniforms caused no immediate astonishment in Potter — 'we are so used in these days to uniforms: what with AFS and ARP and all the other initial letters, we are prepared for any uniform, even a German uniform'. The Germans are depicted as nervous but courteous, and prepared to deal ruthlessly with retaliation should it arise — the gamekeeper sports a black eye after his capture and the shopkeeper's son is shot in the legs and crippled during his efforts to escape.

In Went the Day Well? *a group of German paratroopers, disguised as British soldiers, infiltrate the sleepy rural village of Bramley End and survey the countryside in preparation for a full-scale invasion.*

In the event, however, they are not prepared for the wily ingenuity shown by the lone figure of Bill Purves. He soon realises what is afoot, harkens back to his experiences against 'the bloody Bojers' and an ambush on the veldt 40 years earlier — 'It was as if 1914 to 1918 were an interlude he had hardly noticed at all' — and starts to snipe at the German saboteurs, picking them off one by one. He is wounded but wins the day, somewhat fortuitously, when he lands a shot in a box of explosives and blows up the main party of parachutists. A German lieutenant is mortally wounded, but is still alive when Bill Purves reaches him. He begs to be put out of his misery and the old man duly obliges, killing the lieutenant with his own revolver. Being an experienced poacher, 'Old Purves always felt pity for broken animals'.

Subsequently, the old man lives off his story for a while, exaggerating his accomplishments only slightly when the occasion demands. But he is hardly fêted or anything like that, there are no medals for him and he does not expect such. Indeed he receives just a cold and grudging commendation from the local magistrate who lets him off with a caution on the charge of poaching. But Bill Purves feels gratified, inwardly and quietly so. And the only pang of remorse he experiences is when sometimes, in the privacy of his cottage, he looks at the photograph he took from the body of the dead lieutenant — a photograph of a naked baby romping on a hearthrug. Then he feels uneasy, 'It made him — for no reason that he could understand — feel bad'.

Understatement was the keynote of Greene's short story. It was a characteristic that infused much of British propaganda at the time. It had its strengths, appealing as it did to what can only be described, however unsatisfactorily, as the most nebulous of traditional British traits, reserve. But it also gave rise to increasing concern at the MoI that abroad, at least, British propaganda was in danger of selling the country short. While it was felt, for instance, that 'British propaganda seems to have great influence on American opinion', nevertheless it was also recognized that 'British propaganda in that country may seem to have committed a fundamental error in assuming that the British technique of understatement would have the same reassuring effect on Americans that it has on Englishmen'.[11]

Still, in the spring of 1940, the MoI's specialist advisers were emphasizing that British propaganda to America 'Need not be blatantly bellicose'.[12] In such circumstances Greene's short story fitted the bill. It laid stress upon the extent of British resolve and determination, it highlighted the contribution of everyday, ordinary folk in the struggle for survival and the fight for democracy, and it did so in a characteristically underplayed fashion. The MoI must have been pleased. Clearly, *Collier's* were sufficiently impressed to publish it in the National Weekly.

Thereafter, interestingly, the *Collier's* connection proved to be of value to the MoI in other respects.

In addition to spreading the word in America for itself, one further and very necessary intention on the part of the MoI in the spring of 1940 was to enlist the support, where possible, of American journalists working in London. Such journalists could be of immense help since they provided a direct outlet to American readers and were ostensibly representing neutral and impartial opinion. The MoI fully appreciated how influential this channel of communication might be when it noted that 'The most important of all approaches is, however, that through American news correspondents and broadcasters in this country'. 'Much work has been done in securing facilities for these people', it continued.[13] The war correspondent for *Collier's* in London, Quentin Reynolds, was to be one such beneficiary, and he in turn reciprocated by greatly aiding and abetting the British cause in America.

Quentin Reynolds was to make quite a name for himself as a result of his dispatches, not least for his film reports made directly for the MoI. He wrote and narrated the commentary on three documentary films for the MoI (*London Can Take It, London's Reply to Germany's False Claims,* both in 1940, and *Christmas Under Fire*, in 1941) and appeared as himself in the 1942 Ealing feature film production of *The Big Blockade.* Director Harry Watt, who worked with Reynolds on two of the documentaries, recalls that he was told to get in touch with him by Sidney Bernstein, of the MoI's Films Division, who recommended him in friendly if unflattering terms — 'There's a big ex-pug staying at the Savoy, the *Collier's* man, who might be able to help you'. But his contribution proved to be significant. Watt considers that Reynolds became 'the first star created by documentary' and adds that 'apart from Ed Murrow, Quent was the first outsider to speak up and say we would not be beaten'.[14]

London Can Take It was particularly important in this regard. It was intended primarily for American distribution, though a shorter version was released for domestic consumption under the title *Britain Can Take It.*[15] Its theme was very much expressed in the former title, which Reynolds suggested, and its story was of London in the blitz. Once again, it was told in a deadpan and underplayed style with the emphasis upon a seemingly straightforward and factual narration of events. It was plainly intended as a piece of descriptive reportage and was meant to convey the impression, 'This is how it is in wartime London'.

'These are not Hollywood sound effects', Reynolds points out as he proceeds to show the devastation caused by 'the nightly siege of London'. Actuality is everything ('I am speaking from London'), and there is an insistence upon objectivity ('I am a neutral reporter'). It is a heavily personalized account but the message is one of quiet confidence and continued hope among the people ('London raises her head', 'London

*The villagers suspect nothing and the postmistress (Muriel George) merrily chats
to the men in their new billets.*

looks upwards'), and there is repeated reference to the moulding of a new
'People's Army' and to the high morale of the population despite its
tribulations:

> The People's Army go to work as they did in that other comfortable world,
> which came to an end when the invader began to attack the last stronghold
> of freedom. Not all the services run as they did yesterday, but London
> manages to get to work on time — one way or another. In the centre of the
> city the shops are open as usual — in fact many of them are more open than
> usual.
>
> Dr Paul Joseph Goebbels said recently that the nightly air raids have had a
> terrific effect upon the morale of the people of London. The good doctor is
> absolutely right. Today the morale of the people is higher than ever. They are
> fused together, not be fear, but by a surging spirit of courage the like of
> which the world has never known. They know that thousands of them will
> die. But they would rather stand up and face death than kneel down and face
> the kind of existence the conqueror would impose upon them . . .

It is true that the Nazis will be over again tomorrow night and the night after that and every night. They will drop thousands of bombs and they'll destroy hundreds of buildings and they'll kill thousands of people. But a bomb has its limitations. It can only destroy buildings and kill people. It cannot kill the unconquerable spirit and courage of the people of London.

London can take it.

The film was greeted with much critical acclaim in Britain and went on to enjoy considerable success with cinemagoers. As Mass-Observation assiduously reported to the MoI, it 'received nothing but praise' and topped their popularity list for official films.[16] In America, more significantly, Quentin Reynolds showed it during the course of a lecture tour he made. It was shown without any British credits, of course, and only Reynolds's name appeared on the titles, as war correspondent for *Collier's*. Thereafter, it was booked by Warner Bros for nationwide release in their cinemas. Once more, it proved to be immensely popular. The MoI was delighted and commissioned both Reynolds and Watt to do a follow-up, *Christmas Under Fire*, this time about London during the Christmas of 1940, again for American as well as British distribution.[17] The MoI had a lot to thank *Collier's* for.

The cinema also provided the means whereby the MoI hoped to assuage some of the British fears about invasion during 1940. As *The Lieutenant Died Last* exemplifies what was meant to inspire confidence abroad, so *Miss Grant Goes to the Door* provides evidence of what was intended to boost morale at home. This short film was directed and produced by Brian Desmond Hurst, a feature film director with considerable experience in both Hollywood and Britain. The screenplay and dialogue were provided by Rodney Ackland, and it was based upon a story by Thorold Dickinson and Donald Bull. In short, Graham Greene had nothing to do with the team that made the film, but it might almost have been a filmic rendition of his story. It harps upon the same themes and bears much the same message.

The plot revolves around two sisters who are confronted with the problem of what to do when a German parachutist lands virtually on their doorstep. The church bells are ringing and the invasion is on. The setting is rural and isolated once again, though somewhat more salubrious this time than in the Greene piece. There is a very definite middle class flavour about the Grants' cottage. The parachutist is badly hurt and dies on their hands. But the lonely ladies are greatly relieved when help apparently arrives in the guise of a British officer, a lieutenant. In fact, this is yet another German infiltrator intent upon tracing the whereabouts of the local aerodrome. He wants a map and gives himself away when he mispronounces the name of a nearby landmark. The vigilant Miss Grant spots his mistake and keeps him covered with a revolver, conveniently found on the body of the dead parachutist, while the other sister hops on her bike to alert the Local Defence Volunteers. Help eventually arrives, but not before Miss Grant's kindness almost allows her prisoner to escape. After overpowering her, however, he had been unable to get far because the thoughtful sisters had already immobilized the car and locked up the spare bicycle. The potential saboteur is rounded up and the two sisters are praised for their alertness and vigilance by the commander of the LDV.

There was considerable emphasis upon the simple precautions people might take in order to thwart enemy infiltration and the film was clearly intended to be instructional as well as reassuring and entertaining. Along with other films of a similar nature if different theme — *Now You're Talking, Dangerous Comment, Albert's Savings, Call for Arms, Food for Thought, Salvage With a Smile,* and *Miss Know-all* — it formed part of a series spawned by the MoI which was meant, as Sir Kenneth Clark put it in a BBC Postscript broadcast on 4 October 1940, to 'help people to remember government messages by putting them in a dramatic form'.[18] They were very small scale feature films which were often enjoyed, perhaps not surprisingly, more for their dramatic than instructional content.

In the case of *Miss Grant Goes to the Door*, for instance, which proved especially popular, it was found that audiences liked the 'strong story'. By contrast, the instructional elements were unfavourably received, not least because of some unlikely and improbable features — the success, or otherwise, in dealing with live spies, so it was inadvertently implied, lay in having a dead parachutist conveniently to hand, with a revolver about him. The class base of the characters was also picked up, with comments noting that Miss Grant lived in 'a big house' (a point noted additionally of *Miss Know-all* and in other films, particularly the early 'Careless talk' ones, it happened unfortunately that the spy or gossiper was usually working class).

In the main, however, the film was adjudged a success and was well liked. It was thought that the film did register in significant ways and that, for example, 'The sight of this untrained hand wielding the weapon, however ineffectively . . . was incidental propaganda for a "people's war".'[19] The film did show the people dealing resourcefully with problems that confronted them. It advocated action, no less, which was a good deal more than was advocated in some of the other MoI material forthcoming at the time that was related to the prospect of invasion. 'Stay put and do nothing', for instance, seemed to be the basic message emanating from the official leaflet of instructions, *If the Invader Comes*, which was issued to all households throughout the country in mid-June. Duff Cooper reported that the leaflet had 'a good reception' but recognized that it left most people 'expecting further instructions' and guidance, not least about such essential matters as '(*a*) whether they, the civilians, are to fight, or (*b*) whether they might even take steps to protect themselves'.[20] *Miss Grant Goes to the Door* suffered no such failings.

However, the film did suffer somewhat from the problem that beset much propaganda, especially film propaganda, which was tied in to particular campaigns. In these instances, of course, timing was of the essence. It was vital to get material out in time to be relevant; and doubtless the credibility of a film like *Miss Grant* was undermined slightly because of the time it took in production and before release. In fact, they worked quite speedily on this production: it was completed on 2 July 1940 and released on 5 August 1940. But in between, at the end of July, the Local Defence Volunteers were renamed the Home Guard, for one thing.

The Cockney evacuee George Truscott (Harry Fowler) soon uncovers the face of 'the same old Hun'.

Furthermore, as Ian McLaine recounts, 'from mid-July onwards reports showed people passing from acceptance of the possibility of invasion through to a tendency to doubt its imminence and then, with the exception of people living near the eastern coast, to a stage late in August when expectation of invasion seemed to have almost entirely receded'.[21] There was a sense of widespread relief, in particular, with the passing of those dates that were popularly held to be of special significance — 19 July, when it was thought the invasion would start, and 15 August, the date which it was believed Hitler had chosen for his arrival in Britain.[22]

Yet, if the timing of some of the MoI's invasion campaign material was such that it begged questions about its relevance, effectiveness and ultimate worth, at least officials could reassure themselves, as they did, with the belief that it all helped to guard against complacency. And indeed in the spring of both 1941 and 1942 it was the complacency factor as much as anything else which prompted the MoI to pursue further campaigns on the theme of the continuing possibility of invasion.

In January 1941, for instance, Mass-Observation did a survey of public attitudes to invasion. The results were greatly revealing and carefully nuanced. Of the sample, it found that 'just over half think there definitely will not be an attempted invasion' and only 'a quarter think there will be'. However, it also found that 'both among those who thought there would, and those who thought there wouldn't be an invasion, there was an overwhelmingly strong opinion that the invaders would get no distance'. Among a population, then, which was distinctly sceptical anyway about the likelihood of invasion, most were confident about the outcome, and there was a decided 'unreadiness to suppose even the remote possibility of any serious force penetrating inland'. Moreover, while some people were willing to entertain the idea of plane or parachute landings, they were 'generally quite unable or unwilling to visualize, even vaguely, how these would work'. It was this element, perhaps most of all, which caused concern. Mass-Observation concluded: 'This lack of visualization of what are at least remote possibilities, is not necessarily an asset in terms of morale if by any chance any force penetrated anywhere'.[23]

Complacency had set in and something had to be done. In February 1941 the War Cabinet Committee asked the MoI to produce another leaflet and it agreed to do so. *Beating the Invader* was the outcome and 15 million copies were distributed to all households in the spring of 1941. It was reported not to be a great success, however, and just 49 per cent of the population were estimated to have read it. In effect, 'it still meant that over half the population did not know what the government wanted them to do in the event of invasion'.[24]

More guidance and information were required, but with so many people doubting the prospect of invasion, the MoI soon realized that further propaganda on that theme was hardly likely to prove worth while. Later in the year the Films Division actually declined the suggestion that they should produce another film about future invasion, and on taking office as director general, Cyril Radcliffe informed the Home Defence Executive that 'invasion propaganda would fall dead on the public at present'. Worse, it might even be seen as 'a government stunt to divert attention from the bad news in North Africa, Greece and Crete'.[25] The time was not ripe.

Events early in 1942, however, were to give rise to renewed fears among the population at large that a German invasion might now be imminent. On 12 February three German warships, the *Scharnhorst*, the *Gneisenau* and the *Prinz Eugen*, slipped unmolested through the English Channel on their way back to their base in Germany. Then on 15 February, Singapore fell and 60,000 British troops surrendered to the Japanese. The Home Intelligence weekly report for 16–23 February spoke of 'shock, bewilderment and anger' over the first incident, and of 'silence too deep for words' in response to the latter. Morale had slumped and it was 'the blackest week since Dunkirk'. In particular, it was noted that 'Many people are now said to be taking the possibility of invasion seriously as a direct result of the escape of the German battleships', and that 'This appears to have been heightened by reports that Germany is amassing gliders, and there is said to be some expectation that Hitler may attempt invasion as a "short cut to victory"'. The overall results were both serious and comic. There was a revival in the 'demand for a "clarification of the role of the civilian in the event of invasion", and there is further sarcastic comment on the usefulness of the Home Guards' pikes'.[26]

Within a month of the report, *Went the Day Well?* commenced production. It was not a Ministry of Information film, strictly speaking, in that it was not directly financed or sponsored by that body, a custom which had been largely abandoned anyway by 1942 as far as feature films were concerned. It was made by a commercial film company, Ealing Studios, with Michael Balcon in charge of production and with Alberto Cavalcanti, formerly a documentary film maker and lately arrived at Ealing, as director. But it is difficult to escape the conclusion that it was, in effect, an 'official' film and that it carried the MoI stamp of approval. It was, after all, based upon a story written for the MoI by Graham Greene, though the scriptwriters — John Dighton, Diana Morgan and Angus MacPhail — adapted his piece quite freely since Greene for his part was abroad throughout most of 1942, working for the Secret Intelligence Service in Africa.[27] Also, it made much use of men from the Gloucestershire Regiment who appeared 'by kind permission of the War Office', and whose services would have been secured through the MoI, the usual channel for aid of that nature.

Furthermore, the film was primarily meant to help people 'to visualize', in a vivid and dramatic way, what might ensue in the event of a parachute

Nora (Valerie Taylor) eventually awakens to the fact that the trusted village resident Oliver Wilsford (Leslie Banks) is really a traitor of German origin.

landing by enemy forces and to shake the population out of its inclination towards 'complacency' on that matter. The film was planned then at a time when the MoI felt it still had a considerable job to do regarding invasion propaganda and it went into production at a time when invasion fears were rife. It bore the hallmarks of a MoI production and it marked the culmination of a long invasion propaganda campaign, though that was by no means the only campaign to which it alluded. In fact, the film was in many respects a summation of a good deal of MoI thinking and it neatly encapsulated much of what the MoI stood for by 1942.

The film's title is explained by a brief epigraph that appears at the outset and which honours the villagers who died resisting the invader and defending Bramley End:

> Went the day well?
>   We died and never knew.
> But, well or ill,
>   Freedom, we died for you.

The film itself begins with a prologue which is reassuringly set in the future, at a point in time after the war has finished and victory has been achieved. The church sexton Sims (Mervyn Johns), acts as host and he reveals a memorial in the churchyard to the dead German parachutists who tried taking over the village. He proceeds to recount what happened during the eventful Whitsun weekend of 23—25 May 1942.

The setting is very rural and peaceful, with much more emphasis on the idyllic nature of the English countryside than was evident in Greene's short story — there are quaint cottages, leafy lanes, a windmill on the hillside (Turville in Oxfordshire was used as the location for exterior shooting). The village is self-contained, safe and snug with the war seemingly far away until, that is, the peace and quiet are interrupted by the arrival of lorry loads of 'Royal Engineers'. The villagers are surprised because they were given no warning of any exercise, but they suspect nothing. They warmly welcome the troops and set about finding billets for them. The lieutenant (David Farrar) is taken in by the lady of the manor, Mrs Frazer (Marie Lohr), who also houses a band of evacuee children. The commander (Basil Sydney) is looked after by the vicar (C. V. France) and his daughter, Nora (Valerie Taylor). The troops are billeted in the homes of the villagers and in the church hall.

Contact is immediately established between the German troop commander and the local squire and much respected leader of the community, Oliver Wilsford (Leslie Banks), who is a fifth columnist of German origin. They survey the countryside to facilitate the installation of apparatus designed to disrupt England's entire network of radiolocation, as a prelude to a full scale air and seaborne invasion within 48 hours. That was what the German High Command had planned: but odd things are

Tom Sturry (Frank Lawton) urges 'robust self-defence' upon the villagers and they take up arms to effect an escape when their complacency has been swept aside.

spotted and a few suspicions aroused. One of the soldiers deals harshly with an inquisitive small boy and is severely reprimanded for doing so by the postmistress, Mrs Collins (Muriel George), who compares his methods with those of the Nazis. His sergeant (John Slater) promises to put the man on a charge. Another soldier crosses the figure seven in the Continental fashion, which Nora notices and comments upon. Finally, a nosey Cockney evacuee, George Truscott (played by a young Harry Fowler), finds a bar of chocolate in the commander's kitbag and Nora, once again, spots that it is Viennese chocolate. Armed with her suspicions, she confides in Oliver Wilsford, whom she clearly likes. He, in turn, alerts the invaders and sets off an emergency plan of action whereby the troops forcibly take over the village, seal it off from the outside world and reveal their true identities.

The villagers are rounded up and imprisoned in the church. The vicar is killed when he tries to ring the church bell and warn the local Home Guard, out on manoeuvres, of invasion. The Home Guard, who laugh at the idea that an invasion could seriously be afoot, are killed as they return.

Thereafter, the film revolves around the plight of the villagers and their attempts to enlist help or escape. Several ingenious attempts to pass on messages come to nothing, either by chance or bad luck. One escape from the church is thwarted by the treachery of Wilsford, still unknown as a traitor to all but Nora. The young lad Truscott, however, effects his own escape from the manor house. In the woods, he encounters the poacher, Bill Purves (Edward Rigby) — a leftover from the Greene short story — who knows nothing of what has happened. Once alerted, he covers the lad's escape and loses his life in the process. George Truscott, though badly wounded himself, manages to make it to the next village, where he gets help.

At the same time, a second attempt at escape from the church has proved more successful. Led by Tom Sturry (Frank Lawton), a naval seaman at home on leave, a small band of villagers erect barricades at the manor and start sniping at the parachutists. Nora exacts revenge upon Oliver Wilsford as he attempts to let the besiegers into the house. A fierce fight ensues which is going badly for the villagers until they are finally saved by the arrival of relief forces. Several villagers died bravely during the affray — the postmistress as she tried to alert the telephone exchange, the lady of the manor as she protected the evacuee children from a grenade, the poacher in the woods — but they helped to prevent the German parachutists from gaining more ground than they finally occupied, a small plot in Bramley End churchyard.

Much had changed, then, from the original concept of Greene's story. The plot had been opened up considerably to encompass more than just an invasion story, as relevant as that was in the spring of 1942, to take on board other themes and preoccupations. Throughout the film, for instance, there are regular visual allusions to MoI campaigns. Early on, Nora opens a cupboard to reveal a poster issued by the Ministry of Home Security soon after war was declared on 'Gas attack' and 'How to put on your gas mask'.[28] At the village hall, the German radio operator contacts his superior against the ironic backdrop of a 'Be like Dad, keep Mum' slogan. And in Tom Sturry's cottage, while the German guard scoffs their rations, the Sturry family are symbolically highlighted beside a copy of the MoI's 'Mightier Yet' poster.[29]

Such allusions were incidental, of course, to the major purpose of the film. First and foremost, it was meant to act as a warning against complacency and much of the film was taken up with combating the idea that people might be lulled into a sense of false security regarding the prospect of invasion, and the forms it could take. Thereafter, it tackled the theme of the fifth column, another matter that had figured prominently in official thinking. But the incidental features were not insignificant, and in dealing with its two major themes, the film revealed that it had a good deal more to impart on a variety of issues, not least with regard to questions of class and the depiction of violence.

Some post-war commentators have singled out the class resonances in the film for particular attention. Charles Barr, for instance, has noted:

> The casting of the two leaders, who combine against the villagers, is artful. Basil Sydney and Leslie Banks were the two high naval officers whose pomposity helped to make *Ships with Wings* so alienating. Here, Sydney plays the occupying leader and Banks the treacherous squire. It is like an exorcising of the kind of thirties leadership they represent (its reactionary quality underlined by the fact that Banks' most celebrated role of that decade was *Sanders of the River*). In contrast, the village is saved by the efforts of an unconsidered boy (the Cockney actor, Harry Fowler) and the local poacher (Edward Rigby, veteran of innumerable working class cameos), who contrive between them to get the message of warning through to the world outside.[30]

Raymond Durgnat also feels that the film expresses 'distrust and dissatisfaction with our paternalist betters' and that it captures 'some peace time tensions'. He adds that 'The upper class lady so nicely, so deceitfully, so foolishly, tries to keep the truth from the children', preferring instead to present the invasion to the children 'as a game'. She dies, of course, while it is the 'hard-headed' Cockney lad who gets through, secures help and survives.[31]

There is something in what both these critics have to say, since the film does essentially celebrate its working class figures as heroes: the Quisling appears to represent paternalist middle class leadership, and the upper class lady proves to be largely ineffective (though it is she who saves the children at the film's climax). But they overstate the case — it is the vicar's daughter, after all, who exacts revenge upon the traitor, and there is much evidence throughout of a traditional class structure and social hierarchy. Furthermore, they perhaps ascribe too much in the way of the film's authorship to its director, Cavalcanti. The film might better be seen as virtually a collaborative venture between the film-makers at Ealing and the MoI, and its thinking as representative, if anything, of the new found consensus which evolved during the war. For its part, the MoI was well aware of the strength of 'class feeling' in the country and on occasion, according to Ian McLaine, became overly and needlessly preoccupied with such.[32] It is assuredly true that for all its preoccupation with class, the Ministry sometimes failed to find the appropriate form of propaganda to embrace all classes, not least in the early years of the war. But it did learn: if, in 1940, a film like *Miss Grant Goes to the Door* was found to offer merely 'incidental propaganda' for the notion of 'a people's war', by 1942 the propagandists' priorities had changed and there were many obvious manifestations of the notion. *Went the Day Well?* was but one example.

Similarly, Barr and Durgnat comment upon the 'ruthlessness' and the 'brutality' inherent in the film, particularly in some of the more violent scenes — the shooting of the vicar as he attempts to ring the church bells, the axeing by the postmistress of her German captor before she is bayonetted in turn, the ambushing of the Home Guard, Nora's killing of Oliver Wilsford, the positive glee and relish which the villagers manifest as they snipe at the German parachutists from the besieged manor house, and occasional shots, during the set battle for instance, of such as a dead

The German commander (Basil Sydney) and all his men are killed in a final dramatic battle. The only ground the invaders finally occupied was a small plot in Bramley End churchyard.

body alight with flames from an exploding lorry. Certainly, there is much in the depiction of violence in the film that is chillingly effective and unusual in British films of the period. In part, this must be put down to directorial influence, since Cavalcanti clearly chose to shoot some of the scenes in a manner which served to emphasize the attendant violence — the dramatic close-ups and rapid editing in the axeing scene, accompanied by a rare burst of incidental music, the use of slow motion as Wilsford falls to the ground, shot by a woman who is visibly repulsed by what she has done but who has been impelled to do it all the same. Such creative touches were rare in the film but all helped to enhance its message that, as Barr puts it, 'robust self-defence' was called for when complacency had been swept aside.

But again the links with what the MoI wished to see depicted in the way of violence are worth noting. At an earlier stage in the war it had been quite reserved on the matter. When, in May 1940, the Boultings' film of *Pastor Hall* was shown to officials for their opinion as to its effectiveness, it was noted that Philip Noel-Baker had found the film to be no more than 'a pale reflection' of the events it purported to recreate. 'The truth should be impressed on the public more strongly', he argued. Kenneth Clark replied that 'the public would scarcely tolerate a stronger film'.[33] Within a short while, however, even Clark's feelings on that score were to harden and he was soon advocating that the public must be convinced of German brutality: 'the line we should take in home propaganda was that the enemy were much worse and we should emphasize wherever possible the wickedness and evil perpetrated in the occupied countries'. Subsequently, the Home Planning Committee felt it essential to portray fully 'the evil things which confront us . . . to fortify the will to continue the struggle'.[34] The need for sustained 'Anger Campaigns' gained added momentum when in January 1941, the same month that Mass-Observation reported upon public complacency towards the prospect of invasion, the Policy Committee noted a prevailing attitude among the population 'that a German victory would not make much difference'. 'One facet of the belief that the public were insufficiently hostile towards the enemy', McLaine rightly concludes, 'was a conviction that there existed little comprehension of the consequences of German occupation'.[35] *Went the Day Well?* sought to show just what those consequences might be, and in its violent depiction of those consequences, along with its arguments against complacency and for robust self-defence, it accorded quite neatly with MoI intent.

The film was released finally at the very beginning of November 1942, just when the tide of war started to turn in favour of the Allies. A press notice from the Ealing Studios laid emphasis upon 'the realism of the picture' and 'the utter sincerity' of the characterization, but it recognized the problem implicit in the timing of the film's release, while inevitably trying to stress its continued relevance:

It was a bit of gamble when the picture went into production last March. Would Hitler have decided to risk invading England by the time the film was ready to be shown to the public? So far we have not been invaded, but that doesn't necessarily imply that the threat no longer exists. Undiminished, the danger is still overhead. The big question remains: will Hitler risk it or not?[36]

In truth, though, the danger of invasion was long gone, and the critics said as much. Some, like William Whitebait in the *New Statesman*, suggested 'the warning may yet prove timely' but even he had to honestly admit that 'the temperature is high for invading but low for being invaded. That is a piece of bad luck for Cavalcanti'. However, that did not prevent him from praising everything else about the film, including Cavalcanti's direction, William Walton's score, the acting, and Greene's story — in fact, Graham Greene did exceedingly well by the critics for what was, after all, merely the inspiration and impetus provided by his original short story. Most of all, Whitebait liked the film because there was 'Not a false touch, no England-my-England, or Miniveration'.[37]

Dilys Powell, too, applauded its 'perfect plausibility' and 'the very ordinariness of its characters'. 'At last, it seems, we are learning to make films with our native material', she continued, as she picked up one of the film's essential messages: 'For once, the English people are shown as capable of individual and concerted resourcefulness in a fight and not merely steady in disaster'.[38] To that extent, she spotlighted a feature which probably explains the film's popular success and made it a beneficiary as well as a casualty of the timing of its release. As tardy as the film was in capitalizing upon the public fears of invasion, it nevertheless benefited from the new spirit of 'fighting back' which came with the Anglo-American landings in North Africa and Montgomery's victory at Alamein.[39]

Both *The Scotsman* and the *Manchester Guardian* commented, once again, upon the 'plausibility' of the fifth column element and the theme of 'Nazi brutality', with the latter adding, somewhat condescendingly, that 'The realism of Nazi methods applied in home surroundings is salutary for slothful minds'.[40] But nothing could redeem the film in the eyes of the critic for the *Observer*. While ironically noting that the film 'must be regarded as work of national importance since time, money and manpower have been spent on it', Caroline Lejeune's comments were damning, to say the least:

After *Went the Day Well?* went I home rather sadly, turning over some reflections on war films in general. One is that a film praising the British spirit, as most British films at this time should and will, is obviously the more effective if it presents our enemies with a fair measure of continence. It is a dangerous thing to show your opponents as clowns or bullies, who only get results by treachery, brute force, or the long arm of coincidence. A director who does this merely cheapens his own countrymen, since victory over such people seems empty and meagre.

Another is that any display of hate, except in the hands of an expert director and artists, is to be avoided, since high passions without high performance are less likely to lead to conviction than laughter. A third is that the nearer a plot sticks to life at this tense moment of our fortunes, the nearer it gets to drama. And the fourth is simply that the most patriotic film can lose nothing by the exercise of a little talent and taste.[41]

In the main, however, the MoI must have been well pleased with the film. With the minimum of effort for its own part, it had apparently succeeded in enhancing the propaganda value of several of its more significant campaigns. *Went the Day Well?* provided yet another fine example of the extent to which the commercial cinema was implicitly in tune with what the MoI wished to see put across to the cinemagoing population of the day.

NOTES

1 Policy Committee Paper No. 34, April 1940, pp. 4—5, INF 1/848.
2 'Allied propaganda in the USA', 30 May 1940, INF 1/848.
3 *Collier's National Weekly*, 29 June 1940, pp. 9—10, and 24.
4 See D. G. Wright, 'The Great War, Government Propaganda and English "Men of Letters" 1914—16', *Literature and History*, No. 7, Spring 1978, pp. 70—101.
5 Policy Committee minutes, 10th meeting, 15 March 1940, and 'Book activities of General Division', 18 April 1940, both INF 1/848.
6 Graham Greene, *Ways of Escape*, Harmondsworth, 1981, pp. 69—70. A letter to Mr Greene's literary agent elicited the following reply: 'He left the Ministry of Information early in 1940 but he cannot remember the exact date. He then became literary editor of the *Spectator* for a few months and was already in MI6 in the summer of 1940'. The point was made that *The Lieutenant Died Last* 'was not written under any kind of official pressure as propaganda' and that 'Graham Greene says he has never written any fiction under official guidance and this applies to this story'. Letter to the author from Mr Gerald Pollinger, 13 December 1984.
7 Policy Committee minutes, 12th meeting, 5 April 1940, INF 1/848.
8 Policy Committee minutes, 15th meeting, 18 April 1940, INF 1/848.
9 Policy Committee minutes, 16th meeting, 22 April 1940, INF 1/848.
10 Graham Greene, *Men at Work*, reprinted in Dan Davin, *Short Stories from the Second World War*, Oxford, 1984, pp. 1—7.
11 Mass-Observation File Report No. 629, April 1941, p. 3.
12 Policy Committee Paper No. 33, 26 March 1940, p. 4, INF 1/848.
13 Policy Committee Paper No. 34, April 1940, pp. 4—5, INF 1/848.

14   Harry Watt, *Don't Look at the Camera*, London, 1974, pp. 140−3. Reynolds also did a successful series in the BBC Sunday evening 'Postscript' slot. See *Home Propaganda*, a report prepared by Mass-Observation for the Advertising Service Guild and published in *Change*, No. 2, 1941, pp. 28−9.

15   *Britain Can Take It* was given a theatrical release from October 1940 and a non-theatrical release from December 1940. The commentary for the domestic and overseas versions of the film was reprinted in the *Documentary News Letter*, 1, November 1940, pp. 6−7. The production file at the PRO can be found in INF 6/328.

16   Mass-Observation File Report No. 799, 'Opinion about Ministry of Information Films', 24 July 1941, p. 2.

17   Watt, *Don't Look at the Camera*, p. 145. The film was given a theatrical release in January 1941. See also INF 6/329.

18   Reprinted in the *Documentary News Letter*, 1, November 1940, pp. 4−5.

19   See Mass-Observation File Report No. 394, 'Mass-Observation Film Work', 10 September 1940, p. 3, and File Report No. 458, 'MoI Shorts', 25 October 1940, p. 1. Also, Tom Harrisson, 'Social Research and the Film', *Documentary News Letter*, 1, November 1940, p. 10.

20   Quoted in Ian McLaine, *Ministry of Morale*, London, 1979, p. 69. The Mass-Observation report on *Home Propaganda* did a brief survey of reactions to *If the Invader Comes* (June 1940), and the two other Invasion leaflets that followed, *Stay Where You Are* (August 1940) and *Beating the Invader* (June 1941), in *Change,* No. 2, 1941, pp. 38−41.

21   McLaine, *Ministry of Morale*, p. 77.

22   McLaine, *Ministry of Morale* and Michael Balfour, *Propaganda in War 1939−1945,* London, 1979, p. 189. Mass-Observation confirmed these peaks of expectation as the various 'Morale' reports indicate throughout July and August.

23   Mass-Observation File Report No. 544, 'Attitudes to Invasion', 14 January 1941, p. 4. On Thursday 23 January 1941, the Planning Committee of the MoI discussed the matter of 'Publicity regarding Invasion' and agreed that 'Films Division should prepare another film on the subject'. See INF 1/249.

24   Balfour, *Propaganda in War*, p. 79.

25   Quoted in Marion Yass, *This Is Your War*, London, 1983, p. 33.

26   Home Intelligence Division Weekly Report No. 73, 'Invasion prospects', 25 February 1942, p. 4. INF 1/292.

27   Greene, *Ways of Escape*, pp. 73−96. Also, letter to the author from Mr Gerald Pollinger, 13 December 1984: 'The film was made by his friend, Cavalcanti, when he was in Africa and to this day he has not seen it'.

28   The official campaign urging people to carry their gas masks was not especially successful. See Balfour, *Propaganda in War*, p. 80, M-O File Report No. 544 and *Home Propaganda*, pp. 8−10. In the film, ironically, the poster is not highlighted either but affixed to the inside of a cupboard door and only spotted briefly when Nora opens the door − doubtless an intentional comment.

29   Again, this was not a particularly successful poster on its first appearance, though subsequent variations enhanced its popularity. See McLaine, *Ministry of Morale*, pp. 76, 99, and 251.

30   Charles Barr, *Ealing Studios*, London, 1977, pp. 31—2.
31   Raymond Durgnat, *A Mirror for England*, London, 1970, pp. 15—16.
32   See McLaine, *Ministry of Morale*, pp. 94 and 97—8. And, for the new consensus arising from the war years, see Paul Addison, *The Road to 1945*, London, 1975, pp. 164—5 and 276—7.
33   Policy Committee minutes, 29 May 1940. And Mass-Observation File Report No. 162, '*Pastor Hall* — film shown at MoI for opinion of effectiveness', 2 June 1940. See also File Report No. 472, 'Impressions of Nazi Germany on Film', 29 October 1940.
34   Quoted in Yass, *This Is Your War*, p. 43.
35   McLaine, *Ministry of Morale*, p. 147.
36   'News from Ealing Studios', microfiche on *Went the Day Well?*, British Film Institute Library, London.
37   *New Statesman*, 31 October 1942.
38   *The Sunday Times*, 1 November 1942.
39   Cavalcanti, too, felt that 'The public enjoyed its pathos and its exceptional violence', as he noted later (BFI Microfiche, Programme notes of 14 December 1960). The film found its echoes during the war in the comedy thriller *Warn that Man* (1943), with Gordon Harker and Jean Kent, and, after the war, in *The Eagle Has Landed* (1977), with Michael Caine and Donald Sutherland.
40   *The Scotsman*, 26 January 1943; *Manchester Guardian*, 27 January 1943.
41   *Observer*, 1 November 1942.

7

Mobilizing the Past

The Young Mr Pitt

Historical films have regularly been used as vehicles for propaganda. As a result, they are almost never important for what they tell us about the eras in which they are set, but they may have a good deal to tell us about the periods in which they are made. Quite apart from any other consideration, historical settings have been one outlet for the treatment of controversial subjects. This was particularly true in Britain in the 1930s when the stringently enforced censorship regulations sought to ensure that nothing controversial and nothing offensive to foreign governments reached the screen. So in 1934 when proposed films denouncing anti-Semitism in Nazi Germany were regularly vetoed by the censors as likely to cause offence to a 'friendly foreign country', Gaumont British were able to produce and release *Jew Süss*, a costume film attacking anti-Semitism in 18th century Württemberg. Similarly, Sir Robert Vansittart, removed from his post as Permanent Under-Secretary at the Foreign Office because of his opposition to Chamberlain's policy of appeasement, was able to get his message of national preparedness across by speeches inserted in the script he wrote for the film *Sixty Glorious Years* (1938), the second of Herbert Wilcox's two cinematic celebrations of Queen Victoria. Even more explicit as a national call to arms was Alexander Korda's production of *Fire Over England* (1937). This made a fairly obvious equation between 16th century Spain and Nazi Germany, Philip II and Hitler and the Inquisition and the Gestapo. The propaganda content of this widely praised historical epic is underlined by the lifting wholesale of the sequence of Elizabeth I's rousing address to the troops at Tilbury from that film into the first wartime propaganda film, *The Lion Has Wings* (1939).[1]

Given the value of history for its ability to suggest historical parallels, it is perhaps surprising that comparatively little use was made of history for direct propaganda purposes during the war. There were only a handful of serious historical dramas. David MacDonald's *This England* (1941), tactfully re-titled *Our Heritage* for release in Scotland, pressed into service the English rural myth, which received a powerful boost during the war and was most succinctly encapsulated in the popular song 'There'll always be an England, while there's a country lane, wherever there's a cottage small beside a field of grain.' In this film industrialization is an aberration; rural life and work on the land the ideal. As the opening narration reminds us:

> This England, among whose hills and valleys since the beginning of time have stood old farms and villages. The story of Rookeby's farm and the village of Clevely is the story of them all.

In view of this, it is perhaps not inappropriate that the film should have about it the air of a glorified village pageant.

The story of the farm and the village is told in flashback by farmer John Rookeby (John Clements) to a visiting American journalist (Constance Cummings), part of the ongoing mission to explain Britain to America. It highlights four episodes from Britain's past, all designed to stress her heroic spirit in times of adversity: in 1086 after the Norman Conquest, 1588 during the approach of the Spanish Armada, 1804 during the Napoleonic Wars, and 1914—18 during the First World War. It stresses the timelessness and eternity of England and the English people by having the same actors play the same symbolic roles in each episode: vicar, doctor, blacksmith, publican, and in particular, yeoman farmer Rookeby (John Clements) and farm labourer Appleyard (Emlyn Williams). They are prepared to fight and kill to defend the land. Rookeby leads an uprising of Saxon peasants against their oppressive Norman lord in 1086, and kills him. Appleyard kills the absentee landlord's steward who wants to enclose Rookeby's farm for sheep in 1588. Appleyard and Rookeby both serve in the Great War, the latter being blinded and winning the VC. The film ends with John Clements reciting John of Gaunt's 'This England' speech from *Richard II*, perhaps the most quoted Shakespearean speech of the Second World War. It cropped up constantly on the radio and in patriotic collections, and provided no less than three film titles (*This England, This Happy Breed, The Demi-Paradise*).

In locating the nation's source of strength in an alliance of country gentry and rural working class against foreign aggression in an unyielding defence of the land, the film provided the necessary consensual message for a national effort in wartime. But in coupling this national resistance with a local resistance to oppressive, neglectful or corrupt aristocratic landlords, it adds a distinctly radical element which mirrors the shift to the left in the national mood and the desire for a juster, fairer and more humane post-war society. It is significant that it is Appleyard, the working class 'Hodge' figure, who is the perpetual conscience of the gentleman farmer Rookeby, who, when tempted to abandon the farm for a different way of life, is reminded of his duty to the land. It is perhaps equally significant that Appleyard remains the servant and Rookeby the master. Revolution must, after all, not be carried too far.

This England was neither a terribly good film nor a terribly successful one. *The Times* declared loftily of it:

> The purpose of this . . . film is to celebrate in romantic narrative the essential English virtues. If at the end we do not know quite which of our virtues have been celebrated that is simply because the romantic elements in some of the episodes have got out of hand.[2]

The *New Statesman* thought it 'the sort of patriotic film we do worst' and the *Observer* thought it 'badly handicapped by its format'.[3] The *Monthly Film Bulletin* clinically exposed its cinematic shortcomings:

> This is a film of sentiment, and its film craftsmanship is entirely indistinguished (sic), for its episodic structure robs it of constructional unity and dramatic momentum. In attempting to escape into past ages simply by ringing the changes on costume and wigs, it succeeds no better than other similar films have succeeded before it. It has been conceived theatrically and without proper understanding of the limits and possibilities of the film medium. Not even the production qualities are all that could be desired. That many of the landscapes are model shots, for example, will be obvious even to those unaccustomed to distinguish such niceties.[4]

But as George Orwell perceptively pointed out in *Time and Tide*:

> The keynote is 'our glorious heritage', and as in nearly all patriotic films and literature, the implication all along is that England is an agricultural country, and that its inhabitants, millions of whom would not know the difference between a turnip and broccoli if they saw them growing in a field, derive their patriotism from a passionate love of the English soil. Are such films good for morale in wartime? They may be. It is a fact that many of the events which the jingo history books make the most noise about are things to be proud of.[5]

A rather more familiar format for audiences than the multi-episode reincarnation saga was the straightforward historical biography — the biopic. The war prompted two large-scale political biographies, pursuing more directly applicable historical parallels. Benjamin Disraeli, who had bested Bismarck at the Congress of Berlin and had the additional aggravation value of being Jewish, was the central figure of Thorold Dickinson's *The Prime Minister* (1941); but the Churchillian parallel was more obviously drawn in *The Young Mr Pitt* (1942), dramatizing the career of William Pitt the Younger, who headed the British government during the long years of war against Napoleon Bonaparte's France.

Both *The Prime Minister* and *The Young Mr Pitt* need to be seen in the context of the propaganda aims of the Ministry of Information. A comprehensive programme for propaganda drawn up by the Royal Institute of International Affairs in the Summer of 1939 noted that 'a particularly effective means of propaganda is the idealization of national heroes'.[6] The MoI's own memorandum on film propaganda similarly envisaged 'histories of national heroes' and also suggested that 'ideals such as freedom and institutions such as parliamentary government can be made the main subject of a drama or treated historically.'[7] By 1940 the MoI had developed an attitude to the past which its officials were encouraged to disseminate. This centred on:

> Britain's past record in achieving social justice while at the same time preserving the rights of man. The conjunction of the ideas of Britain as a pioneer of freedom and justice, against both domestic and foreign tyrants, and of balanced gradual social improvement.[8]

Stress was to be laid on the difference between the British way (evolution) and the German way (revolution), the former leading to progress towards democracy and the latter to reversion to tyranny. Both *The Prime Minister* and *Young Mr Pitt* conform to this model of historical propaganda.

The Prime Minister, which was completed in December 1940 and released in March 1941, was a staid and talky film, wholly lacking the dynamism of Warner Bros' Hollywood-made biopics. Effectively it is two films uneasily crammed into one, the first half set in the 1830s detailing the courtship and marriage of the young Disraeli and showing his transformation from dandy novelist to respected statesman, and the second half, set in the 1870s, dramatizing his Prime Ministership and in particular his conduct of foreign affairs. It is this second half which can be seen as a reading of recent events, tinged with a hint of what might have been.

Disraeli (John Gielgud) clearly stands for Churchill: patriot and imperialist, mistrusted as an outsider by the Establishment, he comes to stand above party as a symbol of the nation. But also, in line with the MoI's directives on history, he shows concern for social reform, passing a series of acts (Public Health, Education and Factory Acts), designed to improve the lot of the poor. This programme for reform is significantly achieved by parliamentary methods and not by the revolutionary violence of the Chartists, seen earlier in the film. Disraeli thus stands for 'One Nation' Toryism and is seen to have the backing and the love of the people.

His great opponent, Gladstone, on the other hand, is Chamberlain. He preaches the policies of the National Government of the 1930s: peace, retrenchment, reform. But he is in the pocket of the industrialists and the party Establishment ('The Old Gang'), and his policies are denounced by Disraeli ('Peace at the cost of honour, reform at the cost of the constitution, retrenchment at the cost of national security').

When Disraeli becomes Prime Minister he is handicapped by having a Cabinet full of stalwarts of 'The Old Gang', just as Churchill was. A great Continental alliance of Germany, Austria and Russia threatens to dominate Europe in the 1870s, just as in 1939 the Russo-German treaty gave both Hitler and Stalin the chance to further their territorial ambitions. When in 1878 Russia threatens Turkey, the Cabinet refuse to honour their pledge of support to that country and seek to appease Germany and Russia. But Disraeli insists on mobilizing in support of Turkey ('Peace can be purchased at too great a price'). In 1939 Britain and Turkey had a similar mutual assistance pact, but Turkey can also be seen in the 19th century

The Young Mr Pitt *used historical parallels to point up the current conflict. It contrasted peaceful, democratic Britain (Robert Donat and John Mills) with fanatical, warlike, revolutionary France.*

P.106

context to stand for all those countries lost to Germany by appeasement. Although Gladstone denounces Disraeli as a war-monger, the mobilization halts the Russian advance on Constantinople and at the Congress of Berlin (1878) Disraeli stands up to the dictators and by showing a willingness to fight, brings back to England a real 'peace with honour', a permanent reproach to Chamberlain's 1938 sham.

The contemporary parallels were easily perceived. The trade paper *The Cinema* noted:

> The film is timely too in that the political outlook of Disraeli is mirrored in the European upheaval of today. Then, as now, we had a Prime Minister entirely motivated by his devotion to his country and his high regard for her honour. Then, as now, German diplomacy sought to make the Balkans a cockpit, and then, as now, England pledged her word to go to the assistance of the Turks in the very teeth of the German conspiracy.[9]

The British critics were on the whole respectful rather than enthusiastic. *The Times* summed up their view: while accepting that the life of Disraeli was a potentially powerful subject for the cinema, it felt that *The Prime Minister* was:

> Too inclined to rely on a slow, plodding, unfolding of events by means of a screen which seems full of newspaper headlines, and all too seldom is character seen at its work of moulding these events to its will. The lack of inspiration in the direction, the slowness, the staginess would be even more obvious than they are were it not for the acting of Mr John Gielgud . . . and Miss Diana Wynyard . . . the scenes they share together have a warmth that lights up a film which keeps its dignity throughout but seldom flares into imagination.[10]

The film was not a great box-office success and seems to have made little impact, something which led Gielgud to complain that *The Prime Minister* 'could have been exploited a good deal more than it has been from a wartime propaganda standpoint'. Gielgud thought it was 'a golden opportunity missed'.[11]

A golden opportunity seized, however, was *The Young Mr Pitt*. This grew out of the decision of Francis L. Harley, head of 20th Century—Fox in Britain, to make 'an entertainment film to demonstrate the fighting spirit of the people of Britain in and out of uniform'.[12] At that time, Gainsborough Films were contracted to supply Fox with its British productions and this project was entrusted to their top director Carol Reed by the Gainsborough production chief, Edward Black. The idea of making a William Pitt biopic was Reed's own and emerged from a conversation at Claridge's over dinner with Lord Castlerosse, raconteur, man-about-town and gossip columnist of the *Sunday Express*. Castlerosse had been involved in Reed's abortive plan to make a film of *Rob Roy* in Ireland in 1940 and had subsequently made a cameo appearance as a fat man in a bathchair in Reed's *Kipps* (1941). Now, expanding on the story of Pitt during the Napoleonic Wars and its parallels with the present, he fired Reed with the idea for a film. Castlerosse was engaged to provide a screen story, period anecdotes and dialogue, but for the detailed shooting script, Gainsborough turned to the expert team of Frank Launder and Sidney Gilliat, who had been involved either together or singly in the previous three Reed—Black films: *Night Train to Munich* (1940), *Girl in the News* (1940) and *Kipps* (1941).[13]

The film, described in *Kinematograph Weekly* as 'the most ambitious British production since the war began', eventually ran for nearly two hours and cost £250,000.[14] It took 23 weeks to shoot, from 21 July 1941 to 24 December 1941, and was released in June 1942. It was also beset with difficulties of various kinds during production. The star, Robert Donat, who insisted on a closed set for the film, suffered from the ill-health that was a chronic and increasingly marked feature of his career and this slowed up the shooting.[15] The actor cast as William Wilberforce died at the final rehearsal and John Mills was called in at four hours' notice to take over the part.[16] The brilliant but erratic Wilfrid Lawson was cast as Napoleon, but at an advanced stage in the shooting it was decided that he was neither visually nor vocally anything like Napoleon.[17] He was replaced in the role by Herbert Lom. This necessitated the re-shooting of several scenes. There were also fierce battles over the script between the parties involved in the production. Frank Launder recalled:

> The battles that Sidney and I fought with Carol Reed, Robert Donat and Ted Black were in the main aimed at us showing the human imperfections of William Pitt and giving Charles James Fox a place in the sun. We lost all along the line, Pitt became a paragon of virtue, which he certainly was not, and the part of Fox, by far the more interesting character, was whittled down to give more footage to the heroic Pitt. I have always taken the view that untainted heroes, unless Biblical, are bores.[18]

They actually wanted to have Pitt making a speech in the House while drunk, something that actually happened on several occasions. But neither Reed nor Donat would stand for this. It is not surprising under the circumstances that Launder and Gilliat did lose. It was, after all, wartime and the celebration of a drunken Prime Minister would perhaps have lent more comfort to the enemy than strength to morale at home. Nevertheless, some film critics, with the tiresome propensity of the breed to set themselves up as historical pundits, were to cavil at a depiction of Pitt that was not entirely accurate and at a film which quite properly concentrated on his foreign rather than his domestic policy. But this was absurd: every generation rewrites history to suit its own preoccupations and preconceptions. Carol Reed and Edward Black were giving Britain a William Pitt for the 1940s, quite a different figure from the William Pitt that might have been depicted in the 1930s, the 1950s or the 1980s.

The film opened with a shrewd bid for American sympathy, an entirely appropriate gesture since the United States entered the war in December 1941 and it was as well to seek to dispel the Anglophobia remaining in a country which had been born out of rebellion against the British crown. William Pitt, the Elder, the Earl of Chatham, makes a speech in the House of Lords calling for Britain to end the American War of Independence and make peace. The war is unjust, he says; the colonists are right and America can never be conquered. The camera pans up from the Elder Pitt to a small boy listening intently in the gallery — William Pitt the Younger, thus instantly establishing him as the inheritor of his father's strong pro-American sympathies. Afterwards, Chatham takes wine with his son on the occasion of his birthday, tells him that he is destined for a career in the Commons and warns him 'Do not seek fame through war'.

Time passes, Chatham dies and the country, ruled by a corrupt aristocratic oligarchy, declines. William Pitt, now 24, chafes at the situation: 'We're held in contempt throughout Europe — bankrupt, a third-rate country, our ships scarcely able to control the Channel'. But when the government falls, Pitt is appointed Prime Minister by King George III. He appeals to the Opposition leader, Charles James Fox, to join him in a coalition which will reform the Commons and run the country effectively. But Fox rejects his plea and predicts his downfall. It is the voice of the self-interested politician speaking against the statesman, the man of destiny.

There is a terrifying moment when Pitt enters the Commons for the first time as Prime Minister and is greeted by a hostile opposition who drown out his words with a braying, howling cacophony of animal noises. This will have been far more disturbing to 40s audiences than to present-day audiences, made familiar with such scenes by the broadcasting of Prime Minister's question time in the Commons. Only a handful of faithful friends stand by Pitt, including William Wilberforce, whose association in the popular mind with the ending of slavery (mentioned by Pitt in the film) lends further moral strength to Pitt's cause. When Pitt and Wilberforce are set on by thugs hired by their opponents, they are rescued by two professional boxers who tell Pitt that the people are behind him and he should call an election.

Pitt calls an election, standing on a programme of peace and reform, and in a sequence of vigorously staged election scenes, sweeps to victory. Under Pitt's premiership, there is peace. The scenes of rural calm and harvest bounty that illustrate this end with a peasant sharpening his scythe for the harvest, but Reed cuts from him to scythes in France being sharpened to harvest not the corn but the heads of the aristocracy. The French Revolution breaks out and the sequences which detail it are intercut with speeches by Fox and Pitt. Fox welcomes it but Pitt, who is for reform but against revolution, warns that 'very soon we shall see liberty for the many used as a stalking horse to secure licence for the few.'

With a republic established in France, Talleyrand comes to England as ambassador, and while guaranteeing the security of Holland, proposes to Pitt a pact by which Britain and France would be allies and together rule the world. Pitt rejects the suggestion, France invades Holland and Britain declares war. The war goes badly and British forces are evacuated from Dunkirk. Britain's ally Austria surrenders and Britain faces the enemy alone. For Holland read Poland, for France read Germany, and for Austria read France, for Dunkirk read Dunkirk, and here we have a re-run of 1940.

In the streets the people call for peace: in the Commons, Fox demands peace. Pitt makes a rousing speech, declaring that Britain must face the danger alone. The security of the world is the objective of the war against a danger unequalled in history. Bonaparte takes power in France and so the Churchillian Pitt now has his Hitler to face ('a nation of fanatics, led by an arch-fanatic'). Pitt appoints Nelson to command the fleet and Nelson secures victory at the battle of the Nile. Success makes the war popular again.

In 1799 Napoleon Bonaparte, to gain time to rebuild his forces, suggests peace. The mob, weary of war again, call for peace. Pitt, who knows it is a trick to buy time, refuses to agree but is forced to resign. His successor, Henry Addington, signs the treaty of Amiens, but even while he is making a speech in the Commons about swords being turned into ploughshares, we see in France scenes of ploughshares being turned into swords. The French army mobilizes.

With the return of war, Pitt is recalled to 10 Downing Street and although his health has been undermined by his previous exertions and he knows it will mean his death, he takes the job, calling in the Commons for the complete crushing of Napoleon. Fox at last confesses himself to have been in error and offers his support. As the French prepare to invade, the Home Guard is mobilized. The anxious country learns the news of the great victory of Trafalgar. The threat of invasion has been averted and the bells are rung. At a Guildhall dinner in his honour, Pitt declares: 'England has saved herself by her exertions and will, as I trust, save Europe by her example.'

Throughout the film the historical parallels are clearly drawn. Pitt is Churchill, but a Churchill recast on MoI lines as a leader both of social reform at home and resistance to dictatorship and aggression abroad. Pitt is consistently identified with the cause of the people. This is made clear from the outset, when he is seen as a clear-eyed visionary ('The ideas of yesterday are dead, those of today are dying, we are men of the future') and is contrasted with the reactionary, hide-bound and short-sighted forces of aristocratic privilege and faction, first seen gathered in Brooks' gaming club, an appropriate setting for idlers and parasites. Pitt calls an election in which he stands on a platform of peace and reform and Reed uses two elaborate montage sequences, known jokily as Carol Reed's 'March of Time', to suggest the state of Britain before and after Pitt. Before Pitt, as the narrator (Carol Reed himself) puts it in splendidly empurpled prose: 'The country sprawled aimlessly on a multi-coloured quilt of feckless pomp': ships rot in the harbour, men lie drunk in the street, social contrasts are great (richly dressed gentlemen sweep past ragged beggars in the streets) and a hanged man swings from a gibbet at sunset. This is the world over which the Fox—North coalition presides. But once Pitt becomes Prime Minister with the people's backing, we see a montage suggesting the country galvanized into action: the Industrial Revolution proceeding apace, naval retrenchment strengthening the nation's defences. Pitt confirms his opposition to the previous order of things by making appointments on merit, notably promoting Nelson to command of the fleet over the heads of other more senior admirals ('We must hope to survive their displeasure').

Contrast of a different sort is pointed by intercutting the career of Pitt, the popularly elected politician pledged to peace and reform, with episodes from the career of Napoleon Bonaparte, who is brought to prominence by revolution and seizes power to become dictator, an 18th century Hitler, contemptuous of his foe ('The British are a stupid, illogical race led by a second-rate politician').

Pitt, on the other hand, is given a human side, to stress the cost he paid to give the country leadership. He sacrifices his private life in the inevitable but not obtrusive, and rather touchingly handled, romantic sub-plot. He courts Eleanor Eden, whom he loves but from whom he parts when he realizes that all his time and energy is needed to fight Napoleon. 'You have your own happiness to consider' urges Wilberforce. 'We have the future of this country to consider,' replies Pitt. His health is undermined by

British leaders were seen as heroic but often quirky and humorous individualists, such as Charles James Fox (Robert Morley).

overwork. He ignores his doctor's advice to rest and works on, sustained by port, until it is clear he will sacrifice his life in the end in his country's cause. He allows his financial affairs too to get into such a state that the bailiffs move into Number 10. But Wilberforce and other friends rally round to sort out that set of problems.

Domestically Pitt has a foil in Fox. Churchill too had his Charles James Fox, no aristocrat, no peacemonger, but his foremost parliamentary critic and a thorn in the side of the coalition government — Aneurin Bevan. His biographer, Michael Foot, writes:

> A few at the time and more in retrospect saw a comparison with the part played by Charles James Fox in the French Revolutionary and early Napoleonic wars. Fox thought those wars unjust and unnecessary; there at least the parallel breaks down. But once the thought of this comparison is admitted at all, the likeness between the two men becomes striking. Fox revealed the same paradoxical mixture of impetuous speech and deadly debating skill, of apparent waywardness combined with allegiance to principle. He too made his reputation primarily in opposition, despised the accusations of lack of patriotism since he knew how wide they were of the mark, gave a new meaning to the debased word *charm*, and aroused the same devotion from his friends. To study the life of Fox is to know Bevan better and *vice versa*.[19]

There were other parallels too. Allowing for the time-scale difference, Henry Addington, the ineffectual man who took over as Prime Minister from Pitt and allowed himself to be tricked into signing a peace treaty with Napoleon, is surely another Chamberlain. It may be mere coincidence that a German actor Albert Lieven was cast as Talleyrand, but here was an 18th century Ribbentrop, offering Pitt a similar deal to the one Hitler offered Britain: security for the British Empire in return for a free hand in Europe.

The periodic bouts of war-weariness amongst the people which Pitt resists and overcomes mirror a very real fear which the MoI entertained about the steadiness of the people and the constant need to reassure them about the paramount importance of fighting on. As Harold Nicolson, Parliamentary Private Secretary to Information Minister Duff Cooper, confided to his diary on 2 March 1941:

> I think we can resist the worst, but we shall be so exhausted by that resistance that Hitler may offer us an honourable peace which will be difficult to reject. I have an uneasy feeling that when things get very bad there may be a movement in this country to attribute the whole disaster to the 'war-mongers' and to replace Churchill by Sam Hoare or some appeaser. That will be the end of England. If only we could show people some glimmer of light at the end of the tunnel, we could count upon their enduring any ordeal.[20]

This feeling was prompted in part by the sheer ignorance of the working classes among the mandarins of the MoI, men like Harold Nicolson and Sir Kenneth Clark. It was unfounded. Home Intelligence, set up to monitor morale, reported regularly that there was unprecedented unity across class barriers and continuing solidarity with the war effort. Indeed, on 1 October 1941, in his report on its first year's work, Dr Stephen Taylor, director of Home Intelligence, concluded: 'There is, at present, no evidence to suggest that it is possible to defeat the people of Britain by any means other than extermination'.[21]

Although the Battle of Britain was the victory that Trafalgar was probably intended to parallel, the course of the war caused nature to imitate art. *The Young Mr Pitt* was released in June 1942. In October of the same year, Montgomery and his Eighth Army defeated Rommel at El Alamein, the major turning point of the war, and Churchill, in a speech in the City of London, provided his own parallel to Pitt's curtain speech: 'Now this is not the end. It is not even the beginning of the end, but it is, perhaps, the end of the beginning.'

The whole film adds up to a portrait of an age and of a man, selective of course, sanitized perhaps, but for all that a rousing reminder of the successful prosecution of a previous war against foreign dictatorship and the threat of world domination. The script, whatever the authors' misgivings, is superb, witty, literate, epigrammatic, organizing and deploying the complex tangle of events in the period 1783 to 1805 in such a way as to provide clarity, coherence and narrative drive. The direction by Carol Reed is effective without being flamboyant, carrying the story along with pace, style and force, and highlighting the astonishing central performance of Robert Donat. Donat is quite simply magnificent as Pitt. James Agate called it his 'best film performance' and many of the newspapers concurred. Donat manages the transition from clear-eyed, dynamic, young leader, to ageing, ailing but determined old warrior with total conviction. He delivers the speeches brilliantly. He also enjoys himself hugely playing the Elder Pitt in the first scene, gouty, elderly, gingerly feeding his 14 year old son port ('You shouldn't be upset by a bottle or two of port at your age').

It is hard to believe, given the overall thrust and detailed argument of the script, that no guidance was provided by the MoI. Sidney Gilliat insists that he and Frank Launder received no such guidance,[22] but the MoI input may have come through Lord Castlerosse, who is listed in MoI files as one of the sympathetic journalists to be employed in a press campaign secretly orchestrated by the Ministry to direct popular hatred against the Germans.[23] The MoI planning committee had on 21 June 1940 outlined a home morale campaign which would utilize all available media and would seek to give people a reasonable assurance of ultimate victory, maintain confidence in the authority and efficiency of the government, and show that there could be no truce with Hitler without victory being achieved.[24] A dramatization of the life of William Pitt certainly stressed all those points. Furthermore, the earlier war was in the minds of the Ministry, for Policy Committee Paper 33 had pointed out on 26 March 1940:

> At present the danger of Britain (sic) from Germany is nearly as great as the danger which once threatened her from Napoleon; it was only the unrelenting hatred of large masses of the common people for the French and of a compact body of aristocrats for the French leaders which created the national spirit in Britain that led to Napoleon's defeat. That spirit must now be recreated.[25]

The Young Mr Pitt is almost a textbook demonstration of the MoI's interpretation of history and certainly answered the call for idealizations of national heroes and dramatizations of parliamentary government. It is a film of grit and commitment, but also of humour and humanity. The humour is on the whole the humour of character, one of the glories of English comedy. But here it provides an extra dimension that prevents the film from sliding into over-earnestness. Robert Morley brings superb timing and presence as well as natural authority to the role of Charles James Fox, the opposition leader, striding into a polling booth in the election and announcing majestically: 'Charles James Fox voting for Charles James Fox'. When after being cheered by the mob one minute, he finds stones being hurled through his window at dinner, he turns to his wife and declares with aplomb: 'That, my dear, is life'. Raymond Lovell gives a wholly delightful performance as the vague but good-natured King George III, punctuating his speech with a gruff 'Eh, what', perpetually concerned about the quality of his turnips, anxious to avoid innovation but consistently supportive of his young prime minister. In one priceless scene, he is depicted at Weymouth, taking the sea water and descending from a bathing machine into the sea to the strains of 'God Save the King'. Neither character, however, is pure comic relief. They are 'characters' rather than caricatures, embodiments of the English love of the heroic individual, the eccentric, the larger-than-life 'one-off'.

There is, however, an ideological dimension to this. In Nazi Germany, such figures had no part in the new order, least of all as King or Leader of the Opposition. They are the products of and can only flourish in a free, democratic society where individual, whimsical, self-expression is not only tolerated but encouraged. They must combine when danger threatens — and Fox is last seen drilling with the Home Guards — but otherwise are allowed their eccentricities.

In terms of morale, the film was released at an important juncture, for as Michael Balfour writes: 'after a bout of optimism at the turn of the year which the government regarded as excessive, the period until the end of August 1942 was as gloomy as any in the war'.[26] The optimism had followed the entry of the USA into the war but had been dampened by the loss of Benghazi, the fall of Singapore, the slaughter on the Dieppe Raid and the news of heavy losses in the North Atlantic in the first six months of the year.

In these circumstances, the film was extremely well received. With a few exceptions, the critics were unanimous in praising the film, Donat and Carol Reed. 'A sensitive and absorbing picture, made on the grand scale . . . Robert Donat gives one of the great performances of his career in the central part' said the *News Chronicle*.[27] 'An extremely well-made historical drama, in which Donat's sincere and convincing portrayal of Pitt is matched by Robert Morley's splendid character study of the crafty Fox' declared the *Daily Mirror*.[28] 'The film is in every way outstanding' opined *The Scotsman*.[29] 'A very fine British film . . . magnificently staged, painstaking, amusing, . . . flawlessly directed by Carol Reed and delightfully acted by a distinguished cast' said the *Evening News*.[30] 'The finest historical film we have made . . . The period detail is impeccable, the casting and acting quite superb' declared *Sight and Sound*.[31]

The historical parallels were also clearly understood. Announcing the trade show, *Kinematograph Weekly* said:

> What is happening to England has happened to England before. Where Hitler stands now, Napoleon stood one hundred and fifty years ago. The grim threat of invasion was as strong then as it is now. The British fleet was the bulwark against aggression even as it is today. And where Churchill stands this day, foursquare against the hatred of the Hun, there stood in George III's time a similar man in Number 10 Downing Street, a bold, earnest figure braced with the steadfast faith of the whole people of Britain. His name was William Pitt, and now, at a time when the spirit of Pitt is embodied in Winston Churchill, the great saga of a valiant statesman, who, in his time, defied as brutal an aggressor, has been brought to the screen.[32]

Reviewing it, *Kine Weekly* pronounced it 'Churchillian in power, purpose and poise, and propitiously timed, the picture is an inspiration as well as superb drama. Outstanding general booking, a great British box office achievement.'[33] *Today's Cinema* fervently concurred:

> Outstanding instance of the British film at its most serious best, the finest form of propaganda on our screens today, and first-class entertainment which, while probably making its greatest appeal to discriminating audiences, is a box office proposition no exhibitor can afford to miss. Unreservedly recommended. Here is a British production which not only reflects the greatest possible verdict upon the company concerned in its making, but upon the industry as a whole. Never has any film more perfectly expressed

Pitt received the steadfast backing of King George III, another affectionately observed 'character' (Robert Donat and Raymond Lovell).

the feeling and temper of the British people in times of stress and trouble such as we are passing through today. *The Young Mr Pitt* paints a huge canvas of political history but never obscures the human element, touches the heart with the splendour of its patriotic fervour and stimulates the mind with its fury and argument . . . A heart-warming story of a man who placed his country before love, ambition and ease and who, in the end, gave his life as surely as a soldier on the battlefield, it absorbs the interest to an extraordinary degree, makes a devastating appeal to the emotions, and, by revealing the depths to which a mishandled country can sink, impresses the lesson of yesterday with remarkable vigour and unswerving truth. We feel that no film designed for the purpose has a stronger propaganda value than this simple yet spectacular tale of one man's unremitting labours in the cause of England for it has the force of example, a present day parallel in the threat of invasion, and underlines the almost magical resilience of an unflagging courage. *The Young Mr Pitt* is a film of yesterday for today that will exert a tremendous influence upon tomorrow.[34]

The daily papers shared the enthusiasm of the trades. The *Daily Sketch* announced:

> If you do not see *The Young Mr Pitt* you will be missing a fine film —
> certainly one of the most inspiring made since the outbreak of war, and
> undoubtedly one of the best pieces of propaganda for its unremitting
> prosecution. The parallel between England's perilous position during the
> Napoleonic Wars and her position today is stirringly and astutely drawn. A
> mention of Toulon and Dunkirk reminds us that we suffered early defeats by
> sea and land in that age too — but survived. We are reminded that to dicker
> about peace treaties with a European conqueror is criminal folly — and, in
> the cry flung at the parliamentary gentlemen who wished to wait to see
> which way the Napoleonic cat would jump next, 'Gentlemen, let us create
> events, not wait for them', Pitt the Younger voices the sentiments of the
> British people today.[35]

The *Daily Express* trumpeted:

> Egypt in danger, battles in the Mediterranean, invasion armies across the
> Channel, Europe enslaved and Britain against the world; these are the
> highlights of a brilliant new British picture *The Young Mr Pitt* which Mr
> Winston Churchill was the first in this country to see before he made his
> visit to America. It is a great film because it shows a great nation in action, a
> people highest in temper when lowest in the water. Robert Donat, playing
> the longest part of his career, gives a wonderfully living portrait of the young
> Prime Minister.[36]

The identification of Pitt with Churchill was so complete that it provided the right-wing weekly *Truth* with the opportunity to make a coded attack on Churchill. Its editor Collin Brooks was in close touch with hardline old-fashioned elements in the Conservative party who felt that 'Winston is a difficult leader, and is not a Conservative at all or even, perhaps, by normal standards a statesman — being a creature of 'Palace' favourites, of moods and whims, and overriding egotism under his charm and geniality.'[37] *Truth* devoted a long article to examining the claims of Churchill to be another Pitt on the basis of the film. It praised the film 'as an example of unofficial propaganda . . . which deserves high praise for its influence not only on morale at home but also on the prestige and reputation of this country abroad.' But it goes on to suggest that Churchill should not be adulated but offered constructive criticism. 'To describe Mr Churchill now as another Pitt is frankly overstatement. It is the ardent wish of the nation, however, that as an apt pupil he will become more and more Pitt-like, until he wins us complete victory over our enemies.'[38]

The Young Mr Pitt became one of the four top British box office successes of 1942 — the others were *First of the Few, One of Our Aircraft is Missing* and *Hatter's Castle*.[39] It was also voted as one of the top 20 British films of the war years in the *Daily Mail* National Film Ballot in 1946.[40] Its influence on one intellectual and potentially hostile member of the audience is described in the wartime diary of James Lees-Milne, who wrote on 1 August 1942: 'I saw Robert Donat in *The Young Mr Pitt* and was moved to tears. I feel very ashamed when cheap patriotism makes me weep.'[41] The film was reissued in 1946, cut from 118 to 103 minutes and received again with rapture by *Today's Cinema*.[42] Thereafter it dropped out of sight and has rarely been seen in recent years. But in his history of the British cinema published in 1964, Charles Oakley proclaimed it 'probably the finest historical moving picture ever to be staged in this country.'[43] That verdict surely still stands. *The Young Mr Pitt* is a picture that deserves wider showing and its reinstatement among Britain's finest film works.

It is instructive to compare the relatively limited use of history made by the British cinema for straight propaganda purposes with the extensive use of it made in Germany during the war.[44] This seems to have been deliberate policy on the part of the Propaganda Minister Dr Goebbels, who preferred to work indirectly rather than directly in films to convey his message. Historical parallelism was an important part of his programme. As Dr Fritz Hippler, the Reichsfilmintendant, wrote in 1942: 'The only possible subjects for successful historical films are personalities and events from the past with which people of the present are familiar or with which they can identify. In other words, it must show the meaning of life by means of the timeless authenticity of particular historical events, situations and personalities.'[45]

Historical settings were utilized in films designed to whip up hostility against Germany's two great enemies, the British and the Jews. *The Rothschilds* (1940) and *Jew Süss* (1940) both set out to show the threat posed by the Jews, economic, political, racial and sexual, respectively in 19th century England and 18th century Wurtemberg. *Ohm Krüger* (1941) spectacularly recreated the Boer struggle against the British Empire in South Africa, the occasion when according to the film's programme 'for the first time the entire civilized world realized that England is the brutal enemy of order and civilization'. *Das Herz der Königin* (1940) (The Heart of a Queen) traced the conflict of the pure, noble and romantic Mary, Queen of Scots, with the vicious, scheming and vindictive Elizabeth of England. *Titanic* (1943) featured the unsuccessful efforts of the ship's German first officer to prevent the catastrophe in the face of the unscrupulous machinations of corrupt British aristocrats and plutocrats.

But more importantly, the German cinema was concerned to promote those qualities in the people which would sustain the war effort. First and above all, they promoted the idea of total obedience to an all-wise, all-powerful, all-knowing leader and for this purpose leading figures from

Germany's past were mobilized as proto-Führer figures. They were invariably shown as lonely, dedicated, iron-willed warriors, battling for the glory, unity and future greatness of Germany. *The Great King* (1942) recreated the heroic campaigns of Frederick II the Great of Prussia. The film stressed his refusal to make peace short of total victory over his enemies, his survival of assassination, his mistrust of his Russian allies, who do in fact desert him, his takeover of the running of the war from the high command and the people's trust in his judgement. Goebbels, who was deeply involved in the production of the film, noted in his diary: 'With this film we can make politics too. It is an excellent expedient in the struggle for the soul of our people and in the process of creating the necessary German resistance needed to see us successfully through the war.'[46]

The reports on audience responses suggested that the message was getting through: 'Reports so far assembled from all parts of the Reich on the film *The Great King* all confirm the remarkable and sustained impression made by this work and its very favourable reception by the population, particularly among the general filmgoing public . . . Throughout the film audiences appear to have seen a 'mirror image of our own times'. Many people have compared the King with the Führer . . . The film had managed to give our people . . . some idea of the lonely, glacial atmosphere surrounding a head of state responsible for a nation's destiny.'[47] It was one of the ten top grossing films of the Reich during the war.[48]

Bismarck the 'Iron Chancellor' featured in two films, *Bismarck* (1940) and *The Dismissal* (1942), which together showed him building up the army, abolishing democratic assemblies, imposing press censorship, outwitting the effeminate and intriguing French and Austrians, surviving assassination at the hands of an English Jew and unifying Germany. In the end he is dismissed by the youthful Kaiser Wilhelm II, but the moral of the film is clear. 'Today is no longer important' says Bismarck, 'The Reich survives me. My work is done. It is only a beginning. Who will complete it?' Audiences drew the obvious conclusion.

It was not just political leaders but cultural heroes of Germany's past who were utilized to preach the message: poets (*Friedrich Schiller*, 1940), scientists (*Robert Koch*, 1939; *Paracelsus*, 1943), inventors (*Diesel*, 1942), composers (*Friedemann Bach*, 1941). *Schiller* was subtitled 'The Triumph of a Genius' and this sums up the theme of this cycle of films. All celebrate the struggles and achievements of solitary German geniuses, striving for perfection, knowing they are right, refusing to compromise, sacrificing personal happiness to attain their ultimate goals. All the time they are surrounded by, opposed by and criticized by lesser mortals, who are confounded in the end. Herbert Maisch's *Andreas Schluter* (1942) is typical. It recounts the career of the 18th century architect Andreas Schluter, a significant figure in the sense that Hitler fancied himself an architect, and like Schluter, planned to rebuild Berlin to rival the glories of Ancient Rome. Schluter, dedicated, stubborn and brilliant, is constantly handicapped by the disunity of Germany, the unreliability of a dilettante king, the jealousy of lesser artists and the vacillation and opportunism of politicians. 'Waiting for Hitler' might well be the subtitle of all these films. For the Führer will remove all these vexations and allow the destiny of the German race to flourish, under his own inspired leadership.

These films were invariably lavishly produced with massive sets, elaborate costumes and casts of thousands. But with a few notable exceptions, they are heavy-handed, stodgy and verbose. This is particularly true of many of the biographical films, staged in a leaden monumental style and replete with lengthy, wearisome Nazi rants, delivered by the actors in general as if they were on the verge of apoplexy. The impact of these 'leadership' films should not be underestimated, however. *The Great King, Ohm Krüger, The Dismissal* and *Jew Süss* were among the biggest grossing films at the wartime German box office. A survey published in 1944 revealed that the six most popular films with German youth were *The Great King, Bismarck, The Dismissal, Friedrich Schiller, Ohm Krüger* and *Homecoming,* five of them leadership films.

The failure of the British to use history to anything like the same extent may lie in the conventional wisdom of the film industry, which was that historical films were unpopular with working class audiences. 'History is almost universally condemned' said a survey of 66 exhibitors published in *World Film News* in 1937, speaking of working class audiences.[49] Similarly J. Smithson, Vice-Chairman of the Portsmouth C.E.A., reported in 1936: 'The public do not want too many pictures of the costume and period type, which although brilliant productions, do not in the main particularly interest the proletariat of the kinema. Many of these are all right for high class neighbourhoods but do not generally appeal to the ordinary working class district.'[50]

This relative absence of historical films, particularly historical biographies, compared to the greater use by the Germans, refers only to 'serious' historical films. There was a whole genre of costume dramas, the so-called Gainsborough melodramas, which began in 1943 inaugurated by the same man who had produced *The Young Mr Pitt,* Edward Black. The contract to produce films for Fox ran out in 1942 and Gainsborough became part of the vast Rank Organization, though retaining its own autonomy, personnel and production policies. Edward Black, who died in 1948 at the early age of 48, is one of the unsung giants of British film history. As Alan Wood wrote of him: 'Ted Black unquestionably ranks as one of the greatest figures in British film history, the maker of stars like Margaret Lockwood, James Mason, John Mills and Stewart Granger. He was also one of the few producers whose films, over a considerable period, made money.'[51] He had the ability to sense the popular mood and capitalize on it. The difference is perhaps that in the early years of the war historical films relating directly to the war were needed to keep up morale. After 1943, with the tide of war turning, America and Russia both in, and the Allies making headway, Gainsborough declared their intention of making entertainment films. The public were tired of war films and only two were in fact produced in 1944. Gainsborough hit the jackpot with *The Man in Grey* (1943) and hastened to cash in on their winning formula.[52]

The world of Gainsborough melodrama was not the world of sober statesmen battling to secure the national wellbeing, it was a world of rollicking, rumbustious romps in Restoration or Regency England, of whip-wielding lords and bosom-heaving ladies, of highwaymen, gypsies, moonlit rides, of thwarted love and of steaming passion, a vivid, vibrant world inhabited by such smouldering sex-objects as Margaret Lockwood and Jean Kent, James Mason and Stewart Granger. The titles of the films still evoke in people of a certain age a delighted tremor of recollection —

Pitt sacrifices his chance of personal happiness to devote his energies to conducting the war (Robert Donat and Phyllis Calvert).

The Wicked Lady, The Man in Grey, Fanny by Gaslight, Madonna of the Seven Moons.

Few film genres can have been subjected to such withering critical scorn as the Gainsborough melodramas. In their heyday — from 1943 to 1948 — they were regularly castigated in the press. Take, for instance, the *Manchester Guardian*'s verdict on *The Wicked Lady* in 1946: '*The Wicked Lady* is an odd mixture of hot passion and cold suet pudding, represented respectively by James Mason and Margaret Lockwood. Miss Lockwood, who might well be the life and soul of a dull sherry party, is quite out of place when she tries to shed glamour over a beerswilling thieves' kitchen.'[53] The *Graphic* thought little better of the endearing rococo absurdities of *The Magic Bow* (1946): '*The Magic Bow* is what can fairly be described as a Gainsborough special. It is a luxuriously dressed period piece, totally incredible and of a banality so complete it is almost impressive. Cliché follows relentlessly upon cliché, verbally and pictorially, director and scriptwriter working in the closest harmony to achieve a picture which not even their worst enemy could accuse of being a work of art.'[54] Finally, there is the *Observer* on *The Idol of Paris* (1948): 'Such stupendous imbecility in a film, delivered with such portentous gravity in such excruciating dialogue, demands a sort of recognition.'[55]

Despite this barrage of critical disapproval, the films were great hits with the public and made large sums of money. *The Wicked Lady,* for instance, was the top British moneymaker of 1946 and Gainsborough melodramas were voted second (*The Man in Grey*), third (*Madonna of the Seven Moons*) and fourth (*They Were Sisters*) in the *Daily Mail* ballot for the most popular films of the war years. This very dichotomy tells us as much about the critics as it does about the films. As John Ellis has demonstrated in a notable essay in *Screen* magazine, the British critical establishment in the 1940s was rooted in certain traditions — of documentary realism, of literary quality and of a middle class improvement ethic.[56] Gainsborough melodramas offended against all these criteria of excellence. They were not only not realistic; they were defiantly anti-realistic. They did not derive from respected literary sources, of the kind which earned plaudits for David Lean's beautifully crafted film versions of Dickens, or Carol Reed's atmospheric adaptations of Graham Greene. They were furthermore definitely neither improving nor uplifting. They were rooted, in fact, in that equally critically despised stage melodrama tradition that had packed the working-class audiences into the penny gaffs of the 19th century to thrill to tales of wicked squires, wronged innocents and virtue triumphant.

Not only were the films held in contempt by the critics. They were also looked down on in the industry itself. The managing director of one of Rank's subsidiary companies recalled:

Gainsborough Films . . . was much despised by the other major groups. This was because Gainsborough was a wholly commercial film production organization which assessed public demand of its market, set out to satisfy it and to maximize its products . . . It made no pretence to be arty-crafty or to use spectacular colour or camera angles in any novel way and so was despised by independent producers. It made no appeal to history or to patriotism or to moral uplift, as Two Cities did. Gainsborough based itself on being a factory production line churning out what the public liked . . . The basic theme selected by Gainsborough was 'kitchen' romance pure and simple, aimed at feeding the starved emotions of the great British public who spent night after night in bomb shelters and generally lived a pretty grim existence.[57]

They were also despised by the actors working in them. Stewart Granger called the films 'junk' and James Mason became notorious for his dislike of them.[58]

Only the audiences loved the Gainsborough melodramas. Why? The slick answer is escapism, from the rigours of war and the deprivations of post-war austerity. There is, of course, an element of truth in this. Spectacular costumes, conspicuous consumption and extravagant goings-on did take people out of themselves and help them to forget for a little while flying bombs, clothing coupons and fuel shortages. But there is more to it than that.

First of all, Gainsborough created something which had not previously existed in Britain — 'the woman's picture'. They did so in direct response to a perceived box office need. The war had seen a great upsurge in female cinemagoing. Even in the 1930s women had been great filmgoers, but the huge army of women shift workers and factory girls that the war had called into being, the legion of wives and sweethearts whose menfolk were away serving with the armed forces created a defined and movie-hungry group who responded avidly to Gainsborough's new product. As C. A. Lejeune wrote in 1948 of the war years: 'With the curious reserve of pleasure that is characteristic of the British race, we settled down to enjoy ourselves seriously, even gravely, at the pictures. We were ready for a good cry over something that was far removed from war. We wallowed in the tragedy of *Fanny by Gaslight, Love Story* and *Madonna of the Seven Moons*.'[59] Gainsborough deliberately designed pictures for and geared them towards women filmgoers; pictures that were the British equivalent of the glossy tear-jerking dramas that Hollywood was producing for American female audiences, films built around the talents of Bette Davis, Joan Crawford, Ann Sheridan and Olivia de Havilland.

Stars were all-important to these pictures, larger-than-life icons to undergo larger-than-life trials and tribulations. In providing them, Gainsborough created the first body of genuinely cinema-produced British film stars. In the 1930s stars came to the cinema ready-made from the West End stage, from the music hall, from musical comedy. Only a handful of stars, notably Anna Neagle and Robert Donat, were actually created by the cinema. But in the 1940s Gainsborough films made stars of Margaret Lockwood and Phyllis Calvert, Jean Kent and Patricia Roc, James Mason and Stewart Granger, Michael Rennie and Maxwell Reed. There were women to identify with and take as role models, men to drool over and fantasize about. Stewart Granger, dashing, flamboyant, virile, was Britain's answer to Errol Flynn and Tyrone Power. James Mason, brooding, sneering, smouldering, raping Margaret Lockwood in *The Wicked Lady* and flogging her to death in *The Man in Grey,* provided the same powerful, sexual charge as those dark, cruel, fascinating outsiders of 19th century romantic fiction, Rochester and Heathcliff. The sexual allure of these stars, male and female, was emphasized by their costumes, tight trousers and shirts slashed open to the waist for the men; low-cut, figure-hugging dresses for the women.

But for all the surface appeal of handsome costumes, lavish sets, glamorous stars, highly coloured and highly spiced storytelling, the films also focused attention on two highly relevant subjects, sex and class, areas where established patterns and beliefs were being overturned under the impact of war. The films reflected the much greater importance placed on the role of women in society as a result of the war. By 1943, 90 per cent of all single women between 18 and 40 and 80 per cent of married women with children over 14 were working. Women were also being conscripted into the armed forces. This did not necessarily result in instant equality. Women were for the most part denied equal pay with men and they got less in compensation for industrial accidents than men. But there was an inevitable increase in their sense of responsibility and independence, their mobility and self-esteem. As Mass-Observation noted of women in the services in 1944, they were 'being forced to think for themselves instead of falling back on some opinion taken ready-made from husband or father.'[60] Women like this will have responded sympathetically to Margaret Lockwood's defiant cry in *The Wicked Lady:* 'I've got brains and looks and personality. I want to use them instead of rotting in this dull hole.'

The war also witnessed a change in sexual behaviour and attitudes. Dislocation, both social and psychological caused by bombing, bereavement, conscription and separation put a considerable strain on pre-war behaviour patterns. There were more casual liaisons and a greater degree of sexual freedom as a result of a 'live for today' attitude. In consequence, there was by 1943 a 139 per cent higher incidence of venereal disease than in 1939. There was a doubling of the illegitimate birth rate between 1940 and 1945, with almost a third of all babies, a record 255,460, being born out of wedlock. In 1945 25,000 divorce petitions were filed, compared to 10,000 in 1938. Concern was therefore widely expressed for the stability of the traditional institutions of monogamous marriage and the family unit.[61]

Gainsborough hit on a formula to accommodate both the changing aspirations of women and the traditional social values threatened by the war. So we get a succession of anti-heroines who are independent, aggressive and single-minded in their pursuit of wealth, status and sexual gratification, and whose exploits can be vicariously enjoyed by the audience. But they are always contrasted with the virginal and dutiful good girl, who suffers but in the end gets her man and her happiness, while the bad girl gets her come-uppance. Typically, Margaret Lockwood's Lady Barbara Skelton, the eponymous *Wicked Lady,* having schemed, cheated and murdered her way to the top dies wretched and abandoned when the only man she ever really loved rejects her because of her record and her conduct.

Lady Barbara is the archetype of what Gershon Legman called 'the bitch-heroine'. He was writing in America in 1948 of a parallel development which produced *The Wicked Lady*'s notorious American counterpart, *Forever Amber.* But he could well have been describing Lady Barbara when he wrote:

> The bitch-heroine speaks with a loud voice, moves with a firm stride; one hand always on the reins, the other ever-ready with the whip. She wants what she wants when she wants it, yes and by God, she is going to get it . . . or she will whip, shoot, stab, scrounge, undermine, ruin and drive to suicide, drink or drugs any damn' man who stands in her way . . . She is no accident neither of history nor pathology. She is a wishful dream — Venus Dominatrix — cunningly contrived out of the substance of women's longings. She is presented to the 'emancipated' but still enslaved wives-mothers-and mistresses as a fantasy escape from their servitude to men, to fashion, traditional morality and the paralysing uselessness of being nothing but the show-horses of their owners' success.[62]

The moral of the Gainsborough films may be impeccable but the effect of the films is rather more ambiguous. The sweet and virginal good girl is often colourless and insipid, creating a greater degree of audience identification with the full-blooded bad girl. It was the bad girl, Margaret Lockwood, who was the top female star at the British box office in 1943, 1944, 1945 and 1946, suggesting a degree of identification by the fans that did not occur with, say, Patricia Roc, the long-suffering good girl of *The Wicked Lady.* Similarly it was James Mason, the smouldering, sadistic cad, who was the top British male box office attraction from 1944 to 1947.

Other Gainsborough films elaborated the debate over the role and nature of the new woman in even greater detail. *They Were Sisters* (1944) featured the divergent careers and fortunes of three middle-class sisters, played by Phyllis Calvert, Anne Crawford and Dulcie Gray. Each provided a different role model. Dulcie Gray was the pathetic, tyrannized drudge, driven to her death by a ruthless, domineering husband, the inevitable James Mason. Anne Crawford was the flighty adultress with a string of lovers and an adoring husband who eventually divorces her. These alternatives, what might be called the Victorian and the Bohemian, are rejected by the film in favour of the third, incarnated by Phyllis Calvert, the sensible, balanced, decent and capable sister with an understanding husband who is partner and helpmate. They inherit the children of the other sisters' disastrous marriages and are clearly seen as the ideal embodiment of stable monogamous marriage, shared responsibility and enlightened parenthood.

The two rejected role models from *They Were Sisters* are combined in the splendid *Madonna of the Seven Moons* (1944). For this film Phyllis Calvert plays a beautiful Italian woman with a split personality. Part of the time she is a repressed, saintly, do-gooding banker's wife with no real life or mind of her own. But from time to time she vanishes to take up another existence as a sensuous, wanton gangster's moll, the plaything of swarthy, virile, knife-wielding Stewart Granger. In the end, the conflict of personalities is resolved by her death, saving the life of her daughter, Patricia Roc, who represents a type of healthy modern womanhood. She smokes, drinks and wears shorts, and has a natural, easy, unPuritanical manner but she also marries her boyfriend, a British diplomat, and settles for monogamy and stability.

The corollary of these cinematic depictions of emancipation is the dramatization of the situation from which women were escaping. There were therefore during the war a number of notable films, not usually from Gainsborough, which dramatized the repressive role of the Victorian *pater familias* whose despotic domination over wife and family invariably leads to tragedy, madness and death. In this vein were such memorable productions as *Gaslight* (1940), *Hatter's Castle* (1941) and *Pink String and Sealing Wax* (1945).

But the Gainsborough melodramas not only highlighted sex, they also dealt with the thorny question of class. Margaret Lockwood's anti-heroines in for instance *The Wicked Lady* and *The Man in Grey* were usually penniless or low-born girls who turned to crime to rise in society. Even the pure heroines, like Phyllis Calvert in *Fanny by Gaslight,* are sometimes from humble backgrounds which prevent them marrying the men they love because of class barriers. The villains in such films, men like Lord Rohan and Lord Manderstoke, both played by James Mason, are the worst kind of aristocratic cads and seducers. The clear implication of the films is that social change and a levelling of the barriers is needed. Indeed, one character in *Fanny by Gaslight* actually says: 'In a hundred years this kind of class distinction won't exist any more'. *The Man in Grey* is told in flashback, framed by a modern day sequence in which Phyllis Calvert and Stewart Granger, whose Regency ancestors were separated in part for class reasons, appear to be on the point of consummating the romance.

This is the sort of idea that was coming to be expressed more and more during the war. The notorious early wartime slogan 'Your courage, your cheerfulness, your resolution, will bring us victory', which only emphasized social divisions, was replaced by the deliberate promotion of the concept of 'The People's War'. How far class barriers fell is still debated, but there is no doubt that contemporary observers believed this to be happening, so that George Orwell could write in 1944:

> The obvious class differences still surviving in England astonish foreign observers. But they are far less marked, and far less real, than they were 30 years ago. People of different social origins, thrown together during the war in the armed forces, or the factories or offices, or as firewatchers and Home Guards were able to mingle more easily than they did in the 1914—18 war . . . We are not justified in assuming that class distinctions are actually disappearing. The essential social structure of England is still almost what it was in the 19th century, but real differences between man and man are obviously diminishing, and this fact is grasped and welcomed by people who only a few years ago were clinging desperately to their social prestige.[63]

Any discussion of sex and class had always been treated with the utmost caution by the film censors. There was some relaxation during the war, a relaxation which at last allowed the filming of Walter Greenwood's Depression classic *Love on the Dole*, which had been kept off the screen during the 1930s. But the use of stylized Regency or Restoration settings enabled Gainsborough to highlight current preoccupations without inviting censorial interference.

It is perhaps not too fanciful to suggest that one important reason why audiences liked Gainsborough melodramas was because they spoke to them about the changing nature of women's role in society and the inequities of a hidebound class system, albeit in highly coloured and highly charged surroundings. Once the war was over, the servicemen were demobilized and the great female workforce disbanded, there was a gradual return to a more traditional role for women as wives and mothers. This was matched by a gradual drift away from the mood of radicalism which had elected Attlee's post-war Labour government to the greater conservatism which heralded 13 years of Tory rule. We can perhaps see the beginning of this change of national mood in the gradual decline in popularity of the Gainsborough melodramas in the late Forties. Even more paradigmatic is the fact that in 1947 gutsy anti-heroine Margaret Lockwood was overtaken as top female star at the British box office by the more refined and genteel Anna Neagle, who had captured the public's favour with such nostalgic celebrations of the class system as *The Courtneys of Curzon Street* and *Spring in Park Lane*. Miss Neagle was to hold that position for the next six years and by the time she had relinquished it Winston Churchill was back at 10 Downing Street and the age of affluence was about to replace the age of austerity.

NOTES

1   Jeffrey Richards, *The Age of the Dream Palace*, London, 1984, pp. 257—72.
2   *The Times*, 26 May 1941.
3   *New Statesman*, 21 May 1941; *Observer* review, reprinted in C. A. Lejeune, *Chestnuts in her Lap*, London, 1947, pp. 57—8.
4   *Monthly Film Bulletin* 8, February 1941, p. 14.
5   *Time and Tide*, 31 May 1941.
6   INF 1/724.
7   INF 1/867.
8   Ian MacLaine, *Ministry of Morale*, London, 1979, p. 150.
9   *The Cinema*, 12 March 1941.
10 *The Times*, 5 March 1941.
11 *Kinematograph Weekly*, 24 July 1941.
12 *Daily Mail*, 4 July 1942.
13 George Malcolm Thomson, *Lord Castlerosse: His Life and Times*, London, 1973, pp. 156—7.
14 *Kinematograph Weekly*, 20 November 1941.
15 Margaret Morley, *Larger than Life: a biography of Robert Morley*, London, 1979, pp. 97—8 (on the closed set); *Evening News*, 3 July 1942 (on Donat's illness).
16 John Mills, *Up in the Clouds, Gentlemen, Please*, London, 1980, p. 174.
17 Letter from Sidney Gilliat to author, 4 December 1984.
18 Geoff Brown, *Launder and Gilliat*, London, 1977, p. 104.
19 Michael Foot, *Aneurin Bevan: vol. I (1897—1945)*, London, 1962, pp. 300—1.
20 Harold Nicolson, *Diaries and Letters 1939—45*, (ed. Nigel Nicolson), London, 1967, p. 149.
21 Dr Stephen Taylor, *A Review of Some Conclusions arising out of a year of Home Intelligence Reports*, October 1941; Home Intelligence Report 176, Appendix, INF 1/292.
22 Letter from Sidney Gilliat to author, 4 December 1984.
23 Report of Planning Committee on Home Morale Campaign, 21 June 1940, INF 1/849.
24 Report on Home Morale Campaign.
25 MoI Policy Committee Paper 33, INF 1/848. It is only fair to point out that the parallels between the Napoleonic Wars and the Second World War were much in the minds of commentators. *Time and Tide* (1 March 1941) ran an unsigned article entitled *A Lesson from History: the Invasion Projects of 1803—1805*, pointing out the parallels. Also the right-wing historian Sir

Arthur Bryant wrote two popular volumes of history, *The Years of Endurance 1793—1802*, London, 1942, and *The Years of Victory 1802—1812*, London, 1944, drawing similar parallels.

26   Michael Balfour, *Propaganda in War 1939—45*, London, 1979, p. 249.
27   *News Chronicle*, 4 July 1942.
28   *Daily Mirror*, 3 July 1942.
29   *The Scotsman*, 2 July 1942.
30   *Evening News*, 3 July 1942.
31   *Sight and Sound* 11, Autumn 1942, p. 41.
32   *Kinematograph Weekly*, 28 May 1942.
33   *Kinematograph Weekly*, 18 June 1942.
34   *Today's Cinema*, 17 June 1942.
35   *Daily Sketch*, 3 July 1942.
36   *Daily Express*, 4 July 1942.
37   Paul Addison, *The Road to 1945*, London, 1975, p. 231.
38   *Truth*, 17 July 1942.
39   *Kinematograph Weekly*, 14 January 1943.
40   Dilys Owen, *The Way to the Stars*, London, n.d., appendix.
41   James Lees-Milne, *Ancestral Voices*, London, 1984, p. 83.
42   *Today's Cinema*, 30 October 1946.
43   Charles Oakley, *Where We Came In*, London, 1964, p. 167.
44   On Nazi historical films, see Jeffrey Richards, *Visions of Yesterday*, London, 1973; David Welch, *Propaganda and the German Cinema 1933—1945*, London, 1983; Erwin Leiser, *Nazi Cinema*, London, 1974; Julian Petley, *Capital and Culture: German Cinema 1933—45*, London, 1979.
45   Welch, *Propaganda and the German Cinema*, p. 164.
46   Welch, *Propaganda and the German Cinema*, p. 176.
47   Leiser, *Nazi Cinema*, p. 162.
48   Petley, *Capital and Culture*, p. 105.
49   *World Film News*, February 1937, pp. 6—7.
50   *Kinematograph Weekly*, 9 January 1936. It is worth noting that the only British wartime 'culture hero' film, *The Great Mr Handel* (1942), was a resounding flop.
51   Alan Wood, *Mr Rank*, London, 1952, pp. 145—6.
52   On Gainsborough films see Robert Murphy and Sue Aspinall (ed.), *Gainsborough Melodrama*, BFI Dossier 18, London, 1983. The ending of production of serious historical morale boosters coincides with the adoption of a new policy by the MoI after the advent, in July 1941, of Brendan Bracken as Minister. Bracken reported to the cabinet on 10 April 1942: 'We must stop appealing to the public or lecturing at it. One makes it furious, the other resentful'. So explanation replaced exhortation as the keynote of MoI policy and the historical film as vehicle for exhortation was rendered redundant. Indeed, it was even gently mocked in the MoI film *The Volunteer*, directed by Michael Powell, in 1944. (MacLaine, *Ministry of Morale*, pp. 256—7.)
53   *Manchester Guardian*, 3 January 1946.
54   *Daily Graphic*, 11 October 1946.
55   *Observer*, 7 March 1948.
56   John Ellis, 'Art, Culture and Quality', *Screen*, Autumn 1978, pp. 9—49.

57 Letter to the author, 4 July 1984. The writer wishes to remain anonymous.
58 Stewart Granger, *Sparks Fly Upwards*, London, 1982, p. 92; David Shipman, *The Great Movie Stars — the Golden Years*, London, 1970, p. 379.
60 Mass-Observation, *The Journey Home*, London, 1944, pp. 61—2.
61 Raynes Minns, *Bombers and Mash*, London, 1980.
62 Gershon Legman, *Love and Death*, New York, 1949, p. 58.
63 George Orwell, *Collected Essays, Journalism and Letters*, vol. 3, Harmondsworth, 1982, pp. 38—9. The same phenomenon was noted by foreign observers, such as American journalists, see for instance Stephen Laird and Walter Graebner, *Hitler's Reich and Churchill's Britain*, London, 1942, p. 24; Ralph Ingersoll, *Report on England*, London, 1941, pp. 231—2. It is put in its historical context in Arthur Marwick, *Class: Image and Reality*, London, 1980, pp. 213—30.

8
Signs of the Times

Thunder Rock

On Tuesday 22 July 1941 the executive sub-committee of the MoI's Home Planning Committee, the body responsible for initiating and co-ordinating propaganda on the home front, was deliberating, among other things, whether it should financially support theatrical productions as part of its domestic propaganda effort. It was not the first time the question had been raised. On previous occasions the matter had usually provoked a negative response, and this occasion proved little different. Despite, or perhaps because of, the existence of a brand new Minister of Information, Brendan Bracken, who was but two days into the job, the topic was broached and over in no time. It was agreed once again that 'It was not the Ministry's business to provide financial backing for plays'.[1]

The decision was an unsurprising one in most respects and it is not difficult to fathom the reasons why the sub-committee pursued the policy it did. The MoI's major function, after all, was to mobilize the population at large and its output was generally geared towards reaching as many people as possible at any one time. In comparison with, say, the cinema or the radio, the theatre was rarely a medium with obvious mass appeal. This was especially true of the serious theatre which, for all its artistic achievements, drew its support in the main from the cultural confines of a narrowly based and somewhat elitist audience. Furthermore, the MoI was not in the business of acting as a theatrical impresario. It was not accustomed to the role nor fitted for the task. In the context of a Britain waging total war, it is little wonder that the commercial theatre was left to make its own way, as it had always done. It could be relied upon to do its patriotic bit. If, for its part, the theatre produced hits on the scale that 'Chu Chin Chow' had turned out to be in the First World War, then all very well and good. Theatregoers would be entertained and spirits lifted. But the MoI was not inclined to interfere unduly and the theatre was clearly not afforded a high priority rating on the MoI's shopping list for regular outlets.

Charleston (Michael Redgrave) tends the lighthouse lamp on the isolated Thunder Rock *where he has retreated in disgust with a world hell bent on destruction and war.*

Indeed, in one way the surprise was that the sub-committee meeting on 22 July 1941 had bothered to raise the topic of financial backing for plays at all, since it seemed merely to confirm a policy which had been in force from the outset of the war. But then, of course, as is often the case, the minutes of the meeting did not tell the whole story, and, as one might expect, they hinted at more than they revealed. Doubtless the decision not to provide financial backing for plays was being reaffirmed precisely because it had not proved possible to adhere to it strictly throughout and because it might usefully serve to deter many a theatre manager from thinking that the MoI was little more than 'a soft touch'. The Home Planning Committee was nothing if not a pragmatic body, and the non-interventionist stand which it sought to adopt on theatrical matters very sensibly masked the fact that it did not always turn out to be quite so hard and fast in practice. Certainly, there is evidence to show that it made at least one significant intervention to ensure that a particular play reached as wide an audience as possible.

In the case of Robert Ardrey's play of 'Thunder Rock', for instance, the MoI obviously decided that it warranted some measure of financial support. The play opened on 18 June 1940 at the Neighbourhood Theatre, a small two hundred seat theatre in South Kensington. A month later, on 18 July, Sir Kenneth Clark reported to the Home Planning Committee that 'arrangements had been made for official financial support to enable the play "Thunder Rock" to be brought to a West End theatre'. The point was made that 'This was to be regarded as a contribution to home morale and did not constitute a precedent' and that 'The fact of official support was confidential'.[2] On the same day, with Treasury authority, the MoI invested £600, as against some £400 forthcoming from the firm of H.M. Tennent, to meet the production costs of transferring the play to the Globe theatre.[3] The play was subsequently transferred to the Globe at the end of July.

What had happened, quite simply, was that when the play first opened it had turned out to be a considerable success with audiences and critics alike. James Agate described it as 'a play infinitely superior in craftsmanship, intellectual interest, pure theatre and entertainment value to anything the commercial theatre can offer in these heartsearching days'.[4] The *News Chronicle* said it was 'A tonic to the mind, and a bath to the spirit'.[5] And Michael Redgrave, who starred in the play, recalled, 'The critics heaped praise on us, as a sort of national asset', and, 'our audience found a play which seemed perfectly to catch their mood'.[6]

More significantly, among the first audiences for the play were Diana and Duff Cooper, and it was they who urged Redgrave to transfer the play to a larger theatre. In particular, Duff Cooper, who had become Minister of Information on 12 May 1940, promised to do all he could to help. A meeting was immediately arranged between Redgrave and Treasury officials at which it was reiterated that 'Mr Cooper is very interested in your play'. The question of financial support was discussed and further promises exacted, though it was stressed that 'if this comes up in the House, we should simply deny it'. But the money was forthcoming and the play transferred to the Globe, where it proved 'so successful that the Treasury was repaid'.[7]

Clearly, in this instance, Duff Cooper's personal intervention was instrumental in securing the necessary funds, but what was it about this play from an obscure American playwright — a play which had closed after just 23 performances on its New York premiere in November 1939 — that prompted Duff Cooper to make such an intervention and to see it as 'a contribution to home morale'? Why did it stir the critics sufficiently for them to regard it as some kind of 'national asset' in the difficult days of summer 1940? What 'mood' did it capture?

Robert Ardrey, born in 1908 and educated at Chicago University where he learned his craft under Thornton Wilder's tutelage, was very much influenced by what he described as 'the theatre of social protest' that emerged fitfully in America during the mid to late 1930s. Clifford Odets'

1935 hit 'Waiting for Lefty' made a profound impression on Ardrey and inspired him to write 'Star Spangled', his first play which opened to moderate success in 1936. Though by no means a Marxist, he was increasingly drawn to that lively coterie of left-wing artists and intellectuals which constituted the Group Theatre, a dissident offspring of the Theatre Guild, that was to last, despite constant in-fighting and back-biting, from 1933 to 1940.[8]

Ardrey's second play, 'Casey Jones', was in fact produced by the Group Theatre, with Elia Kazan directing. It opened in New York in 1938, at much the same time that his third play, 'How To Get Tough About It', was being given its premiere. Both flopped, but to have two plays opening simultaneously in New York was sufficient to recommend Ardrey to Samuel Goldwyn, who hired him as a scriptwriter and shipped him off to Hollywood. Ardrey's sojourn in Hollywood was disastrous and short-lived and he returned East to continue his play writing.

He spent the autumn of 1938 on the Atlantic seaboard of the island of Nantucket. 'Every night I passed the lighthouse at Sankaty Head', he recalled, and it was there he conceived the idea of 'Thunder Rock': 'The Munich Crisis reigned on the radio and in the newspapers that came daily from the mainland. When the resolution of the crisis favoured peace for our time, like many another I found myself overwhelmingly convinced that war was inevitable'.[9]

The play was written in the winter and spring of 1939, on a visit to New Orleans, and was rewritten in Connecticut during the summer of 1939. Elia Kazan was greatly taken by the play and promised to stage it as quickly as possible, while its issues were still 'relevant'. In the event, Harold Clurman, the Group Theatre's founder, took on the direction of the production, though Kazan took the helm when Clurman fell ill a few days before its premiere. It opened at the Mansfield Theatre, New York, on 14 November 1939, with Luther Adler in the leading role of Charleston, the lighthouse keeper. To the immense surprise of everybody concerned with the production, it closed after little more than a week's run. Relevance was to be the play's undoing in an America still at peace, and where feelings of isolationism were strong.

Some considerable time after the event, Robert Ardrey gave the following reasons for the play's initial failure in the United States:

> No one believed that there was a war. Particularly in our most intellectual circles, it was fashionable to assert that the Powers had made a deal, that the little shooting then taking place was window-dressing, and that there would never be a war.[10]

And then, readily acknowledging the benefits of hindsight, he proceeded to analyse what he felt were the play's strengths and weaknesses:

I have come to believe it an imperfect play. Its cast includes no villains, the antagonist must exist in the minds of the audience. If the audience is cynical or satisfied or subjected to no sense of pressing danger, then the play does not exist. But if the audience is haunted by lethal fear or spiritual despair, then the play will be as large as the fear is intense. It is strictly a play for desperate people.[11]

Despite the play's dismal failure in New York, Herbert Marshall, then the director of the Neighbourhood Theatre, felt it had potential as far as London audiences were concerned. He sent it on to Michael Redgrave, who when he got down to looking at it during an enforced convalescence in May 1940 thought it 'one of the most exciting plays I had read'. He was especially attracted to the part of Charleston, the protagonist of the piece.

Charleston's tortured imagination conjures up images of industrial hardship for workers like Briggs (Frederick Cooper) in mid-nineteenth century Britain . . .

B·B·1·86.

. . . and of imprisonment for Ellen Kirby (Barbara Mullen) who campaigned for women's rights.

The play follows several classical lines of dramatic exposition, not least in its careful and confined delineation of time and place. It is set throughout in the Thunder Rock lighthouse on Lake Michigan and takes place over three days in the summer months immediately preceding the outbreak of war in 1939. David Charleston, an American, has retreated there in disgust with a world which appears to be drifting towards war, and weary of his seemingly futile life as a journalist and political commentator. He is intent upon isolation, seclusion, contemplation and a quiet if ordered life as the lighthouse keeper. He is determined that the outside world should not intrude upon his existence if he can help it. He will have nothing to do with it, scorns contact with it and prefers not to have any books or a radio around the place to remind him of its turmoil.

This proves difficult, however, and the play's essential message that 'No man is an island' is emphasized over and over again by a succession of characters, real and imagined, who parade before him and attempt to shake him out of his complacency. At the outset, Charleston's privacy is invaded by the arrival of Inspector Flanning, who brings supplies and does his monthly check to see that everything is functioning properly. But Charleston is nothing if not efficient and Flanning knows full well that he will have no problems on that score, even if he does not understand what motivates the lone keeper, whose book on European affairs he picked up cheaply in a drug-store. With Flanning comes Streeter, an aviator for the lighthouse service, and an old friend of Charleston's.

Charleston and Streeter reminisce at first, but their meeting serves as the first significant clash of ideas in a play which is given over almost exclusively, and unusually, to a discussion of ideas and competing philosophies of life. What begins as an amiable chat soon deteriorates into a full-blooded confrontation when Streeter reveals that he is shortly to give up his job for the sake of joining the Chinese in their fight against Japanese aggression. 'I can't just stand by and watch', argues Streeter. He feels the need to be involved, to do something. Charleston, by contrast, believes that he has been involved enough already to know that there is no point in 'crusading'. He is disenchanted, disillusioned and pessimistic: 'I say the world's hell-bent for destruction . . . Society itself is a lost cause . . . For all humanity, I make one wish — let the people die off fast'.[12]

It is a bleak vision of the world and once the visitors depart, the discussion over it continues in earnest, but this time it takes place within the mind of Charleston himself. To lend substance to this conflict of ideas, however, and to give credence to the many arguments, Ardrey usefully employed the dramatic device of filling the stage with creatures of Charleston's tortured if lively imagination. In his solitude, Charleston creates a fantasy world of ghosts. He communes with them, they challenge and confront him. They personify and personalize the debate going on within him. They are the ghosts of people who drowned some ninety years earlier, immigrants to America, fleeing from poverty or persecution in Europe. A plaque in the lighthouse commemorating their death in 1849 on the packet Land o' Lakes, which went down near Thunder Rock, gives rise to David Charleston's flights of fantasy. He proceeds to imagine what they might have been like as people, what it was that they were escaping from, and what their hopes and aspirations were. He chooses as his confidant the captain of the vessel, Captain Joshua, and together they view the figments of David Charleston's fertile imagination.

Initially, the audience is given only a superficial and slight impression of the chosen band of passengers, five of them in all. But Joshua chides David for making them 'silly and shallow' and accuses him of being 'as afraid to face my people and my times as you are to face your own'. Thereafter, he delves deeper into their characters. There is Briggs, a working man from the English potteries, who dreams of escaping poverty, illiteracy and poor health in gold-rich California but who recognizes he will probably not make it that far; Miss Kirby, a fighter for women's rights in her home country, who now hopes she might just be able to attract a husband among the Mormon community in Salt Lake City; Dr Kurtz, 'the tragedy of greatness unachieved', a pioneer of anaesthetics in Vienna who was hounded out of the city because of ignorance and superstition and who will settle instead for a quiet practice in Wisconsin; his daughter, Melanie, filled with bitterness at the expense of her former courage and optimism; and his wife, Anne Marie, who remembers only the happiness of times past. Now, as Kurtz puts it, they are 'groping about in an alien land for all the second prizes — wealth, peace of mind'.

Charleston rebukes them for their despair and for giving up. He tells them of the advances that have been made since their death and recites the names of great men and women who have successfully fought the battles against exploitation, ignorance and prejudice. In so doing he comes to a greater awareness of his own condition and spiritual malaise. He discovers new strength and hope.

At the play's end there is considerable emphasis upon finding the right 'leaders' and the men and women of 'courage, and honesty, and vision'. David finally switches on the radio that Flanning left behind, only to hear that Poland had been invaded, war was about to be declared in London and that the station will be holding a symposium on the subject, 'Can America avoid the impending European conflict?'. In a powerful speech delivered to Streeter, now also returned as a ghost, Charleston says:

> We've reason to believe that wars will cease one day, but only if we stop them ourselves. Get into it to get out of it, Street. Problems can only be solved by doing them. We've got to create a new order out of the chaos of the old, and already its shape is becoming clear. A new order that will eradicate oppression, unemployment, starvation and wars as the old order eradicated plague and pestilences. And that is what we've got to fight and work for, Street; not fighting for fighting's sake, but to make a new world of the old. That's our job, Street, and we can do it.

At the last, when Flanning returns to make his regular check, David announces that he is resigning, leaving the lighthouse service, and Thunder Rock: he is returning to the fray.

It is little wonder the play made such a powerful impression on those who saw it during the summer of 1940, especially on its opening night audience of 18 June. It was, as Ardrey so rightly noted, 'strictly a play for desperate people', and it could not have been better suited to its times. Barely a month or so earlier the country had experienced a leadership crisis, the departure of one prime minister, Chamberlain, in virtual disgrace, and the arrival of another, Churchill, in whom so many hopes were placed. At the end of May, it had witnessed the turmoil of the Dunkirk evacuation, with the British army in seeming disarray. J. B. Priestley, in the first of his radio 'Postscripts' on 5 June, emphasized the measure of victory snatched from the jaws of defeat — 'the way in which, when apparently all was lost, so much was gloriously retrieved' — with an inspiring little talk in which he described Dunkirk as 'another English epic', and paid homage to the 'little boats', the 'Queens', the 'Belles', the holiday steamers, that 'made an excursion to hell and came back glorious'.[13] Then, on 18 June, on the second night after the most recent setback, the fall of France, here was a play which offered a message of restrained hope in the midst of apparent despair. It is not difficult to appreciate why the play was so well received on its first night, among an admittedly small circle of theatregoers.

But to understand whatever success 'Thunder Rock' enjoyed, one can only see the play in the context of its immediate circumstances. Ardrey was not a great playwright and this was not a great play. Neither his nor his play's reputation have survived beyond the war and it is now little more than a museum piece. None of his subsequent efforts enjoyed much British success. But he clearly did have something meaningful and

Charleston's own experiences as a radical journalist in the 1930s brought him into conflict with the directors of the Daily Argus, *who favoured appeasing the emergent Fascist powers, and with the editor (Miles Malleson), who cut his copy.*

pertinent to say to British audiences in that summer of 1940. He hit a note which found its echo in the work of others who came to share his view of war as 'the midwife of social progress'. It is interesting, for example, to compare some of the sentiments expressed in Charleston's final speech with the following extract from one of J. B. Priestley's 'Postscripts', broadcast on 21 July 1940, just over a month after Ardrey's play had opened, when Priestley's inspiration gave way to idealism:

> This bring us to the second, and more truthful, way of looking at this war. That is, to regard this war as one chapter in a tremendous history, the history of a changing world, the breakdown of one vast system and the building up of another and better one. In this view of things Hitler and Mussolini have been thrown up by this breakdown of a world system. It's as if an earthquake cracked the walls and floors of a house and strange nuisances of things, Nazists and Fascists, came running out of the woodwork. We have to get rid of these intolerable nuisances but not so that we can go *back* to anything: there's nothing that really worked that we can go back to. But so that we can go forward, without all the shouting and stamping and bullying and murder, and really plan and build up a nobler world in which ordinary, decent folk can not only find justice and security but also beauty and delight . . . I tell you, there is stirring in us now, a desire which could soon become a controlled but passionate determination to remodel and recreate this life of ours, to make it the glorious beginning of a new world order, so that we might soon be so fully and happily engrossed in our great task that if Hitler and his gang suddenly disappeared we'd hardly notice that they'd gone. We're even now the hope of free men everywhere, but soon we could be the hope and lovely dawn of the whole wide world.[14]

Furthermore, while not a Briton himself, of course, Ardrey was obviously doing with his one play what few other British playwrights of the day were doing. Indeed, one eminent critic, Harold Hobson, who was present when 'Thunder Rock' was first shown, roundly castigates British playwrights, in his 'personal' history of British theatre, for noticeably failing to provide what he provided — 'where he inspired, they depressed'; he singles Ardrey out as being the 'sole inspirer'.[15]

By the same token, the special and pressing circumstances of the time account for the MoI's particular interest in the play and explain why, above and beyond Duff Cooper's personal intervention, the MoI was willing to give it financial support to move into a larger theatre. As the former Secretary to the Home Planning Committee, Michael Balfour, recalls:

> The grant to 'Thunder Rock' needs to be seen as an example of the kind of thing which could happen in the summer of 1940 and at few other times. The prevailing spirit was that no holds must be barred, no sacred cows preserved, if it was a question of getting something done which someone thought might help to avoid defeat. If we did avoid defeat, everyone would

be too relieved to ask awkward questions; if we didn't, there'd be nobody to ask questions of'.[16]

The play enjoyed a successful run at the Globe, with Walter Hudd eventually taking over the part of Charleston from Redgrave. Subsequently, American interest in the play revived somewhat and it was afforded a prestigious production in the American sector of Berlin. Within six weeks of VE day, it was running in Vienna and by the autumn of 1945 it was being presented in Budapest and Prague.

Almost inevitably, however, the play had also awakened interest in film circles. The Boulting brothers proceeded to sign a contract in the autumn of 1941 whereby their Charter Films would produce the film for Metro-Goldwyn-Mayer on a budget of £63,500, the entire amount to be provided by M-G-M, who would then have distribution rights throughout the world.[17] Roy Boulting was to direct and John Boulting to produce. Several actors were contracted to repeat the roles they had created in the original stage production, with Redgrave as Charleston, Frederick Valk as Dr Kurtz and Barbara Mullen (a later addition to the stage cast) as Miss Kirby. James Mason and Lilli Palmer were brought in to add star quality to the parts of Streeter and Melanie respectively, and Finlay Currie brought his wealth of talent as a character actor to bear in the role of Captain Joshua.

Jeffrey Dell and Bernard Miles were engaged to write the screenplay. Miles had a particular affinity for the play since he too had been a member of the original cast, in the part of Briggs, and he was also familiar with the way the Boultings worked, having acted in two of their earlier wartime efforts — as the kindly concentration camp SS guard in their feature film of *Pastor Hall,* in 1940, and as a member of the Home Guard with visions of a better Britain after the war was won in their MoI short of *The Dawn Guard,* in 1941 (yet another fine example and exponent of the 'new world we are fighting to build' ideology).[18]

The screenplay was ready in the spring of 1942. It was presented for pre-production scrutiny to the British Board of Film Censors on 17 March 1942. Both the readers passed it as 'suitable for production as a film', though one of them took offence at the actual words with which Streeter admonished Charleston for isolating himself on Thunder Rock and wished to see the line, 'pick your nose, examine your navel', deleted.[19] Subsequently, the Boultings were given a 'special release' from the services to get on with the production. They spent ten weeks filming in the Denham studios, and once completed the film was shown to the trade in September 1942. It was given a London premiere at the very beginning of December 1942 and put on general release in February 1943.

Though it remained essentially faithful to Ardrey's original text and it retained much of his dialogue, albeit understandably truncated and occasionally transposed, the resulting film is as interesting for its points of difference as for anything else. The times had changed and the medium of

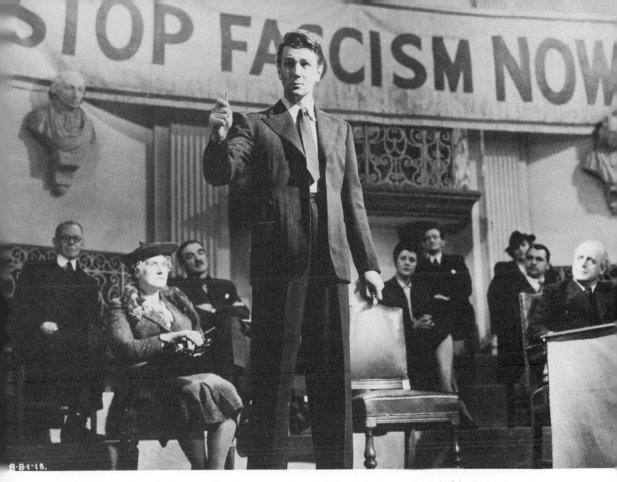

He was compelled to embark on a personal crusade to warn of the dangers of Fascism.

communication was different. Both the scriptwriters and the production team very wisely appreciated that, of necessity, the film would need to be opened out to accommodate the transition from one medium to another and to incorporate additional features born of new found circumstances. A lot had happened in two years, and clearly the thinking was that if the film was to prove as relevant as the play had been, then further elaboration upon its themes was required.

Some of the additions were pretty straightforward and obvious. There was a lot more in the way of scene setting for one thing. At the film's outset, before turning the focus of attention upon the Thunder Rock lighthouse, there is a snappily edited prelude in the offices of the lighthouse service as the company wonder who it is that is consistently failing to cash his pay cheques, before they hit upon Charleston. Charleston, for his part, is made into an Englishman and each of the ghostly passengers is afforded a little potted history to explain their background. The hardship of Briggs's life in the potteries is shown and the difficulties of Ellen Kirby's life as she seeks to escape a repressive father and a narrow-minded fiancée, only to suffer several periods in jail at the hands of a harsh legal system which will brook no opposition from her cause. Dr Kurtz's character is fleshed out with scenes which depict him administering anaesthesia to save a patient, being censured by a medical board of inquiry when his efforts prove unsuccessful, and subsequently being stoned by a howling mob and hounded out of Vienna. Melanie and Anne Marie are similarly developed and some play is made of the immigrants' difficulties in transit with a dramatic storm on the lakes serving as a fateful highlight.

In short, much of the additional material was there to aid character development, to eke out the plot and to provide a visually arresting film. But there was more besides, and by far the most interesting additional sequence occurs when Captain Joshua confronts Charleston with lacking the courage to face his own time. In his defence, Charleston produces his book, *Darkening World,* and a visual montage follows in which the audience is treated to glimpses of his career in the making, during the turbulence of the 1930s.

The purpose of the sequence was clear. The montage was intended to lend added substance to Ardrey's vision of Charleston as a committed and campaigning commentator. Charleston was meant to represent and to epitomize 'that brilliant school of radical foreign correspondents, mainly British and American, which dominated the international press between the wars . . . plugging the theory of the "evitable war" from the early 1930s onwards'.[20] In addition, it was intended to depict the conflict which had ensued when the sympathies of those correspondents had sometimes put them at odds with the newspapers they served, by no means an uncommon occurrence.

But beyond the general nods in the direction of Ardrey's inspiration, the sequence was also invested with specific meaning as far as the British context was concerned. Turning Charleston into an Englishman was only part of it. Further allusions were evident, as indeed were the sympathies of the film's creators — Dell, Miles and the Boulting brothers. They were seeking to capitalize upon the prevalent mood of disillusion with the policy of appeasement and all it stood for.[21] *Their* Charleston was meant to be a combination of the likes of G.L. Steer, G.E.R. Gedye and Norman Ebbutt. The fictitious books they ascribe to their Charleston, *Darkening World* and *Report from Inside* — there was only one mentioned in the Ardrey play and it was never referred to by title — were meant to stand comparison with such real works as Robert Dell's *Germany Unmasked* (1934) and *The Geneva Racket* (1940), Douglas Reed's *Insanity Fair* (1938) and *Disgrace Abounding* (1939), Edgar Mowrer's *Germany Puts the Clock Back* (1938), and, ultimately, 'Cato's' *Guilty Men* (1940). In the film's carefully detailed and finely woven world of allusion, furthermore, the conflict which inevitably occurs between Charleston and his paper's board of directors, over the matter of cutting his copy, can only be read as taking place at *The Times* (for all that it is coyly referred to as the '*Daily Argus*').

The retrospective sequence delves into Charleston's *Darkening World* and by a mixture of acted fictional scenes and actuality newsreel material highlights the major international incidents of the 1930s. It begins in 1931 at the League of Nations ('Chapter 1: Scene at Geneva') where David meets 'M. Henri Bouchon' and is assured that hopes for 'a new form of international morality' are high. But all such hopes are dashed when the Japanese delegate reports back to his cabinet that the League is made up of 'too many timid voices' and that Britain and America are hardly likely to act if Japan marches into Manchukuo. Then, Charleston and Streeter happen to find themselves at the Italian frontier when Anthony Eden calls for sanctions to be imposed in the wake of the Italian invasion of Abyssinia ('Chapter 3: Fascist Italy Moves'). Streeter's remark that 'We could do with a few more like Eden' provokes an incident with the border police and lands the two of them with a hefty fine, while their friend, an Italian journalist, is taken off to jail.

The chapter on Spain is dealt with solely by the means of an assemblage of newsreel footage from the Spanish Civil War. Interestingly, however, at one point there is superimposed a *Daily Argus* billboard proclaiming 'Guernica bombed', in what is surely the sequence's first obvious attempt to equate David Charleston's newspaper with *The Times*. (The coverage of Guernica by *The Times* had been the source of much debate in its day. On 28 April 1937, two days after the Basque town had been bombed, it published G. L. Steer's report stating not only that the town had been bombed but also that it had been bombed by German planes which were fighting for Franco's insurgent forces. It thus became, as one historian has commented, the first British newspaper 'to implicate Germany directly in the bombing of Guernica'.[22] The article caused a furore in Germany. Just as significantly, it produced a speedy admission from *The Times* that it had been over-hasty in printing Steer's uncorroborated article.)

Subsequently, Charleston is seen attending a Nazi rally in Germany ('Chapter 10: German Strength') and writing a pro-Churchill report about the might of German rearmament. His worst fears about the 'complacent and comfortable' response being fostered to the looming threat are confirmed in conversation with some French friends — 'We have the Maginot, you have the Channel'. In an attempt to stir people out of their lethargy and, most of all, to get his message across, he returns to London and confronts his editor, who he says has been slashing his articles to pieces — 'Spain, Abyssinia, Austria, concentration camps, German rearmament, the whole sad story'. At a meeting of the board of directors, he is accused of viewing the world through 'left-wing spectacles' and his warnings are greeted with the retort, 'The Fascist nations are young, Charleston. Like puppies they bark a lot, but they won't bite'. The board meeting at the *Daily Argus* could be taking place anywhere and the paper is purposely given the circulation of a popular daily — 1,300,000. But Charleston's major adversaries at the meeting, played by the actors Miles Malleson and Alfred Sangster, are made up in such a way as to bear a striking resemblance to Geoffrey Dawson and Robert Barrington Ward, respectively. It is *The Times* the film is talking about, and the allusion this time is doubtless to the case of Norman Ebbutt. Though, in retrospect, Dawson has been largely exonerated from the charge of cutting Ebbutt's reports, nevertheless, at the time the film was made, it was 'an integral part of the demonology of appeasement that Ebbutt's dispatches from Berlin were censored by Dawson with an eye to appeasing the Nazis'.[23]

Thereafter, Charleston resigns, writes *Report from Inside,* and embarks on a personal lecture tour of Britain with the slogan, 'Britain awake, stop Fascism now'. But his audiences are sparse. Thoroughly disillusioned, he walks into the street and drops into a newsreel theatre. The voice of the Gaumont British News commentator, Ted Emmett, can be heard recounting that 'Nazi tanks enter Sudetenland'.[24] The camera scans the ranks of the cinemagoers. They sit impassive and oblivious, and only break into life when the newsreel ends and is followed by a Popeye cartoon. The world does not care, and David walks out into the night.

In general, then, the retrospective section of the film dealing with Charleston's career served as a vindication of those elements that were broadly anti-Fascist in British circles throughout the 1930s. Its message was very much one of 'Look, they were right all along'. In particular, it served as an indictment against *The Times* for the outspoken support it gave to Neville Chamberlain's policy of appeasement. In this respect, the film found its inspiration in much of the post-appeasement literature of the day, not least the work of Jeffrey Dell's namesake, Robert Dell, a vehement anti-Nazi, whose book, *The Geneva Racket,* which was published in 1940 and reprinted in 1941, was as powerful an anti-*Times* tract as one could expect to find.[25] If Ardrey's play was well suited for Britain in the summer of 1940, then the film which Dell, Miles and the Boultings created was best fitted for Britain in the period which followed immediately thereafter.

Not surprisingly, given that the film was very much a film about ideas, *Thunder Rock* won some acclaim for that alone and it was taken up by the critics on the quality papers in particular. C. A. Lejeune, especially, wrote a long and enthusiastic review for the *Observer:*

> This industry of ours — the industry that so many conspire successfully to keep in its infancy — is beginning to have growing pains. Twice in one season the British studios have engaged the mature mind on equal terms. Twice in one season they have produced a film that is neither pettish, nor infantile, callow nor smartly precocious, a film that seeks neither to distract nor to inflame, but to suggest ideas to those who are willing to receive them. Twice in one season, a British director has seen in the functions of the cinema not its limitations but its freedom. Two months ago we had Noël

Coward's *In Which We Serve.* Now we have the Boulting brothers' version of Ardrey's play 'Thunder Rock'.

Thunder Rock is not an easy film to follow. It makes tough seeing. You have to be in your seats at the beginning, you have to stay till the end, you have to keep your wits alert, to enjoy it. The piece is worth the effort. It hasn't got the simple emotional clues of the Coward film. Possibly the stature is that much smaller in that the appeal is through the brain and not the heart. *Thunder Rock* is not complete without your collaboration. *In Which We Serve* was a statement in itself, human, undeniable, irresistible. Coward, from a long life of technical experience, interpreted an age-old wisdom. The Boultings' piece is younger, sharper, more blundering and more experimental. Frightened of nothing else in this world, it is still a little frightened of simple feeling. But what a stimulus to thought it is, this good, brave, outspoken, unfettered picture . . .

I hope you will like *Thunder Rock.* I like it very much. I like its sincerity and its fervour. I like the assumption of intelligence in the audience. I like the honest acting — Michael Redgrave's, Frederick Valk's, Lilli Palmer's, Barbara Mullen's. I like Mutz Greenbaum's clear-cut camerawork, which will throw a figure askew through a freak of distorted thought, but slip from time present to time past without a fadeout or dissolve. I like the unselfconscious courage of a film that knows what it should do and goes ahead and does it. I like a piece that doesn't give a hang whether it is popular or unpopular. I like its frank speech, so distinct from the mumbo jumbo of the average refined, inoffensive, pie-faced British picture.[26]

The critic for the *Manchester Guardian* was also impressed but had clearly seen the play and was more inclined to draw comparisons between the two:

Robert Ardrey's 'Thunder Rock', still the best new play of the war, has been faithfully translated to the screen by John Boulting, with Roy Boulting as director and editor, and Michael Redgrave in the part he originally played on the stage. The result is a really intelligent film, more moving in parts than anything this country's studios have produced before and more interesting technically than anything since *Citizen Kane* — which, thanks to Mutz Greenbaum's camerawork, it sometimes resembles. Its only fault is that it uses the freedom of photography to diffuse the theme instead of concentrating it . . . In the play this dramatic conflict in one man's mind is confined compactly enough within the blank walls of a lighthouse; in the film it is projected into the world at large. Some day 'Thunder Rock' will inspire a cinematic masterpiece in the *Caligari* tradition. Meantime this version will do very well.[27]

And William Whitebait in the *New Statesman* was similarly inclined to downgrade the film, when compared to the play, and, indeed, to condemn the cinematic insertions:

Whether you go to *Thunder Rock* or not depends on whether you have seen the play. If you have, the film is bound to be disappointing. Not that it isn't tastefully photographed and well acted — better acted, indeed, with Redgrave in his old part, and Bernard Valk, Lilli Palmer, Barbara Mullen assisting, than on the stage. The situation still holds, and the moments of uneasy hovering between real and unreal are smoothed out . . . Charleston's dilemma hasn't been vulgarized or simplified at all; and that is a meritorious achievement. 'It's so elegant, so intelligent', we may murmur, as the film ends and a diversion called *Fraidy Cat* takes its place on the screen.

But still something has been missed. Not the point; that is even underlined. Not the characters; we see more into their lives than we did on the stage, and Charleston himself dives back into pre-war episodes when, so far from escaping, he pursued the world. What has been lost, or partly lost, is that compactness of symbolism, drama, poetry and ideas that made 'Thunder Rock' a remarkable play. The stage jammed everything into the lighthouse, a headpress in which the escapist mind could think its thoughts; this compression has been scattered in the film, which begins with comic scenes in an office, hundreds of miles away, and keeps on opening corridors in different directions. Hitler at a sports meeting in Nuremberg, Vienna a hundred years ago, the doomed boatload crossing Lake Michigan, cafés and conferences in Geneva, Guernica: all these are, so to speak, 'thrown in'.

The effect is not only to slow down the action and create parentheses, but to break the spell by which alone such a drama can succeed. One method, on the screen, would have been to make everything more subjective and to use photographic imagery to take us a step nearer the conflict in Charleston's mind. It mightn't come off, but it is a possibility. The present *Thunder Rock* is a compromise between stage and screen, with the screen honourably losing.[28]

Opinions were divided, then, over the extent of the film's achievements: and the film's reception at the box office did little to settle the matter, since it enjoyed only middling success, though it was reissued in 1947.[29]

As the Boulting brothers were to find with their production of *Fame is the Spur,* just a few years later, it was one thing to invest a film with meaning and a message for the times in which it was made, it was yet another to convince people that the results merited more than just passing attention.[30]

NOTES

1   Planning Committee minutes, 22 July 1941, INF 1/249.
2   Planning Committee minutes, 18 July 1940, INF 1/249.
3   Paul Morley Titmuss, *Commercial Feature Film Production and the Ministry of Information,* unpublished MA Thesis, Polytechnic of Central London, 1982, p.37.
4   Quoted in the introduction by E.R. Wood to Robert Ardrey, *Thunder Rock,* London, 1966, p.16.

5   Quoted in Michael Redgrave, *In My Mind's Eye*, 1983, p.133.

6   Redgrave, *In My Mind's Eye*.

7   Redgrave, *In My Mind's Eye*, p.134.

8   For the relationship between the Group Theatre and the American cinema of the day see William Alexander, *Film on the Left*, Princeton, New Jersey, 1981, *passim*.

9   See the introduction by Robert Ardrey to *Plays of Three Decades*, London, 1968, p.19.

10 Ardrey in *Plays of Three Decades*, p.21.

11 Ardrey in *Plays of Three Decades*, p.22.

12 There were slight changes made for the first British production of Ardrey's text, not least with regard to the ending of the play where Ardrey originally introduced a new character who takes over Charleston's job in much the same disillusioned vein. For the background to the British production see Herbert Marshall's obituary on Robert Ardrey (1908 — 1970) in *The Bulletin of the Center for Soviet and East European Studies*, No. 24, Spring 1980. My thanks to Professor Marshall for providing me with a copy of this and for other information.

13 Reprinted in J.B. Priestley, *All England Listened*, New York, 1967, pp.3 — 7.

14 Priestley, *All England Listened*, pp.51 — 8.

15 Harold Hobson, *Theatre in Britain, 1920 — 1983*, London, 1984, pp.117 — 18.

16 Letter from Michael Balfour to the author, 4 November 1984.

17 Interview with Roy Boulting, 19 November 1984. Roy Boulting recalls that the deal was 'made memorable to us by the fact that we had a producing and directing contract which penalized our company financially in proportion to the sum by which we might exceed the budget figure. We did in fact "go over" by £367, and found ourselves very gratified when Sam Eckman, then head of M-G-M in this country, indicated that he would not exercise his contractual rights, which would have involved our receiving £1,000 less. In all our years in film-making, this was to prove a unique experience.'

18 *The Dawn Guard*, produced by John Boulting, directed by Roy Boulting, and with Percy Walsh and Bernard Miles, was given a theatrical release in January 1941 and a non-theatrical release in March 1941.

19 *British Board of Film Censors Scenario Reports*, 1941 — 3, pp.32 and 32a (17 March 1942; bound volume, British Film Institute Library, London).

20 Quoted in Franklin Reid Gannon, *The British Press and Germany 1936 — 1939*, Oxford, 1971, p.3.

21 See Paul Addison, *The Road to 1945*, London, 1975, pp. 110 — 12, and 127 — 63.

22 Gannon, *The British Press and Germany*, p.113.

23 Gannon, *The British Press and Germany*, p.123. See also the more recent account, Iverach McDonald, *The History of The Times, vol. V: Struggles in War and Peace, 1939 — 1966*, London, 1984.

24 The Gaumont British Newsreel story is not actually seen, doubtless for economy's sake, and does not in fact exist with the commentary as read over the soundtrack. It appears that Ted Emmett wrote a special commentary for the newsreel he is supposedly reading in *Thunder Rock*, though it does combine elements of actual commentaries for stories that were included in GB Issue No. 481, from August 1938, and GB Issue No. 499, from October 1938.

25   It has proved difficult to ascertain whether Jeffrey Dell and Robert Dell were in fact related. According to *Who's Who in the Theatre* (8th revised edition, 1936), Jeffrey Dell was born in 1899 and was the son of John Edward Dell. *Who Was Who Among English and European Authors 1931—1939* (1978) tells us that Robert Dell was born in 1865 and christened Robert Edward Dell.

26   *Observer,* 6 December 1942.

27   *Manchester Guardian,* 6 April 1943.

28   *New Statesman,* 12 December 1942.

29   The American response was equally divided, if James Agee's review in *The Nation* on 4 November 1944, is anything to judge by. He thought the film 'well produced and on the whole very well acted'. 'There were moments when it really moved me', he continued, and 'it is not only on the side of the angels but sometimes takes their side with passion and some eloquence'. He was 'glad of some outspoken virulence against some of the people — those, next to the Nazis, most often blamed — who did most to get this world into this war', but he had reservations about a play which 'came late enough to be safe'. And he concluded: 'To find oneself, and others, approving this sort of intrepid *esprit d'escalier* is not only shaming but frightening'. (Reprinted in *Agee on Film,* New York, 1958, p.122.)

30   Much the same thing happened to the Boultings with their film of *Fame is the Spur* (1947). See the chapter on the film in Jeffrey Richards and Anthony Aldgate, *Best of British: Cinema and Society 1930—1970,* Oxford, 1983, pp.75—87.

9

Naval Cavalcade

In Which We Serve

Noël Coward discovered upon the outbreak of war what others have discovered both before and since — that having a sense of humour, particularly a deadpan sense of humour, can be fatal to one's credibility. People find themselves unable to tell when you are being serious and when not. It makes them feel uncomfortable. It is a matter of convenience for most people to be able to pigeon-hole others, it tidies up the landscape of life; you know where you are. It was just this propensity for one-dimensional role conferral that led some foolish folk to conclude that Coward's play 'Cavalcade' was a cynical piece of topical exploitation or even a spoof rather than what it actually was — a manifestation of a deeply held love of his country.

Like all truly creative people, Coward was a complex being, in whom a variety of emotional and temperamental strands ran side by side and sometimes criss-crossed, creating fascinating paradoxes which undiscerning critics were too often apt to ignore. A censorious sentimentalist, a moralistic cynic, a workaholic playboy, a patriotic hedonist, he simply did not fit any known pigeon-hole. But most complicating of all was his sense of humour. This did not endear him to political activists either of the right or the left, who are often painfully earnest and seem to view a sense of humour as redundant or even subversive, whereas it is in fact nature's secret balancing ingredient, preventing the onset of terminal fanaticism. Coward was to find himself attacked by newspapers and politicians on the left and the right as he tried to 'do his bit' for the war effort. But he was to weather the attacks and to succeed in touching the hearts of the British people at war.[1]

The stock image of the frivolous playboy was reinforced by various unfortunate wartime episodes. The publication of his *Middle East Diary* (1943) gave his concert tour of Allied bases the undeserved air of a de luxe holiday and furthermore caused considerable offence in America by his criticism of two weeping Brooklyn soldiers he encountered in a military hospital. His song 'Don't let's be beastly to the Germans' was intended as a satire on those wanting soft treatment for the enemy: it was taken instead as an endorsement of that policy and raised a storm of protest. His trial on currency offences in 1941 added further fuel to the flames.

The approach of the war had served to crystallize Coward's attitude to his country. He realized quite clearly and decisively that:

> I did love England and all it stood for. I loved its follies and apathies and curious streaks of genius; I loved standing to attention for 'God Save the King'; I loved British courage, British humour and British understatement; I loved the justice, efficiency and even the dullness of British colonial administration. I loved the people — the ordinary, the extraordinary, the good, the bad, the indifferent — and what is more I belonged to that exasperating, weather-sodden little island with its uninspired cooking, its muddled thinking and its unregenerate pride, and it belonged to me whether I liked it or not.[2]

Coward passionately opposed appeasement and detested Chamberlain, its principal champion. This is made clear in Frank Gibbons' fierce anti-appeasement speech in *This Happy Breed* and in the declaration of war sequence in *In Which We Serve* in which Chamberlain is heard saying on the wireless: 'You can imagine what a bitter blow this is to me' and AB John Mills chips in with 'It isn't exactly a bank holiday for us'.

Convinced of the imminence of war, he was anxious to offer his services:

> I knew in my innermost heart that if I were intelligently used by the government, preferably in the field of propaganda, where my creative ability, experience of broadcasting and knowledge of people could be employed, I could probably do something really constructive.[3]

But when he consulted Winston Churchill, then still on the back benches, what he should do to help the armed forces in the event of war, Churchill's advice was 'Go and sing to them, when the guns are firing — that's your job'.[4]

But Coward wanted a more active and participatory role. So he eagerly accepted an offer from Sir Campbell Stuart to set up a British propaganda bureau in Paris, which would liaise with the French Ministry of Information in disseminating Anglo-French propaganda to Germany. Stuart, Lord Northcliffe's right-hand man in the department of enemy propaganda at Crewe House in the First World War and currently chairman of the Imperial Communications Committee, had been brought in by the government in 1938 to plan covert propaganda operations in the event of war. Stuart chose Coward 'not as a playwright, but as a man of great ability who wanted to serve his country in her time of trouble quite properly in some other way than as an actor'.[5] Nevertheless, the fact that Coward, Francophile and French-speaking as he was, was a playwright may have been deemed an extra qualification, if only because the French Minister of Information, Jean Giraudoux, was also a playwright.

Whatever meeting of minds there may have been, however, proved unproductive. Coward was installed in Paris as soon as war was declared and set up his bureau, but little was achieved because of bureaucratic indecisiveness and chronic lack of direction from the top. When it was suggested that the RAF might drop leaflets containing speeches by Mr Chamberlain and Lord Halifax over Germany, Coward tartly reported in a memorandum that there was not going to be time to bore the enemy to death. He was reprimanded. By April 1940, he was so frustrated that he asked Stuart for a change of assignment and was sent to the United States to report on American reactions to the war.

He flew back to England on 9 June 1940, to find that Stuart had been replaced by the incoming Churchill government. The new Minister of Information, Duff Cooper, had nothing in England for Coward to do and suggested that he return to America to continue monitoring attitudes. The Ministry of Information paid for his passage to New York and the British Ambassador in Washington, Lord Lothian, 'assured me that I could be of considerable service if I travelled about the States for a while and talked to key citizens, notably news editors and tycoons in various cities, about England and the British war effort'.[6] This he did at his own expense. But still chafing to do something constructive, he accepted an invitation from the Australian government to visit Australia, make a series of broadcasts about the British war effort and give concerts for the troops and for the Australian Red Cross. Between November 1940 and February 1941 he raised £12,000 for Red Cross charities and broadcast first in Australia and later in New Zealand about the war effort. The broadcasts were subsequently published both in Britain and Australia with proceeds going to the Red Cross.[7] Coward later noted in his autobiography that they prompted 'many letters from people in out-of-the-way places, saying how comforting it had been to hear news of home at first hand.'[8]

Although Coward recorded that the press were on the whole generous to him in Australia and New Zealand, he was under constant attack at home. As Sir Campbell Stuart recalled: 'Coward's was an appointment for which I was much criticized.'[9]

Early in 1940, the 'Peterborough' column of the *Daily Telegraph* reported that Coward had been seen 'sauntering along the Rue Royale in naval uniform'.[10] In fact Coward had refused Stuart's suggestion that he should receive an honorary rank and service uniform in his propaganda job. On 10 March 1940 the *Sunday Pictorial* ran a two-page feature on 'The Civilians in Uniform' with a photograph at the top of young men preparing for action ('They're wearing the uniform which is the pride of the fighting men') and a list of eight prominent civilians whom they accused of masquerading in uniform.[11] Noël Coward was at the top of the list and the newspaper poured scorn on the suggestion that he was working for the

In Which We Serve *was based on the exploits of Lord Louis Mountbatten and his ship* HMS Kelly. *Noël Coward portrayed Mountbatten as briskly authoritative.*

Ministry of Information and said he was merely entertaining the troops. It called for Parliamentary questions about the situation. Coward received many abusive anonymous letters about the matter.

Then, when Duff Cooper sent him to America, a leader in the *Sunday Express* denounced him:

> The despatch of Mr Noël Coward to the States can do nothing but harm. In any event, Mr Coward is not the man for the job. His flippant England — cocktails, countesses, caviare — has gone. A man of the people, more in tune with the new mood of Britain, would be a better proposition for America.[12]

The *Daily Mirror* took up the attack:

> Mr Coward, with his stilted mannerisms, his clipped accent and his vast experience of the useless froth of society, may be making contacts with the American equivalents . . . but as a representative of democracy he's like a plate of caviare in a carman's pull-up.[13]

On 6 August questions were asked in the Commons and critical comment came from all sides of the House — from Conservative Commander Sir Archibald Southby, from Socialist Emanuel Shinwell and from Liberal Edgar Granville. The Parliamentary Private Secretary to the Ministry of Information, Harold Nicolson, defended Coward's despatch to the United States, saying: 'His qualifications are that he possesses a contact with certain sections of opinion which are very difficult to reach through ordinary sources.' But Mr Granville echoed the newspaper comment when he asked: 'Does the Parliamentary Secretary recognize that the gentleman does not appeal to democracy in America and does not represent democracy in this country and will he bring him back to this country?' Captain F.J. Bellenger (Labour) suggested that Coward was just getting out of Britain to save his own skin. 'I think that is grossly unfair' replied Nicolson.[14]

What all this demonstrates is that Coward was still a prisoner of his image. For many he was still the brittle sophisticate, the cynical social butterfly, the world-weary roué with dressing-gown and cigarette holder. He was a figure indistinguishable from the characters he had created when as *enfant terrible* of the West End stage he had shocked some and delighted others with his satirical revue lyrics mocking home, church and Empire and plays about scandalous goings-on in high society. It was an image totally at odds with the new populist spirit abroad in the war. The key figures of the age encapsulating this mood were men who spoke to the people, for the most part in non-metropolitan accents, of what concerned them most closely, men with 'the common touch', like J. B. Priestley, Ernest Bevin, Lord Woolton (known to his officials as 'Uncle Fred'), Dr Charles Hill, 'the Radio Doctor', Tommy Handley and Archbishop William Temple, 'The People's Archbishop'. Coward with his clipped, much imitated self-parody of an upper-class accent was apparently miles removed from this image.

Yet by birth and origins Coward was no toff. Born into a lower middle class family in Teddington, Middlesex, he was the entirely self-made product of his own talent. He had achieved his success by working for it and all his life remained a stern believer in and unbending practitioner of hard work, self-discipline and the stiff upper lip. 'Determined to rise above it' was his regular reaction to setbacks and disasters. His father was a travelling salesman and his family had lived in genteel poverty in a succession of London suburbs, his mother reduced to taking in paying guests to make ends meet. The achievement of success against this background inevitably made him a staunch defender of the status quo, a fervent patriot, a man with a deep love of England, the Empire, the royal family, some of whom he was to count as personal friends. Equally he believed firmly in the class system:

> Personally I have always believed more in quality than quantity, and nothing will convince me that the levelling of class and rank distinctions and the

contemptuous dismissal of breeding as an important factor in life, can lead to anything but dismal mediocrity.[15]

His love of England, Empire and status quo had become clear as early as 1931, when as Britain was going off the gold standard amid a mood of national disquiet, he had written 'Cavalcade', a panorama of life in Britain between 1900 and 1930, a nostalgic celebration of the English class system and a hymn to duty. It ended with the entire cast singing 'God Save the King' and Coward making his celebrated curtain speech: 'I hope this play has made you feel that, in spite of the troublous times we are living in, it is still a pretty exciting thing to be English.'

He expanded on his political beliefs in his eight broadcasts in Australia. He showed himself at one with other commentators in perceiving the lowering of class barriers and the strength of democracy in action. It was Coward — of all people — who was praising 'the provinces':

> The provinces of England have, I think, contributed more to the glory of the country than the streets of Mayfair, and perhaps one of the few benefits that emerge from this war will be the final destruction of those false snob values which have imposed themselves upon the honest heart of London. As a matter of fact, a change is already taking place in the ARP canteens, in buses and tubes and air raid shelters. There is a new comradeship growing in London between people of all creeds and classes. All they are enduring makes it increasingly apparent that true democracy needs no veneer.[16]

It is important to stress that Coward sought not the abolition of class distinction, but a greater sympathy and understanding between classes.

He stressed Britain's partnership with the Dominions and with the United States and the importance of the English-speaking peoples maintaining peace and justice after the war: 'The future lies with us — I mean the English-speaking peoples of the world — if only we are strong enough and wise enough to deal with it efficiently. With all our faults, and there are many, we have an integral sense of justice and fair play. The much laughed at or berated 'old school tie' decency should not be too wittily dismissed.'[17] There are echoes of Orwell here and elsewhere in Coward's broadcasts. Like Orwell, he stressed the decency and unity and patriotism of the people. Like Orwell, he spoke of the national passion for gardening, the richness and flexibility of the English language, the scandalous downgrading of patriotism by the intelligentsia between the wars. Where he parted from Orwell was in endorsing the Churchillian war aim of victory and national security: 'We have two aims — to win the war and then to win after the war. We have to create security for ourselves, for France and all other Peoples threatened and overcome by the Nazi regime. This aim takes precedence of any others'.[18] Orwell, on the other hand, lined up with Priestley in seeking a better, indeed a Socialist Britain after the war. What Coward celebrated was the shorter term, the unconquerable spirit of the British people, but there was room for both viewpoints in the national struggle; both room and necessity.

Coward's contribution to the war effort should not be underrated: the Germans certainly did not underrate it. After the war, when the official Gestapo arrest list to be implemented in the event of a German conquest of England was found, the name of Noël Coward was there along with those of such luminaries as J. B. Priestley, Rebecca West, Alexander Korda and Winston Churchill.[19] Coward wrote patriotic songs ('London pride' most notably). He made patriotic broadcasts both at home and in the Empire. He toured army camps, naval bases and the war fronts in the Middle East, South Africa, Burma and India, performing in concerts for the forces. His repertoire frequently included two of his most enduring contributions to patriotic lore, the toast from 'Cavalcade' and the song 'Mad Dogs and Englishmen', originally intended as a smart, albeit affectionate satire of the *pukka sahib* tradition, but converted in wartime into a defiant affirmation of the national spirit.

It was when he returned from the Far East that he broadcast on the Home Service (19 November 1944) about the 'Forgotten Army' in fulfillment of a pledge to General Slim. He denounced the press for ignoring them, talked of the dreadful conditions they were enduring and of their indomitable courage and fortitude ('We are forever in the debt of these extraordinary men, who are keeping the flame of our national pride and honour burning clearly in the far away corners of the world').[20] As a result of the broadcast, he received congratulations from the King and Queen, 2,000 letters of thanks from relatives of the men serving in the East and 'a full page of unqualified abuse from John Gordon in the *Sunday Express*'.[21] He was also appointed an adviser to the BBC on the content and quality of forces broadcasting.

It was, however, with his films, and in particular *In Which We Serve,* that he was to make his greatest contribution. He was initially reluctant to become involved in the film industry:

> I had generated in my mind a strong prejudice against the moving picture business, a prejudice compounded of small personal experience and considerable intellectual snobbery. I had convinced myself, with easy sophistry, that it was a soul-destroying industry in which actors of mediocre talent were publicized and idolized beyond their desserts and authors, talented or otherwise, were automatically massacred. Of all my plays, only 'Cavalcade' had been filmed with taste and integrity. The rest . . . had been rewritten by incompetent hacks, vulgarized by incompetent directors and reduced to common fatuity.[22]

So when just after opening in his new play 'Blithe Spirit' on 2 July 1941 he was approached to make a film, he refused. The offer had come from the Italian emigré producer Filippo del Giudice, managing director of Two Cities Films. He had entered into a distribution agreement with Columbia

Pictures and had produced for them *Unpublished Story*. Charles Thorpe of Columbia suggested getting a top playwright to script the next film and mentioned Coward as a possibility. Del Giudice, Thorpe and producer Anthony Havelock-Allan saw Coward and offered him complete control of cast, director, subject and crew, if he would agree to write and star in a film for them. The genesis of the film can be followed in the pages of Coward's diary.[23]

On 3 July he dined with Lord Louis and Lady Edwina Mountbatten and heard the full story of the sinking of *HMS Kelly*, which Mountbatten had commanded in the Battle of Crete. He thought the story 'absolutely heartbreaking and so magnificent'. The seed of a screen story was planted in his mind, a story that would contain 'all the true sentiment, the comedy, the tragedy, the casual valiance, the unvaunted heroism, the sadness without tears, and the pride without end.'[24] On 18 July he went to the Ministry of Information and talked to Sir Gerald Campbell about his idea of doing a naval propaganda film for Columbia. Campbell 'thought it was a magnificent idea and was most helpful.' On 22 July Coward put the idea to Mountbatten who was 'wildly enthusiastic and said the Admiralty would support me all out'. He was, however, very anxious that the film should not be directly about him and Coward assured him that it would not. Coward then talked to Thorpe and del Giudice, who agreed to give him complete control of the project. He promised to provide a story outline in three weeks and after that they could discuss shooting dates and other details. On 28 July at the Mountbatten's country house, Broadlands, after further discussions with Lord Mountbatten, Coward worked out the story for the film, which was at that stage to be called *White Ensign*. Mountbatten supplied many incidents and details from the story of the *Kelly* and the next day Coward worked on further naval details and completed the story outline.

Although Coward had agreed to Mountbatten's stipulation about depicting him, Lord Louis did not like the first draft:

> The very first script he showed me had the captain married to Lady Celia Kinross, living in a large country house with a Rolls-Royce and a driver. 'Noël, this is the limit!' I said, 'this is pointing straight at me'. He agreed, and so the car was turned into a Ford without a driver and his wife lost her title, and they lived in a small villa.[25]

Nevertheless many of the incidents and even speeches were taken directly from Mountbatten's career.

Once the script had been approved by the producers, Coward joined *HMS Nigeria* for a short cruise in the North Sea, in order to get a feel of the atmosphere and conditions. Then he set to work on the script, which he began on 6 August and completed on 2 September. He envisaged it, as he explained to his mother, as 'a naval "Cavalcade" '.[26]

By now the press had got wind of the project and the *Daily Express* began to make mischief. Lord Beaverbrook had long-standing vendettas against both Coward and Mountbatten and the chance to get at them both was too good to miss. On 29 August, there was a front page story in the *Express* announcing that a £150,000 film was to be made by Noël Coward and Columbia Pictures centred on the war exploits of Lord Mountbatten.[27] It announced that Coward would direct and also appear, possibly as Lord Louis. Coward rang his 'staunchest supporter at the Admiralty', Captain Brooking of the Press Division, about the article and learned that both Brendan Bracken, the Minister of Information, and Walter Monckton, the director-general of the Ministry, had asked him if he did not consider it a mistake that Coward should act in the film. Brooking told them that he thought it 'an excellent idea'.[28]

The controversy surrounding the film highlights several important issues. First, the individual services were able to sponsor propaganda

In his portrayal of Mountbatten, called Captain Kinross in the film, Noël Coward stressed his concern for his crew.

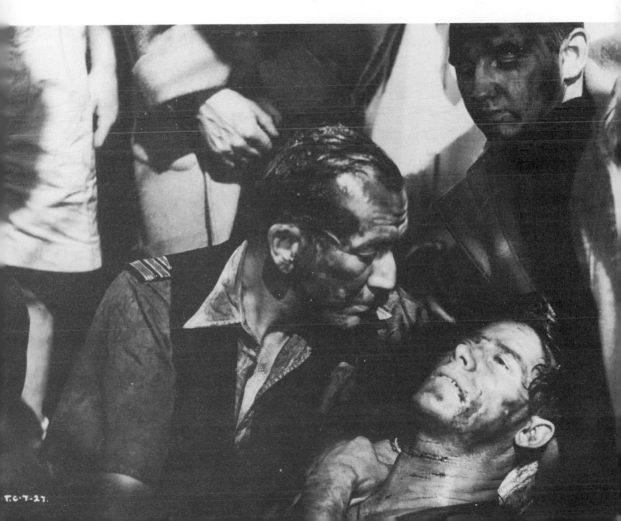

films about themselves without specific reference to the MoI and the Admiralty backed the Coward film from the start, largely due to Lord Mountbatten:

> Dickie's personal enthusiasm cut through many strings of red tape and set many wheels turning on my behalf. From the beginning he saw the idea as a tribute to the service he loved, and he supported me through every difficulty and crisis until the picture was completed.[29]

Coward indeed admitted that he could never have made the film without Lord Louis' 'constructive criticism, his gift for concentration, his confidence in the film and in me.' Nevertheless, there was continued opposition from the Ministry of Information, which had powers over the granting of certain facilities and also the important question of export licences for the film. It used all these powers in trying to block another film it disapproved of, *The Life and Death of Colonel Blimp*.[30]

The Ministry's principal concern seems to have been that Coward was inappropriate casting in a role based on a real-life war hero and the King's cousin. It was the albatross of the frivolous playboy image again. It did Coward little good to deny that his central character was Mountbatten but he continued to try:

> There had never been any question of my portraying Lord Louis Mountbatten . . . Captain D in *In Which We Serve* was conceived, written and acted to the best of my ability as an average naval officer, whereas Mountbatten was then, and is now, very far from being an average naval officer.[31]

The denials were not believed and Sidney Bernstein of the Films Division of the MoI, a personal friend of Coward's, was detailed to dissuade him from appearing.[32] He tried and failed.

The press campaign continued. On Wednesday 17 September 1941 the *Daily Express* ran a story by Jonah Barrington, the film correspondent, headed 'The Battle of Noël':

> When I published the story that Noël Coward would play the part of Lord Louis Mountbatten, hero of the destroyers *Javelin* (torpedoed) and *Kelly* (sunk off Crete), an official denial was issued. Nevertheless, I am now informed that a fight is still going on to put Coward in the leading part. The scenario, it is contended, is based on a cavalcade of naval exploits and not on the adventures of Lord Louis alone. There are two schools of thought on this position: 1, Those who support Mr Coward; 2, Those who think that a film about the Navy should be produced in the same way as the RAF film *Target for Tonight*, with real naval men in the leading parts.

The article went on to elaborate on the need for authenticity in approach and personnel and to suggest that 'it is wrong to have a professional actor dressed in the peaked cap and the gold braid of a British naval officer.'[33]

This last point was so absurd, in view of the regularity with which actors had in the past been seen portraying naval officers, that Coward was undoubtedly correct in interpreting this as an *ad hominem* attack. He telephoned the Admiralty ('Brooking furious') and wrote to Mountbatten about it. Captain Brooking contacted Walter Monckton at the MoI to demand that pressure be brought to bear on the *Express* to desist from their attacks.

But the attacks continued, and on 30 September Barrington reported that he had been to the Admiralty himself to suggest that 'there was criticism against Mr Coward dressing in the clothes of a British naval officer'. The Admiralty assured him that Coward would undergo 'exhaustive tests' before casting was approved, though Coward himself would have the final say. An actual naval officer could not be released from active service to play the part, though lesser ranks would be released to appear as extras in the interests of authenticity.[34]

In due course Coward defended himself in the press, telling the *Observer:*

> It is probably from my point of view the most serious and the most sincere job I have done. Feeling as I do about the Navy, if in my picture there is anything vulgar, anything insincere, I should be forever ashamed . . . I'm only playing [Captain Kinross] because I want to show how ordinary I can be, not just that smart, witty Noël Coward but just a commonplace, simple human being.[35]

He made a more telling response to the *Express* persecution in the film *In Which We Serve.* He used a shot of the front page of a discarded copy of the *Daily Express,* dated January 1939 and proclaiming 'No war this year'.

Coward was at work on the second draft of the script in October 1941 when he was summoned for contravening currency regulations, in respect of failing to declare monies held in the United States in accordance with a law of 26 August 1939. He pleaded not guilty and argued that he had spent these monies to finance his fact-finding missions for the MoI. He was fined £200 on that charge and later £1,600 on a related charge, although he might have been required to pay up to £61,000 and his counsel G.D. Roberts QC declared: 'He is a loyal Englishman who emerges from this ordeal with his honour entirely untouched.'[36]

With this ordeal over, he plunged back into work, viewing and studying British wartime documentaries in detail for technique and atmosphere in order to get the right visual feel for his film. He assembled his production unit, the most important of whom were editor David Lean, who was chosen as co-director, Ronald Neame as director of photography and Anthony Havelock-Allan as associate producer. Lean and Neame had both worked on a number of films that had impressed Coward and he wrote of the trio: 'From these three I had wholehearted, intelligent and affectionate cooperation from the beginning to the end.'[37] Indeed they subsequently joined together to form Cineguild and to produce three more Coward pictures (*Brief Encounter, Blithe Spirit* and *This Happy Breed*).

Coward was also unfailingly backed by Filippo del Giudice ('His English was appalling and his enthusiasm boundless'). This support was crucial as another problem emerged, that of finance. The film was originally budgeted at £60,000, but as planning proceeded and estimated costs rose, the budget passed £100,000. Columbia withdrew and del Giudice persuaded C.M. Woolf of General Film Distributors to step in. However, when estimated costs reached £180,000, even before shooting began, Woolf pulled out. Shooting began without a backer and it was not until six weeks into the project that Sam Smith of British Lion agreed to back and distribute the film, which eventually cost £200,000.

Coward later recalled the period of preparation:

> On looking back on the seven months between the original conception of *In Which We Serve* and the day on which we actually began shooting, I find I can see them only in terms of montage — endless conferences; hours in Wardour Street projection rooms looking at British films; casting discussions, technical discussions; days at sea in destroyers; drives to and from Denham Studios in winter weather; arguments about the budget of the picture; moving into a dank cottage so as to be near the studios; crises, triumphs, despairs, exultations; tests in the Gaumont British studios at Shepherds Bush; hours of staring at myself on the screen — heavy jowls, no eyes at all; lighting wrong, lighting better; visits to shipyards in Newcastle; to dockyards in Plymouth and Portsmouth; endless discussions with experts — naval experts, film experts, shipbuilding experts, gunnery experts; and last, but by no means least, the nerve-wracking business of my court proceedings at Bow Street and the Mansion House.[39]

The script had been read, checked for inaccuracies and approved by Lord Louis Mountbatten on 12 December, but on 17 December there was another bombshell. The MoI had been sent a copy of the final script, for del Giudice worked closely with the Ministry and the service organizations in the production of entertainment films that would aid the war effort. (It was del Giudice that Paul Kimberley, as director of the Army Kinematographic Service approached for a feature film that would do for the Army what *In Which We Serve* had done for the Navy: the result was *The Way Ahead*. It was del Giudice too whom the MoI approached to make a feature film on British colonial administration in East Africa: this led to *Men of Two Worlds*. Indeed del Giudice assured Jack Beddington in a letter (7 November 1942): 'It is the policy of this company not to make any films whether on subjects connected directly with the war or not without the approval of the Ministry of Information.'40) There was therefore consternation when Beddington wrote to the Admiralty stating 'unequivocally that in the Ministry's opinion the story was exceedingly bad propaganda for the Navy, as it showed one of HM's ships being sunk in enemy action, and that permission would never be granted for it to be shown outside this country'.41 This information was relayed by Beddington himself to Coward by telephone. Coward wrote in his diary 'Absolutely appalled by this utterly infuriating impertinence.' He called Mountbatten, who said that he would take charge of matters and asked for a copy of the script to show the King and Queen. Mountbatten got Admiralty clearance for the script from Admiral Sir Tom Phillips, Vice-Chief of Naval Staff, and armed with this Coward and Mountbatten had a meeting with Brendan Bracken and Jack Beddington. According to Coward, 'Dickie went off like a time bomb, and it was one of the most startling and satisfactory scenes I have ever witnessed. I actually felt a pang of compassion for the wretched official, who wilted under the tirade like a tallow candle before a strong fire.' After that there was no further opposition from the Ministry.42

By now the film was called *In Which We Serve,* from a phrase in the naval prayer recited every morning on board ship. Shooting began on 5 February 1942 at Denham Studios and continued until 27 June. Coward duly cast himself as Captain Edward Kinross (Captain D), and took charge of the shooting. A tremendous disciplinarian, he insisted on every member of the cast being word-perfect on the first day. Every member of the unit, actors and technical staff alike, received copies of the complete script three weeks before shooting began. John Mills, cast as AB Shorty Blake, wrote in his diary on 5 February 1942: 'This is the only way to make pictures — efficiency, drive, enthusiasm and a perfect script. Actors also word-perfect.'42 Some 250 naval ratings and a unit of the Coldstream Guards were supplied to act as extras. The authenticity of naval procedure was ensured by Commander 'Bushy' Clarke and Lieutenant Charles Compton, who successively acted as 'ward-room and bridge advisers', and Terry Lawlor, who had been Mountbatten's cabin hand on the *Kelly*, was 'lower decks adviser'. The film was given the official imprimatur of approval by a visit to the set by the King and Queen and the two princesses on 8 April.

With Coward taking one of the leading roles and having no previous experience of directing, he had chosen David Lean to co-direct, but Lean soon became the effective director, as Coward, bored by the technicalities and impatient with the inevitable delays and retakes, confined himself to instructing the actors and ensuring that Lean achieved the overall 'feel' and mood that he required. Nevertheless, it remains Coward's film, with Lean taking the responsibility for translating into cinematic form the conception of the author-star-producer-composer.

In Which We Serve is a film of love: love of England ('England may be a

The film depicted the families of the crew and showed all classes pulling together for the war effort. Celia Johnson, Daniel Massey and Ann Stephens played the middle class family.

very small island, vastly overcrowded, frequently badly managed, but it is in my view the best and bravest country in the world'); love for the Navy ('I love the Navy, I inherited my affection for it, all my mother's family were Navy . . . They've got the best manners in the world and I love the sea and Navy discipline'); love for Lord Mountbatten ('Dickie's militant loyalty, moral courage and infinite capacity for taking pains, however busy he is, is one of the marvels of this most unpleasant age. I would do anything in the world for him').[44]

It is chronologically the last grand summation of his feelings about his country, the counterpart and successor, in a sense the synthesis of 'Cavalcade' and 'This Happy Breed'. All three had been prompted by crises and proclaimed his faith in the essential soundness and steadiness of the British people. 'Cavalcade', which was first presented at Drury Lane on 13 October 1931, emerged in the wake of the General Strike, the Wall Street crash and the onset of the Depression. The end of civilization as we know it was daily predicted. Coward's play interwove the lives and fortunes of two families and a single home: the upper middle class Marryots and their servants, the lower class Bridges'. It drew on the nation's experiences of victory and defeat, joy and loss, and wove them into the tapestry of national myth, in which the nation's tragedies (the death of the Old Queen, the Boer War, the sinking of the *Titanic,* the First World War) became personal tragedies. But the final toast not only contained a message of hope but also the essence of the play and of Coward's world-view:

> Let us drink to the future of England. Let us couple the future of England with the past of England. The glories and victories and triumphs that are over and the sorrows that are over too. Let's drink to our sons who made part of the pattern and to our hearts that died with them. Let's drink to the spirit of gallantry and courage that made a strange heaven out of unbelievable hell and let's drink to the hope that this country of ours, which we love so much, will find Dignity and Greatness and Peace again.

In seeing the present as part of a continuum, the past alive in memory and tradition, Coward again links with both George Orwell and Humphrey Jennings, who used the same term 'pattern' in their search for the secret of what makes England England.

'This Happy Breed', written in the spring of 1939, in the wake of Munich and under the shadow of war, traced the effect of the events of the period 1918—39 on the Gibbonses, a lower middle class family in Clapham. It did not in fact open in London until 30 April 1943, when W.A. Darlington called it Coward's 'tribute to John Citizen, the ordinary Englishman' and declared 'for the first time in his brilliant career, we have him writing with sympathy, understanding and admiration of the common man.'[45] In fact, Frank Gibbons, as played on stage by Coward himself, expresses many of the author's views on England. Frank soliloquizes to his baby grandson at the end of the play in a speech cut from the film version of 'This Happy Breed':

> You belong to a race that's been bossy for years and the reason it's held on as long as it has is that nine times out of ten it's behaved decently and treated people right. Just lately, I'll admit, we've been giving at the knees a bit and letting people down who trusted us and allowing noisy little men to bully us with a lot of guns and bombs and aeroplanes. But don't worry — that won't last — the people, themselves, the ordinary people like you and me, know something better than all the old fussy politicians put together — we know what we belong to, where we come from and where we're going. We may not know it with our brains, but we know it with our roots. And we know another thing too, and it's this. We 'aven't lived and died and struggled all these hundreds of years to get decency and justice and freedom for ourselves without being prepared to fight fifty wars, if need be, to keep 'em.

There is no desire on Coward's part to do away with the class system. What he is doing in his plays and films is to mobilize it in defence of the status quo, to highlight the strengths of each individual class and to show how by pulling together they can win through. *In Which We Serve* combines 'Cavalcade' and 'This Happy Breed'. The Kinrosses are the Marryots reincarnated, the upper middle classes in the service of the nation. Coward himself described them: 'Ordinary upper middle class family. Private income, £600 or £700 a year. Small country house outside Plymouth, ordinary, pleasant wife, family, one boy and one girl, Cocker spaniel called Trafalgar.'[46] The Hardys are the Gibbonses, complete with endlessly complaining mother-in-law. *In Which We Serve* adopts a similar narrative pattern of interweaving public events and private lives, telling the story of *HMS Torrin* and its crew from its commissioning in 1939 to its sinking in the Battle of Crete in 1943. En route it takes in the outbreak of war, Dunkirk, the Battle of Britain and the Plymouth Blitz.

The film is dedicated 'to the Royal Navy, whereon under the good providence of God, the wealth, safety and strength of the Kingdom chiefly depend'. Significantly, the seamen in the film are not conscripts but regular Navy. The service, duty and discipline are their life even before the war, a war which both Captain Kinross and CPO Hardy as seasoned professionals believe inevitable. 'This is the story of a ship' says Leslie Howard in the prologue to the film and the ship is clearly meant to serve as a metaphor for Britain, and the commitment to her that is expected of all in wartime. This feeling is visually encapsulated when after an initial montage of the building and launching of the ship, she is commissioned as *HMS Torrin.* The crew is lined up for the raising of the ensign and then can be seen through the fluttering flag, serried ranks, marshalled in perfect discipline.

Commitment, discipline and dedication become clear in the action sequences and are pointed up by a famous episode based on fact. In action in the North Atlantic amid a raging storm, Shorty Blake (John Mills) stands by his gun, although concussed, and continues firing, while a young stoker (Richard Attenborough) panics and leaves his post. On their safe return, the Captain addresses the crew, telling them how proud he has been of them all but one. One man panicked, has been reprimanded and will not be punished further. Kinross blames himself for not having got his creed across to all his men. When later the stoker dies of wounds sustained in action, the captain tells him that he'll write to his family and tell them they can be proud of him.

The film opens with the sinking of the ship in the Battle of Crete, on 23 May 1941. The survivors, covered in oil, swim across to a raft and cling there, keeping their spirits up by singing 'Roll out the barrel', their plight rendered doubly difficult by persistent German strafing. Clinging there, each of the three main characters, Captain Kinross (Noël Coward), CPO Walter Hardy (Bernard Miles) and AB Shorty Blake (John Mills) recall their families, establishing the diverse elements that make up the crew and also the harmony between them. In rapid succession three Christmas dinners are seen, establishing a mutuality of interest. AB Shorty Blake is seen at home with his working class family, parents, sister and brother-in-law, Bert, a marine. They quarrel about the relative merits of their respective services, but they end up toasting each other's units, in particular toasting the *Torrin,* in which the whole family join. In the lower middle class home of the Hardys, complete with devoted wife Kath and grumbling mother-in-law Mrs Lemmon, CPO Hardy makes a touchingly formal speech which ends up with a toast to the *Torrin.* At the Kinrosses, there is an officers' party with a toast to the King. There Alix Kinross (Celia Johnson) makes a speech welcoming Maureen, newly engaged to Flag Officer Michael Wilding, to the sisterhood of naval wives. She talks of the constant moving round, the poor pay and a permanent and undefeated rival for their husbands' affections — the ship. But she toasts *Torrin:* 'God bless this ship and all who sail in her.'

Whatever else may divide them, they are united in love of the ship, i.e. the country. Now the lives begin to overlap. On a train Shorty meets Freda Lewis (Kay Walsh), who turns out to be Hardy's niece. Shorty and Freda are married and travelling by train to Torquay for their honeymoon, meet the Kinrosses, who wish them well and reveal that they too spent their honeymoon in Torquay. There is the common experience of separation: Walter and Kath Hardy part at home, Shorty and Freda Blake at the dockyard, Maureen and 'Flags' at the station. There is the agony of loss, sustained both at sea and at home: 'Flags' is killed at Crete. Mrs Hardy and Mrs Lemmon are killed in the Plymouth Blitz. There is the agony of waiting: after the sinking of the *Torrin,* we see Shorty's wife and mother and Alix Kinross all waiting in their homes for news and then the outpouring of relief and joy when news arrives to say that Kinross and Shorty are safe.

The central element in most of these scenes is restraint, emotion that is not repressed but kept in check. The feelings can clearly be seen on the faces of the characters but they are not flaunted. This restraint is common to characters of every class. 'There's no use making a fuss is there', says Kath Hardy to her grumbling mother as bombs rain down on Plymouth. Alix reads *Alice in Wonderland* to the children to quiet them. Shorty breaks the news to Walter of Kath's death and, tears glistening in his eyes, he thanks Shorty quietly for telling him the news and goes up on deck to be alone. There is restrained emotion too in the sequence of the return from Dunkirk. *The Times* singled this scene out for particular praise:

> The camera moves down a line of men drawn up on a quayside; their faces are empty with exhaustion, and there is no sound except the faint notes of a military band 'off-screen'. From the destroyer the sailors look down silently. Nothing is said, for there is nothing to say. That is the aftermath of Dunkirk stated theatrically, and the theatrical terms are magnificent.[47]

There is, however, an upbeat ending, as the captain makes a final speech to the survivors of the *Torrin:*

> Now she lies in 1,500 fathoms and with her more than half our shipmates. If they had to die — what a grand way to go. Now they lie all together with the ship we loved and they're in very good company. We've lost her but they're still with her. There may be less than half the *Torrin* left but I feel that we all take up the battle with even stronger heart. Each of us knows twice as much about fighting and each of us has twice as good a reason to fight. You will all be sent to replace men who've been killed in other ships and the next time you're in action — Remember the *Torrin.*

He shakes hands with each man individually as the crew leaves. The final shots show Coward on a new ship ordering 'Open fire', and Leslie Howard speaks the final words:

> Here ends the story of a ship, but there will always be other ships, for we are an island race. Through all our centuries the sea has ruled our destiny. There will always be other ships and men to sail them. It is these men, in peace or war, to whom we owe so much. Above all victories, beyond all loss, in spite of changing values in a changing world, they give us, their countrymen, eternal and indomitable pride. God bless our ships and all who sail in them.

The finished film was first shown on Sunday 17 September 1942 in aid of naval charities. Coward was well pleased with it: 'There it was, once and for all, well directed, well photographed and well played, and, above all, as far as I was concerned, an accurate and sincere tribute to the Royal Navy'.[48] When the press notices appeared, he was even more gratified, noting in his diary:

> Read the London notices of the film, which are absolute superlatives. Nothing but 'great picture' and 'finest film of the war' etc. The most gratifying thing of all is that even the commonest journalistic mind has observed that it really is a dignified tribute to the Navy.[49]

Perhaps the most gratifying verdicts will have been those from the arch-opponents of the project. The *Daily Express* described *In Which We Serve* as 'a great film of the Royal Navy' and went on 'it is a fighting film, but it is also a human, deeply moving film, sweeping from the high seas into the homes and hearts of men, and their womenfolk quietly awaiting the news of triumphs and disasters'.[50] Coward also received a letter of congratulation from Jack Beddington. Even more remarkable was a letter from the Minister, Brendan Bracken (9 October 1942), asking him to make a similar film about the Army:

> I hope you will consider very carefully my suggestion that you should make a

film about the Army. I have never seen a really good film about the Army and I am sure you could make one which would be as rousing a success as *In Which We Serve*.[51]

Coward declined on the grounds that he had little knowledge of or acquaintance with the Army and it was his 'many, many years' of contact and friendship with the Navy which had enabled *In Which We Serve* to succeed.

The trade papers were ecstatic. *Today's Cinema* called the film:

Not only a memorable British achievement and grand entertainment but a box office proposition to rejoice the hearts of all showmen . . . a stirring story told without theatrical flourishes, treated on finely spectacular lines — a story to stir the heart, uplift the flagging spirit and rouse the lethargic — a story that brings to vivid life the gallantry of the Navy as coldly worded reports have failed to do.[52]

Kinematograph Weekly declared:

There has never been a more comprehensive, a more emotionally stimulating, a more thrilling war film or a greater woman's picture than this. Neither has there been one better equipped to present the British point of view abroad. Outstanding general booking, the greatest achievement in the annals of the British screen.[53]

The newspaper critics were equally impressed. In the *Observer,* C.A. Lejeune called it 'one of the most heart-warming, heart-stirring films this country has ever produced, either at peace or in war'.[54] Dilys Powell in *The Sunday Times* called it 'the best film about the war yet made in this country or in America'.[55] The weeklies and monthlies joined in the praise. The *Monthly Film Bulletin* called it 'the finest war drama yet produced and because of the strength of its understatement and recognition occasionally of human weakness, is propaganda of the very best sort. It should be seen by all.'[56] *Sight and Sound* called it 'the best war film made so far'.[57] One of the few dissentient voices was that of William Whitebait in the *New Statesman* who thought it a 'good, nearly a very good film' but added:

In Which We Serve is far too long, too much centred upon Mr Coward. How often we have to stare at those familiar features fronting the gales, bobbing up in the waters, while another dive bomber swoops over or another order has to be given from the captain's deck. Too many speeches to the crew, too many Christmas gatherings and tear-jerks all in a row.[58]

But he was very much in a minority and out of tune with the public mood. Winston Churchill had the film run for him several times and always ended up in tears. It was shown to the Royal Family at Buckingham Palace and impressed the King enough to want to honour Coward with a knighthood.[59] But the ordinary cinemagoing public loved it too. They made it the most successful British film of 1943 at the British box office and second only to *Random Harvest* as the top box office attraction from Britain or America.[60] The *Daily Mail* poll of 1945 listed it as the eighth most popular film of the war years.[61] Many of the film fans who wrote to *Picturegoer* for J. P. Mayer's survey of British filmgoers and their preferences singled out *In Which We Serve* as one of the highlights of their film viewing. One of them, a 16 year old junior female assistant in an accountants office, listed *In Which We Serve* and *The Way Ahead* among her favourite films, noting: 'These films, besides being so interesting to us, will be very valuable in the years to come. They show the true British spirit in the years of the war.'[62]

There has been far less enthusiasm for the film in recent years. It has been fashionable for critics to downplay Coward's patriotic works and dismiss films like *In Which We Serve* as 'museum pieces'.[63] But they are deeply felt, expertly crafted and still have the power to stir and move. Their success with the general public suggests that the ordinary cinemagoer responded, in a way which intellectual critics find it hard to appreciate, sympathize with or even comprehend, to Coward's blend of emotional patriotism and personal restraint, decency and discipline, family and nation.

Similarly, some of the structural criticisms are merely academic. It has been pointed out for instance that the 'subjectivity' of the various remembrances is repeatedly violated in that 'although the flashback begins in the context of one person's memories, it often ends in the middle of another's. Events that the character who is remembering is not involved in are somehow conjured up (for example, three Christmas dinners are in Captain Kinross' flashback, although he was present at only one of them).'[64] But there is no evidence that anyone at the time cared two hoots about this or even noticed it. What was true for audiences was the sentiment and that overrode all other considerations.

Coward's view of his characters both in *In Which We Serve* and *This Happy Breed* has been called both false and patronizing, but in writing about the lower middle classes he was writing about the stratum of society in which he had been raised and for whose speech and mores he had an acute sense of recall. He was easily able to evoke the upper class, moving as he did in high society and counting among his friends both Lord Louis Mountbatten and the Duke of Kent. But even more revealing about the authenticity of Coward's view of his characters is a Mass-Observation report of March 1941 on reactions to the Portsmouth Blitz. The observers reported that there were few signs of defeatism, though the constant pressure was having an effect on the people. They singled out as the most representative reaction that of the working class woman who told them:

Sometimes I say if we could stand Monday, we could stand anything. But sometimes I feels I can't stand it any more. But it doesn't do to say so. If I says anything my girls says to me: "Stop it, Ma! It's no good saying you can't stand it, you've got to!" My girls is ever so good.'[65]

This is exactly the tone, even to the dialogue, of the scene between Kath Hardy and Mrs Lemmon in the Plymouth Blitz sequence in *In Which We Serve*. As to the naval scenes, Lord Mountbatten said of the film: 'He produced a film which as far as I was concerned was exactly like life at sea. All the survivors of the *Kelly* agreed that it was quite staggering to find how true the whole film had been.'[66] Since it was based on his own experiences, there can hardly be better testimony than that.

Indeed what people at the time were impressed by was the film's realism. The visual feel can probably be attributed to David Lean, though it was certainly something Coward was anxious to aim for. The film opens with a Griersonian documentary montage of ship-building and shipyard:

The working class family of crew member, John Mills, were played by Wally Patch, Kathleen Harrison, Jill Stephens and George Carney.

heroic proletarian faces, sparks flying, as welders and rivetters work, the hammering and banging, the honest sweat. The action scenes are graphically shot, edited and staged, with rapid cutting and emphatic close-ups — engagement with the enemy, attack, the ship hit and abandoned, a dizzying sequence of men leaping over the side, Kinross remaining on the bridge to the last and finally being swept overboard by a great wave.

The realism in the depiction of naval life has already been noted, but it is important to recall that this was something new in war films. As Mass-Observation noted in 1941: 'The Navy has done much less to tell people about itself, photograph itself, film itself or produce books about itself than either of the other two services'.[67] Such previous films as there had been (*Convoy, Ships with Wings*) had devoted themselves exclusively to the officers; *In Which We Serve* was the first film to give equal screen time to the other ranks. Even the language had a salty authenticity that would have been censored in the pre-war cinema ('A bloody miracle', 'Here come the bastards back again').

Although Coward noted in his diary that he was trying hard to 'eliminate Noël Coward mannerisms', he was not always successful. He was least convincing and most mannered in the familiar, much-parodied staccato fashion in the domestic scenes with his wife:

Alix: Does the chintz look all right?
Teddy: Absolutely first-class.

But he was more relaxed and more convincingly authoritative with the crew. Celia Johnson, a quite remarkably beautiful and sensitive actress who in a sense embodied the soul of the upper middle class, was wholly convincing throughout and particularly moving in her Christmas Day speech. There was also excellent and highly praised work from Bernard Miles, John Mills, Joyce Carey and Kay Walsh, supported by a large and unfailingly excellent cast, in which Richard Attenborough made a notable impact as the cowardly stoker.

Much of the adverse criticism derives in fact from the film's resounding endorsement of the existing class system, bonded together by mutual sympathy and sent forth to war. This was recognized at the time but, unlike now, was not seen to invalidate the emotional truth of the film. The *Documentary News Letter* ran a perceptive review which still holds true:

This is an exceptionally sincere and deeply moving film . . . And it is one of the best war films ever made. Even after a second viewing of *In Which We Serve* these points still operate, and it is all the more necessary to try and formulate a straight critical attitude to the mood and purpose of the film. In doing this, one is paying Coward the compliment of treating his film seriously, not merely as an emotional or a patriotic success, but also as a considered attempt at propaganda. . . . Firstly, the story in all essentials looks backward from the present. The future, except in terms of the continuance of the Navy and its traditions, doesn't get a look-in at all. In fact the whole structure of the film, with its ingenious and surprisingly successful flashback continuities, depends on an attitude which looks no further than today and accepts no perspectives other than the strictly parochial. This is fair criticism, and one which Coward would probably not only accept, but would also argue the reasons why he chose these limitations. Secondly — and this arises from our firstly — the social structure of the British community is presented as a fixed and settled structure; nowhere is there any suggestion that the present war represents a revolution not only in thinking but in class relationships. This point must not be misunderstood, because Coward is one of the first people to put across with truth and realism the character and behaviour of three different income groups . . . It would be easy to go on from here and develop an argument that *In Which We Serve* is consciously or unconsciously fascist in intention, and one could have a field day on this line by taking up the whole relationship between the captain and his crew. It would be easy, but quite erroneous, for what Coward has done here is to delineate with considerable accuracy the atmosphere and behaviourism of a disciplined group of men on a warship . . . All of which adds up to the fact that Coward has produced a superb piece of ad hoc, short term propaganda — a film which because it is sincere and not mawkish, realistic in effect . . . and truthful in its delineation of ordinary people, is something which will at the least of reckonings be a positive factor on our own screens and on many screens abroad.[68]

Looking back in 1947 at the films of the war years Dilys Powell was able to pinpoint accurately what it was about the film that made it so meaningful to the cinemagoers of the war:

The emotional impact of *In Which We Serve* was immense. The experiences of civilian and fighting men were presented as essentially one, bound together by ties of human love and devotion; nobody but felt that he had a stake in this drama. If we look at the film with a detached and critical eye we must recognize the technical skill, the command of the medium which has gone into its making. The authority with which the complex strands of the narrative are handled, the mastery of simple, unemphatic dialogue, the easy, unobtrusive use of camera angle and movement, all are here. And the acting was pretty near faultless . . . *In Which We Serve* . . . set a new standard in the English cinema. There was nothing experimental, certainly nothing revolutionary in the style of *In Which We Serve.* What makes it historically important in the British cinema is its use of two significant motives: documentary background and the native theme . . . Noël Coward in *In Which We Serve* took a handful of typically British men and women and made from their stories, ordinary enough in themselves, a distillation of national character . . . Coward's film spoke for the Navy, to some effect, for tough though the British sailor holds himself, admirals and ratings alike were observed in tears at its performance.[69]

The film's emotional truth, its tribute to endurance, self-sacrifice, stoical humour and team spirit, qualities inadequately subsumed under the shorthand term 'the stiff upper lip', are what endeared this film to the nation. They impressed foreign observers too and helped to shape the image of the British people in the collective consciousness of our allies. *In Which We Serve* was chosen by the United States National Board of Review as the outstanding film of 1942 and Coward was awarded in 1943 a special Oscar for his outstanding production achievement in *In Which We Serve*.[70] The Russian director V.I. Pudovkin wrote of the film:

> It's a splendid job, overwhelming in its complete and well-thought out frankness. One of my comrades called it profoundly national, and I fully agree with him. The picture is English through and through. You can see the real face of England in it. The scene in which the captain, taking leave, shakes the hand of a whole file of his compatriots, and each conducts himself as though he were like no one but himself, and yet at the same time all are like each other, will remain long in memory.[71]

What Coward in fact did was to give visual life to the picture of wartime England painted by George Orwell. For Orwell, the English were gentle, private, patriotic, old-fashioned, law-abiding, anti-intellectual, deeply moral and profoundly class-ridden. These are exactly the qualities mirrored in *In Which We Serve*. More importantly perhaps, Orwell put his finger on that mood which caused such a response to Coward's film:

> In any calculation one has to take into account its emotional unity, the tendency of nearly all its inhabitants to feel alike and act together in moments of supreme crisis . . . the nation is bound together by an invisible chain . . . it resembles a family . . . it has its private language and its common memories and at the approach of an enemy it closes its ranks.[72]

The qualities perceived by both Coward and Orwell were those with which Coward also imbued the characters of his next and equally successful film, *This Happy Breed* (1944). Like *In Which We Serve,* it became the top British box office success of the year. In fact, Coward, apart from writing the play, viewing the rushes and making comments and suggestions as nominal producer, had comparatively little to do with the film. It was the work of the triumvirate which Coward had assembled to help him make *In Which We Serve* — David Lean, Ronald Neame and Anthony Havelock-Allan. It starred several of the *In Which We Serve* cast, notably Celia Johnson, John Mills and Kay Walsh, with Robert Newton as Frank Gibbons. Coward pronounced it 'on the whole very well done'. The publicity for *This Happy Breed* emphasized Coward's role in it:

> Noël Coward has no equal as a writer depicting the British character. The heroine of his new story is . . . No. 17 Sycamore Road, Clapham, SW. The world will love and respect the 'Gibbonses' who live in this house. Their

kind survive wars, zeppelins, Heinkels, the Kaiser, strikes, political upheavals, despairs, jubilations, the same as you.[73]

Where *In Which We Serve* was essentially a film about the present (i.e. the war and fighting it), *This Happy Breed* was its analogue and counterpart — a film about the past and the future, a film which avoided the war altogether, something which by 1944 filmgoers were anxious to do. It evoked the imminent end of the war in fact, with narrator Laurence Olivier declaring that with the return of the troops, 'hundreds and hundreds of houses are becoming homes again'. But it also presents a selective view of the events of 1919—39 in such a way as to assuage any guilt feelings the lower middle class may have entertained about their endorsement of the National Government and its appeasement policy. For this Clapham cavalcade intermingles the joys and sorrows of the Gibbons family, Frank and Ethel, and their three children (marriage, births, deaths, quarrels and reconciliations) with the great events of the age (the Empire Exhibition, the General Strike, the Abdication, the Munich Crisis). It does so in such a way as to endorse the lower middle class in their suburban streets as the backbone of England. For although the younger Gibbonses flirt with change, they settle in the end for the tried and true. Son Reg flirts with radical politics but is tamed by marriage. Communist son-in-law Sam similarly finds domestic bliss a happy substitute for world revolution. Daughter Queenie rejects her background as 'common' and runs away in search of the bright lights. But she too eventually settles for marriage to the boy next door and shows every sign of becoming the archetypal supportive wife and mother that Ethel has been throughout. Marriage, home and the family are thus seen to be playing a profoundly political role by depoliticizing the lower middle class and deploying them in defence of the status quo.

The film is in fact a plea for a return to 'normalcy' after the war. Frank's philosophy is 'it's up to us ordinary people to keep things steady'. This involves Frank and/or Ethel during the course of the film rejecting Communism and Fascism, filing reverently past the coffin of King George V, breaking the General Strike and denouncing appeasement. In discounting what Ethel calls 'that Bolshie business', Frank expounds his and Coward's Conservative evolutionary philosophy:

Oh, there's something to be said for it, there's always something to be said for everything. Where they go wrong is trying to get things done too quickly. We don't like doing things quickly in this country. It's like gardening, someone once said we was a nation of gardeners, and they weren't far out. We're used to planting things and watching them grow and looking out for changes in the weather . . . What works in other countries doesn't work here. We've got our own way of settling things. It may be slow and it may be a bit dull, but it suits us all right and it always will.

When the ship is sunk, the survivors determine to carry on the fight in other ships.

Once again, the film struck a chord in audiences, for it was the first time that the suburban middle class had been portrayed in the round. The sort of incarnation it was used to previously was Ivor Novello's hilarious satire on Clapham mores and manners *I Lived With You.* Here they were being taken seriously and treated with respect. *The Times* thought *This Happy Breed* 'excellent' and the *Manchester Guardian* called it 'an essential "photo" for John Bull's family album'.[74] William Whitebait of the *New Statesman,* who had expressed reservations about *In Which We Serve,* was completely bowled over by *This Happy Breed:*

> It would be hard to overpraise the skill, the feeling and the enhanced fidelity of the film . . . how exactly right are the accents, the clothes, the ideas, the shindies and celebrations. A Mass-Observation report on 'Sycamore Rd., Clapham' would no doubt provide us with the same detail, exhibited under glass; Mr Noël Coward sees it very much alive.[75]

Concerned that he may have overpraised the film, Whitebait went back to see it several months later and wrote a second review for the *New Statesman:* 'Not only is *This Happy Breed* true to life, to emotions, as well as exteriors, but there is the camera magic woefully absent from so many documentary-inspired stories.'[76]

C.A. Lejeune recorded the reaction of some of the audience:

> This film about the suburbs has gone out into the suburbs and the suburbs have taken it to their hearts. All the Gibbonses of Greater London have flocked to see themselves on the screen. Women in fish queues, fruit queues, cake queues, bus queues and queues for queues have passed the word to each other over their baskets. We have been amused, touched, entertained and edified by the film. It has gone straight to our address; or, as we say genteely in our suburb, *Chez Nous.* Nor is the enthusiasm for the film confined to Metroland. The Gibbonses are a large family; they are found all over the British Isles. There are plenty of Gibbonses, too, serving in Normany, Italy and the Middle East. No film in my memory has brought in more letters of appreciation . . . One man speaks with a kind of flame about a smoky evening sky over the roofs of Clapham. Another refers to the solid sense of family. A third comments on the nice use of Mr Coward's 'London pride' as background music. A flying officer in the Balkan Air Force writes that he has seen the film on three consecutive nights, with an enthusiastic audience of Dominion and Allied troops who 'were seeing England, the real England, for the first time' . . . Our correspondent describes *This Happy Breed* as 'a documentary; the unembellished facts of a life that is lived daily and consecutively till it is finished' . . . Yet *This Happy Breed* is not just a photographic and microphonic record of suburban life in the years between the two wars. If it were, nobody would care to see it. Art does not consist in repeating accurately what can be seen and heard around us. Art must try to conjure up, with the help of familiar symbols, things that are not perceptible to human eyes and ears. It must be a kind of second sight, what Baudelaire calls a 'sorcellerie evocatoire'. And *that,* I think, is the special quality of Mr Coward's film; a film that finds in a house in a row the symbol of the nation.[77]

This Happy Breed also figured strongly among the preferences of the *Picturegoer* survey respondents, with a 15 year old schoolgirl paying it the backhanded compliment 'it was so ordinary and so natural that it seemed a little odd', and a 24 year old Admiralty typist declaring:

> the two BEST British films ever made — *In Which We Serve* and *This Happy Breed,* such realism, such tradegy (sic) and humanity, these people were us, were our Fathers and Mothers after the last war, were our husbands and brothers in this war, the troubles and trials were what we have had to endure, the upsets and misunderstandings of every day. I thank Noel Coward for bringing to the screen the best there is of human nature.[78]

If *In Which We Serve* was resoundingly a film of the present (1942), its Army counterpart, Carol Reed's appropriately named *The Way Ahead*

(1944), looked to the future. For while *In Which We Serve* celebrated the professional Navy moving from peace to war under its existing hierarchy, *The Way Ahead* showed a conscript force of civilians being welded together, men of widely differing classes and backgrounds, united by a common purpose and effort but coming to a wider understanding of each other's lives and aspirations. Its officer was no upper middle class gentleman regular. Lieutenant Jim Perry was a former garage mechanic and territorial who believed in explaining things to his men in order to carry them with him. The emphasis of the film was on equality, the creation of a new citizen army rather than the mobilization of the existing force. As the press handout put it:

> *The Way Ahead* is the story of the Tommy of Today. Your husband, my brother, their son, the man next door, the chap at the pub, the boy from the city . . . A group of men join the Duke of Glendon's Light Infantry . . . the honour of the regiment, of the Army is safe in the keeping of the ordinary man. He was a civilian, he became a crusader. But that's not what he calls himself. As Tommy, we salute him, in this British film.[79]

In an earlier chapter mention was made of two key voices speaking for England in the darkest days of the war. Here in these two films the two voices can be heard again. *In Which We Serve,* with its quarterdeck speeches, flags, hymns and ceremonial, is in the Churchillian vein. Coward himself hero-worshipped Churchill and the film became one of Churchill's favourites. It was a film rooted in the traditions of the Navy stretching back to Nelson and the Armada. Carol Reed, on the other hand, made a film about the mobilization of the man in the street for a war effort that promised social and political change. It was a film in the Priestley vein, and if we can see in the socially concerned officer and tough professional sergeant who lead the army unit echoes of Attlee and Bevin, then this was indeed the way ahead.

NOTES

1   On Coward's life and career in general see Sheridan Morley, *A Talent to Amuse,* Harmondsworth, 1974; Cole Lesley, *The Life of Noël Coward,* London, 1976; Charles Castle, *Noël,* London, 1974. Coward's own account of his war years is contained in his autobiographical volume, *Future Indefinite,* London, 1954, in his *Middle East Diary,* London, 1944 and in Graham Payn and Sheridan Morley (ed.), *The Noël Coward Diaries*, London, 1982.
2   Coward, *Future Indefinite,* p. 139.
3   Coward, *Future Indefinite,* p. 52.
4   Coward, *Future Indefinite,* p. 51.
5   Sir Campbell Stuart, *Opportunity Knocks Once,* London, 1952, p. 191.

6   Coward, *Future Indefinite*, p. 156.
7   Coward, *Australia Visited — 1940*, London, 1941.
8   Coward, *Future Indefinite*, p. 165.
9   Stuart, *Opportunity Knocks Once*, p. 191.
10 *Daily Telegraph*, 19 February 1940.
11 *Sunday Pictorial*, 10 March 1940.
12 *Sunday Express*, 4 August 1940.
13 *Daily Mirror*, 7 August 1940.
14 H.C. Deb. vol. 364, August 1940, pp. 33—4.
15 Coward, *Future Indefinite*, p. 27.
16 Coward, *Australia Visited*, p. 5.
17 Coward, *Australia Visited*, p. 58.
18 Coward, *Australia Visited*, p. 14.
19 David Lampe, *The Last Ditch*, London, 1968, p. 177.
20 Noël Coward 'The Forgotten Army', Home Service broadcast, 19 November 1944, BBC Written Archives, Talks Scripts, Microfilm 98.
21 *Sunday Express*, 26 November 1944.
22 Coward, *Future Indefinite*, p. 206.
23 Payn and Morley (ed.), *Diaries*, pp. 7—20.
24 Coward, *Future Indefinite*, p. 208.
25 Castle, *Noël*, p. 174.
26 Letter from Noël Coward to his mother, quoted by Morley, *A Talent to Amuse*, p. 277.
27 *Daily Express*, 29 August 1941.
28 Payn and Morley (ed.), *Diaries*, p. 10.
29 Coward, *Future Indefinite*, p. 208.
30 *Daily Express* (11 November 1941) reported friction between the MoI and the Air Ministry over a proposed 85 minute, £150,000 colour film of RAF night-time bombing raids, set up without reference to the Ministry. On the 'Blimp Affair' see Jeffrey Richards and Anthony Aldgate, *Best of British*, Oxford, 1983, pp. 61—74.
31 Coward, *Future Indefinite*, p. 209.
32 Caroline Moorehead, *Sidney Bernstein*, London, 1984, p. 149.
33 *Daily Express*, 17 September 1941.
34 *Daily Express*, 30 September 1941.
35 *Observer*, 8 February 1942.
36 Roberts' quote is in *Daily Express* 31 October 1941, which carried a report of the trial. Coward's account of the affair is in *Future Indefinite*, pp. 219—23.
37 Coward, *Future Indefinite*, p. 211. The filming of *In Which We Serve* is recounted in *Future Indefinite*, pp. 210—31.
38 On the financing of the film, see Alan Wood, *Mr Rank*, London, 1952, pp. 130—1.
39 Coward, *Future Indefinite*, p. 213.
40 Letter from Filippo del Giudice to Jack Beddington, 7 November 1942, INF 1/224.
41 Coward, *Future Indefinite*, p. 210.
42 Coward, *Future Indefinite*, p. 211.
43 John Mills, *Up in the Clouds, Gentlemen, Please*, London, 1980, pp. 176—7.

44   On England: letter from Coward to his mother, quoted by Morley, *A Talent to Amuse,* p. 277; on Navy, Castle, *Noël,* p. 173; on Lord Louis Mountbatten, Payn and Morley (ed.), *Diaries,* p. 15.
45   *Daily Telegraph,* 1 May 1943.
46   *Observer,* 8 February 1942.
47   *The Times,* 24 September 1942.
48   Coward, *Future Indefinite,* p. 231.
49   Payn and Morley (ed.), *Diaries,* p. 18.
50   *Daily Express,* 24 September 1941.
51   Brendan Bracken's letter to Noël Coward, 9 October 1942, and Coward's reply, dated 12 October 1942, are in INF 1/224.
52   *Today's Cinema,* 25 September 1942.
53   *Kinematograph Weekly,* 1 October 1942.
54   C.A. Lejeune, *Chestnuts in her Lap,* London, 1947, p. 79.
55   *The Sunday Times,* 29 September 1942.
56   *Monthly Film Bulletin,* 9, 1942, p. 142.
57   *Sight and Sound* 11, Winter 1942, p. 68.
58   *New Statesman,* 25 September 1942.
59   The knighthood was scotched by the publicity surrounding the currency case. Coward was eventually knighted in 1970.
60   *Kinematograph Weekly,* 13 January 1944.
61   Dilys Owen, *The Way to the Stars,* London, n.d., appendix.
62   J.P. Mayer, *British Cinemas and their Audiences,* London, 1948, p. 173. cf. pp. 171, 177, 195, 227, 214, 228.
63   See for instance John Lahr, *Coward the Playwright,* London, 19892, pp. 92−113 and Clyde Jeavons, *A Pictorial History of War Films,* London, 1974, p. 113.
64   Alain Silver and James Ursini, *David Lean and his Films*, London, 1974. p. 17. This book also discusses in detail Lean's contribution to *In Which We Serve.*
65   Mass-Observation File Report 606, March 1941.
66   Castle, *Noël,* p. 174. It should be noted that the lower decks sometimes had a more ambivalent response to Coward's film. The historian J.D. Marshall recalls that the 'happy ship is an efficient ship' speech was irreverently parodied by the other ranks: 'A happy ship is an efficient ship, and an efficient ship is a fish and chip shop'. Marshall, himself a serviceman in those days, believes: 'The average sailor loved to see patriotic stuff on the screen, although he might grumble like blazes when with his mates. Imagine the glow of pride, however, when sitting with wife, girl friend or 'tart wot I picked up' in the cinema. IWWS did have a real attempt at representing not only sailors at war, but families.' He stresses that the working class characters 'did NOT represent lower deck speech and manners . . . But they were a curious approximation or common denominator' (Letter from J.D. Marshall to author, 22 January 1985). On his way to the Middle East, Coward was closely questioned by the other ranks about the film. 'They were all delighted with the fact that the lower deck had been presented in the film not as comic relief but as an integral and vital part of the story' (Coward, *Middle East Diary,* p. 9). This fact may well have done much to compensate for any inaccuracy in Coward's depiction of working class folk.

67 Mass-Observation File Report 967, November 1941.

68 *Documentary News Letter* 3, October 1942, pp. 143—4.

69 Dilys Powell, *Films since 1939,* London, 1947, pp. 25—8.

70 *New York Times,* 24 December 1942, called it 'one of the most eloquent motion pictures of these or any other times. There have been other pictures which have vividly and movingly conveyed in terms of human emotion the cruel realities of this present war. None has yet done it so sharply or so truly as *In Which We Serve.'* The film earned $1.80 million in the USA (James Curran and Vincent Porter (eds), *British Cinema History,* London, 1983, p. 165).

71 *Documentary News Letter* 5, 1944, p. 2.

72 George Orwell, *Collected Essays, Journalism and Letters* 2, Harmondsworth, 1971, p. 88.

73 BFI *This Happy Breed* microfiche.

74 *The Times,* 24 May 1944; *Manchester Guardian,* 29 May 1944.

75 *New Statesman,* 27 May 1944.

76 *New Statesman,* 21 October 1944.

77 Lejeune, *Chestnuts in her Lap,* pp. 116—18.

78 Mayer, *British Cinemas and their Audiences,* pp. 176, 214.

79 Vincent Porter and Chaim Litewski, 'The Way Ahead: Case History of a Propaganda Film', *Sight and Sound* 50, Spring 1981, p. 113.

10
England, Their England

Fires Were Started

One of the most remarkable developments of the war years was the way in which the documentary, its technique, approach and ethos, entered the mainstream of British film-making. Ian Dalrymple, head of the influential Crown Film Unit, noting this development in an article in October 1941, attributed it to four factors which interacted under the impact and dictates of the war.[1]

The first was the existence of the documentary movement, nurtured and promoted by John Grierson and his followers in the 1930s. Dalrymple described it as 'a movement to apply the complicated motion-picture medium to the recording of life and human beings, their actions and even thoughts and motives — and almost their instincts — in their essence and integrity . . . Characteristics of these films were that they relied on the reconstruction of a small section of, or incident from, or activity of real life for their drama; that the players were the people themselves; and that the camera was not confined . . . to the studios.'

The practitioners of the documentary found themselves in demand with the coming of war: first, to provide instructional films for the services; secondly, 'to record the events of this critical chapter in our history and the behaviour of our people through the ordeal for the edification and, we hope, admiration of posterity'; thirdly for propaganda. Dalrymple elaborated on the idea of British wartime propaganda:

> When we make propaganda we tell, quite quietly, what we believe to be the truth. The Nazi method is to bellow as loudly and as often as possible, what they know to be absolutely and deliberately false. This being our conception of propaganda — that we should attempt to tell the truth — what was more natural than that the government should make use of the documentary movement as their method of film propaganda? We say in film to our own people 'This is what the boys in the services, or the girls in the factories, or the men and women in Civil Defence, or the patient citizens themselves are

like, and what they are doing. They are playing their part in the spirit in which you see them in this film. Be of good heart and go and do likewise.' And we say to the world 'Here in these films are the British people at war.' And the world is either moved or it is not moved. It has seen the truth and it can make up its own mind.

This sums up the projection of 'The People's War', which was one of the cardinal principles of the Crown Film Unit.

So during the war documentaries flourished as never before. But even more remarkable was the fusion of documentary realism and feature film entertainment. In some cases, feature films were directly inspired by and based on existing documentaries. *The Way Ahead* (1944), Carol Reed's tribute to the ordinary British conscript, was an expanded remake of the army instructional film *The New Lot.* Several instructional films made for the forces were deemed successful enough as entertainment to be released commercially to civilian cinemas, notably the Army's *The Next of Kin* and the RAF's *Journey Together.* Furthermore, several feature-length documentaries adopted a conventional dramatic narrative structure to tell reconstructed true-life stories of the war using their original participants (*Target for Tonight, Western Approaches*). Documentary realism became one of the critical tests of the successful entertainment feature. It was one of the factors, for instance, prompting the well-nigh unanimous praise of Noël Coward's *In Which We Serve.* It was also the reason why Michael Balcon recruited some of the leading documentarists, notably Cavalcanti and Harry Watt, to feature film-making at his Ealing Studios.

But in the field of wartime documentary one name stands out, and that of a man who is in some ways the least typical of all the documentarists — Humphrey Jennings. Jennings, Cambridge intellectual, poet, painter, literary critic, film-maker, had scattered his talents in many directions before the war. He had been an organizer of the International Surrealist Exhibition in London in 1936 and a founder member of Mass-Observation. But with the outbreak of war he found his questing mind more and more drawn to the war effort and its relation to the nature of England and the English. In his work the propaganda objectives of 'How we Fight' and 'Why we Fight' often imperceptibly merged. He found the ideal medium for his purpose in the cinema and in particular, documentary film. In one way his films were intensely and deliberately personal, but in another, by addressing themselves to the nature of the nation, they were resoundingly public.[2]

In an essay on contemporary theatre in the 1930s, he had denounced both the bland commercialized entertainment and the didactic political drama of his day and had pointed admiringly to the short period at the end of the 16th and beginning of the 17th century when:

> several Englishmen used 'theatre' as they found it, for their own purposes of poetry and analysis of behaviour — *connaissance* — we have no word for it,

naturally. That these may still be constructed by Englishmen there seems just a possibility, but that they can or will use the theatre as a means is hardly possible since in one way or another it is precisely against these things . . . that the present theatre's activity is directed.[3]

Jennings not surprisingly therefore turned to the sponsored cinema for his 'own purposes of poetry and analysis'.

Working for the Crown Film Unit and producing mainly short films for non-theatrical distribution at home and overseas, Jennings in his language and his imagery managed to distil something of the soul of the nation, something that was officially recognized by the award of the OBE in 1946. *London Can Take It* (1940), co-directed by Harry Watt, depicted how London was standing up to the Blitz. *The Heart of Britain* (1941) examined the effects of the war on the provinces. *Words for Battle* (1941) unforgettably matched inspired images to inspirational texts. *Listen to Britain* (1942), co-directed by Stewart McAllister, evoked the myriad sounds of the nation at war. *The Silent Village* (1943) movingly recreated the Lidice massacre in the Welsh village of Cwmgiedd. *A Diary for Timothy* (1944 – 5) interpreted the events of the last winter of the war for a newly born child. Jennings' only full-length feature film was *Fires Were Started* (1943), which hewed to a straightforward narrative line unlike most of his other films which relied on creative montage for their effect. But what all the films shared was the will to fight on to the end, defiance of the enemy, a triumphant celebration of ordinary people and an unashamed rejoicing in the richness of British culture. Together they decisively shaped and defined the image of Britain at war that was to be circulated round the world and handed on to the generations to come.

Jennings' approach was unabashedly poetic. Lindsay Anderson has dubbed him 'the only real poet the British cinema has yet produced'.[4] Jennings' idiom was 'painterly'. His Crown Unit colleague Pat Jackson recalled:

> It was terribly like a painter in a way; it wasn't a storyteller's mind. I don't think the dramatic approach to a subject, in film, really interested him very much. It was an extension of the canvas for him. Patterns, abstractions appealed to him enormously, and those are what people remember most, you know.[5]

The imagery he achieved in his films was crucially influenced by two movements in particular. The first was Surrealism. The aim of the Surrealists — to present 'a solidified dream-image' — was achieved by the technique of juxtaposing apparently incongruous elements in order to upset traditional modes of perception and thus liberate the unconscious as 'an instrument for the exploration and revelation of the material world.'[6] So striking images were consciously planted in his films. In *Fires Were Started* the shot of a terrified horse being led to safety through the smoke

Fires Were Started dramatized the work of the Auxiliary Fire Service during the Blitz.

struck many observers. It was present in the script and had been designed in advance of shooting. Similarly the shot of a one-legged man moving slowly through the rubble creates ripples in the mind. It was not in the script, but was a faithful reproduction of something Jennings had witnessed after an air raid and incorporated in his poem 'I See London'.

The other influence was Mass-Observation, which Jennings had founded with the anthropologist Tom Harrisson and the poet and sociologist Charles Madge. Paul C. Ray has called it 'Surrealism in reverse', in that where Surrealism sought to project the imagination on to the objective world in order to transform it, Mass-Observation tried to recover the imagination that had produced the objects and images of the real world.[7] The poet Kathleen Raine said that Mass-Observation inspired both Madge's and Jennings' poetry:

in which an imagery of precise and objective realism, gathered from the daily human (and especially urban) scene, from the habitat of common man, is informed with a content not only supremely imaginative, but infused with the imagination of the collective mind of which it is an eloquent, if unconscious expression; a listening to the dreaming . . . of a nation or a world, itself unaware of the purport of its own fantasies.[8]

The same description could be applied to Jennings' films, where he sought not to invent but to discover images from literature, history and real life which would reveal the inner truth. The startled horse and the one-legged man in *Fires Were Started* are examples of this. But perhaps the best known example is the recurrent image of the dome of St Paul's, which, defiantly etched against the night sky in *London Can Take It,* became one of the most memorable images of the Blitz. It recurs in *Words for Battle* when on Churchill's line 'we shall never surrender', Jennings cuts to St Paul's towering above the rubble. In 'I See London' Jennings writes: 'I see the dome of St Paul's like the forehead of Darwin'. The dome thus symbolizes the intelligence of the scientists and paradoxically a building that is a testament of faith becomes a monument of reason. But it enshrines Jennings' belief in the survival of London, England, the British people, his faith in the triumph of all the things that England stands for, one of which is tradition as embodied in the classicism of Sir Christopher Wren and another of which is scientific progress, which he traced back to the reign of Charles II, the age not only of Wren but of Newton. Connections, interrelations and fusions like this were integral to his view of England.

But an approach like this aroused the fury of the documentary purists, who sought a rigorous objective realism devoid of poetic frills. Their voice was regularly to be heard in *Documentary News Letter* where *Words for Battle* was reviewed with withering scorn:

> *Words for Battle* is an illustrated lantern-slide lecture, with Olivier's curate-like voice reverently intoning various extracts from poetry, verse and topical political speeches . . . Altogether an extraordinary performance, the effect of which on morale is quite incalculable. The man who must feel most out of place is poor old Handel. As he stood on his gaily coloured barge conducting the Water Music that was to bring him back into royal favour he can hardly have guessed that it would come to this.[9]

Edgar Anstey, in the *Spectator,* was equally dismissive of *Listen to Britain,* which he described as 'an expensive Crown Film Unit production . . . which will not encourage anyone to do anything at all':

> By the time Humphrey Jennings has done with it, it has become the rarest piece of fiddling since the days of Nero. It will be a disaster if this film is sent overseas. One shudders to imagine the effect upon our allies should they learn that an official British film-making unit can find time these days to

contemplate the current sights and sounds of Britain as if the country were some curious kind of museum exhibit or a figment of the romantic imagination of Mass-Observation.[10]

But Jennings' films were successful both at home and abroad and any fears that they might have been too arty-crafty for mass audiences seem to have been wide of the mark. Lady Forman, who as Miss Helen de Mouilpied had been deputy head of non-theatrical distribution at the MoI, arranging for showings of films in factories and village halls for people unable to reach a cinema and for specialist groups (Home Guard, Civil Defence, Women's Organizations etc.), recalled:

> One of the NT (non-theatrical) films . . . which was liked and applauded was Humphrey Jennings' *Listen to Britain.* All sorts of audiences felt it to be a distillation and also a magnification of their own experiences of the home front. This was especially true of factory audiences. I remember one show in a factory in the Midlands where about 800 workers clapped and stamped approval.[11]

Roger Manvell, who was Films Officer for the South West (1940—43) and later North West of England (1943—45), made a practice of including a Jennings film in all his programmes. The reason for this was:

> the poetic and emotional life they gave the programmes as a whole. I do not exaggerate when I say that members of audiences under the emotional strains of war . . . frequently wept as a result of Jennings' direct appeal to the rich cultural heritage of Britain going back . . . to Shakespeare and the Elizabethans, to Purcell and to Handel. People found themselves being brought suddenly and movingly into touch with what was at stake if indeed the Nazi forces . . . invaded and took over the conduct of their lives.[12]

Ian Dalrymple reported in 1942 on an unofficial try-out of *Fires Were Started* in Wales before an audience 'entirely Welsh and mostly "tough" (miners etc.)':

> The reception was most enthusiastic. The film seemed to be a revelation to most as to what had been going on in other parts of the country.[13]

It has been customary for critics to refer to the films as 'Jennings' films', but like all films, they were necessarily collaborative, and the question of who was ultimately responsible for creating a film has once again been brought centre stage by Dai Vaughan's important book on Stewart McAllister.[14] The book is part of a wider attempt to retrieve and resolve the role of the editor in the creation of films. In emphasizing McAllister's role in the films, Vaughan was fastening on an important area, because they depend a good deal on editing for their effect.

McAllister, born in Lanarkshire and a student at Glasgow School of Art, was seven years younger than Jennings, a shy introvert animated by a passionate love of documentary. He worked on almost all the major Jennings documentaries and several of his colleagues emphasized McAllister's contributions, crediting him with several key sequences in *Listen to Britain* — the build-up of airplane sound over the cornfield; the cutting on a chord from Flanagan and Allen in the factory canteen to Dame Myra Hess at the National Gallery.[15] Since a quarter of the footage for *Listen to Britain* was drawn from pre-existing sources, an ever greater stress than usual was laid on creative editing. But then McAllister's importance to that particular film was acknowledged in the joint credit, directed and edited by Humphrey Jennings and Stewart McAllister. This credit was not repeated on any other film.

Jennings and McAllister clearly worked closely together, but the process remains mysterious. Ian Dalrymple recalled:

> Humphrey and McAllister had a strange effect upon one another. Humphrey was frightfully well organized in shooting. He'd have the most marvellous luck, too, because sort of symbolic things happened the whole time; and because he'd been a painter and in fact was still daubing with paint when he had a moment, he had a wonderful gift for choosing the exact place to put the camera. So he'd go out and shoot madly and all the stuff would come in to McAllister, and McAllister would brood over it on the Movieola. When Humphrey had finished shooting, he would join McAllister in the cutting room and nothing would happen for weeks, apparently. You wondered when the hell anything was going to emerge, and of course London end got a bit restive. Then all of a sudden, overnight, somehow everything went together — doink. And there was what I thought a mini-masterpiece in each case.[16]

Nevertheless, it is hard to accept that the overall conception, the continuing preoccupations, the structure even of the films are not ultimately those of Jennings. Jennings prepared the scripts beforehand, outlining the ideas he sought to express in much greater detail than he has often been given credit for. He certainly improvised on location to incorporate images and ideas that appealed to him, but always within the masterplan. Jennings' Surrealist background gave him a full appreciation of the value of juxtaposition of images, one of the features of the short films. On the other hand, McAllister did not edit *A Diary for Timothy*, a key Jennings work which strongly relates both visually and thematically to the rest of his work. Furthermore, there is no attested evidence of specific interest on McAllister's part in England and the English, not perhaps too surprising in a Scot.

Vaughan is unable finally to determine individual responsibility for specific shots in the film but suggests that the methods and approaches of the two men meshed and they worked closely together. Vaughan defines McAllister's creative personality as consisting in:

> a certain way of connecting images; a linkage, relying upon a delicate balance between the compositional and the conceptual, wherein each image may assume a symbolic quality, but of a transitory symbolism, limited to context and in no way antagonistic to the shot's status as witness to a vanished moment.[17]

Jennings, as his colleagues recalled, believed in a similar juxtaposition. 'He tried to get two ideas on the screen at the same time' said editor R. Q. MacNaughton.[18] Charles Madge talked of Jennings' aim as 'the combination of many effects, each utterly insensible alone, into one sum of fine effect.'[19] McAllister had written as early as 1933: 'It is agreed, I think, that our delight in all the arts depends greatly on what may be called "pattern".'[20] Jennings belief in pattern is also well attested and will be developed later. What emerges is that McAllister's belief in pattern as artistic form harmonized directly with Jennings', but in Jennings' case this artistic form was a reflection of a wider world view of the pattern of British history and of English life and culture. It is this consistent and coherent world view which ultimately marks Jennings out as the directing intelligence of the films, for all the major contribution that McAllister undoubtedly made in realizing it in shaped imagery. The films continue to be, in my submission, Jennings' films.

Jennings' world view was crystallized by the war and in a very real sense his films stand alongside George Orwell's essays *The Lion and the Unicorn* and *The English People* in articulating a robust Socialist patriotism, a full-blooded love of England and the English centred on an unashamed admiration for the qualities of the common man. This set both Orwell and Jennings apart from the general run of left-wing intellectuals, who as Orwell scornfully pointed out had little time for their own country:

> The really important fact about so many of the English intelligentsia [is] their severance from the common culture of the country. In intention at any rate, the English intelligentsia are Europeanized. They take their cookery from Paris and their opinions from Moscow. In the general patriotism of the country they form a sort of island of dissident thought. England is perhaps the only great country whose intellectuals are ashamed of their own nationality. In left-wing circles it is always felt that there is something slightly disgraceful in being an Englishman and that it is a duty to snigger at every English institution, from horse racing to suet puddings.[21]

This was not a view to which either Orwell or Jennings subscribed. Their love of England ran deep. They shared an affection for the countryside; indeed both had affinities with the same part of rural England, Suffolk. Jennings was born in the Suffolk village of Walberswick and it was from the River Orwell that Eric Blair, born in Motihari, Bengal, chose his pen-name. Both were middle class left-wing intellectuals who set off deliberately to find the real character of England. Orwell took the road to Wigan Pier and wrote graphically and movingly about his experiences and encounters in 'darkest England'. Jennings took the road to Bolton which became the centre of Mass-Observation's operations in the north and the place where it began to study the English people close-up by anthropological techniques. When Jennings turned to film-making with the GPO Film Unit, his first important effort was *Spare Time* (1939), sometimes called his 'Mass-Observation film'. It is an exploration of working class leisure in Bolton, Sheffield and South Wales, which contains passages on pigeon fancying, whippet racing, football, bicycles and choirs. It parallels exactly Orwell's investigations into the submerged culture of the proletariat — the seaside postcard, boys' papers, the pub. Interestingly both ignore the cinema, which A. J. P. Taylor called 'the essential social habit of the age' but which so many middle class commentators disliked because they believed it induced passivity and apathy in the working class. Jennings, like Orwell, admired those things which escaped 'culturization', processing

The film traced the integration of a newcomer into the fire-fighting unit.

into a genteel and bloodless middle brow respectability. He gave as examples beer ads, steam railways, Woolworths and clairvoyants. Orwell looked to comic postcards, the back garden, suet puddings and 'the nice cup of tea'.

Jennings' grand synthesis came in *Family Portrait* (1950), a film commissioned for the Festival of Britain, which was his equivalent of Orwell's *The Lion and the Unicorn,* and echoed its findings. Jennings, like Orwell, observed that the British loved public pomp (pageantry, tradition) and private domesticity (the fireside, the garden). Both saw a country full of such paradoxes and both sought for the pattern which would make sense of them. Orwell defined the problem:

When you come back to England from any foreign country, you have immediately the sensation of breathing a different air. Even in the first few minutes dozens of small things conspire to give you this feeling. The beer is bitterer, the coins are heavier, the grass is greener, the advertisements are more blatant. The crowds in the big towns, with their mild knobby faces, their bad teeth and gentle manners, are different from a European crowd. Then the vastness of England swallows you up, and you lose for a while your feeling that the whole nation has a single identifiable character. Are there really such things as nations? Are we not 46 million individuals, all different? And the diversity of it, the chaos! The clatter of clogs in the Lancashire mill towns, the to-and-fro of lorries on the Great North Road, the queues outside the Labour Exchanges, the rattle of pin-tables in the Soho pubs, the old maids biking to Holy Communion through the mists of the autumn morning — all these are not only fragments, but *characteristic* fragments, of the English scene. How can one make a pattern out of this muddle? But talk to foreigners, read foreign books or newspapers, and you are brought back to the same thought. Yes, there is something distinctive and recognizable in English civilization . . . It has a flavour of its own. Moreover it is continuous, it stretches into the future and the past, there is something in it that persists, as in a living creature.[22]

The word 'pattern' recurs throughout *Family Portrait.* Jennings stresses the variations in weather, landscape and race. But he sees this compensated for in the alliance of industry and art, science and agriculture, the mingling of poetry and prose. Jennings concludes by looking out from Britain to Europe and to the Commonwealth:

We have become both inside the family of Europe, and the pattern overseas. We are the link between them. For all that we have received from them, and from our native land, what can we return? Perhaps the very things that make the family, a pattern, possible — tolerance, courage, faith. A world to be different in — and free — together.

For in the end he has reached the same conclusion as Orwell. 'England is, if anything, a family' said Orwell. 'We like to think of ourselves as a family' said Jennings. The family above all other images epitomizes the ideal of diversity within unity.

Jennings' love of England centred on three basic principles: his admiration of the common people, his instinctive belief in individualism and his love of English culture. The war had been a revelation to him in that it had shown him the real worth and strength of ordinary people. This comes through in his letters to his wife, Cicely, whom he had evacuated with their children to the United States. He wrote to her on 20 October 1940 of the Blitz:

> Some of the damage in London is pretty heart-breaking but what an effect it has had on the people! What warmth — what courage! What determination! People sternly encouraging each other by explaining that when you hear a bomb whistle it means it has missed you! People in the north singing in public shelters: 'One man went to mow, went to mow a meadow.' WVS girls serving hot drinks to fire-fighters during raids explaining that really they are 'terribly afraid all the time'. . . . Everybody absolutely determined: secretly delighted with the *privilege* of holding up Hitler. Certain of beating him; a certainty which no amount of bombing can weaken, only strengthen[23]

After encountering the Welsh miners of Cwmgiedd during the filming of *The Silent Village,* he wrote to Cicely on 10 September 1942:

> I never thought to live to see the honest Christian and Communist principles daily acted on as a matter of course by a large number of British — I won't say English — people living together. Not merely honesty, culture, manners, practical Socialism, but real life, with passion and tenderness and comradeship and heartiness all combined. From these people one can really understand Cromwell's New Model Army and the defenders of many places at the beginning of the Industrial Revolution.[24]

It was this indomitable spirit that Jennings celebrated and honoured in his films: the ARP men and WVS women of *The Heart of Britain* who talk directly and simply and movingly of their work; the Welsh miners of *The Silent Village,* refusing to submit to the Nazi yoke; the fire-fighters of *Fires Were Started;* the four central figures of *A Diary for Timothy,* whose lives intermesh in the last full year of the war — Goronwy the miner, Bill the engine driver, Alan the farmer and Peter the fighter pilot, all doing their bit with courage and calmness.

Closely related to his feeling for the people, was his belief in individualism. He saw it as integral to English character, as he outlined in a lengthy review for *The Times Literary Supplement* of the anthology *The Character of England:*

> The English travel in trains; not a company, but a collection of individuals; first turning each carriage into a row of cottages — the word compartment is

a word of praise — and then sitting in each corner with the same blank denial of any other presence that the lovers show in the park. The English live in cities, but they are not citified; they very seldom produce, for example, that characteristic symptom of a city, the mob. They are urbane without being urban; creating their own environment within their own being, they can dwell in the midst of 20 miles of paving stones and pretend, with the aid of a back green or even a flower pot, that they are in a hamlet on the Downs. Or so it seems to the outsider. Perhaps the English have something different in their heads.[25]

This belief surely lies behind the inclusion in *Fires Were Started* of the quote from *Macbeth,* spoken by Rumbold:

Ay, in the catalogue, ye go for men; as hounds and greyhounds, mongrels, spaniels, curs, shoughs, water-rugs and demi-wolves are clept all by the name of dogs; the valu'd file distinguishes the swift, the slow, the subtle, the housekeeper, the hunter, every one according to the gift which bounteous nature hath in him clos'd.

So just as the firemen are all fire-fighters and all men, each is uniquely himself. This was a cardinal point of British propaganda, given the stock image of the German as a faceless, heel-clicking, identikit automaton. But it also sprang from deep within Jennings himself. As his close friend Gerald Noxon recalled:

To say that Humphrey Jennings was a typical Englishman is, of course, a contradiction in terms, for the most characteristic quality of the English is their untypicalness, their eccentricity. In fact he was most English in his eccentricity, which happened to include a complete lack of what are often considered English characteristics — snobbishness, intellectual and social hypocrisy, insularity, arrogance and indifference.[26]

The picture is completed by Jennings' immersion in English culture. Kathleen Raine wrote that 'in the tradition of Chaucer and Blake, Humphrey Jennings had a sense of the organic whole of English culture'.[27] Gerald Noxon amplified this point:

In his formative years . . . Humphrey had been influenced particularly by certain English writers and artists of the past — by Shakespeare and Marlowe, of course, but more unusually perhaps by John Milton, John Bunyan, John Constable and William Blake. The works of these men remained in Humphrey's background as a permanent frame of reference. Their kind of Englishness was Humphrey's kind of Englishness.[28]

Poetry and music in particular exerted an influence on Jennings. In his *T.L.S.* review, he stressed that the English 'have a power of poetry which is the despair of the rest of the world'. He encapsulated that feeling in what has been justly called 'this exquisite little masterpiece', *Words for Battle*.[29] In it he employed the technique of startling juxtaposition in matching images to words. Using Blake's *Jerusalem* to accompany a sequence of the evacuation of children from London, he cuts on 'Bring me my chariot of fire' to a low-angle shot of a steam engine leaving Waterloo. In the notable finale, as Laurence Olivier speaks the words of the Gettysburg address ('That we here highly resolve that the dead shall not have died in vain. That the nation shall under God have a new birth of freedom and that government of the people, by the people and for the people shall not perish from the earth.'), a line of tanks rumble past Lincoln's statue and across Parliament Square, dissolving to a succession of shots of men and women of all nationalities in the uniforms of the allied nations as they mingle in the streets of London.

Music, particularly English music, was integral to Jennings' films: classical music like Handel, Vaughan Williams, Elgar and Purcell; Welsh hymns; popular songs; folk songs; dance band music. One film, *The True Story of Lilli Marlene,* told the story of the German song which with characteristic illogic the British Eighth Army had appropriated as its own. *Listen to Britain* created a symphony of sound, evocatively blending all kinds of music, the natural sounds of the country, the man-made sounds of factory and city streets, the official (Big Ben, the BBC, the RAF Band) and the unofficial (children dancing in the playground, 'Music while you work', train sing-songs), until the whole swells into a choral rendition of *Rule Britannia,* the fitting apotheosis of all that has gone before. It is this very richness and diversity, Jennings is telling us, that give the strength of purpose to ensure that the national effort ends in victory.

Several commentators have stressed the importance to Jennings of music not just as background but as structure to his films. William Sansom records:

> He always stressed his need for music in the film; and I think it is plain that, apart from any material music he used, his films were composed in the swelling—dying, theme and repeat-theme notation of a kind of musical composition.[30]

Even a cursory look at *Fires Were Started* and *The Silent Village* reveals a very definite three movement structure, which give these films something of their classical shape and feel.

Fires Were Started in fact brought together many of Jennings' preoccupations and gave visual form to his feelings about England and the English. It stressed the heroism of ordinary men and women in the Blitz, carefully characterizing them as distinctive individuals. It placed them securely in their culture, with popular songs resonating through the action ('One man went to mow', 'Please don't talk about me when I'm gone', 'Out with my barrow and my moke all day', 'Ah, sweet mystery of life'). Their own actions are underscored by the heroic symphonic music of William

Alwyn and placed in the wider context of English culture by quotations from Sir Walter Raleigh ('Oh, eloquent, just and mighty death') and from Shakespeare's *Macbeth,* the past being quickened by its contemporary relevance.

The film was the result of a proposal to make a feature-length film about the fire service. Besides paying tribute to their heroism, it would also serve to fulfil the demand that was being made for propaganda for teamwork. As a memorandum from the Public Relations Committee of the Civil Defence put it:

> The simple idea that we would like to see brought to life is that the action of the people of Great Britain today provides the finest example of teamwork the world has ever seen . . . In time of war, we make the most of what we already possess and faith in the power derived from voluntary team work is immeasurably superior to that of a nation dragooned for war. But to make the most of our national genius and to mobilize quickly our inherent strength, we must through propaganda make the idea of teamwork more articulate, conscious and dynamic.[31]

The idea to assign Jennings to the film came apparently from Harry Watt, the tough and canny Scottish director whose *Target for Tonight* was one of the top documentaries of the war. 'We must try to get Humphrey to do an action picture because everything is so static with Humphrey. All his set-ups are static. The people are static' he told Ian Dalrymple.[32]

Jennings agreed to do it and set about gathering detailed accounts of fire-fighting from Liverpool and London.[33] One of them was an account of fighting a fire at Woolwich Arsenal on 10 September 1940. Another was an account of procedure at fire stations in the event of air raids. The first draft for the script, an outline of ideas clearly based on these reports, was completed by 25 October 1941:

> The station would send out its crew as described in the Woolwich report and everything would proceed very much as in that report, except that it would be the warehouse which would be alight and the curtain of water would have to be thrown in the narrow street between the warehouse and the factory.

It was also intended from the outset that one of the firemen would be killed, which was in line with the MoI's desire to stress the need for sacrifice in winning the war:

> It will end up with one man definitely giving his life to make sure that the curtain of water is kept up between the warehouse and the shell dump.

More detail, including a threatened munitions ship, was worked into a second version of the script, completed by 22 November. A further version, broken down into sequences, was completed by 16 December.

Three more scripts appeared during January until a final, detailed shooting script, dated 27 January 1942, was ready. The copy in the Jennings Papers at the British Film Institute is very full and is scrawled over by Jennings with changes and alterations. Images such as the frightened horse being led through the smoke and the finding of Jacko's tin hat in the ruins are carefully described and were obviously pre-planned. There is also mention of a sing-song around the piano in the fire station, although the specific song is not named. This is important in the light of statements made about Jennings' method of work. William Sansom stated that there was:

> No script. A general scheme of course, which we did not know about. The film was shot both on and off the cuff. Dialogue was always made up on the spot — and of course the more germane for that — and Jennings collected detail of all kinds on the way, on the day, on the spot.[34]

Ian Dalrymple said: 'I was always in trouble with the London end because there was never any script. That wasn't the way Humphrey worked. He'd have a bit of a note on an old envelope or something, a few words to remind him of various things'.[35] Statements like this have led to the belief that Jennings' films were improvised. They were not. He was certainly ready to improvise where necessary. He would incorporate interesting details encountered during filming, like the penny-whistle blower who is introduced into the introductory sequences. He improvised the details of the sing-songs, though he had always intended that there should be one, and his letter to Cicely during the Blitz reveals that he had heard people in shelters singing 'One man went to mow'. It was just the sort of real-life detail he liked to recreate. Scenes in the script were shortened and tightened. The dialogue, of which there was too much and too literate, was pared back, to be supplemented by ten pages of Cockney dialogue from AFS fireman Maurice Richardson, which is dated 13 February 1942, and by improvisations worked out with fireman Fred Griffiths on the set. But it is clear that the film was carefully scripted and structured before shooting began and even if Jennings kept the details in his head, they were worked out.

Jennings selected real firemen from stations around London, seconded for the duration of filming. They were Leading Fireman Fred Griffiths, a Cockney taxi driver who had joined the AFS before the war; Leading Fireman Philip Wilson-Dickson, previously in an advertising agency; Leading Fireman Loris Ray, a sculptor; Fireman T. P. Smith, a former waiter; Fireman John Barker, a Manchester businessman; Fireman Johnny Houghton, and Commanding Officer George Gravett, a regular with the London Fire Brigade. Bill Barrett, the new man, was played by the writer, William Sansom.

The film was produced by the Crown Film Unit for the Ministry of Information with facilities provided by the Ministry of Home Security, the

Fires Were Started acknowledged the need for individual heroism.

Home Office and the National Fire Service. It went through a variety of working titles: *NFS, Heavy One Rides Again, The Bells Went Down, I Was a Fireman* and eventually *Fires Were Started*. The budget was originally estimated at £10,498 8s 2d, but shooting overran and the cost eventually worked out at £13,283 18s 4d. The original shooting schedule was to be 5 February to 2 May, but due to 'unavoidable hold-ups' it went on until October. Exteriors were shot on location with the fire staged at St Katherine's Dock, and interiors taken at Pinewood Studios, the headquarters of the Crown Film Unit.[36]

William Sansom described the shooting:

He dealt well. Democracy the rule. Christian names all round, discussion and beer together after work. He gave us the sense of making the film *with* instead of for him.[37]

Jennings described the filming in Stepney and Wapping to his wife, Cicely, in a letter of 12 April 1942:

> The place and the people illuminating beyond everything. The river, the wharves and shipping, the bridge in Wapping Lane smelling permanently of cinammon, the remains of Chinatown, the *Prospect of Whitby* and another wonderful pub called the *Artichoke,* which is our field headquarters. Reconstruction of a fire in the docks . . . For the last two months we have been working at this down here for 12 hours a day six days a week; we are now roughly half way through and pretty exhausted; the results peculiar and very unlike anything I have had to do with before; popular, exciting, funny — mixture of slapstick and macabre Blitz reconstruction . . . It has now become 14 hours a day, living in Stepney the whole time, really have never worked so hard at anything or I think thrown myself into anything so completely. Whatever the results it is definitely an advance in film-making for me — really beginning to understand people and making friends with them and not just looking at them and lecturing or pitying them. Another general effect of the war.[38]

The film that resulted from all this activity, initially known as *I Was a Fireman,* although made in 1942, looks back to 1940 to recreate one night in the Blitz. The opening title explains that this film takes place before August 1941 when the unified National Fire Service was created by a merger of various independent brigades of regular and auxiliary firemen. It is one of the key works in creating the mythic image of the London Blitz. Those heroic figures silhouetted against the blazing inferno sweeping the dockside warehouse etched themselves into history, embodying the epic of the ordinary men and women who calmly and courageously took up the defence of their city.

The myth of the Blitz was established almost instantaneously and is enshrined in such official publications as the MoI's *Front Line 1940−41: the Official Story of the Civil Defence* (1942), which paints in words the same picture of the heroic firemen that Jennings creates in images (e.g. 'Sometimes he stood firmly on a flame-lit roadway . . . knees a little bent and body braced against the thrust of the water through his hose'.) *Front Line* ends with a quotation from Churchill which epitomizes the tone and mood of the account:

> I see the damage done by the enemy attacks; but I also see, side by side with the devastation and amid the ruins, quiet, confident, bright and smiling eyes, beaming with a consciousness of being associated with a cause far higher and wider than any human or personal issue. I see the spirit of an unconquerable people.

Jennings' film dramatizes the experiences of Heavy Unit One, a single fire engine and its crew stationed at a dockland fire station. Like the rest of his work, it is carefully structured, falling into three distinct movements: the build-up, the fire, the aftermath. Unusually for him, he adopts a conventional linear narrative form. Within it, however, he inserts a number of typical Jennings images, all of them drawn from reality and observation. There is the startled horse being led to safety through the smoke, the one-legged man hobbling on crutches past the ruins, three large women wheeling a rickety pram through the confusion, a solitary tree in full blossom in the station yard, a graceful sailing barge gliding down the Thames, a barrage balloon floating majestically above the river. The river is a recurrent image, gliding serenely and timelessly on in peace and war. Jennings' shots of it capture the mood of his poem 'I See London':

> I see the grey waters of Thames, like a loving nurse, unchanged, unruffled, flooding between bridges and washing up wharf steps—an endlessly flowing eternity that smooths away the sorrows of beautiful churches—the pains of time—the wrecks of artistry along her divine banks—to whom the strongest towers are but a moment's mark and the deepest-cleaving bomb an untold regret.

All these images are images of life continuing amid the crisis, but they also help to give the film the feel of the 'solidified dream-image' of the Surrealists.

The pace of the first section of the film is relaxed, centring on the depiction of routine. We are introduced to each of the crew of Heavy One in turn, as the film cuts back and forth from them as distinctive individuals to the life of the streets and docks going on as usual – the picture of normality. The crew gathers at sub-station 14Y with a litany of 'good mornings': cheerful Cockney taxi driver Johnny Daniels; jaunty tobacconist 'Jacko' with his permanent cigarette; Scottish intellectual Rumbold, nicknamed 'The Colonel'; chirpy B. A. Brown; pleasant Vallance and quiet Walters. They are introduced to a new man, advertising copywriter Bill Barrett, who is put in Johnny's hands to be shown the ropes. The fire engine is cleaned and over that scene we hear the voices of the girls in the control room receiving the routine daily reports on the state of the fire-fighting equipment and appliances, a device which has the effect of integrating the girls at headquarters with the work of the men on the ground. The crew go through their drill and then Johnny shows Barrett over their patch. The role of the newcomer has the effect of identifying the audience with the new man and explaining to them through him the functions of the Auxiliary Fire Service.

As night falls, they wait for the air raids to begin. The blackout is put up. The men chat and in the recreation room there is beer, snooker, darts and table-tennis. When Johnny discovers that Barrett can play the piano, he gets him to 'tickle the ivories'. Johnny and B. A. do a comic Sand Dance to his improvised rumba until they are all sent off to get kitted up. As they return, Johnny gets Barrett to strike up with 'One man went to mow', which is taken up by each in turn of the crew as they come in. This is a conscious but potent artistic device to show the newcomer integrated into the group, which earlier one of the girls has affectionately dubbed 'The Crazy Gang'. The same sing-song device is used to great effect by such Hollywood masters as John Ford (*How Green Was My Valley*) and Howard Hawks (*Rio Bravo*). The air raid siren sounds during the last verse of the song and with it the first movement of the film ends.

Events begin to move rapidly and the pace of the editing speeds up too. Guns and bombs are heard. Control begins to plot the locations of fires and order out appliances. As each of the crews in turn leaves, Heavy One join in 'Please don't talk about me when I'm gone', a comic variation on John Pudney's war-time lament: 'Do not despair for Johnny Head-in-Air'. At last Heavy Unit One is ordered out to fight a warehouse fire in Trinidad Street, which threatens a munitions ship moored nearby. The firemen run out their hoses and set to work. The water runs out and they turn to a nearby sunken barge for further supplies. Their fire-fighting is intercut with headquarters receiving and relaying information, a process which continues even when a falling bomb causes a shower of debris in the control room. The firewoman on the telephone simply dabs her cut forehead, apologizes for the interruption and carries on. This has the effect of demonstrating the very real danger faced by all members of the service, whether on the ground or at headquarters. It also shows them all facing danger with the same dedication and composure.

To get a better angle of attack on the fire, Jackie, Rumbold and Sub-Officer Dykes go up on to the roof and direct their hose into the heart of the blaze. Dykes is injured and has to be lowered to the ground. Jacko carries on alone, flames licking around his feet, until he is overcome and falls to his death amidst the blazing rubble. There is an enormous explosion from the warehouse, as if to signal the extent of the loss of a single heroic individual in the struggle. More appliances and hoses arrive from other forces and the fire is gradually subdued. This fact is reported to control. Dawn breaks, the 'All Clear' sounds and the second movement ends.

The aftermath shows the results of the fire in the bleak, grey light of morning: smoke, rubble, water and men physically and mentally drained. Clearing up, Barrett finds Jacko's battered helmet. A mobile canteen arrives with the 'nice cup of tea', that distinctively British symbol of normality. The men are stood down. A workman coming on duty observes laconically 'Bad night'. 'Bad night', replies Johnny, 'You wanna go down the road. There's a boat down there, good as new. She ain't got a scratch on 'er, a sight for sore eyes'. That is the justification for their work.

But there is a price to be paid. In the tobacconist's corner shop, the type so well described by Orwell, Jacko's wife awaits his return. She listens to the wireless: 'It does not appear that casualties are likely to be heavy'. Back at the station the crew of Heavy One sit silent, smoking cigarettes or drinking tea until B. A. barks 'Come on, chums, snap out of it'. The film ends with the funeral of Jacko, the coffin borne by his surviving comrades, the trees of the graveyard leafless. But the grief and formality give way to a sense of triumph as the scene dissolves to the prow of the munitions ship moving safely out to sea. The fire comes to symbolize the war itself, beaten by organization, teamwork and individual sacrifice: the film itself, the distillation of the qualities of the People's War.

Watching *Fires Were Started,* one is reminded time and again of John Ford, in the integration of the outsider into the group round the piano (*How Green Was My Valley*); in the ritual formality of the funeral (*Wee Willie Winkie*); in the barrack-room camaraderie, the discipline, the fortitude and the humour (the cavalry trilogy); the classical precision of the shooting framing the romantic and patriotic celebration of the common man. It is perhaps no coincidence that Lindsay Anderson, one of the foremost champions of Jennings' work, is also one of the leading admirers of Ford. What he discerns in them both is a pure and consistent poetic truth.

Fires Were Started, using real firemen, real locations and authentic episodes, fulfilled all the criteria laid down by Ian Dalrymple for a documentary. According to William Sansom it was literally true:

> As a practising fireman I could say this: the film was true to life in every respect. Not a false note — if you make the usual allowances for the absence of foul language which was in everybody's mouth all the time.[39]

There is a sprinkling of words ('bastard', 'bleeding', 'bloody') which would not have been sanctioned in pre-war years, though they are sparingly used, but more important than the literal truth is the mythic and poetic truth of the film. It transcends the mere photographing of reality. Jennings' placing of his camera, staging of the action, tempo of the editing, do not merely record, they celebrate the men and their struggle. The crew are individually characterized by the consistent use of close-ups, while their activity shows them acting as a team, pitted against the elements — night, fire, water. With no sight of and little mention of the enemy, the fire becomes almost an abstract symbol of struggle, highlighting the qualities that the nation needs at its moment of supreme crisis.

The film's overrunning of its shooting schedule was a matter of continuing concern because Ealing Studios were at the same time making their own feature film about the AFS, *The Bells Go Down.* The Ministry of Information sent a memorandum on 20 November 1942 urging the Crown Film Unit to get *I Was a Fireman* completed and released before the Ealing film because whichever fire service film came first would receive considerable publicity and 'this should have a substantial effect on bookings and profits'.[40] This refrain was to run through Crown's dealings with the distributors, with whom a bitter wrangle developed.

During the war there was an unofficial distributors' rota under which the principal commercial distributors undertook in turn to handle the release of official films. It was the turn of General Film Distributors (GFD) to handle *I Was a Fireman*. An agreement was drawn up by which the distributors agreed to handle the film for home theatrical distribution and got the rights for five years. The MoI retained the rights to overseas distribution and non-theatrical showings to the forces, but agreed not to show it until at least six months after the commercial release. £1,000 was earmarked for advertising and the cost of striking 50 prints of the film was to be deducted from the receipts. Thereafter 20 per cent of the box office receipts were to go to the distributors and 80 per cent to the Ministry.[41]

But there was an immediate problem. GFD chiefs Arthur Jarratt and C. M. Woolf refused to take the film as it stood. They wanted a change of title and cuts in the first reel to speed it up. Jack Beddington, Films Division director, wrote to Ian Dalrymple on 26 November 1942:

> I would not accept their judgement for one moment did I not feel myself that the film can be much improved both from a propaganda and entertainment point of view.[42]

Fires Were Started *celebrated not only individual heroism but also team effort.*

He wanted much of the introductory build-up cut and a narrator introduced 'both to point the dialogue and give added emphasis to the value of the munitions ship motif'. He also wanted it made clear that the action took place two years ago, 'before the new efficiency and organization of the present National Film Service'. Dalrymple, unwilling to cut, enlisted the aid of C. A. Lejeune, the respected film critic of the *Observer,* who was shown the film and wrote at Dalrymple's suggestion to Jack Beddington:

It should be shown quickly, it should be shown widely and it should be shown in its present form . . . I think it is one of the finest documentaries we have ever made. I am quite sure it will bring prestige to the unit and to British films generally. I can guarantee that what I may call 'my' public will like it, and I have enough faith in the good heart of the wider public to believe that they will like it too. I have never known a film as honest and human as this one fail to get its message through. If it were my film, I should be very proud of it.[43]

Jennings, who had been informed of developments, wrote angrily to his wife on 18 November 1942:

All sorts of people — official and otherwise — who apparently had not had the courage to speak out before, suddenly discovered that that was what they had thought all along, that the picture was much too long and much too slow and that really instead of being the finest picture we had produced (which was the general opinion till then) it was a hopeless muddle which would only be 'saved' by being cut right down and so on. Well of course one expects that from spineless well-known modern novelists and poets who have somehow got into the propaganda business — who have no technical knowledge and no sense of solidarity or moral courage. But worse, the opinion of people at Pinewood began to change. All this arising out of the criticism of one or two people in Wardour Street, who had other irons in the fire anyway and who fight every inch against us trespassing on what they pretend is their field. In the meantime Lejeune of the *Observer* has seen it and said it was easily the finest documentary ever made and that to touch it would be like cutting up Beethoven![44]

But on 9 December 1942 Arthur Jarratt forwarded to Beddington a report from the GFD publicity manager in Preston who had attended a showing of the film at the New Victoria Cinema, Preston, on 4 December, where *I Was a Fireman* had been shown in place of the advertised second feature:

The audience did not appear to be unfavourable, but, on the other hand, there were no enthusiastic comments. In conversation with members of the local press, police and fire-fighting representatives, I gathered the concensus [sic] of opinion to be that the film was deplorably slow for the first half-hour; . . . the blitz sequences were, on the other hand, particularly good, and even the fire authorities approved this . . . I would suggest that the film would make a good second feature up here, provided a good strong first feature was played with it.[45]

On 16 December 1942 Beddington informed S. C. Leslie of the Ministry of Home Security that 700−800 feet was definitely going to be cut from the first three reels because 'it is too long at the beginning'.[46] Negotiations with GFD continued to drag on and Sidney Bernstein began negotiations with Columbia Pictures to take over distribution on the same terms as those offered to GFD and an agreement, dated 1 February 1943 was drawn up. But Columbia were unable to promise a speedy release date and as *The Bells Go Down* was now completed, the matter became urgent. Negotiations with GFD resumed and on 19 March 1943 agreement was reached. Crown would cut the film from 74 minutes to 65, the title would be changed to *Fires Were Started* and there would be an opening title setting the historical context. In return GFD promised a West End opening on 29 March with general release on 12 April.[47]

Leslie Furniss of the GFD Publicity Department wrote on 16 April to J. D. Griggs, press officer of the MoI, to report that the crew of Heavy Unit One had made personal appearances at the Hammersmith and Holloway Odeons in connection with the film: 'I know you will be glad to learn that the boys received an ovation at both houses and the stunt was generally a big success.'[48]

Fires Were Started did beat *The Bells Go Down* into release and thus scooped the publicity; but it is worth comparing the two films briefly. *The Bells Go Down,* directed by Basil Dearden, is in many ways typical of Ealing's mature war films.[49] It follows much the same story line as Jennings' film — the training of a fire-fighting unit, camaraderie between the men, the Blitz, and the death of one of the heroes. It incorporates impressive documentary footage of training and fire-fighting, employs a narrator and precise dating for events to give it an authentic feel. But where it differs from *Fires Were Started* is in the elaboration of the home life, love life and personal background of the characters, and the employment of actors, notably Tommy Trinder, James Mason, Philip Friend and Mervyn Johns, to play the firemen. The two films share a sense of community, teamwork and individualism. But there is an inevitable artificiality about the studio exteriors and some of the romantic sub-plots.

The Times, reviewing *The Bells Go Down* on 15 April, concentrated on this area of difference between the two films:

> *The Bells Go Down* is unfortunate in that it so quickly follows the documentary film *Fires Were Started.* It is by no means true that a documentary film must, by the very virtue of its office, be better than an imaginative reconstruction of events, but here the film which was acted by men who were actually in the N.F.S. is superior at nearly every point . . . Their methods of approach are not dissimilar, and it is only in the casual moments, at the times when the men and the films are off duty, as it were, that the difference between them becomes apparent . . . (Tommy Trinder's) cockney humour and good spirits are admirable so long as they spring

The film stressed above all the resilience, humour and determination of Londoners under attack.

naturally from character and circumstance but there are moments when they are forced and deliberate, and the artificiality in them and in a story which depends too much upon unconvincing personal relationships cuts a jagged tear across an otherwise commendable design.[50]

Press reaction to *Fires Were Started* was, on the other hand, almost uniformly ecstatic: 'inspiring and dramatic' (*Daily Mirror*); 'magnificent, stirring and often deeply moving' (*Star*); 'a vivid piece of British social wartime history that speaks for itself' (*Daily Herald*); 'a noble and convincing tribute to the firemen' (*Daily Mail*); 'Thrilling and admirably made' (*News Chronicle*); 'an impressive testament to the courage of a fine body of Spartans' (*Manchester Guardian*); 'the scenes, largely recon-structed, have an authenticity which is moving and terrifying, and the acting and presentation seem to me to set a new standard in this kind of documentary' (*The Sunday Times*). Even the *Documentary News Letter,* usually the scourge of Jennings' films, joined in the praise:

Who would have thought that a film about the blitz could seem timely and important now? It is the great achievement of *Fires Were Started* that you're just as interested and the film means just as much now as if it had been made and shown in the middle of the raids; and it will mean just as much in a few years' time when the war is over. And this makes it, with the original *Merchant Seamen,* the best of the Crown films . . . Jennings must be held entirely to blame for the three or four occasions when, with somebody playing the piano or reading or reciting poetry (in his worst *Words for Battle* manner), he goes all arty for a moment . . . Never mind, these faults in the end do not detract from what is the real strength of the film — the best handling of people on and off the job that we've seen in any British film.[52]

One of the few dissenting voices was that of Campbell Dixon, whose review in the *Daily Telegraph* was headed 'Fires were started — but too slowly':

Humphrey Jennings takes an unconscionable time to get started — about a reel is devoted to 'good mornings' and other preliminaries — and when the test does come the spectacle is disappointing . . . I wish I could report that the film completely recaptures the atmosphere of the night of (say) 29 December 1940, but it does not.[53]

He was promptly rapped over the knuckles by William Whitebait in the *New Statesman:*

I think he misses the point, which is that by focusing our attention on a single 'incident' during a night in the Blitz, Humphrey Jennings builds up, without either hurry or failure, a drama that could not well be surpassed in excitement and intensity. The daylight scenes . . . stress the delay before nightfall and help to create suspense. We are given time to see into the daily routine and individual characters of the station personnel, and without this previous intimacy the later sequences of the men in action, fighting a warehouse fire in which one of them is killed, would lose half their effect . . . *Fires Were Started* creates its own tempo, which quite rightly is not that of the dramatic feature film — and brilliantly justifies it.[54]

The stature of the film has steadily grown over the years. Jim Hillier writes of it: 'It is the masterpiece not only of Jennings but also of the British documentary school and the whole British cinema'.[55] Daniel Millar calls it 'the highest achievement of British cinema'.[56] Sir Denis Forman described it as 'one of the most precious possessions of the cinema; it is without doubt the crowning achievement of the British documentary school'.[57] Lindsay Anderson summed up the general opinion when he declared: 'No other British film made during the war, documentary or feature, achieved such a continuous and poignant truthfulness or treated the subject of men at war with such a sense of its incidental glories and its essential tragedy'.[58]

In the years since the war, historians, whose stock in trade is the debunking of myths, have examined the events of the Blitz in detail. Evidence has emerged that there was some looting, some panic and some unrest in the East End about shelter-provision. But the general picture of a courageous, determined and good-humoured people surviving everything the Luftwaffe could throw at them remains.[59]

As for the firemen, there was another dimension to their story that was publicized even at the time. It was in 1941 that AFS member Michael Wassey published his highly critical *Ordeal by Fire,* complaining bitterly of the lack of recognition of the AFS and their lack of parity with the regulars in pay, compensation, status, conditions and promotion opportunities. But for all this discontent, Wassey declares of an AFS, drawn from all classes and all walks of life:

> After nearly two years of living, sleeping, eating, laughing, suffering and fire-fighting and going literally through fire and water together, they have been welded into a solid phalanx of fire-fighters with one and all 'mates', understanding of one another, tolerant, comradely, and all one loyal, though sometimes not happy, family.[60]

But a year after Wassey's book, the AFS got their recognition and their tribute in Jennings' film, which inscribed for all time in the national record the courageous reality at the heart of the myth.

NOTES

1   *London Calling* 109, October 1941, pp. 6—7. On his work at the Crown Film Unit, see Dalrymple, 'The Crown Film Unit. 1940—43', in Nicholas Pronay and D. W. Spring (eds), *Propaganda, Politics and Film 1918—1945,* London, 1982, pp. 209—20.

2   On Jennings' life and career, see Anthony W. Hodgkinson and Rodney E. Sheratsky, *Humphrey Jennings: more than a maker of films,* Hanover and London, 1982; Mary-Lou Jennings (ed.), *Humphrey Jennings: Film-maker, Painter, Poet,* London, 1982; Alan Lovell and Jim Hillier, *Studies in Documentary,* London, 1972, pp. 62—132; John Grierson et al., *Humphrey Jennings 1907—1950: a tribute,* London, n.d.; *Film Quarterly,* 15, Winter 1961—2, Humphrey Jennings issue. Specifically on *Fires Were Started,* see Philip Strick, 'Great Films of the Century no. II — *Fires Were Started', Films and Filming* 7 (May 1961) pp. 14—16, 35, 39, and Daniel Millar, 'Fires Were Started', *Sight and Sound* 38, Spring 1969, pp. 100—4.

3   Geoffrey Grigson (ed.), *The Arts Today,* London, 1935, pp. 215–16.
4   Jennings (ed.), *Humphrey Jennings* p. 53.
5   Elizabeth Sussex, *The Rise and Fall of British Documentary,* Berkeley, 1975, p. 144.
6   Paul C. Ray, *The Surrealist Movement in England,* Ithaca, 1971, pp. 38–66.
7   Ray, *The Surrealist Movement,* p. 177.
8   Kathleen Raine, *Defending Ancient Springs,* London, 1967, pp. 47–8.
9   *Documentary News Letter* 2, May 1941, p. 89.
10 *Spectator,* 13 March 1942.
11 Pronay and Spring (eds), *Propaganda, Politics and Film,* p. 230.
12 Hodgkinson and Sheratsky, *Humphrey Jennings,* p. xiii.
13 Memorandum from Ian Dalrymple to R. H. Weaitt, Films Division, MoI, 23 October 1942, INF 6/985.
14 Dai Vaughan, *Portrait of an Invisible Man,* London, 1983.
15 Vaughan, *Portrait of an Invisible Man,* p. 83.
16 Sussex, *British Documentary,* p. 144.
17 Jennings (ed.), *Humphrey Jennings,* p. 61.
18 Hodgkinson and Sheratsky, *Humphrey Jennings,* p. 30.
19 Jennings (ed.), *Humphrey Jennings,* p. 47.
20 Vaughan, *Portrait of an Invisible Man,* p. 137.
21 George Orwell, *Collected Essays, Journalism and Letters* (Harmondsworth, 1971), p. 95. Orwell and Jennings both died in the same year, 1950.
22 Orwell, *Collected Essays,* pp. 75–6.
23 Jennings (ed.), *Humphrey Jennings,* p. 25.
24 Jennings (ed.), *Humphrey Jennings,* p. 33.
25 *The Times Literary Supplement,* 7 August 1948.
26 *Film Quarterly* 15, Winter 1961–2, p. 21.
27 John Grierson et al., *Humphrey Jennings,* p. 4.
28 *Film Quarterly* 15, Winter 1961–2, p. 21.
29 Hodgkinson and Sheratsky, *Humphrey Jennings,* p. 57.
30 *Film Quarterly* 15, Winter 1961–2, p. 28. C. A. Lejeune, for instance, has noted 'a certain deliberate symphonic shape' (*The Observer* 28 March 1943) and Sir Denis Forman compared *Fires Were Started* to a Mozart concerto (NFT Programme Note, 1958).
31 Memorandum from the Committee of the Director of Public Relations of the Civil Defence Executive Sub-Committee, 13 January, 1941, INF I/849.
32 Sussex, *British Documentary,* p. 146.
33 These accounts and Jennings' treatments, drafts and scripts for *Fires Were Started* are in the Humphrey Jennings Collection, Box I, in British Film Institute.
34 *Film Quarterly* 15, Winter 1961–2, p. 27.
38 Jennings (ed.), *Humphrey Jennings,* p. 31.
39 *Film Quarterly* 15, Winter 1961–2, p. 29.
40 Memorandum from E. H. to Mr Watson, 20 November 1942, INF 5/88.
41 Agreement between MoI and General Film Distributors, 10 June 1943, INF 1/212.

42   Letter from Jack Beddington to Ian Dalrymple, 26 November 1942, INF 1/212.
43   Letter from C. A. Lejeune to Jack Beddington, undated, INF 6/985.
44   Jennings (ed.), *Humphrey Jennings,* p. 35.
45   Report by J. A. Bardsley, dated 4 December 1942, enclosed with letter of 9 December 1942, from Arthur Jarratt to Jack Beddington, INF 1/212.
46   Letter from Jack Beddington to S. C. Leslie, 16 December 1942, in reply to one from him, dated 15 December, inquiring about the progress of *I Was a Fireman.* On December 18, Leslie wrote back: 'I found the opening passages a bit long and am quite prepared to believe that I shall share your view about the cuts when I see the film.' The Ministry of Home Security regarded the film as an important work of propaganda and were anxious to see it released as soon as possible. INF 1/212.
47   Letter from Jack Beddington to Frank Ditcham, Managing Director of GFD, 19 March 1943, INF 1/212.
48   Letter from Leslie Furniss to J. D. Griggs, 16 April 1943, INF 1/212. The Ministry retained the original length and the original title for its non-theatrical showings. Posterity, while preferring Jennings' original version, which is the one currently available, has also preferred to adopt the commercial title as more evocative and resonant. So the full version has since become universally known as *Fires Were Started.*
49   On *The Bells Go Down* in the context of Ealing's wartime films, see Charles Barr, *Ealing Studios,* London, 1977, pp. 13 – 38.
50   *The Times,* 15 April 1943.
51   *Daily Mirror,* 25 March 1943; *Star,* 27 March 1943; *Daily Herald,* 26 March 1943; *News Chronicle,* 27 March 1943; *Daily Mail,* 25 March 1943; *Manchester Guardian,* 9 April 1943; *The Sunday Times,* 28 March 1943.
52   *Documentary News Letter* 4, 1943, p. 200.
53   *Daily Telegraph,* 24 March 1943.
54   *New Statesman,* 3 April 1943.
55   Lovell and Hillier, *Studies in Documentary,* p. 98.
56   Millar, 'Fires Were Started', p. 102.
57   NFT Programme Note, 1958.
58   Jennings (ed.), *Humphrey Jennings,* p. 57.
59   On the Blitz, see Constantine Fitzgibbon, *The Blitz,* London, 1970, and Tom Harrisson, *Living through the Blitz,* Harmondsworth, 1978.
60   Michael Wassey, *Ordeal by Fire,* London, 1941, p. 36.

11

The War the Documentarists Won

Western Approaches

By the spring of 1941, the 'Battle of the Atlantic' (a phrase coined by the Germans but adopted by Churchill in March 1941) was as much a source of concern in MoI circles as it was to Churchill himself. It posed a particular problem for the propagandists in so far as they were prevented for security reasons from saying too much about it in detail. German claims for Allied shipping sunk were invariably exaggerated and the tonnage claimed for April 1941, for example, of some 1,000,211 tons sunk — reportedly the equivalent of the yearly peace time output of British shipyards — was grossly higher than the real figure of 653,960 tons.[1] Yet a decision by Churchill in April to discontinue publishing weekly figures of losses prevented the MoI from contesting the German claims in anything other than the broadest terms — and that was just one of the problems. In addition, of course, it had to contend with the fact that heavy losses were still being sustained. How, then, should the MoI publicize a vital part of the war effort when so much was apparently set against it?

A meeting of the Planning Committee, held on 3 April 1941, highlighted the many sources of the MoI's dilemma when raising for discussion the matter of the 'Treatment of the Battle of the Atlantic'. Sir Kenneth Clark pointed out that 'owing to the withholding of news for security reasons, the public in Britain and in the United States were not stirred by the Battle of the Atlantic and did not feel that it concerned them', and that 'This state of affairs called for action but it was hard to decide what to do until the Ministry could tell how much could be said'. In the event it was decided to hold a meeting on 7 April with representatives of the Admiralty and the Ministry of Shipping 'to explore the ground'. But it was further noted:

While the departments concerned declared that the dangers of the Merchant

Navy must not be stressed for fear of scaring seamen out of signing on for service, the ship owners held that seamen could only be persuaded to serve if the dangers were stressed, though in combination with emphasis on the vital importance of the job done. It was agreed that publicity at home had to take into account both the encouragement of merchant seamen — where womenfolk were probably the key — and the creation of interest among the public as a whole.[2]

For its part, the Films Division was in a position to set a precedent. It could oblige almost immediately with a production on the topic of the Merchant Navy, though it was readily available more by chance than by design. Jack Holmes had virtually completed a film on the subject in the summer of 1940 but it got held up thereafter. Then it had the working title of *Able Seamen* and was being made for the GPO Film Unit. By the time it came out finally in May 1941, doubtless as a result of the impetus provided by the Planning Committee's discussion of the matter, it was a Crown Film Unit production and bore the new title of *Merchant Seamen.* The *Documentary News Letter* for May 1941 criticized the length of time it had taken for *Merchant Seamen* to be put on the screen but felt that had in no way detracted from its obvious qualities and claimed, 'There has never been a documentary before quite so good in handling of people, whether actors or real men in the street'.[3] The film was given a theatrical release from June and put on non-theatrical release from September.

For all its success with *Merchant Seamen,* however, the Films Division of the MoI was still evidently on the look-out for further projects that might enhance its revived interest in the Merchant Navy as a propaganda subject. Late in 1941 it received a submission which merited particular attention because it came with Admiralty approval.

On 28 November 1941, Captain C. A. H. Brooking of the Admiralty's Press Division wrote to the director of the Films Division, Jack Beddington, enclosing 'an outline treatment for a film dealing with Atlantic convoys which I have received from Mr Owen Rutter'. While noting that 'there are one or two other projects with the same theme', Brooking was especially attracted to the proposal because 'this deals with the subject from a rather different angle and it has the makings of a good propaganda film'. He emphasized, furthermore, that 'The Admiralty favours the idea and the Commander-in-Chief Western Approaches is prepared to give full co-operation provided that the film is made on a proper official basis and not merely as a commercial speculation'. He inquired, finally, whether the Crown Film Unit might be inclined to take on the production.[4]

Any proposal that had the backing of the Admiralty and Admiral Sir Percy Noble demanded to be looked at carefully, and Beddington's reply of 1 December was certainly enthusiastic. But as he pointed out, in fact, his head of production at the Crown Film Unit, Ian Dalrymple, had already received Rutter's submission and had independently declared it to be 'extremely interesting'. It very much fitted in with their plans. Consequently, it was proposed to proceed further with the treatment though it was stressed, once again, that 'It will be very important for us to keep this distinct both from *Merchant Seamen* and from *Coastal Command,* on which we are engaged at present'. It was anticipated that preparation of the project would take some time but, as Beddington wryly noted, 'in view of the weather this is perhaps not of vital importance'.[5] Time and the weather were to play a recurring and influential part in the film's progress.

Owen Rutter, a former army officer, a writer and a naval historian, had some experience of the cinema and was nothing if not ambitious in his outline of what was initially called 'HM Escort'.[6] The general idea of the film was to depict 'the working of the convoy system' and its particular aim was 'to show how closely the ships under the White Ensign and the Red Ensign work together in time of war, and how the Royal and Merchant navies together form British sea power'. 'The treatment will be documentary, the actors being the naval, mercantile marine and RAF personnel who are engaged in the operations', he stressed, and 'Every scene will thus carry conviction by its authenticity'. The leading character was to be the senior officer commanding a Royal Navy escort which takes a merchant convoy out to sea, hands it over in mid-Atlantic to a relief escort of United States destroyers, and then picks up in return a homeward bound convoy of ships.

But to enhance the documentary flavour of the film, Rutter anticipated that the focus of attention should shift constantly throughout to encompass a variety of naturalistically depicted scenes — at the headquarters of Western Approaches (as plans are laid, courses plotted and surveillance made), at the offices of a shipping company (as arrangements are completed and ships' masters briefed), on the deck of '*HMS Strongbow*' (the destroyer at the head of the convoy), on the bridge of '*SS Leander*' (the commodore's leading ship), and out at sea (with 60 ships steaming 12 abreast in columns of 5, with escort vessels in attendance). To lend dramatic impact to his story Rutter contemplated a couple of incidents in which, on the voyage out, an air attack is made but beaten off, and, on the return, the convoy is attacked by a submarine and one ship is sunk. At the last, to emphasize that 'The life of the sea goes on', Rutter wished to see the film return to the Western Approaches operations room, as the commander-in-chief watches a Wren plotting the position of the next outward bound convoy.

In all it was a grandiose project and clearly to take it on would entail a massive commitment on the part of Films Division. However, Arthur Calder Marshall, a production specialist, was convinced that 'naval subjects of this type will always be extremely popular, and extremely good propaganda, especially for shipyard workers, the state of affairs in shipyards being such that at the moment we can make no films of shipbuilding'. He did have some fears about the matter and thought, in particular, that 'The question of security really governs the whole film . . . A lot of this material of Rutter's is extremely interesting and will be very novel to a film audience if it is allowed to be shown but if not there may be a tendency that the resemblance to *Merchant Seamen* becomes greater and greater as we go on'. But such reservations did not stop Calder Marshall from concluding: 'My feeling is that despite the precautions imposed by security reasons, there still will be a very valuable and very interesting propaganda film'.[7]

In the event, Films Division decided to proceed with the project. On 11 December 1941 Dalrymple sought formal permission from Beddington to develop the subject which was henceforth to be known as *Western Approaches*. He too had some worries — 'The difficulties of production are well known with sea subjects, not necessarily any longer through lack of Admiralty will to co-operate, but owing to the shortage of ships and personnel'. But, as he pointed out, the odds were on their side on this occasion. Rutter is 'well established with Sir Percy Noble and Commander Walker assures me that the Admiralty is also in favour'. He felt they should be able to get what they required in the way of help. In consequence, he proposed to complete a script and re-examine the feasibility of production at the end of February 1942. Finance was required, however, and he sought permission to spend some £250 in preparing the script — £50 to purchase the outline from Rutter, £50 to employ Rutter for five weeks from 22 December as technical writer and as liaison with the Admiralty, and the remainder to be spent on allotting one of Dalrymple's staff to work with Rutter and on various travelling expenses that might be involved. In addition, Dalrymple recommended that if they went into production, Rutter should be subsequently re-employed as a Naval Liaison Officer at £10 per week for whatever number of weeks might be required.[8]

Not surprisingly, permission was quickly received to proceed with preparation of the script but immediately thereafter Dalrymple encountered the first of the many problems he was to experience in bringing the project to fruition. Initially, his problems were of a minor nature and were concerned solely with financial and administrative detail. Authority was granted to spend up to £250 but no undertaking could be made to re-employ Rutter until the production had been given a definite go-ahead and a budget allocated. Should the film go into production then the proposal to engage Rutter further would 'require to be reported to Establishments for their concurrence and this point will be covered when a budget is received'. 'In the meantime', Dalrymple was firmly if politely told, 'will you be good enough to regard the authority as covering only the expenditure to the script stage'.[9]

At the outset of 1942, however, Dalrymple was presented with the larger of his immediate problems when he found to his amazement that there were plans afoot for a film along the same lines elsewhere, and they emanated from no less a quarter than the Admiralty itself. The property had also landed in the laps of Captain Simmons-Yates, Commander Hunt and Lieutenant Cox and they had grandiose ambitions of their own. They contemplated a Technicolor production to be called 'They Sail Again', which would be financed by General Film Distributors, directed by Harry Watt and written by Paul Holt. Dalrymple acted speedily. He pointed out that *Western Approaches* was at 'a more advanced stage', that it had already received the blessing of the Admiralty, and, finally, that Watt though 'an extremely able director' was 'not under contract to them'.[10] He hastily arranged a meeting at the Admiralty for 21 January and took along Owen Rutter and Pat Jackson, whom he intended should direct the film, to lend support to his case.

The meeting was a great success, as Dalrymple recorded in a long memorandum to Beddington on 26 January 1942. It was agreed that the Admiralty would drop its project and the Crown Film Unit should proceed alone with its plans. Dalrymple had got what he wanted; but clearly the meeting had been mutually beneficial. In addition, the discussion had raised some interesting new questions which Dalrymple, being an experienced producer, wisely saw fit to incorporate in his latest submission regarding their own production of *Western Approaches.*

In particular, Dalrymple was greatly taken by the idea of working with Technicolor and he now favoured it for their film. He gave the following reasons for seeking permission to do so:

1   Colour is still sufficiently a novelty to attract patronage. In other words, it sells propaganda.
2   The first British *naval* subject in Technicolor will attract enormous notice.
3   For the Admiralty's purpose . . . colour is used considerably for recognition.
4   Colour will have a most salutary effect on revenue.
5   Films of the sea shot round these shores are usually drab to look at.
6   In propaganda films, colour automatically adds 100 per cent value — due to uniforms, flags and other patriotic emblems, insignia, etc.
7   It will be particularly useful to distribute the film in the United States.

Then, Dalrymple outlined the advantages and disadvantages of the various methods which might be employed to finance the film. It could be raised privately — Technicolor had approached the Admiralty of their own accord with the offer of entirely financing 'They Sail Again', through J. Arthur Rank, and their offer still 'holds good'. In that case, as Dalrymple pointed out, the offer would be conditional upon the film being distributed by GFD and Rank would expect 'a major participation in the profits' from their investment of £22,500 (the Technicolor estimate for the Rank interest). Furthermore, the film might be made 'with our own personnel but it would be difficult to avoid all interference'. Or, alternatively, the film could be made with money found from the Treasury, 'in which case there is a moral obligation to allow GFD to distribute it but all production profits would accrue to the Treasury'.

Dalrymple did wonder whether GFD would be as interested in promoting a film in which they were merely given distribution rights when they had offered a stake in the production, but on that score he concluded emphatically: 'In my view, the film will sell itself'. He estimated that if done by the Crown Film Unit, the film could be made on a budget of £15,755 (including the costs of shooting some 6,000 feet of film in Technicolor, 4,000 on location and a further 2,000 in the studio). He therefore advised that finance should be sought of the Treasury — 'The Treasury should not refuse private finance and turn down our application for Technicolor' — and that distribution should be offered to GFD.[11]

As attractive as it was, Dalrymple's proposition did not win the unanimous support of all sections of the Ministry. The Finances Division, for example, felt compelled to point out that previously colour had only been used on one film, *Plastic Surgery,* for 'reasons which were peculiar to that film'. The anticipated cost of £16,000, furthermore, would put undue strain on a programme which had authorized expenditure for that year up to £62,000 and which estimated for an average provision of £10,200 per film. The question was raised whether anything could be charged to the Admiralty vote and, of course, whether the film might not be better made by private enterprise — 'There may be difficulty in convincing the Treasury that it is in the public interest for this film to be made at the public expense rather than by the commercial interests who are apparently willing to make it at their own expense with the aid of facilities from the Admiralty'.[12]

The honorary films advisers also had some comments to make regarding the likely expense. When asked for his opinions on the matter, Colonel A. C. Bromhead recorded on 9 February 1942 that he felt lots of extra production charges might be expected in view of both the ambitious subject matter and the use of Technicolor. In consequence, he recommended that the print order for the film would need to be carefully controlled and restricted, and certainly the number used for the British market should be less than on *Target for Tonight.* In any case, it would cost more than £16,000 since, additionally, it was impossible to estimate for the costs of naval facilities and personnel. Yet for all that, he favoured using colour since 'black and white too often yields disappointing monotonous results' and because 'the booking potential will be increased and the commercial security reinforced'. In his opinion, 'all the costs of the film, if well produced in colour, should be recouped with a comfortable margin' and, furthermore, there was 'no room or necessity for private finance or participation'. The Treasury should finance the film and pocket the profits. It was 'a vital, national story' and 'just the kind of factual feature film which the Films Division should undertake'. Sidney Bernstein, the other adviser, added tersely that he 'agrees generally with Colonel Bromhead'.[13]

For his part, Jack Beddington already felt that Dalrymple should 'go ahead in Technicolor' and that it was 'much better to finance it ourselves'. Elsewhere in the MoI, S. G. Gates agreed with the views expressed by the Films Division director and the honorary films advisers, when noting:

(1) I regard this film as peculiarly suitable for showing in America where, as we have always recognized, the highest quality is needed to ensure success. This consideration reinforces the technical and commercial arguments in favour of using colour.
(2) I feel strongly the film is unsuitable for private enterprise and peculiarly suitable for the Crown Film Unit. I am sure that on security grounds alone, the Admiralty would prefer us to make it. Moreover if, as I believe, the film has a good chance of success in the United States of America, it would be a pity to lose the chance of increasing the prestige of British Government films over there.[14]

In effect, then, all of Dalrymple's opinions were vindicated. His arguments that the film should be made in Technicolor and financed by the Treasury without recourse to commercial investment or interference were accepted, at least within the ranks of the Films Division and the MoI. In addition, there were the tangible arguments to be weighed in favour of getting the film done in-house — for security reasons and to enhance the prestige of official British films abroad. With some grace, the Finance section duly relented and it only remained now to convince the Treasury of the worthiness of their cause.

In a memorandum which displayed considerable acumen in marshalling its arguments, H. G. C. Welch wrote to R. J. P. Harvey at the Treasury, on 18 February, on the subject of *Western Approaches*. He sought financial provision to produce the film in Technicolor for £16,000 exclusive of the costs of Admiralty facilities. A special outlay for production, incidental to the use of colour, would be required up to £4,350, and additional costs for distribution would amount to £20,000−£25,000 on the basis of 210 prints for commercial distribution in the United Kingdom and North and South America, and 50 prints for free distribution. Welch sought authority to proceed but asked that the authorized programme of £62,000 for the current year up to 30 November should not carry the £16,000 needed for *Western Approaches.* He wondered whether the sum needed might be treated as an agency service for the Admiralty over and above the budget allotted to the authorized programme, and continued:

> I may add that we have had tentative offers from the trade for a joint film arranged on lines which would no doubt follow, perhaps not very closely, those of *49th Parallel.* We are anxious to avoid any such arrangement. The fact that we have been approached does however indicate that the subject of the film is regarded by the trade as a profitable one.

He concluded by drawing attention to the points in favour of the film being made in colour, for America, and by the Crown Film Unit, for security purposes. An assurance was given finally that 'We should consult you again before incurring expenditure on distribution'.[15]

The Treasury's response was both heartening and worrying. Authority was granted to go ahead at a cost of £16,000 exclusive of Admiralty facilities, but considerable doubt was expressed about the idea of setting any costs against the Admiralty vote and it was emphasized that the film was already in production and 'was presumably budgeted for (in black and white it is true) within the allocation of £62,000'. It was pointed out, furthermore:

> It is a little disturbing to find that your Films Division are already apparently talking in terms outside this allocation. It is of course important that the Ministry's expenditure on films should not exceed the ration and I hope therefore that you will be able to agree that these production costs should be regarded as falling within that ration in the normal way.[16]

The film had money to go into production, then, but the ball was very much back in the MoI's court as far as the matter of overall financial provision was concerned. Welch wrote to Beddington querying whether the Crown Film Unit should really be planning more work than its programme could reasonably carry and drawing attention to the fact that the Finance Division had already raised the same question in January. Of the £62,000 allocated to the Films Division some £46,000 was being earmarked for the purposes of making four commercial films that would be given a theatrical release. Yet, as Welch pointed out, £16,000 of that was now being allotted to *Western Approaches,* and a film he referred to as the 'Fire Special' (doubtless a reference to *Fires Were Started,* see page 233) had already gone into production with a budget estimated at £12,170. In short, something like £28,000 had been given over to just two films, and only £18,000 remained for the two other commercial films to be put into production before 30 November 1942.[17] Could it be done?

Beddington replied in his characteristically indomitable fashion. He was determined that the Films Division programme should go ahead as planned, not least with regard to *Western Aproaches* which had clearly now become something of a pet project. 'The matter will continue to be watched carefully', he conceded, but, he added:

> I fear it is not practicable to give an assurance that the Crown Film Unit's programme of theatrical films will be confined to four and completed within £46,000. The figures for expenditure on this class of work were an estimate and circumstances are constantly changing. The entry of the United States into the war for instance is a new development which affects the Crown Film Unit's work very closely. The great success of certain Crown Film Unit productions is another factor which must be borne in mind.[18]

By the end of March 1942, however, Dalrymple was comparatively free to get on with the main job in hand, making a film. He had money at his disposal, though Finance were pressing for 'a detailed budget as early as practicable' before he could spend much of it,[19] and a script had yet to be completed. There were other vital matters to be dealt with immediately as well, such as the ordering of Technicolor film stock, which was manufactured in America and could take months to arrive (now 30,000 feet of special Monopack stock to be paid for in dollars and requiring, of course, tricky negotiations with Finance and the Treasury who were anxious to avoid dollar expenditure[20]), and the engaging of a naval liaison officer, which was done finally through Alfred Holt and Company in Liverpool (with a considerable amount of help from Beddington personally who contacted an old friend at the company for advice[21]). All of this took time, however, and it became increasingly clear that the whole project would take many months to complete. Certainly, Beddington's first thought that the film might be completed 'before early summer' now looked to be out of the question.[22] They had, after all, yet to go into production.

Throughout the early months of 1942, the director of the film, Pat Jackson, was for his part experiencing life on the convoys, with trips up the east coast and to Gibraltar. In addition, he was scouting in Liverpool for merchant seamen to take part in the production.[23] Like Rutter, he was adamant that the characters he wanted portrayed should be played by 'real people, no actors'. However, the script which he produced finally on 17 June 1942 differed in most other respects from Rutter's original conception and treatment: it was very much his own work. In particular, Jackson's script shifted the focus of attention considerably from the Royal Navy to the Merchant Navy. There was still to be a convoy but this time it was intended to follow it on its journey from New York to Britain, and to stay with the one convoy throughout. Yet again, there was meant to be a considerable amount of film spent observing such features as the ships' masters' conference and life in the Western Approaches operations room, but the emphasis was largely to be placed upon just one ship, the *Leander,* its officers and crew.

There was also, however, a distinct innovation. The story of the convoy was to be juxtaposed throughout with a story about the trials and tribulations endured by the survivors from the *Jason.* Their ship had been sunk by a German submarine and they were crammed into a lifeboat, with scarce resources and an injured crew member, hopeful of being rescued or making their way back to land. Their chances are increased when the *Leander* picks up their distress signal and speeds to their aid. But they are subsequently diminished when it becomes apparent that the German submarine is using the lifeboat as a decoy to lure yet another ship into a trap. The climax of the film was to be a battle for survival between the U-boat and the merchantman.[24]

There were, in short, a good many changes between Rutter's treatment

For Western Approaches, *the Crown Film Unit's most prestigious documentary of the war, director Pat Jackson determined to recreate as faithfully as possible the harsh and dangerous conditions of life at sea for men of the Merchant Navy. The scenes on the stranded lifeboat of the* Jason *were shot out at sea.*

Merchant seamen were recruited to play the parts of the hapless crew . . .

and the final script put forward for consideration by Jackson. His script would have been circulated for further comment anyway but, in this instance, the matter assumed added importance. For one thing, the Finance Division had twice repeated its call for 'a detailed budget' for the film and on the last occasion it curtly pointed out that a detailed listing of the likely expenditure had been requested, in the first instance, almost four months earlier.[25] It was difficult to prepare an accurate budget without an adequate script. For another, so many hopes and expectations were riding on this one horse, not to mention a considerable amount of money, that it was increasingly essential for the Films Division to know whether it had a sure fire bet or not.[26] To determine that the various advisers needed something tangible to work upon.

In the event, Pat Jackson did exceedingly well from the readers' reports. Arthur Calder Marshall, for example, heartily endorsed his script and pronounced it a definite winner. It was 'a first class story', he confirmed, and 'a first class script'. 'The "popular" story is a suspense story, a rescue', he stated, and continued:

The film differs from a feature made with the same story, even the same motive, by the amount of footage given to the various operations guided or recorded by the operations room, so that the film does give one a feeling of a message at a second level — which is that in the war, or in fact in life today — the history of the individual is intimately tied up with the history of all sorts of other people.[27]

The script won approval in most quarters. Other aspects of the production were not progressing as smoothly. Perhaps because they too had read the script and formed their own conclusions, Dalrymple suddenly found that the Admiralty were no longer proving to be as co-operative and enthusiastic as they had promised. 'The Admiralty have adopted an unhelpful and intransigent attitude towards the production of the film', he complained bitterly to Beddington, and he continued, 'As the request came originally from them for such a film to be made, there would seem to be little need for them to return to the antediluvian attitude of the first two years of the war'.

Inevitably, Dalrymple had wanted to arrange for the provision of certain

. . . and the rescuers on board the Leander *. . .*

. . . who speed to their aid . . .

naval craft, with fuel and personnel to operate them. Western Approaches
were prepared to grant them, but final permission for all such facilities to
be used had to be sought of the Admiralty — and the Admiralty were
promptly vetoing Dalrymple's requests. His anger was evident:

> I think it is a bit much when we attempt to make films which will properly
> show aspects of the Royal Navy's work that we should be recommended (as
> has been suggested by Lieutenant Shaw, Press Division) to confine our
> attentions to a studio tank and in general to follow Mr Noël Coward's
> production methods. Apart from the fact that we are unable to budget at
> £125,000, we have not got 50 tons of steel and have not got a stage on which
> to build a complete destroyer, this suggestion would not seem to harmonize
> with recent pronouncements of Admiralty Press Division officers on the
> subject of authenticity.[28]

A meeting between Dalrymple, Beddington and Captain Brooking from the Admiralty quickly settled that matter, however, and won the promise of renewed support and assistance. But as soon as that problem was over and done with, to everybody's apparent satisfaction, the question of finance reared its head again.

Once the script was completed, it had proved possible to proceed with a final estimate of the costs of the sort that Finance were demanding before the film could embark upon full scale production. An estimate was forthcoming on 5 August 1942 and it more than bore out all Bromhead's warnings regarding the extent of extra production charges. The expected cost of the film had doubled: it now stood at £32,390 and that figure did not include a sum for £1,285 which the MoI had already spent on purchasing Technicolor stock for silent work on the film. The project had been greatly revised, of course, and expanded. It was now planned to be an eight reel film instead of six reels, the cut length would be in the region of 8,000 feet and they hoped to work on a negative cutting ratio of 12 to 1. The budget was calculated on the basis of 11 weeks location shooting, 9 weeks in the studio and a further 2 months to film convoy material. And finally, it had proved possible to cost the seamen's expenses with £2,500

. . . only to encounter the problems of attack from a marauding German submarine.

being earmarked for wages and £2,400 for subsistence. A starting date for filming was given as approximately 1 September 1942.[29]

To nobody's surprise, Finance were not very happy. A memorandum was sent to the Deputy Director General of the MoI, Bamford, pointing out that the direct costs of the budget and the additional sum for film already bought came to some £33,675 in all. When a figure for overheads was added (£16,837 — estimated at 50 per cent of direct costs), and a probable additional cost (estimated at £2,500) for certain sequences related to the convoy, which it transpired the production team wanted to film in America, then they were broadly speaking of a film which would cost not less than £53,012. Any delays in the production of the film, of course, would increase those costs. 'Colonel Bromhead and Mr Gates approved the film when it was expected to be £16,000', it was noted, before adding, 'You will no doubt wish to obtain their further observations now and to consider whether the proposal should go forward to the Treasury'.[30]

Luckily for Beddington, Dalrymple and Jackson, the project gathered a measure of support thereafter which few production teams during the war years could have enjoyed. If nothing else, it was a test of the extent to which there was truly a commitment to the use of film in the propaganda cause.

Bamford did indeed consult Bromhead, the Films Adviser, and once again Bromhead declared that 'it is strong enough in story taken and particularly in dramatic suspense to carry the length of seven or eight reels and a production cost of £50,000 or so'. He repeated all the arguments in its favour he had earlier mentioned, not least with regard to the film's propaganda potential which he stated to be 'very high, such a film is wanted now for all the world accessible to us'.[31]

Subsequently, Bamford wrote to his Director General, Cyril Radcliffe, arguing that 'This ambitious proposal should have your authority'. For his part, he was convinced that 'This film should be produced by the Crown Film Unit and should be undertaken as a matter of urgency'.[32] Radcliffe, in turn, also endorsed the production. He commented that 'The project should go ahead in view of the paramount value of this film for home propaganda and I hope abroad'. Though he added a note of caution regarding 'this very considerable venture' when stating: 'We are bound to recognize that if this film is not a success in exhibition, we shall have to adapt the future policy of the Crown Film Unit accordingly'.[33] In short, there was now more than just hopes and money being invested in this one film: it looked very much as if the future of the Crown Film Unit was also at stake.

The Treasury, too, echoed the same theme and issued the same dire warning when it came their turn to pass judgement on the proceedings. A meeting between the Deputy Director General, Bamford, and Treasury officials agreed that 'subject to confirmation from a higher authority', the film should proceed on the basis proposed. However, it also resulted in a grim prognosis:

> The Treasury emphasized that we were risking a good deal by putting all our eggs in one basket and that if this film did not come up to expectation, the whole programme of the Unit would have to be reconsidered.[34]

And when permission was finally received to proceed into production, the official letter from the Treasury continued in the same vein. Authority was granted to spend between £50,000 and £70,000 on the film which had been formerly estimated at £16,000 in direct costs. The substantial increase, it was noted, was being put down to several reasons: the costs of the services of merchant seamen to be employed on location work; the high proportion of complicated studio work; that the film was in colour; that it was now eight reels. But the point was made during the course of the summation:

> To invest up to £70,000 of public funds in a particular film inevitably involves a measure of risk. There is nothing more uncertain than a film success, but in view of the importance of the subject from the propaganda standpoint and also in view of the success of the ambitious ventures of the Crown Film Unit so far undertaken, you felt that the risk was worth taking. In the considered view of the Film Advisers to the Ministry, the film *Western Approaches* was likely to be a box office success and they were confident that the film would pay for itself and possibly make a profit as well.

The letter continued to summarize the contents of the discussion between the MoI and the Treasury raising, in the process, a matter which had been agreed earlier in the war between the two parties and revealing, incidentally, just how carefully Bamford had been scrutinized as to the extent of MoI resolve and commitment to the film, and how much he had needed his wits about him:

> We wondered whether the project conflicted with the recommendations made in the 13th Report of the Select Committee on National Expenditure that the Ministry should not assume direct responsibility for the production of feature films by the provision of public money. From our discussion, however, it seemed clear that the Select Committee had not this kind of film in mind but rather the entertainment film in the production of which stars are employed. There will be no stars as such in *Western Approaches* and in your view, which we accept, the film does not conflict with the Select Committee's recommendations.

The message was clear, then, and there could be no mistaking it. The

Crown Film Unit's head was on the block and the Ministry was in line as well. To conclude, however, the Treasury could not let the subject drop without explaining in detail precisely what it was they were anxious to avoid. In particular, they wished to ensure that 'the production of this film should not mean an increase in the staff of the Crown Film Unit, which has almost doubled in a year'. Then, there should not be 'any further expansion until we see how the Unit comes out of this, its greatest test'. Finally, the production could go ahead but 'apart from the special team of Technicolor experts, it should not involve the employment of additional staff by the Crown Film Unit beyond that already authorized'.

It was reiterated that subject to those conditions, the Treasury were 'content that the project should proceed'. With a last flourish and a neat touch of irony — whether intentional or not it is difficult to decide — the Treasury letter ended: 'We would only wish you and the Crown Film Unit all success'.[35]

Bamford, for his part, noted quite simply — 'This seems to be a fair summary of the discussions with the Treasury'. Though, with more than a dash of weary resignation mixed with stolid determination, he added: 'The important thing now is to get ahead quickly'.[36]

The production crew for *Western Approaches* had started to do just that. By the time that final confirmation to proceed reached them during the first week of September 1942, most of them were already ensconced in the Station Hotel at Holyhead. As the production manager, Dora Wright, sensibly put it later in her first location report, it was decided to proceed 'so as not to lose the artists'.[37] Given a team of 14 technicians and 22 artists, however, it was almost inevitable that new found expenses would soon be entailed, of a sort they had never bargained for. When one of the merchant seamen fell asleep while smoking, the unit manager, Gerry Bryant, had to compensate an irate landlady for the loss of bed linen. £13 8s 6d was paid out to replace the items and the case of 'the sordid matter of the burnt bedding' duly entered the log and the expenses lists.[38]

There were other more profound difficulties to contend with as well. The technical problems were horrendous. They were shooting all the scenes that took place in the stranded lifeboat of the *Jason* and were doing so several miles out at sea with the weather worsening constantly as winter began to set in. Seasickness was rife and the whole crew, artists, equipment and a bulky Technicolor camera (which with its three negatives took time to load) were crammed into one small lifeboat, subject to freak winds and sudden squalls. As Jackson recalls: 'The platforms at the end of the lifeboat put the boat out of trim. When we put weights in, to bring the boat into trim, the boat became so sluggish that it was slopping water over. The water was creating shorts in the cables and everything else'. Inevitably, there were delays and progress was slow, but 'eventually somehow we licked it'.[39]

The lifeboat sequences were completed off Holyhead by the first week of March 1943. It was intended that the next location shooting should take place in Northern Ireland where they hoped to film gun deck sequences before moving into the studios on 27 March. But an initial reconnoitre revealed that the ship provided by the Admiralty was landlocked. The Northern Ireland location was cancelled. Their entry into the studios was also postponed. They finally got into the studios in April and the interior shots were completed by 24 June.

Thereafter, on 15 July a smaller crew was dispatched on a seven week voyage to America and back to shoot footage of the convoy at sea, action shots of the convoy at work and dock scenes in New York. By this time 'the really extraordinary difficulties which have surrounded the making of the film' were inevitably giving rise to fears that 'the budget figure is likely to prove wide of the mark'.[40] By 5 July the total cost of the film was being estimated at between £85,000 and £100,000 as against the £70,000 authorized by the Treasury. It was proposed to seek authority for an additional £30,000.[41] Bamford concurred:

> I agree there is nothing for it now. It is distressing that the original budget and time schedule have been so far exceeded. I understand that the best we can hope for now is that the film will be ready next Christmas. However Mr. Gates tells me that the material so far shot is very good indeed and that in the Admiralty's opinion, as expressed by General Tripp, the U-boat story will still be quite topical when the film is ready.[42]

Treasury authority was duly received, without a murmur this time.[43] But Bamford's hopes that the film would be ready by Christmas were also to prove wide of the mark.

On the unit's return, at the end of August, the sequences featuring the German submarine were filmed in Fishguard and destroyer scenes were taken between 4 and 12 October in Liverpool. By 26 October, after five more gruelling days at sea, they had completed what they hoped would be the last of the important location shooting.

They were immediately confronted with a problem of inter-service rivalry. Coastal Command demanded a credit on the film. The Royal Navy had received a credit when the Crown Film Unit had made a film in 1942, under Jack Holmes's direction, essentially about *Coastal Command,* and now Coastal Command wanted one in return on the Admiralty's film of *Western Approaches.*[44]

Ironically, Jack Holmes was for his part now the director of the Crown Film Unit, having taken over after Dalrymple's resignation in May 1943,[45] and he sought Dora Wright's advice. She pointed out that 'The whole film is an epic of the Merchant Navy' and added, caustically:

As regards the Admiralty's part in *Western Approaches* you know, of course, that they only appeared in the Masters' Conference, where for political reasons and on the recommendation of the Admiralty and the Air Ministry, we featured the American side of the air escort question.[46]

Wright's reply raised as many questions as it answered. For as Holmes subsequently noted: 'My own view is that Dora Wright's point about the small amount of footage allotted in the film to the Royal Navy is one that should not be stressed in view of the fact that I believe the Admiralty originally asked for the film to be made'. He suggested, therefore, that in replying the emphasis should be placed upon the fact that the major purpose of the film was to pay tribute to the Merchant Navy during the worst days of the Battle of the Atlantic, it did not seek 'to explain the working of the convoy system or even the methods to protect convoys from attack' — much had indeed changed since the original conception of the film, and that 'strictly speaking the title *Western Approaches* is a misnomer', since 'Most of the action in the film takes place in mid-Atlantic, out of reach of Coastal Command patrols'.[47] By such means were Coastal Command assuaged.

Mollifying Coastal Command was one thing, however; completing the film itself was another. On 29 November the crew returned for a week to Liverpool to re-shoot material which had not come out well in the processing (a tricky business in itself since it required the film to be shipped to Hollywood, with consequent delays on the journey out and back, and, of course, the presence over there of a naval official to supervise the processing of the film under security conditions). Not until the end of 1943 was Pat Jackson in a position to get down to editing the film.

By the time that Dora Wright produced her second production report, on 25 January 1944, she was at last able to announce that they had seen a final rough cut on the screen and the fruits of some 18 months work on the film.[48] The actual production process had taken 18 months but in all, of course, the film had been in the works for well over two years — and there was still no exhibition print to show for it. It was little wonder that, on reading the report, Beddington was prompted to remark, 'There is no doubt that Jackson has done a wonderful job but we have not seen the film yet'. Or that somebody cryptically added: 'Yes, let us see the film first, soon I hope'.[49]

When Dalrymple, who had retained his interest in the film, saw the latest version, 'more or less finished', in February 1944, he was highly enthusiastic about it. 'I think it's the finest camera study of humanity I've seen', he stated, and 'in addition it has sheer elemental excitement'. He wrote to Beddington that it 'should be fine box office in this country with the normal energetic exploitation, which even the biggest fictional films must have to put them over, after all'. He was full of praise for Pat Jackson: 'Pat Jackson has done a memorable job and deserves an OM'. But incredibly, in view of the arguments marshalled to defend the film at an earlier stage, he concluded: 'The Americans won't understand a word, and what should they care about the finest documentary since *Nanook*?'.[50]

To nobody's surprise, however, the difficulties were not yet at an end. A musical soundtrack still had to be recorded and laid. The Denham Recording Studios were booked for 11 April but two sessions would be required and an orchestra of 'no less than 48 musicians'. The whole thing would cost £521, according to the musical director, Muir Mathieson, including a fee of £100 for the composer, Clifton Parker. Somebody, somewhere wished to query the costs, but fortune favoured the film to the last. The assistant director of the Films Division, R. Nunn May, stated that it would be 'absurd to try and economize on the music sessions for this important and very expensive film'.[51] The recording sessions could go ahead. A final dubbing was scheduled to start on 17 April and to last until 26 April and the film was to be handed over to the Technicolor laboratories by the end of April. The production of show prints was to be done in England, but a first colour print was not expected before the beginning of July, at the earliest, because Technicolor required a week for each of the nine reels and, in any case, they already had Laurence Olivier's production of *Henry V* to hand.

Technicolor, for their part, had become thoroughly disillusioned with their experiences over the film. As a result, the managing director had written to the MoI at the end of March stating emphatically that they 'No longer offer the use of Monopack negative to any British production until after the war'. 'Under war conditions it is quite impossible for us to continue with the use of Monopack for any British production', he asserted, though their commitment to *Western Approaches* remained as strong as ever. He felt certain that 'Nobody will be disappointed with the final result', and, in particular, he wished to stress, 'For what our opinion might be worth . . . we think that the Ministry will have in *Western Approaches* their best picture of the war'.[52]

There remained, however, the problem of how quickly prints might be ready for distribution to the cinemas. It was suggested, within the Films Division, that the completion and delivery of the film could be speeded up: 'They may be useful for theatrical distribution in the USA and delay now endangers good autumn release arrangements'.[53] One sure way of achieving this was by giving it a higher priority and by putting it 'higher up the Government production schedule', to take it out of the feature release print schedule, and to regard it, according to Technicolor, 'as part of the one million feet of film per month we allocate to Government production'. On the Technicolor reckoning of 8 May, a complete answer print would be ready by the end of August and release prints were scheduled for October and November.[54] To beat those schedules, the film simply had to be given a new priority. Unfortunately, for once, the film lost the day. Nunn May replied that *Western Approaches* had to remain within the feature print release schedule.[55]

One thing the Films Division knew, and Technicolor did not, was that suddenly and surprisingly *Western Approaches* was encountering difficulties over censorship. On the 5 May 1944 the Ministry of Information received notification from the British Board of Film Censors that the film had been viewed and that exception had been taken to one feature. The BBFC wished the MoI to 'Delete the word "Bloody" when it occurs'.[56] It was a simple enough stricture but it was another time consuming problem and potentially bothersome. E. Hudson, the London Contacts Officer, wrote to Jack Holmes and relayed the gist of a conversation he had had with J. Brooke Wilkinson, the secretary to the BBFC. He recounted:

> *Western Approaches* went to the BBFC today. Mr Brooke Wilkinson rang me to say that he considers the film is one which should go for general distribution. At the same time he cannot give it even an 'A' certificate as long as it contains the word 'bloody'. He asserted, and I did not argue with him on the point, that they had never allowed this word except (during the war) as applied to a German. He added, for our encouragement, that during the last war a film called *The Better 'Ole* was made which originally contained 144 swear words. These were expunged at his request and the film was a smashing success. It will suffice if the offending word is blurred in each case.[57]

Holmes immediately got on to Nunn May about the matter and asked whether he could see Brooke Wilkinson about it. 'We feel that there may be some confusion at the BBFC', he pointed out. He knew full well that what the BBFC said was 'true of the word "bastard" (which is also used in *Western Approaches* in an anti-German context) but "bloody" has been used in a number of war films (mostly ours) and in at least two pre-war films (one ours and the other by George Bernard Shaw!)'. He added, finally, that 'Jackson says it is impossible to blur the words'.[58]

Subsequently, a list was compiled of the films which had indeed used the offending word 'bloody' and got away with it, so that they might be prepared for any ensuing arguments. It comprised the pre-war films *North Sea* and *Pygmalion* and, as Holmes had indicated, the wartime films *Men of the Lightship* (where 'bastards' had also been used), *Squadron 992, Coastal Command, Fires Were Started* (with 'bastards' in evidence once again), *San Demetrio London* (an Ealing feature film which had also used the offending words 'Bloody Venus'), and *Tunisian Victory* (where 'Poor Bloody Venus' had appeared as well).

The Films Division was well and truly ready, then, for any possible confrontation. But for all that, some measure of restraint was applied and an accommodation was sought with the BBFC. Too much time, money and energy had been expended to fall at the last hurdle. Within a week of receiving the BBFC's formal notice, Nunn May was able to report that:

> Pat Jackson has removed six 'bloodies', leaving five which he regards as 'dramatically important'. One of these refers to a U-boat and is presumably therefore permissible. Of the remaining four, two occur during the rowing sequence when the men are angry and almost exhausted. It may help with Brooke Wilkinson that there has been a genuine attempt to meet his point.[59]

Pat Jackson recorded that: 'I hope in view of our recent purge the Ministry will be successful in taking Mr Censor by storm'.[60] Subsequently, Nunn May wrote to Brooke Wilkinson, on 8 June, after more excisions had been made, to proudly boast:

> We have expunged no less than twelve 'bloodies'. Three remain, with legitimate dramatic effect. We hope that in the rather special circumstances of this case and in the assurance that we shall not regard it as in any way a precedent, you may see your way to pass the film with these three scenes as they stand.[61]

Within a few days J. Brooke Wilkinson replied that 'Lord Tyrrell has granted permission for the word "bloody" to be used on the three occasions you mention, and I have now given instructions for the certificate to be issued'.[62]

One last problem surfaced on 6 September when Technicolor wrote to say that they had discovered a flaw while printing the final reel of the film. There was a flare in the picture, on a close-up of Griffiths, the gunner of the *Leander* who dies in the final shoot-out with the submarine. 'To emphasize our strong objection to the release of the picture with the scene in its present form', they were willing to place a camera crew and the necessary amount of negative at the disposal of the Films Division, in order that the scene might be reshot.[63] But things had gone too far for any reshooting now. Dalrymple replied that he would be 'reluctant after all this time to put up a case to the MoI for any further production expenditure on this film'. Besides, Jackson was out of the country and he felt a number of other scenes were 'as bad'.[64]

He was right. Nobody would have contemplated further expenditure at such a late stage on a film which at the last count had incurred direct costs of £57,041 and which with Crown overheads at £28,520 made a total production cost of £86,292.[65] The film was allowed to proceed, blighted shot or not. An answer print was accepted on 5 October 1944 and the film was passed by Film Security Censors and accepted by the Production section on 6 October 1944. A show copy was received that same day, almost three years after the project had first been broached.

It only remained now to publicize the film and to await the public response. Already numerous charities were seeking to book the film for charity premieres. Beddington declared himself well pleased with it. He wrote to Jackson to say that he thought it was 'brilliant' and 'a great achievement'.[66] To Dalrymple, he commented: 'I think *Western Approaches* is one of the landmarks in all film-making and I am glad to tell you that the Minister thinks it is the best film he has ever seen'.[67]

But in view of the very high costs the film had incurred it was necessary to drum up as much support for it as possible and to spread the word about it far and wide, in order to ensure its commercial success. The press officer at the Films Division, J. D. Griggs, felt that:

> *Western Approaches* will stand up to all the publicity we can give it. And although it would have been much easier to sell at the time the Battle of the Atlantic was at its height, nevertheless, even with the prevailing 'escapist mood' it should be possible to whip up public interest in the work of the Merchant Navy, without which D-Day and everything since then, would not have been possible.[68]

Ironically, given one of the film's avowed intentions, he then went on to lament the lack of any 'stars' in it, since he was prevented from using such as a selling point. He would have liked, for instance, to arrange radio interviews with the men but 'unfortunately we have no *names* so that the usual film personality programmes are not necessarily open to us'. However, he did proceed with the charity premieres and arranged a series of special showings of the film to which were invited a long list of 'prominent' names and organizations. Grigg's pitch was nothing if not obvious. 'It is the biggest film this Ministry had handled', he informed them, and 'When you see it, I think you will agree that it is in many ways as important for the Merchant Navy as *In Which We Serve* was for the Royal Navy'. But it seemed to work, for all that.

Western Approaches enhanced its reputation considerably as a result of these special showings. 'It is a splendid form of entertainment', commented Beaverbrook, as he congratulated the Crown Film Unit 'for having produced one of the best films of the war, if not the very best'.[69] The Ministry of War Transport deemed it 'a magnificent tribute to the Merchant Navy'.[70] The Office of War Information felt it would prove 'extremely popular'.[71] 'I think it is the most exciting film that has been made in the war', noted the film-maker Frank Launder, and added, 'It is surely a complete justification for the continuance in peace time of the Ministry's Films Division'.[72] The film producer Filippo Del Giudice saw it first at a special showing and went back to see it twice more thereafter. He thought it 'a real triumph for the Crown Film Unit' and 'a great achievement'. And he complimented Beddington on 'your foresight in establishing such a

brilliant organization for documentary films. The industry will be grateful
to you, apart from this film, for the discovery of so many new talents who
will one day undoubtedly be great assets to British film-making'.[73] Not
surprisingly, in view of the pre-release acclaim it had already received, the
film was taken up by the Ministry for us in liberated territories and
rendered into various foreign languages for the purpose.[74]

Western Approaches was given a trade show on 9 November 1944, a
press show on the 5 December, its London premiere at both the Warner
Theatre, Leicester Square, and the Regal, Marble Arch, on 8 December
1944, and it was put on general release, finally, from 15 January 1945.

After the opening credits, there follows a dedication:

Western Approaches is a vast area of ocean control covering thousands of
square miles of the Atlantic. In these waters is set this single incident in the
fiercest and longest sea battle in history. The players are not professional
actors but serving officers and men of Allied Navies and Merchant Fleets.
This film is dedicated to them and to their gallant comrades who made
possible the victory of the Allied cause.

Subsequently, the film unfolds very much in the fashion as summarized
by the official synopsis of the film and just as Pat Jackson had intended in
his script of June 1942:[75]

Western Approaches, made as a tribute to the Merchant Navy, tells the story
of 22 men, survivors of a torpedoed merchantman, the *Jason,* who spend 14
days in a lifeboat in the Atlantic. The Master of the *Jason* is in the lifeboat
with his crew, including the ship's boy, and a man wounded in the head
when the U-boat surfaced and machine-gunned the crew as they took to the
boats.

Meanwhile another convoy is preparing to sail from New York. At the
Masters' Conference the arrangements are discussed and the Masters are
told that a Hudson will escort them on the first part of the journey. The
convoy set sail but an old French merchantman, *La Belle France,* develops
engine trouble and the whole convoy has to slow down. One of the other
ships, *Leander,* cannot keep station as she is too sluggish in answering the
helm at the slow speed. The Commodore gives her permission to go on
ahead and wait for the convoy in the morning.

A lurking U-boat has spotted the *Jason*'s lifeboat and picked up the
distress signal which is being sent out on the small portable transmitter in
the boat. Realizing that this may bring a ship to the rescue, which will
provide a sitting target for his last two torpedoes, the U-boat commander
decides to wait and see what happens. In the morning the *Leander* picks up
a faint distress signal from the lifeboat.

Back in the lifeboat the men see a smudge of smoke on the horizon and fire off two distress rockets. At the same moment, while all the other men are gazing at the smoke on the horizon, the wounded man sees the periscope of the U-boat. At first the men think it is delirium, but then someone else sees it too. At once they realize that they are being used as a decoy and try to signal to the approaching *Leander.* Their own safety is no longer of importance to them, the *Leander* must leave them to their own fate and turn away before the U-boat can attack her. Their signals are partly successful. The *Leander* dodges the first torpedo, but the second hits her forward. The Master orders the men to the boats but remains, concealed with some of the men, including the gunner.

The U-boat commander, believing the *Leander* has been abandoned, surfaces to finish her off with gunfire. A duel follows and the U-boat is sunk, but not before the gunner of the *Leander* has been killed. The men of the *Jason* are taken on board, and the *Leander,* though badly damaged, proceeds under her own steam.

The film received as rapturous a response after its press showing as it did from the earlier private showings. *The Times* said it had 'the immense advantage of being both authentic and austere' and described it as 'a memorable film'.[76] Jympson Harman, in the *Daily Mail,* called it 'the most realistic sea picture ever put on the screen'.[77] The critic on the *Manchester Guardian* echoed the same sentiments and deemed it 'a memorable and authentic film'.[78]

In particular, Richard Winnington of the *News Chronicle* was much taken by it. He had written a report on the film's progress in May 1944 and fancied it then. By the time it came out, he was even more enthusiastic:

There has never been a film so surrounded by modesty and self-effacement as this magnificent British story of the Atlantic convoys . . . For a whole year we have known we are going to see that epic production *Caesar and Cleopatra* some time in 1945; *Wilson* and *Since You Went Away* already loom large in our lives. How can they — how could any film — live up to these premature ecstasies? But if advance publicity has its drawbacks, so too has the complete absence of it. For citizens like me can get comfort from the thought that such films as *Western Approaches* lie ahead.

The film is devoid of heroics although it is impregnated with heroism. The wrecked crew in the lifeboat who try to warn their rescuers of the lurking U-boat and the captain of the *Leander* who suddenly decides to alter his course to pick up the lifeboat are men playing the parts they normally live and they give us the common currency of bravery as no screen actors could. They are seamen, and their selflessness in danger is automatic and unstated.

I have seen this film three times and its quality becomes more marked with each viewing. It is perhaps the feel of the sea itself evoked at moments with an exquisite blend of colour, sound and shape — the flapping of a sail, the cry of a bird, the clanking of chains, the elusive changing face of the Atlantic. In this delicate use of sound, embracing at times the best Technicolor effects of the sea ever photographed, lies perhaps the film's great freshness.

Refreshing, too, are those ordinary British voices whose accents sound without false emphasis and a story that, although fictionally conceived, mirrors a thousand untold tales of the Western Approaches during the most vicious sea war the world has ever known. And that story has shape and drama and austerity.

You will not find here the suave technique of the commercial product; you may think it in some ways an untidy sort of picture; but you will have been as near to the Atlantic as the imagination of a first class director and the camera can get you. And the life of the merchant sailor is not noted for tidiness.[79]

As Winnington intimated, comparisons were inevitable. The most obvious comparison likely to be forthcoming was between the official MoI film of *Western Approaches* and the commercially produced Ealing feature film of *San Demetrio London,* released early in 1944, on much the same theme — though it was set in 1940 — and also dedicated to the officers and men of the Merchant Navy. Such a comparison was made in the pages of the *New Statesman,* when William Whitebait reviewed the film. But *Western Approaches* was still considered to be the better of the two:

Here is one more achievement to add to our list of notable English documentaries. *Western Approaches* deals — and deals nobly, as the theme deserves   with the Merchant Navy. In undertaking this film the Crown Film Unit had set itself a considerable task; that of improving on *San Demetrio.* For there could be no question that *San Demetrio* 'covered the ground', and pretty successfully, thanks to an approach less impersonal than would at one time have been conceivable in documentary circles. It gloried in the facts, and it told a story. If, by severe standards, this was fiction, then it was a fiction with the realism uppermost; an adventure was reconstituted, as nearly as could be imagined to the real event.

If one looked at the film more closely there were cracks: studio sets and the real thing didn't attain a complete homogeneity, the actors taking part occasionally reminded us by a gesture that they were actors under restraint. Accept the human touch, then, accept the necessary dramatization, but tighten realism to a yet higher pitch — this was the lesson to be learnt, and the Crown Film Unit, by accepting it, have immensely enlarged their method.

Much of the drama in *Western Approaches* is provided by a small boatful of men adrift in the Atlantic, and the situation is made even more actual and more dramatic than similar scenes in *San Demetrio.* The men, talking and singing, growing more silent, resting more, grimacing, passing the canisters of water, seeing an aircraft in the clouds, listening to the throb of a lurking submarine, stir and oppress us by their exaggerated closeness. They are as real as the waves and the sky. Possibly actors in a studio could have achieved the same effect, but I very much doubt it.

The Crown Film Unit spent many months at sea taking these shots, and the results justify the method. They have brought back a magnificent photographic haul, which glitters in the memory: the convoy, rough seas, sunset and moonlight, men in open boats, on decks and in cabins. Events move to a climax as the lifeboat, an old merchantman and a Nazi submarine come to an inevitable meeting point, like the iceberg and the liner in Hardy's poem. The enemy, for once, aren't caricatured — a minor tribute to the film's truthfulness.

My only criticism of *Western Approaches* is that the Technicolor is uneven in some sequences, so that a picture postcard blue may suddenly intrude among more subtle graduated shots, and one effect of realism on the soundtrack is that we can't always hear what is being said. But these are unimportant flaws in a film that is top of its class.[80]

The film did have its detractors. C. A. Lejeune, in the *Observer,* felt that 'The main trouble with *Western Approaches* is that a good deal of its message has already been conveyed in other pictures'. While praising its 'sense of immediacy' she felt that the film erred in placing too much emphasis upon ' "ordinary" people and "natural" dialogue'. In her opinion, the film lacked 'poetry'.[81] In the opinion of most of the critics, however, the film was a decided success. It won a measure of esteem and acclaim which survived the war intact and which it continues to enjoy today, unlike many films from that era. As one commentator put it quite recently: '*Western Approaches* still stands as one of the finest feature documentaries of the war'.[82]

It was a very different kind of documentary, though, and that fact must not go unrecognized. Like *Target for Tonight, Coastal Command, Desert Victory* and a few others, *Western Approaches* was one of those feature-length documentaries which Paul Rotha has described thus: 'Technically very well made, they were not in the traditional line of peace time documentary and, with some exceptions, they were not made by technicians from the pre-war British documentary group'.[83]

Rotha's point was well made — these films really bore little relationship to the traditional product emanating from the mainstream of the documentary movement, except in the broadest sense, and they were hardly likely to benefit the movement *per se*. The makers of those 'social and informational documentaries' were largely engaged during the war, as Rotha well recognized, on the production of films for the non-theatrical field, with all the inevitable constraints that brought regarding production resources, size of intended audiences, and such. Virtually all the directors of the large scale feature documentaries, furthermore, moved eventually if unsurprisingly into commercial feature production (Harry Watt to Ealing, for example, Pat Jackson to Metro-Goldwyn-Mayer). And, as Rotha noted,

'They have migrated as individuals, not as a group, which means that their influence on behalf of the documentary idea over commercial production will be fragmentary'.

However, if the prestigious feature documentaries did little to advance the cause of the 'documentary idea', being essentially celebratory rather than ruminative in character, they were at least popular, something else that Paul Rotha appreciated: '*Target for Tonight, Desert Victory, Western Approaches* and other famous feature-length documentaries received a wide commercial distribution in the cinemas earning considerable revenue . . . The public wanted to see these films because they were dramatized actuality, with all the physical excitement and dramatic action of raid and battle and shipwreck'.[84] They were films which captured the heart more so than the mind, and the war the documentarists won was very much the war the Ministry of Information wanted them to win.

NOTES

1   Michael Balfour, *Propaganda in War 1939—1945,* London, 1979, p. 272.
2   Planning Committee minutes, 3 April 1941, INF 1/249.
3   *Documentary News Letter* 2, May 1941, p. 88.
4   Brooking to Beddington, 28 November 1941, INF 1/213. There are also files on *Western Approaches* in INF 5/103—109, inclusive, and INF 6/370. But unless otherwise stated, all references in the notes henceforth come from the major file on the subject, INF 1/213.
5   Beddington to Brooking, 1 December 1941.
6   The 1934 film *Once in a New Moon,* directed by Anthony Kimmins, was based upon Rutter's book *Lucky Star.* See Tony Aldgate, 'Comedy, Class and Containment: The British Domestic Cinema of the 1930s', in James Curran and Vincent Porter (eds), *British Cinema History,* London, 1983, pp. 265—7. Rutter's ten page outline of 'HM Escort' is appended to Brooking's letter.
7   Calder Marshall to Beddington, 29 November 1941.
8   Dalrymple to Beddington, 11 December 1941.
9   Campbell to Dalrymple, 19 December 1941.
10 Dalrymple to Beddington, 14 January 1942.
11 Dalrymple to Beddington, 26 January 1942.
12 Memorandum by H. G. C. Welch, 3 February 1942.
13 Bromhead to Beddington and Welch, 9 February 1942. And handwritten note on same re Bernstein, 10 February 1942.
14 Beddington handwritten note, 30 January 1942. Memorandum from Gates, 14 February 1942.
15 Welch to Harvey, 18 February 1942. The 50 prints were to be distributed as follows: 22 dominions and colonies; 10, Russia; 1, China; 7, Free French and Belgian Africa; neutral countries in the East, 10.

16 Harvey to Welch, 3 March 1942. He also queries the number of prints for free distribution. Beddington's handwritten comment of 6 March suggested: 'It may be necessary to tell the Treasury that we expect considerable profits from this film'.

17 Welch to Beddington, 5 March 1942.

18 Beddington to Welch, 9 March 1942.

19 Campbell to Dalrymple, 24 March 1942.

20 See Welch to Beddington, 18 May 1942, and Campbell to Dalrymple, 21 May 1942, *inter alia*. Negotiations with Technicolor were going on throughout.

21 Beddington to Alfred Holt and Co., 12 June 1942. He sought Chief Officer Large, whom they had used before, in the first instance but he proved unavailable. In the event, Beddington's contact, Roland H. Thornton, produced Chief Officer Morgan for what he described as 'this MoI racket', subject of course to 'some proper financial arrangement' being made with the company.

22 Beddington to F. Hill, the Kinematograph Renters Society Ltd, 30 January 1942.

23 Pat Jackson's account of the production events can be found in Elizabeth Sussex, *The Rise and Fall of British Documentary*, Berkeley, 1975, pp. 148–51. He and Dalrymple had already worked together on *Ferry Pilot* (1941) and *Builders* (1942).

24 Shooting script for *Western Approaches*, 17 June 1942.

25 Campbell to Wright, 9 July 1942, and 17 July 1942.

26 The Technicolor bill thus far amounted to £1,285. By 9 July 1942, further incidental expenses in respect of scripting and preliminary work amounted to £850 and by 4 August this had risen to £1,050.

27 Memorandum by Calder Marshall, 15 July 1942.

28 Dalrymple to Beddington, 11 August 1942.

29 Estimate of costs, *Western Approaches*, 5 August 1942.

30 Welch to Bamford, 12 August 1942.

31 Memorandum by Bromhead, 15 August 1942. Beddington's handwritten note of 20 August 1942 stated, 'I entirely agree with Col. Bromhead's conclusion'.

32 Bamford to Radcliffe, 21 August 1942.

33 Radcliffe to Bamford, 27 August 1942.

34 Bamford to Gates, 7 September 1942.

35 Harvey to Bamford, 14 September 1942.

36 Bamford's handwritten note on same, 15 September 1942.

37 Wright to A. W. Osborne, 12 May 1943.

38 Bryant to Osborne, 22 December 1942. The crewman eventually left the production.

39 Sussex, *The Rise and Fall of British Documentary*, p. 148.

40 E. L. Mercier to Beddington, 18 May 1943.

41 Welch to Bamford, 5 July 1943.

42 Bamford to Welch, 6 July 1943.

43 W. E. Phillips to Welch, 12 July 1943. They may not have been so sanguine had they realized that British Information Services had booked the production

crew into the Lexington Hotel in New York. They soon moved out to a cheaper hotel when they gathered that after paying five dollars a day in hotel bills, they had just four dollars left of a nine dollar a day subsistence allowance to live on. The intense heat did not help. One artist took to wearing his 'white ducks' as the 'only suitable attire'. As a result his laundry bill was 'quite fantastic'.

44 F. Gillman to N. Lloyd, 23 October 1943.
45 Dalrymple's letter of resignation to Beddington, 10 May 1943, is found in part in Sussex, *The Rise and Fall of British Documentary*, p. 151.
46 Wright to Holmes, 30 October 1943.
47 Holmes to Nunn May, 8 November 1943.
48 Wright to Osborne, 25 January 1944.
49 Memorandum by Beddington, 9 February 1944. It is difficult to decipher the initials on the handwritten note of 11 February to same, but they could well belong to Sidney Bernstein.
50 Dalrymple to Beddington, 29 February 1944.
51 Memorandum by Nunn May, 30 March 1944.
52 K. Harrisson to Beddington, 30 March 1944.
53 Archibald to Beddington, 4 April 1944.
54 L. W. Oliver to Nunn May, 8 May 1944.
55 Nunn May to Oliver, 15 May 1944.
56 J. Brooke Wilkinson to MoI, 'Minute of exception', 5 May 1944.
57 Hudson to Holmes, 6 May 1944.
58 Hudson to Nunn May, 6 May 1944. The subsequent list of films is undated and unsigned.
59 Nunn May to Archibald, 12 May 1944.
60 Jackson to Nunn May, 12 May 1944.
61 Nunn May to Brooke Wilkinson, 8 June 1944.
62 Brooke Wilkinson to Nunn May, 12 June 1944.
63 Oliver to Dalrymple, 6 September 1944.
64 Dalrymple to Oliver, 13 September 1944. The flare is plainly visible to this day.
65 Memorandum by Welch, 9 October 1944. The final direct costs of the film, as of Osborne's estimate on 19 June 1945, amounted to £58,164 excluding a sum of £494 for customs duty which 'need not be regarded as a Crown Film Unit cost'.
66 Beddington to Jackson, 6 October 1944.
67 Beddington to Dalrymple, 26 October 1944. His first draft noted that '. . . the Minister thinks it the best film we have made', but that was subsequently amended to read '. . . the best film he has ever seen'. Dalrymple replied on 3 November 1944 stating, among other things, that 'The job was done and the Treasury was not exactly without money through the film'.
68 Griggs to Beddington, 10 October 1944. Requests for charity premieres were forthcoming from the King George's Fund for Sailors, the Lord Mayor of Liverpool's War Fund, and the YWCA Wartime Fund. Special showings were arranged on 16 October, at 11am and 3pm, on 17 October, at 6pm, and on 19 October, at 3pm.
69 Beaverbrook to Beddington, 6 November 1944.

70   Ministry of War Transport to Beddington, 12 December 1944.

71   Office of War Information to Beddington, 13 December 1944.

72   Launder to Arthur Elton, 17 October 1944.

73   Del Giudice to Beddington, 15 January 1945.

74   Memorandum by S. Nolbandov, 13 November 1944.

75   The synopsis can be found in INF 1/213 and on the microfiche for the film held at the British Film Institute Library, London.

76   *The Times*, 10 November 1944.

77   *Daily Mail*, 13 November 1944.

78   *Manchester Guardian*, 18 November 1944.

79   *News Chronicle*, 11 December 1944. For Winnington's earlier piece on the film see the *News Chronicle* for 23 May 1944.

80   *New Statesman*, 9 December 1944. For a detailed discussion of *San Demetrio London* see Charles Barr, *Ealing Studios*, London, 1977.

81   *Observer*, 10 December 1944. Edgar Anstey retaliated in the *Spectator* on 15 December 1944, where he concluded: 'Has not Pat Jackson, the film's director, achieved more by assuming, firstly, that his characters are not dull, and, secondly, that real life and the common people need not be "theatrical" in order to be dramatic?'.

82   Sussex, *The Rise and Fall of British Documentary*, p. 147.

83   Paul Rotha, 'Documentary is Neither Short Nor Long', a privately circulated memorandum dated 9 August 1946 and reprinted in *Rotha on the Film*, London, 1958, p. 229.

84   Rotha, *Rotha on the Film*, pp. 228–9. INF 1/199, 'Receipts from commercial distribution of films, summary of statement 18 prepared for evidence for the Public Accounts Committee in May 1944', reveals that *Target for Tonight* made £73,636, *Coastal Command* made £47,797 and *Desert Victory* made £77,250. In addition *Close Quarters* (1943, director Jack Lee) made £13,740. The summary was prepared before *Western Approaches* went on release, of course. Unfortunately, despite the mass of documentation relating to *Western Approaches*, it does not appear that there are any papers recounting how much profit this film made.

12

Our American Cousins

The Way to the Stars

When the *Daily Mail* polled its readers in 1945 to ascertain the most popular film of the war years, the winner with 500,000 votes was *The Way to the Stars*, a victory rendered all the more remarkable by the fact that by 1945 war films were generally unpopular and the next four films in the *Mail* poll in order of popularity were the Gainsborough melodramas *The Man in Grey, Madonna of the Seven Moons* and *They Were Sisters* and then Laurence Olivier's *Henry V.*[1]

The film's success can be explained in a number of ways. First, it was one of the finest collaborations of the richly productive alliance of the playwright Terence Rattigan, the writer - producer Anatole de Grunwald and the director Anthony Asquith. The collaboration began when Asquith directed the film version of Rattigan's play *French Without Tears* (1939), an adaptation made by Rattigan and de Grunwald with Ian Dalrymple. The partnership was consolidated during the war on six films (*Quiet Wedding, Uncensored, English without Tears, The Demi-Paradise, Cottage to Let, The Way to the Stars*), on which they worked in various permutations.[2] It carried on after the war with seven more films, including Asquith's two final works *The VIP's* (1963) and *The Yellow Rolls-Royce* (1964).

Second, *The Way to the Stars* was a film rooted in observation and personal experience. Terence Rattigan, who had achieved considerable success with his comedy *French Without Tears*, had joined the RAF in 1940 and been posted to Coastal Command as a pilot officer air gunner and wireless operator.[3] He was later promoted to the rank of flight lieutenant and became gunnery officer with 422 Squadron. His RAF service opened up an entirely new area for his writing, and in 1941 between flying duties he wrote a play, *Flare Path*, which achieved an enormous success when staged in 1942. It was directed by Anthony Asquith.

Set in the residents' lounge of a hotel close to an RAF bomber base in

Lincolnshire, it charted the reactions of the service wives to their husbands' absences on a night raid over Germany, an experience which deepens the various relationships explored. As Rattigan's biographers Michael Darlow and Gillian Hodson put it:

> The real achievement of *Flare Path* . . . was that it caught precisely the public mood of the moment. It was the major reason for Rattigan's amazing popular success, and arguably his chief claim to enduring reputation, that he managed to mirror and focus the public and private concerns of a vast British audience over a period of almost 20 years. This audience extended beyond middle class theatregoers to millions of cinemagoers in every part of the English-speaking world and from every stratum of society.[4]

Criticisms of the play centred on the contrived 'happy ending' when one husband believed killed turns up alive, an unconvincing romantic triangle and some rather stagey working class characters. It is interesting to note that when Asquith and Rattigan reworked some of the material from *Flare Path* in *The Way to the Stars,* all these unsuccessful elements were omitted.

Third, the film eschewed combat and action scenes in favour of exploring the emotional impact of the war on the leading characters. It was thus not so much a film about the fighting of the war as of living with and through the war. Like *In Which We Serve,* it was a film about human emotion and the British character. It is noticeable that the same aspects are singled out for praise in the contemporary reviews, namely that the film is British, it is real and its keynote is understatement. Dilys Powell, writing in 1947, set the film in its context, saying that Asquith succeeded 'admirably in capturing the emotion trembling beneath the laconic phrase, the controlled emotion . . . Beautifully played by John Mills, Michael Redgrave and Rosamund John, the film holds, for anyone who has lived through the years of air battle over England, an incomparable quality of regret for the massacre of youth'.[5]

C. A. Lejeune in the *Observer* noted the same quality:

> Mr Asquith's work is one more proof that the British film has at last attained its majority. It has one great merit, rare in Hollywood pictures these days, of emotional restraint. The intimate scenes between Miss Rosamund John, Mr Redgrave, Mr Montgomery and Mr John Mills are beautifully charged with a feeling that never spills over. These people are real people, and like real people, they do not make much of their private emotions. Again and again the audience is left to resolve its own tensions, an operation that is painful, unusual and good for the soul.[6]

Ernest Lindgren wrote in the *Monthly Film Bulletin:*

> No other film has so subtly and truthfully portrayed the life of the airman in

The Way to the Stars *eschewed scenes of combat to depict the stresses of command (Michael Redgrave, Basil Radford and John Mills).*

war, its problems, its hazards, its exaggerated casualness towards death, its courage, its humour, its comradeship.[7]

Richard Mallet wrote in *Punch:*

Not for a long time have I seen a film so satisfying, so memorable or so successful in evoking the precise mood and atmosphere of the recent past.[8]

The *Daily Sketch* thought the film:

sensitive and intelligent — it has . . . a close relation to reality . . . the story is credible, the characters true, the dialogue lifelike . . . the film, as a whole, has a lovely atmosphere, a simplicity which is almost satisfying, and in all its admirable emotional restraint it is far more moving than any picture deliberately designed as a tearjerker.[9]

But depiction of the reality of the wartime experience of the RAF was only one objective of the film — the other was the promotion of Anglo-American friendship.[10] During 1942 Terence Rattigan had been seconded temporarily from the RAF to work on the screenplays of *The Day Will Dawn,* a film about the Norwegian resistance, and *Uncensored,* a story of the Belgian resistance. In March 1943 he was seconded again to work with another screenwriter in the services, the American Captain Richard Sherman, on a film which was intended to deal with a British airfield during its transition from RAF to USAAF use. The Ministry of Information, anxious to promote Anglo-American cooperation and understanding, had set up and backed the project, arranging for Rattigan's release and the provision of service facilities. The Hollywood company 20th Century—Fox had agreed to produce the film, with Merle Oberon starring and William Wyler directing. Wyler shot a lot of footage of preparations for and the undertaking of a bombing raid, but decided to use it not in a fiction film but in a documentary. The result was one of the most celebrated documentary films of the Second World War — *Memphis Belle.* But the MoI was left with the Rattigan—Sherman script *Rendezvous,* which it was still anxious to use. Fox had pulled out of the deal and so the Ministry had two options open to it. It could commission the film as a fully fledged MoI feature and finance it with government funds, as it had *49th Parallel,* or it could sell the script to a commercial producer with an offer of full service facilities. This latter procedure involved the Ministry in much less expenditure and effort, and was the one they had used in the case of *The Way Ahead.* The treatment for this Army film had been produced at the suggestion of the War Office by army personnel, Captain Carol Reed, Lieutenant Eric Ambler, Major David Niven and Private Peter Ustinov. It was then sold to Two Cities Films for £250 on terms which included one third of all UK profits to the government, and Ministry approval of script, stars, producer and final cut.[11] The Ministry opted for a similar procedure in the case of *Rendezvous.*

Therefore on 4 June 1943 Jack Beddington, head of the MoI Films Division, wrote to L. P. Baker, president of the Kinematograph Renters Society, to put out feelers for an acceptable producer. On 23 June 1943 Baker replied that three companies had expressed interest (Alexander Korda Productions in association with MGM, General Film Distributors and Paramount Film Service) and he left it to Beddington to make the next move.[12] In the event, Two Cities undertook the production, under the aegis of GFD, with whom they had had a distribution arrangement since September 1942. Two Cities were in a way the logical choice since they had already produced the definitive Army and Navy films and *The Way to the Stars* was to be, by common consent, the definitive RAF film.

It seems to have been Anatole de Grunwald who, having learned of the project from Rattigan, interested Two Cities' chief, Filippo del Giudice in it. As director, they turned to Anthony Asquith. Both De Grunwald and

Asquith would have had a good idea of the propaganda angles needed, as both were members of the MoI ideas committee, set up in late 1941, to bring forward new ideas for propaganda films and to discuss and criticise those already made.[13] Asquith, the son of the former Liberal Prime Minister had, after a highly praised film about Gallipoli, *Tell England* (1930), had a very uneven directorial career in the 1930s, with several lengthy periods of unemployment. But he became a very busy director of important propaganda films during the war (*Freedom Radio*, 1940; *Cottage to Let*, 1941; *Uncensored*, 1942; *We Dive at Dawn*, 1943; *The Demi-Paradise*, 1943) as well as several MoI shorts (*Channel Incident*, *Rush Hour*, *Two Fathers*). He was also the director of the highly praised instructional film for GIs *A Welcome to Britain* (1943).[14] De Grunwald, a White Russian exile, educated at Cambridge and a self-confessed Anglophile, was a highly experienced screenwriter turned producer. He had worked on many films during the war, notably such outstanding celebrations of England and the English spirit as Leslie Howard's *Pimpernel Smith* and *The First of the Few*, and *The Demi-Paradise*, which featured Laurence Olivier as a solemn Russian engineer discovering the delights of the English way of life.

During 1944, de Grunwald worked with Rattigan and Asquith preparing a new screen treatment based on the Rattigan—Sherman scenario and incorporating elements of *Flare Path*. Then Rattigan alone wrote the complete shooting script from the treatment.[15] It was finished by September and on 20 September 1944 Two Cities signed a formal contract with GFD for distribution of the film, to be called either *Rendezvous* or *This Side of the Ocean*.[16] Ultimately the title of the film was to be *The Way to the Stars*, a reference presumably to the motto of the RAF, *per ardua ad astra*.

The film-makers were given full cooperation by the British and American air forces. This was a clear sign of official approval of the project, as was the fact that the script received the formality of BBFC approval as late as 16 February 1945, when shooting was well advanced. Asquith and De Grunwald assembled a formidable cast of British actors, headed by Michael Redgrave, John Mills, Rosamund John, Trevor Howard, Basil Radford and Renee Asherson. For the leading American part they secured the release of Douglass Montgomery. The son of an American mother and a Canadian father, he had been serving with the Canadian Army since 1941. Little remembered now, he had had a busy career as a Hollywood star in the 1930s. But his refusal to sign long term contracts and his periodic returns to the stage prevented his consolidating his position as a major film star. His great assets were his sensitivity, openness and charm, which he had displayed to considerable effect as a young First World War soldier in James Whale's masterly *Waterloo Bridge* (1930). Other American parts were played by American actors resident in Britain such as Bonar Colleano and Hartley Power.

Shooting began at RAF Catterick in Yorkshire in September 1944. But by the time the film was completed, it was clear that the war would be over before the film went on general release. So a new beginning was devised and added, showing a disused and overgrown airfield, with the main story told in flashback.[18] This made *The Way to the Stars* not only the last war film of the war but also the first war film of the peace and precursor of the post-war cycle of films such as *Angels One Five* and *The Dambusters*. Thus it was at the same time a realistic recreation of what had occurred but also a cause to rejoice in and celebrate a noble period in our history.

The film opens with a long, expressive tracking shot through a now deserted airfield where sheep graze. There is a close-up of a sign which shows us that this is Halfpenny Field, mentioned in Domesday Book. This and the grazing sheep give us the feel of rural timelessness, in which the recent hurly-burly of war is but a passing episode. The war is already part of history. Then the camera tracks through the control room and the crew rooms, picking up various items which subsequently appear in the film: a

The Way to the Stars *also dramatized the ordeal of the women who wait (Michael Redgrave and Rosamund John).*

telephone number scribbled on a wall; a crumpled 'Lucky Strike' cigarette packet; an abandoned pin-up photograph; an enamel sign from a pre-war German train. These objects are all that remain of the people who lived and loved and died there over five years of war. The whole sequence superbly evokes the feeling of the recent past, recollected with sadness and pride.

Like the ship in *In Which We Serve*, it is the airfield in *The Way to the Stars* which provides the continuity. Also like *In Which We Serve*, the film recapitulates the highlights of the war, the war in the air this time, with sequences which take place in 1940, 1942 and 1944. But except for an enemy air raid on Halfpenny Field early on, the film concentrates on the effect of the events in the air on the women who wait at the 'Golden Lion' hotel in Shepley and the officers who wait at the field for their comrades to return.

The film intertwines two major themes. The first is the reactions of the characters to the impact of war on their lives. The principal audience identification figure is Peter Penrose (John Mills), a former secondary school master, who starts out as a rookie pilot and ends up as ground controller after the USAAF has taken over the base. No sooner has he arrived and been introduced to Squadron Leader Carter (Trevor Howard), the Commanding Officer, than Carter is killed and Flight Lieutenant David Archdale (Michael Redgrave), Peter's room-mate, becomes C.O. David too is killed. Later, Peter becomes a friend of Captain Johnny Hollis (Douglass Montgomery), the American flyer whom all the characters take to their hearts. He is also killed.

These losses are invariably received with a pain that is doubly moving by its restraint. There is no flag waving, no soupy soundtrack music, no over-the-top emotionalism. As Campbell Dixon put it at the time, declaring that 'few films have been more essentially English', 'Just imagine how Hollywood would have treated it — the tears from the women, the maudlin sentiment from the dead man's friends and at least one big bout of hysteria from somebody.'[19] The Englishness is thus seen to lie in emotional restraint. It is most succinctly expressed in the two John Pudney poems, 'Missing' and 'Johnny-in-the-clouds', which in the film are the work of David Archdale and provide one of the recurrent motifs of the narrative. The best known is 'Johnny-in-the-clouds', which gave the film its American release title and its epilogue, spoken by Redgrave. Sparely and economically, it underlines one of the principal morals of the film, about not making a fuss when people die but working for a better world so that the sacrifice shall not have been in vain.

> Do not despair
> For Johnny-head-in-air;
> He sleeps as sound
> As Johnny underground.

Fetch out no shroud
For Johnny-in-the-cloud;
And keep your tears
For him in after years.

Better by far
For Johnny-the-bright-star,
To keep your head,
And see his children fed.

Thus, the airmen return silently from the raids, which invariably involve the loss of one or more of their comrades. David Archdale announces the death of his close friend Carter and Peter Penrose relates David's death with a similar forced matter-of-factness ('Bad show'). David's wife, hotel manager 'Toddy' (Rosamund John), receives the news of his death from Peter without emotionalism, in the same way that the last parting of David and 'Toddy', interrupted by the eternally complaining Miss Winterton, was made without fuss. He just squeezes her shoulder and departs, using the same gesture that Trevor Howard uses in that other tribute to emotional restraint *Brief Encounter,* when parting forever from Celia Johnson, trapped by a gossiping neighbour in the refreshment room at Milford Junction. The same kind of emotional ellipsis is applied to the visual structure of the narrative, notably in indicating the death of David. He and Peter quarrel over David's desire to ground Peter because the latter is strained and over-tired. They leave on a raid and David forgets his lucky lighter. There is a telling close-up of the lighter. Then a hand closes round it and raises it to light a cigarette. It is Peter, who has returned from the raid. David has not. All these scenes are flawlessly acted by a cast who convey with rare poignancy and sensitivity the painful realities of grief and loss. The mood and atmosphere of the times are also notably captured in the sequence of the dance at the base where the young Jean Simmons sings 'Let him go, let him tarry,' casting a spell of innocence, youth and transience over the uniformed men and women who must soon return to the grim business of killing and being killed.

The imminent danger of death dictates the necessity of seizing happiness while you can. David marries 'Toddy' and fathers a son before he is killed. Peter, although in love with Iris Winterton, niece and companion of the querulous, selfish Miss Winterton, breaks with her rather than land her with the prospect of widowhood. But it is a breach which causes them both pain and is healed by 'Toddy', who tells Peter that she knows what has upset him and assures him that she does not regret marrying David and would do it again in similar circumstances. Encouraged by this, Peter proposes and is accepted by Iris, who knows the situation as well as 'Toddy' and will take the risk.

The film's second theme is provided by the Anglo-American angle. The arrival of the Americans at Halfpenny Field is marked by mutual

The film explored the roots of Anglo-American antagonism (Tryon Nicholl, Bonar Colleano and John Mills).

incomprehension, dislike and ridicule. When USAAF Colonel Page first arrives at the base he finds Flying Officer 'Prune' Parsons (David Tomlinson), doing an impersonation of boastful Americans. Similarly American Lieutenant Joe Frizelli (Bonar Colleano) dismissively impersonates the British, not realizing that Peter Penrose is in the room. Only a few English officers remain when the Americans take over and while the Americans noisily play handball, the British disdainfully take tea in the mess ('We must try to rise above it').

The Americans are set up as noisy, boastful, insensitive intruders, dramatizing the characteristics that the British are known to have found most offensive. Frizelli and his pals go to the 'Golden Lion' at Shepley, cause a scene because of language and etiquette differences and throw their weight around. These scenes interestingly parallel similar ones in Asquith's instructional film for GIs on how not to behave in Britain. Frizelli also sounds off about how easy the war is going to be now they are in it, in the presence of Penrose, who listens without comment. But Frizelli is chastened and enlightened by his first combat experience in the first US air raid on Germany on 17 May 1942. The Americans admit they were wrong to say it would be easy to bomb Germany and Penrose buys them drinks. Thereafter the Americans are gradually calmed and civilized by contact with the British, but they also have a beneficial effect on the residents' lounge of the 'Golden Lion', transforming its atmosphere from stuffy, repressed, genteel decorum to cheerful, uninhibited exuberance. English and American airmen drink together, sing and dance so gleefully that at the end a waitress declares half-admiringly and with an eye to the audience: 'You Americans and you RAF — there's nothing to choose between you.' The very British 'Tiny' (Basil Radford) even joins in a baseball game. It is simply a matter of each side adjusting to the other's ways with a little sympathy and give-and-take.

But what links Britain and America in the end is shared sacrifice. Johnny Hollis, the acceptable face of the USA, returns from a mission with a bomb stuck in his plane's undercarriage. He refuses to bail out because the plane would crash on Shepley. He tries to land but the plane blows up. 'Toddy' tells Joe Frizelli that 'as long as this town lives, he'll be remembered here.' Johnny, although offered the chance to return home as an instructor, had stayed on to finish the job because he felt that America had come late into the fight. He strikes up a friendship with 'Toddy', she providing female companionship and he sharing with her his feelings about his wife and children at home. Noticeably too, like Archdale and Carter, Johnny smokes a pipe, the infallible badge of a good chap. His friendship with 'Toddy', his devotion to his family and his belief in the war all mark him out as a man of the same stamp as David Archdale. They are consciously linked by the film. 'Toddy' gives Johnny David's lucky lighter, and at the end she lets Joe Frizelli read David's poem 'Johnny-in-the-clouds'. Joe realizes what it means and says it might have been written for Johnny. We hear Redgrave's voice on the sound track reciting it as Joe and Peter Penrose stroll back to the base, symbol of the uniting of Britain and the USA in a common cause hallowed by the loss of friends they have loved.

The critics appreciated the way the Anglo-American angle was presented and dealt with. Richard Winnington wrote in the *News Chronicle*:

> In this film's frank handling of the hostility between two groups of fliers, the tried and the untried, and its gradual breaking down into respect and friendship, a valuable and delicate service has been done for Britain and America.[20]

C. A. Lejeune in the *Observer* went so far as to call it:

> the only film I have ever seen that succeeds in explaining the Englishman to the American, and the American to the Englishman with good humour, good sense and clarity. It does this in the frankest possible way, by admitting that

any difference that exists between British and American manners must necessarily present itself to the American as an inferiority on the part of the British, and to the Englishman as an inferiority on the part of the American; but that there are certain things deeper than manners, which both nations admit to be superior, and which they have in common.[21]

It is interesting to note that *The Way to the Stars* is almost entirely about middle class officers. The only non-officer is Sergeant 'Nobby' Clark (Bill Owen), treated as an equal by Penrose and Archdale, but not an important character. This contrasts with *Journey Together*, scripted by Terence Rattigan for John Boulting and the RAF Film Unit, a film which stresses the friendship between upper middle class Cambridge under-graduate Jack Watling and working class cockney Richard Attenborough. But alongside this there is an Anglo-American angle, which has the British pilots sent to Arizona to train and there overcoming language difficulties and etiquette variations. The pilots are befriended and looked after by the chief American flying instructor, Edward G. Robinson, and his wife, Bessie Love.

Both films were sponsored by official bodies, the MoI in the case of *The Way to the Stars* and the RAF in the case of *Journey Together*, made as an RAF training film but commercially released by RKO in 1945. Both films set great store by stressing the growth of understanding and sympathy between Britons and Americans and this reflected a wider official concern.

The average Englishman's view of America had been powerfully shaped and influenced by the movies. As Sir Denis Brogan wrote in 1942 in a book designed to explain the British to America and lessen mutual ignorance and intolerance:

For the average moviegoer . . . America is the films . . . The America he sees in the films is an energetic, precedent-breaking, very amusing, fabulous country where anything goes and anything is possible.[22]

This was an immensely attractive picture, particularly to the young. But the view was greatly affected by the massive influx of US troops in the wake of America's entry into the war. The American GIs bathed in the glamour automatically conferred on them by the movies and armed with such scarcities as cigarettes, chocolate, chewing gum and nylons, arrived and began, in the words of one commentator, 'to treat Britain as an occupied country'.[23] George Orwell reported in his letter from England to *Partisan Review* (3 January, 1943), on the mutual antipathy between the British masses and the Americans:

There is widespread anti-American feeling among the working class, thanks to the presence of the American soldiers, and, I believe, very bitter anti-British feeling among the soldiers themselves. I have to speak here on second-hand evidence, because it is almost impossible to make contact with an American soldier. They are to be seen everywhere in the streets, but they don't go to the ordinary pubs, and even in the hotels and cocktail bars which they frequent, they keep to themselves and hardly answer if spoken to. American civilians who are in contact with them say that apart from the normal grumbling about the food, the climate etc., they complain of being inhospitably treated and of having to pay for their amusements, and are disgusted by the dinginess, the old-fashionedness and the general poverty . . . If you ask people why they dislike Americans, you get first of all the answer that they are 'always boasting' and then come upon some more solid grievance in the matter of soldiers' pay and food. An American soldier gets ten shillings a day and all found, which . . . means that the whole American army is financially in the middle class, and fairly high up in it . . . The Americans are given foodstuffs, otherwise reserved for children, and also imported luxuries which obviously waste shipping space. They are even importing beer, since they will not drink English beer. People point out with some bitterness that sailors have to be drowned bringing this stuff across.[24]

The film sought to highlight the sources of Anglo-American friendship and dispel the negative image of the 'Yanks' (Douglass Montgomery and Rosamund John).

This constituted a considerable shift of view, since as Orwell observed in *Tribune* (17 December 1943): 'Before the war, anti-American feeling was a middle class and perhaps upper class thing, resulting from imperialist and business jealousy and disguising itself as dislike of the American accent etc. The working class, far from being anti-American, were becoming rapidly Americanized in speech by means of the films and jazz songs.'[25]

Orwell's impressionistic view of the grievances between the two peoples is confirmed by the Home Intelligence unit, which monitored feeling towards the US troops in its weekly reports from the summer of 1942 when large numbers of GIs began to arrive. At this time there was 'an inclination to anticipate problems and difficulties where they [the GIs] were expected' and HI noted that the prospect of an 'American invasion' aroused little enthusiasm in the populace at large.[26]

Once the Americans had arrived, the complaints about them were early established and never varied throughout the rest of the war. They were criticized for their high pay and heavy drinking, their boastfulness and their casualness, and their behaviour with girls.[27] 'Overpaid, oversexed and over here' genuinely did summarize the causes of anti-American feeling. Another perhaps unanticipated problem arose between Britons and Americans: 'The kindness meted out to coloured Americans by their British hosts is said to be resented and misunderstood by the white Americans, who do not mix with them'.[28] Coloured troops consistently gained high praise from the British civilians, as for instance in the report for 23 November 1944: 'There is praise for their quiet, considerate and well-mannered behaviour'.[29]

The complaints divide almost equally into those inspired by envy and those produced by ignorance. In time, the latter diminished but the envy always remained. The popularity of the GIs with British women, reflected in the departure to the USA of some 70,000 'GI brides' at the end of the war, and the Americans' attitude towards women continued to be a cause for complaint. On 8 June 1944, HI reported criticisms of US troops for 'accosting, making love in public, having intercourse in telephone booths, leaving contraceptives about and for "indiscriminate" choice of women'. But the women came in for even greater censure. They were said to make most of the running in many cases: 'Blame of the girls is more widespread and sometimes stronger than the men. Their predatoriness is particularly censured: some girls are said to be 'dunning' as many as three or four US soldiers to provide for their coming child'.[30] As late as March 1945 another perennial complaint was still surfacing. A BIPO survey about feelings towards America, while noting general approval from 73 per cent of those questioned, recorded that 'American boasting about its part in the Allied operations and a failure to give Britain sufficient credit for her part in the fighting . . . came in for a share of the criticism.'[31]

But it is important to put all this in perspective. Mass-Observation examined Anglo-American antipathy in detail in two major surveys into attitudes towards Americans in 1943:

> These demonstrated that Americans have never been regarded wholly as foreigners but more as distant cousins. As relations they are much criticized, particularly as it is less easy to forgive relations such 'foreign' habits as they may have. Their behaviour is measured against a standard of British behaviour, and where it deviates it is made a point of much adverse comment. Other foreigners are judged against a far less exacting yardstick of foreign behaviour . . . As more Americans have arrived in this country and thus increased the chances of the average person meeting them, many of the pre-conceived favourable ideas were dispelled, yet at the same time specific 'like' factors have tended to increase. Generally speaking coloured rather than American troops have made themselves particularly popular with people of this country . . . At the present time a vociferous minority is strongly critical of the Americans in this country, while a majority have no complaints. A survey of American soldiers' views of the British revealed some strong feelings: though a majority liked England and the British, many strongly criticized the way in which children begged for sweets, the way Americans were being 'done' by what some considered the low moral tone of British women.[32]

A BBC Listener Research Report on the state of British public opinion towards the Americans in 1942 and 1943 confirmed this view:

> There would appear to be no basis for alarmist statements to the effect that American troops are universally unpopular, though their much higher pay is a source of considerable ill feeling. In general, they are accepted as including, like all large groups of men, both good and bad. Inevitably it is the behaviour of an obtrusive minority which is noticed, however unrepresentative that behaviour may in fact be, so that drunkenness and an overbearing attitude of white to coloured troops creates a bad impression far out of proportion to the real incidence of such occurrences. The British people are, too, somewhat shocked by what they feel to be a slovenly appearance or bearing of American troops, and this makes a very great many doubt whether the American soldier will ever be the equal of the British. It is only fair to add that American soldiers' generosity, to children for example, is quickly appreciated, and such significant comments as 'They are really decent chaps when you get to know them' were not infrequent. In a word, bearing in mind the potentialities of misunderstanding and discord, the relationship between American troops and British civilians is much more satisfactory than many sanguine observers might reasonably have expected.[33]

Two continuing factors helped to diminish the initial hostility. One was increasing appreciation of the American contribution to the war effort. HI regularly reported comments like 'Genuine pleasure has been expressed at the part played by the US forces in the Tunisian victories and confidence in their fighting qualities is said to have thereby increased'.[34] Increased

The Way to the Stars remains a lasting memorial to the role of the Allied air forces and the sacrifice of 'the Few', whose youth and transience is captured in the dance sequence when Jean Simmons sings 'Let him go, let him tarry'.

acquaintance between the two peoples improved the position too, and this was deliberately fostered by MoI-backed local committees and regional organizations. Such contact led to reports, like that of 25 November 1943, that recently arrived US troops had been described as 'a pleasant surprise', because they were quiet, courteous and friendly. This had the effect of enlisting positive sympathy on the side of the GIs. So that HI could report: 'People are thought . . . to be more tolerant and more willing to be favourably impressed; unfriendliness towards American troops is criticized, and exploitation by retailers, landlords and taxi drivers strongly condemned.'[35]

As the most popular and accessible of the mass media, movies were pressed into action to promote the Anglo-American alliance. In Hollywood there was a rash of films sympathetic to Britain and the British war effort,

such as *Mrs Miniver, The White Cliffs of Dover* and *Forever and a Day.*
An hour-long film *A Welcome to Britain* (1943) was commissioned by the
War Office from the Ministry of Information and paid for by the Treasury.
It was then handed over to the American Office of War Information for
showing to US troops. It was devised and directed by Anthony Asquith,
assisted by writer Sam Spewack, director Irving Reis (of the OWI) and the
actor Burgess Meredith, who acted as guide and narrator. With sympathy
and humour, Burgess Meredith expounded to his audience the role,
function and etiquette of the English pub, explained the rationing system
and the privations suffered by the British and called in on a lesson being
given by elderly schoolmaster 'Mr Chips' (Felix Aylmer), who explained the
geography of Britain. He met Bob Hope, who explained English currency,
visited a British restaurant to learn about the fixed prices and limited
menus, encountered some prostitutes in the blackout and warned 'watch
your step', and in a forthright section on racial prejudice explained that
there were fewer social restrictions on blacks than in America and the
coloured man would be made more welcome in Britain than at home. At
the start Meredith is told by Lieutenant General Jacob Devers, US Army
chief (European theatre of operations): 'Next to winning the war, the most
important thing on earth is the friendly relations of the Allied nations. We
Americans know how to meet death but we are not always so good at
meeting life'. His view is echoed by the British Adjutant-General, General
Sir Ronald Adam, who declares: 'This film is intended to further the
object which you and I have so much at heart — greater understanding
between our armies and our peoples'.

The film seems to have achieved the stated objective. It was rapturously
received by the British critics who saw it. The *Daily Mail* thought it
'should do more than any other single stroke to create a genuine Anglo-
American understanding'.[36] The *News Chronicle* thought 'this production
will serve its purpose admirably and should, I think, be released to
audiences here if only on the grounds of its admirable qualities of
entertainment.'[37] Dilys Powell summed up its appeal best in *The Sunday
Times:*

> I see a good many propaganda films, some of them startlingly effective in
> defeating their own ends. I have not yet seen a film more successful than
> *Welcome to Britain* in disposing the mind to accept. To accept what?
> Nothing very hard and fast; merely that the British have ways different from
> American ways, that their food is, in wartime anyway, not so good, that they
> are quieter and slower, that their money and spelling are eccentric, but that
> taken all in all, they are quite a decent, friendly lot.'[38]

The Sunday Times indeed joined *The Times,* the *News Chronicle,* the
Daily Herald and the *Manchester Guardian* in calling for its release to
British civilian audiences.[39] It never was generally released, but it is
interesting to note that the style, message and approach of *A Welcome to*

Britain re-appeared in *The Way to the Stars* to help promote the Anglo-American friendship angle. This approach seems also to have appealed to GI audiences, as the 1943 Annual Report of the British Division of the OWI reported that a poll of test audiences of American troops had shown virtually unanimous approval of *A Welcome to Britain*.[40]

In Britain, decisive cinematic steps were taken to make America acceptable to the general public. One way of demonstrating adherence to a common cause was the integration of an American outsider into a predominantly British fighting group. In *Pimpernel Smith* (1941), the brash American student David Maxwell, initially reluctant to join Smith's archaeological expedition, becomes in the end his chief disciple. In *San Demetrio London* (1943), the objectionable and unpopular 'Yank' (Robert Beatty) becomes part of the team that saves the tanker and brings it safely to port. In *Flying Fortress* (1942) a worthless American playboy (Richard Greene) is regenerated by joining the RAF. *The Foreman Went to France* (1942) saw an American secretary (Constance Cummings) joining forces with a British trio, Welshman (Clifford Evans), Cockney (Tommy Trinder) and Scot (Gordon Jackson) in rescuing vital machinery from the Nazis.

The historical background to the special relationship was stressed in a brace of turgid costume epics, *Penn of Pennsylvania* (1941) and *Atlantic Ferry* (1942), which contained speeches looking forward to future cooperation between the two countries after English settlers found the colony of Pennsylvania in the 17th century and Scottish pioneers establish regular steamship sailings across the Atlantic in the 19th century. *Penn*'s producer, Richard Vernon, announced that he had long been struck by the similarity between Penn's views and those of President Roosevelt, and the film's eponymous hero was billed in the advertising as 'The Briton who laid the foundations of the American constitution and forged the first links in the unbreakable chain that binds together the two nations.'[41]

But it was not until 1944 that feature films about GI's in Britain reached the screen. In Michael Powell's *A Canterbury Tale,* one of the latterday Canterbury pilgrims who are spiritually awakened by the beauties of the English countryside is a GI, Sergeant Bob Johnson, played by the real-life GI Sergeant John Sweet. But this complex and fascinating film mystified audiences and was not a box office success. It was not, in fact, until 1945 that two such films appeared which were box office successes, and by then the problem was apparently diminishing.[42]

Both films were the work of mainstream commercial producers but received very different critical responses. *I Live in Grosvenor Square* was produced and directed by Herbert Wilcox with a cool calculation, identified by C. A. Lejeune, who described it as:

> an organized and successful assault on our emotions that is guaranteed to produce rivers of tears on both sides of the Atlantic. Using every cinematic cliché known to man; from the Duke — blessings on his white hairs and

golden heart — who can bear the loss of his acres with fortitude, but does love his cup of tea, to the patient Mom in Arizona, who wipes her hands on her apron, adjusts her glasses and composes herself to read the fatal message from overseas, it is designed by a cool head to appeal to a warm heart. To my mind, it is Herbert Wilcox's cleverest picture, advocating an alliance between democratic America and aristocratic England, while being careful not to implement it . . . The whole effect is contrived by the writer and director and is due to them alone. A certain impression of sincerity is required, and that both Miss Neagle and Mr Jagger . . . provide remarkably well. The rest is simply an illusion produced by the machinery of a good box office film.[43]

The film opens with the words: 'Just before D-Day there were over three million Americans in Britain. This is a record of what happened to one of them.' It carefully sets up and disposes of differences between the two nations in language, customs and etiquette and establishes the alliance by the time-honoured convention of a love affair which personalizes the two nations — America as Sergeant John Patterson (Dean Jagger) from Flagstaff, Arizona, in peace time a construction engineer working on the Boulder Dam and now serving with the USAAF, and England as Lady Patricia Fairfax (Anna Neagle), granddaughter of the Duke of Exmoor (Robert Morley), and now serving with the WAAFs. Patterson and his Jewish sidekick Sergeant Benjie Greenberg of Brooklyn (Pfc. Elliott Arluck) are billeted on the Duke of Exmoor's Grosvenor Square mansion. They encounter hostility from the old housekeeper, Mrs Wilson, which disappears when she discovers that Patterson lost his father in the First World War, just as she had lost her husband (i.e. a record of shared national sacrifice in the past). John falls in love with Patricia and is accepted by the Duke, whom he calls 'Pop', as a surrogate son (the Anglo-American alliance). Pat's fiancé, Major David Bruce (Rex Harrison) gallantly steps aside in the light of their love (British self-sacrifice). But John, returning from a mission with a crippled plane, crashes it trying to avoid the village and is killed, exactly like Johnny Hollis in *The Way to the Stars* (American self-sacrifice). A memorial to the plane's crew is unveiled in the village church and the Duke hands over a US flag to a boy from the local school, stressing the blood ties between Britain and America. The film ends with David Bruce leading his paratroopers in a raid on Europe, piloted by an American Eagle Squadron pilot who has married an English girl and declares: 'Some day I'd like to see a bridge across the Atlantic'. The words of the Walt Whitman poem 'Two Together' are flashed on the screen.

To avoid alienating a war-weary public, the film was billed and publicized as 'Not a War Film! Not Propaganda! But a love story that bridges the Atlantic.' It may not have been a war film in the narrow sense of the word, but propaganda it most certainly was. *Time* magazine described it as 'probably the most pro-American picture ever made outside the USA'.[44] But British critics expressed serious reservations about the British social setting depicted in the film. The *Daily Telegraph, The Sunday Times* and the *Daily Herald* all complained about the stereotyped and limited social setting, which they feared would simply confirm Americans in their view that Britain was hopelessly class-ridden and outdatedly aristocratic.[45] Edgar Anstey in the *Spectator* called it 'a British imitation of an American film about Britain' and complained of 'distorted and damaging fantasies of our own British life'.[46] The *News Chronicle* declared: 'I should say whatever level of British society you inhabit, this snob-ridden nonsense would bitterly offend you. The box office will probably prove me wrong.'[47]

The box office did indeed prove him wrong and it was a considerable hit both in Britain and in America, where it was released by Fox under the title *A Yank in London.* But the critics rather overreacted to the setting and they did so because of the long-standing commitment of the British critical establishment to documentary realism and a faithful depiction of British life in all its aspects. This perhaps led them to overlook the fact that one of the film's purposes was to tackle the perennial American criticism that Britain was class-ridden and dominated by a privileged aristocracy. These are the very criticisms that John Patterson voices when asked for his view of Britain. But the film carefully shows the dismantling of this aristocratic dominance and the acceptance of change by the ruling class. Exmoor Castle is requisitioned for use by American troops, the aristocracy is shown as suffering like everyone else from rationing restrictions and a by-election in the Duke's pocket borough ends in defeat for his Conservative nominee and the election of a working class independent. Britain is seen therefore as engaging in the transition from aristocracy to democracy and thus constituting a fit partner in the war effort for 'the land of the free and the home of the brave'.

Certainly the film shuffles and deploys all the known stereotypes in the interests of the Anglo-American alliance. On the one hand, there is the sturdy, upright WASP hero with all the integrity of the classic Westerner. He has a likeable comic Jewish sidekick and a patient, devoted mother, played by the classic American Mom-ikon, Jane Darwell. On the other hand, there is the lovably eccentric Duke who patiently accepts all the changes in his circumstances, the democratic Lady Patricia, who not only falls in love with the Yank but is to be seen jiving in the GI club and thus giving the lie to British snobbishness, and Major David Bruce, the classic British officer and gentleman who accepts defeat in love and in the by-election with equanimity, makes speeches about the meaning of democracy and service and fights gallantly for his country. It was unquestionably calculated, undeniably cliché-ridden, indisputably soap-opera: but the public loved it.

Both critics and public, however, loved *The Way to the Stars*, which has remained a lasting memorial to the Anglo-American effort, to the wartime role of the RAF and to the sacrifices of 'the Few'. It was the latter aspect which perhaps made *The Way to the Stars* such a special film for so many people. The critic of *Time and Tide* spoke for them when he wrote:

> It's five days since I saw *The Way to the Stars* and I am still asking myself why this unassuming picture moved me so much . . . So many pompous things have been said about the Battle of Britain that the imagination shies from it. This film makes it possible to dwell on it again, in poetry, in freshness and with the perspective of history . . . Everyone who remembers it will have their own evocations. It was the jokes which brought 1940 back to me most in the film. The ones about nuns and parachutists. The history books will omit them, and omit too the temporariness, the feeling that the world will end tonight and why worry since tomorrow can't possibly happen. The pilots talk in their odd new Elizabethan idiom, of which Mr Rattigan is a master, of cars and girls and borrowing enough money from the adjutant to get tight tonight. Seldom of flying, never of dying.[48]

The *Daily Mail* put it more succinctly, but no less relevantly, when it called the film 'a masterpiece of understatement'.[49] It was unknowingly echoing Winston Churchill's comment on *Flare Path*.[50] For Rattigan, Asquith and De Grunwald had succeeded triumphantly in capturing and exploring with sympathy and understanding that much-mocked but nevertheless central aspect of Englishness.

NOTES

1   *Daily Mail,* 24 April 1946. There was a popular novelization of the script, Dilys Owen, *The Way to the Stars,* London, n.d. It contains the results of the *Daily Mail* ballot in an appendix. The film also topped the poll in a ballot organized in his Granada Cinemas by Sidney Bernstein for the best film, British or American, since VE Day (Maud Miller (ed.), *Winchester's Screen Encyclopedia,* London, 1948, p. 219).

2   *Quiet Wedding* (1940) was directed by Asquith and scripted by de Grunwald and Rattigan; *Cottage to Let* (1941) was directed by Asquith and co-written by de Grunwald; *Uncensored* (1942) was directed by Asquith and co-written by Rattigan; *The Demi-Paradise* (1943) was directed by Asquith and written and produced by de Grunwald; *English Without Tears* (1944) was directed by Harold French and written by Rattigan and de Grunwald.

3   On Rattigan's life and career, see Michael Darlow and Gillian Hodson, *Terence Rattigan: the Man and his Work,* London, 1979.

4   Darlow and Hodson, *Terence Rattigan,* p. 113.

5   Dilys Powell, *Films Since 1939,* London, 1947, p. 30.

6   C. A. Lejeune, *Chestnuts in her Lap,* London, 1947, p. 151.

7   *Monthly Film Bulletin* 12, 1945, p. 70.

8   *Punch,* 15 June 1945.

9   *Daily Sketch,* 8 June 1945.

10   On the background to and making of *The Way to the Stars,* see Darlow and Hodson, *Terence Rattigan,* pp. 101—36, and R. J. Minney, *Puffin Asquith,* London, 1973, pp. 111—22.

11   Vincent Porter and Chaim Litewski, 'The Way Ahead', *Sight and Sound* 50, Spring 1981, pp. 110—16.

12   Letter from L. P. Baker to Jack Beddington, 23 June 1943, INF 1/224.

13   The Ideas Committee was formed at the instigation of the Screenwriters Association which wanted closer contact with the MoI. It consisted of Anatole de Grunwald, Rodney Ackland, Leslie Arliss, Sidney Gilliat, Frank Launder, Angus Macphail, J. B. Williams, Gordon Wellesley, Anthony Asquith, Michael Powell, Leslie Howard, Jack Beddington, Roger Burford. *Kinematograph Weekly,* 25 December 1941.

14   On Asquith's career see Minney, *Puffin Asquith,* and Peter Noble, *Anthony Asquith,* BFI New Index Series no. 5.

15   The credits read 'screenplay by Terence Rattigan from a story by Terence Rattigan and Anatole de Grunwald based on a scenario by Flt Lt Terence Rattigan and Captain Richard Sherman'.

16   Memorandum of agreement between Two Cities and GFD, 20 September 1944, INF 1/224. In the event, it was released by United Artists, for reasons I have been unable to ascertain.

17   BBFC Scenario Reports 1945, no. 106/106A.

18   The introduction was influential enough to be copied directly in Henry King's *Twelve O'Clock High* (1949), a Hollywood film set in a USAAF base in England.

19   *Daily Telegraph,* 8 June 1945.

20   *News Chronicle,* 9 June 1945.

21   C. A. Lejeune, *Chestnuts in Her Lap,* London, 1947, p. 151.

22   D. W. Brogan, *The English People,* London, 1943, pp. 233—4.

23   Angus Calder, *The People's War,* London, 1971, p. 356.

24   George Orwell, *Collected Essays, Journalism and Letters* 2, Harmondsworth, 1971, pp. 320—1.

25   George Orwell, *Collected Essays, Journalism and Letters* 3, Harmondsworth, 1982, p. 76.

26   Home Intelligence Report 95, 30 July 1942, INF 1/292.

27   HI Report 168, 23 December 1943.

28   HI Report 92, 9 July 1942.

29   HI Report 216, 23 November 1944.

30   HI Report 192, 8 June 1944.

31   BIPO Survey of British Attitudes towards America, March, 1945, INF 1/327A.

32   Mass-Observation File Report 2021, Survey of work in 1943.

33   BBC Listener Research Report on changes in the state of British public opinion on the USA during 1942 and 1943, HI Report 175, 10 February 1944.

34   HI Report 144, 8 July 1943.

35   HI Report 164, 25 November 1943.

36   *Daily Mail,* 1 January 1944, overseas edition.

37   *News Chronicle,* 23 December 1943.

38   *The Sunday Times,* 20 February 1944.

39 *The Times,* 24 December 1943; *Manchester Guardian,* 6 April 1944; *Daily Herald,* 23 December 1943; *News Chronicle,* 23 December 1943.
40 Report of the British Division of the OWI, 1943, section 4a, INF 1/327A.
41 *Kinematograph Weekly,* 13 February 1941.
42 On *A Canterbury Tale* see Jeffrey Richards and Anthony Aldgate, *Best of British,* Oxford, 1983, pp. 43—59.
43 *Observer,* 22 July 1945.
44 *Time,* 18 March 1946.
45 *Daily Telegraph,* 24 July 1945; *Sunday Times,* 22 July 1945; *Daily Herald,* 21 July 1945.
46 *Spectator,* 27 July 1945.
47 *News Chronicle,* 21 July 1945.
48 *Time and Tide,* 16 June 1945.
49 *Daily Mail,* 24 April 1946.
50 Darlow and Hodson, *Terence Rattigan,* p. 119.

13

'National Pride and Prejudices'

Tunisian Victory

Much has been written about Frank Capra's film activities during the Second World War. Not surprisingly, commentators have tended to concentrate their attention on the important series of seven films he produced for the US Army under the title, *Why We Fight* (1942–5), 'the centrepiece of the Army's troop indoctrination programme', as it has been correctly described.[1] Occasional, albeit significant, scholarly contributions have also been forthcoming on related orientation projects, such as *The Negro Soldier* (1944) and *Know Your Enemy — Japan* (1945).[2] Of late, however, the spotlight has been turned upon Capra's role in the course of official Anglo-American efforts to co-operate in the making of two prestigious documentaries intended to celebrate the Allied cause. The first sought to record the successful outcome to the last North African campaign, while the second was concerned with the war in the Far East theatre and was meant to outline the strategic value of the Burma campaign.[3]

These collaborative ventures attracted a considerable amount of high level support and interest in their day but, as recent accounts have emphasized, the experiments did not prove to be especially easy for the participants. Both attempts were bedevilled by squabbles in production, by professional rivalry and, to borrow Frank Capra's own words, by 'national pride and prejudices'.[4] Nor, indeed, were the results particularly worthwhile as propaganda. In the case of the Burma campaign film, in fact, there was no visible result, at least in the form of a joint production. Having sought to act in unison between autumn 1944 and spring 1945, the American and British contingents felt compelled, quite simply, to go their separate ways. Colonel Frank Capra quickly produced *The Stilwell Road* for the US War Department. And by the outset of November 1945, Lieutenant Colonel David Macdonald and Captain Roy Boulting (producer and director, respectively) had finished work on *Burma Victory* for the British Ministry of Information.[5]

In the case of the earlier proposal for a documentary on the North African campaign, the concerted efforts of the American and British production teams, under Capra and Major Hugh Stewart (with Boulting's help, once again), did finally bear fruit in *Tunisian Victory*. This was first shown in New York and London on 16 March 1944, some seven months after Capra and Stewart had embarked upon their combined enterprise, and fully a year after the end of the campaign it purported to cover. Even among the American film critics, who greeted it favourably on the whole, there were those like Bosley Crowther of the *New York Times* who felt compelled to point out that 'the most obvious encumbrance on this picture is the fact that it is woefully late'.[6] Among British critics, the film's tardy arrival was the least of its problems and just one of several faults found with *Tunisian Victory*. Campbell Dixon of the *Daily Telegraph* thought it guilty of 'sins of omission' and believed it 'shows signs of having been edited largely for the American public'.[7] 'The moral of the film, which is obvious enough, is lost in a lot of sentimental and incredibly well-meaning vapourings', concluded the *Documentary News Letter*. It detected 'the fell hand of Capra's Hollywood', as did many British critics who greatly disliked the introduction of Burgess Meredith and Bernard Miles on the soundtrack and the 'pie in the sky' message of the film's ending.[8] All were agreed that *Tunisian Victory* fared badly in comparison with the 'sober' documentary style employed in its hugely successful predecessor, *Desert Victory* (1943), which had been made by Macdonald and Boulting of the British Army Film Unit with no input from either American sources or personnel. All were agreed, furthermore, that with *Tunisian Victory* Capra had simply 'poached' for his own nationalist ends what was intended initially to be a joint Anglo-American venture.[9]

The charge that Frank Capra had, in effect, 'poached' *Tunisian Victory* for his own purposes stuck and, indeed, gained added credence with subsequent disclosures forthcoming from some of the Britons and Americans who were most closely involved in its production. J. L. Hodson, for instance, who co-wrote the commentary for both *Desert Victory* and *Tunisian Victory*, was one member of the team who felt the joint exercise had actually proved beneficial. Yet, for all that, he revealed in the second volume of his wartime diaries that he had constantly found it necessary to do 'a little fighting to prevent our picture on the Tunisian campaign becoming disbalanced in favour of America'. 'After all', Hodson argued, 'we did most of the dirty work and had twice as many casualties'.[10] It is perhaps little wonder there were arguments in production since, as Hodson noted, the protagonists seemed to disagree over so much else besides:

We dined with Capra the other evening — Stewart, Boulting, and I. During our talk Capra said the public was always right in its judgments but I said that I thought, on the contrary, they were usually wrong, and that it was

'Preserve integrity — make it real. Use the stuff shot by the photographers with the troops and only that — even if the resultant picture is poor.' A genuine shot from the war front included in the film of Tunisian Victory.

only a minority of folk who kept the best art going, whether music or pictures or plays or books. For every lover of Shakespeare and Beethoven there are a hundred who prefer swing music and Rudolph Valentino. But maybe we were both wrong and the truth lies about midway.[11]

In the third volume of his diaries, Hodson outlined more about the precise nature of the problems encountered over *Tunisian Victory*:

No war documentary can be made with absolute integrity and truth, some reconstruction is inevitable if the story is to be properly told. A short part of *Desert Victory*, and this not the least effective, was reconstructed. The battle of Hill 609 in the new Tunisian film was 'shot' by the Americans in America . . .
    There are two schools of thought. The first says: 'Preserve integrity — make it real. Use the stuff shot by the photographers with the troops and *only* that — even if the resultant picture is poor. Keep the reconstructed stuff

'Make a good picture. If the "real stuff" isn't good enough, fake some that's better. The result is all that counts.' Reconstructed material, shot by Capra's unit, for 'the battle of Hill 609'.

down to, say, 5% of the whole. We realise the picture may lose something that a lot of "fake" material would give it but integrity counts higher than that'. The other school says: 'Make a good picture. If the "real" stuff isn't good enough, fake some that's better. The result is all that counts'.

The second, as I understand it, is the American view, and the Anglo-American picture of the Tunisian campaign pretty well conforms to it. And the result? Well, I think it's a good picture — it is at once something more and something less than *Desert Victory*. It certainly lacks the truth and sincerity of *Desert Victory*.[12]

Roy Boulting, by contrast, who worked on all three films in the *Victory* trilogy, derived scant pleasure from *Tunisian Victory*. 'Capra wanted to suggest that the campaign had been won by the American forces', he reiterated, and 'we had great battles with him . . . [to] get the US contribution in proportion'.[13] 'It wasn't an easy situation by any means', agreed Hugh Stewart, who felt that Capra's minimal account of the events in his autobiography amounted to a tacit, if honourable, admission of guilt over his poaching activities: 'In the book he wrote about his life, he very much skipped over this whole matter of the Tunisian business because he was honest enough to realise that, from the American point of view, it wasn't a terribly satisfactory thing to do'.[14]

Ironically, though perhaps somewhat predictably, it was Capra's voluble compatriot and colleague, John Huston, who described 'this fiasco in England' in the most forthright terms. It was 'a hell of a dirty trick we played on the English', he frankly admitted, and Capra was nothing if not 'very coony' in his dealings with the British Army Film Unit over 'the Joint Operation Film'. Unlike his British counterparts, however, who were understandably inclined to stress the nationalist motives behind Capra's moves, Huston was intent upon emphasizing a more mundane and practical purpose. For Huston, a further significant key to understanding Capra's dealings with the AFU lay in the fact that his 834th Photographic Signal Detachment suffered from a distinct lack of 'really good camera coverage' on the campaign in North Africa. They had the footage on 'the battle of Hill 609', of course. But that was clearly insufficient, as they had found when first trying to make a film of their own. Moreover, it was 'fabricated combat film' which had been shot in the Mojave Desert, California to complement other reconstructed material shot in Orlando, Florida. By comparison, as Huston soon discovered, 'the English had wonderful material'.[15] Capra was already well aware of this. The American premiere of *Desert Victory*, in March 1943, revealed just how rich the AFU's sources could be. His contacts advised there were more riches in store. Despite Hodson's subsequent claims to the contrary, he was highly sensitive to the accusation that he resorted to 'reconstructed stuff', in preference to 'actual shots from the battlefields'.[16] In fact, Capra was always keen on acquiring such. But it was difficult to obtain. From the spring of 1943, though, Capra proved more determined than ever to lay his hands on as much front line footage as possible. Undoubtedly, as Huston intimated, the vital matter of film supply was a further element in explaining Capra's interest in the AFU from the outset. It constituted a major reason for his sojourn in London from August to November of 1943.

How, then, did it come about that Frank Capra, a leading film director in the foremost film-producing country in the world, could ever find himself without adequate supplies of materials commensurate to his film compilation purposes? For an answer to that question, and a good many other questions besides, one must look at what Capra has to say both in public and private.[17] Capra's autobiography, *The Name Above the Title*, is replete with references to the problems he encountered winning recognition and resources for his unit. He spends much time there discussing 'the Great Celluloid War' which ensued between 'the Know-It-Alls of Hollywood and the Got-It-Alls of the Pentagon' over such heated issues as securing a public release for the first film in the *Why We Fight* series, *Prelude to War*. In that instance, he was finally successful.[18] But 'the Army proved a hotbed of intrigue', as David Culbert has rightly commented, and much energy was constantly expended in protecting Capra's detachment from the 'diehard opposition of officers in the field, and rivals in the Signal Corps and Office of War Information'.[19]

Nowhere were Capra's difficulties more acutely felt than in everyday practical matters such as obtaining film — whether stock footage or current, domestic or foreign. Again, his autobiography cites the obstacles Capra confronted in buying 30 cans of 'historical newsreel footage' from Pathé News in New York (done at his own expense, for 3,000 dollars, with little prospect of repayment); in viewing more recent foreign material such as Leni Riefenstahl's *Triumph of the Will* (a question, at least initially, of security clearance); and in acquiring both German and Japanese newsreels for the previous 20 years (which resulted in a reprimand and 'dire threats' from Signal Corps superiors because he expropriated film intended for their use).[20] If getting hold of library footage was difficult, obtaining first-hand front line material was worse. A major problem lay in the competition from the Signal Corps. There should never have been such competition, really, since much Signal Corps Army Pictorial Service activity was geared, principally, to the production of training films — 'the "nuts and bolts" type of visual aids', as Capra put it, 'to explain the "hows" of war, not the "whys"'. Capra's Photo Signal Detachment, assigned since its inception in May 1942 to Special Services, was meant to fulfil the latter objective and engage in propaganda designed to win 'the struggle for men's minds'.[21]

But competition existed in abundance. Despite the increasing number of people with feature film experience at the US Army's disposal, the 'American forces were still finding their feet in regard to certain specialised areas of production'.[22] Documentary in general and compilation film in particular were largely unknown territory to many recruits from the mainstream cinema. And Capra's ignorance of the documentary realms, which he honestly admitted, was by no means exceptional: 'I hadn't the foggiest idea how to make a documentary. To me, documentaries were ash-can films made by kooks with long hair'. They all had to learn the art and, despite his scathing comment, Capra was obviously keen to acquire the necessary skills to make the 'documented, factual-information film' he had been enjoined to do by no less a person than the Army Chief of Staff, General George C. Marshall.[23] Others in the APS, such as Colonel Darryl F. Zanuck, were as ready to please their masters, just as ambitious to extend their horizons, accustomed to building up film empires, and every bit as 'coony' in achieving their aims. Thus, in practice, the dividing line between the intent and purpose of units such as Capra's and Zanuck's often become blurred. Disputes over domain and demarcation invariably followed, as producers vied for film sources.

Capra was compelled finally to complain about the problems caused by Signal Corps rivals and did so in a memorandum he wrote on 12 November 1942 to his immediate superior, Colonel Edward L. Munson Jr. 'I have no particular objection to them making semi-propaganda and information films', he stated, 'but then we shouldn't be making them too'. There was 'so clearly a duplication of effort', he continued, and 'also, they get first crack at all domestic and foreign films, leaving us to beg, plead and steal what crumbs we can'. Capra concluded: 'if we don't get a clear definition of duties between us we will be constantly in competition for the same material and certainly will be giving the Army uncorrelated viewpoints'.[24] A reply followed within a week. It tactfully avoided a full answer to the larger tricky question of jurisdiction but promised better things in regard to warfront footage, not least from the campaign in North Africa:

> the OSS and Film Pictorial Service have 75 cameramen covering the North African push. The film will be shipped to London, developed there, pooled and made available to British newsreels. It will then be shipped to the US and made available to newsreels, Signal Corps and Special Service. What the priority of one outfit over the other is, I do not know, but I think that all of us will have a crack at whatever we want.[25]

Such promises were not easily fulfilled. The British newsreels found they had to wait a long time for material.[26] Capra did better but discovered there was little he could do to speed up an interminably slow process. Besides, he was immediately diverted and preoccupied with other issues of significance. *Prelude to War*, for instance, was released in that month of November 1942 and it became mandatory viewing for all military personnel. But the first broadsides in the looming battle to obtain a wider release for the film were already being fired by hostile critics such as Lowell Mellett of the OWI.[27] In addition, on another front, Capra was heavily engaged in negotiations with Walt Disney Productions 'to greatly increase the size of the "Capra Unit" within the studios'.[28]

In the event, Capra found that some more film was forthcoming. Certainly, Colonel William J. Donovan's agents from the Office of Strategic Services came up with welcome material which included 'current enemy newsreels [stolen] for me in border countries'.[29] It was not enough, though. Furthermore, even as the bulk of the North African film was being received in the USA, it was imposing severe strains upon a system ill equipped to cope with it. Captain Leonard Spiegelgass outlined 'the new problems of the film shot in overseas areas' to Capra, at the outset of December 1942:

Not only is the running of it a gargatuan [sic] task, and one which we are utterly unequipped to handle, but it is bewildering to try to imagine to what use it is all going to be put. With the [Army-Navy] Screen Magazine people, we must come to some kind of understanding. Otherwise, we shall be shipping you miles of unusable film or, conversely, preventing you from having material that is relevant and desirable.[30]

Once again, the difficulties remained unresolved. On 13 February 1943, for instance, Major Emmanuel Cohen was prompted to complain that 'the problem of getting film is still a serious one'. His note also hinted that Capra was not altogether happy with the American material on the North African offensive which was finally coming through since he plainly preferred to see it used overseas but not domestically.[31] Some people, less choosey, were willing to rush into production with whatever they had managed to acquire, if only to be the first. Thus, Darryl F. Zanuck, who corresponded with Capra about the 'difficult, painstaking job' he had been 'working day and night' to complete, finished At the Front in North Africa (1943) as speedily as possible. To do so, he had 'gone through the problem of blowing up 16 mm to 35 mm in Technicolor'. Nevertheless, he guaranteed, 'The effect is wonderful when you finally get it'.[32] Not everybody agreed. The result was certainly, as Richard Dyer MacCann notes, a 'pioneering effort' which offered the 'first evidence of what might be done in the way of reports from battlefields, and was an important response to the early leadership of the British in this respect'. Yet, as MacCann concedes, the film did little to enhance Zanuck's reputation in the realms of actuality production and, in its day, evoked decidedly 'mixed critical reactions'. Time magazine thought it unsatisfactory and concluded that Zanuck 'tried to dress up the film with arty shots of tank treads, dawns, sunsets and many another ill-placed frippary'. Plainly, being first was no guarantee of a good film or critical success.[33]

Capra was anxious to avoid such pitfalls. To compensate, moreover, for the problems experienced with the American sources of film supply, he looked increasingly to those who had provided the undoubtedly 'early leadership' in warfront reportage. The vital factor was to establish regular and dependable channels of communication with 'official' British outlets. In this, he was greatly aided by the presence on his staff of Pamela Wilcox. Wilcox had worked for some time with the National Film Board of Canada but, from the beginning of 1943, she was seconded to Capra's Special Service Unit. Her specific assignment was to assist in the production of the film Know Your Ally — Britain (1943) but she soon proved to be a 'most useful member' of the team in many other respects, as well.[34] Wilcox was given the task, for example, of liaising with the Director of the Film Division at the British Information Service in New York, the former United Artists executive, George Archibald, and of ascertaining BIS willingness to supply information and film materials. She was not to be disappointed. A long memorandum to Capra from Wilcox, in the spring of 1943, catalogued the full extent of Archibald's offer to help. Some of it amounted to no more than the promise of help, some brought immediate and tangible benefits. Though Archibald stressed there were matters he could not handle, 'being chiefly concerned with the distribution of British films', he was not without influence at the Ministry of Information in London — he was the US representative, after all, of its Films Division — and this he was plainly willing to exert on Capra's behalf. For one thing, Archibald offered to assist in obtaining as complete reports as possible of all official film production activity. Wilcox recounted:

> the monthly dope sheets which catalogued in great detail every film being shot in England, and which are brought out every month by the Ministry, will be received here as quickly as mail will allow. This means that we shall have a 3 month vista into all production activity in England, which will give us in advance an idea of what subjects are already being covered by Ministry units, thereby saving Special Service a great deal of wasted production in England.

On the matter of viewing MoI Films, Wilcox reported that Archibald was already making arrangements:

> to ensure that a print of all British films will be made available to Special Service and will be handed over to Private [Richard] Griffith [Film Production Section, Special Service] in New York for viewing. This means that we will be able to see all British films 'ad lib' and then as we need material we can apply for it in the usual manner.

In regard to Capra's request for MoI Films Division help in actually shooting material for his production of *Know Your Ally — Britain*, Wilcox could only report back Archibald's latest information. Ian Dalrymple, head of production at the Crown Film Unit, had been given the project and word of his progress was expected imminently. But, as Wilcox indicated, there were reasons for the delay:

> It must be faced that it is due, in part, to the lack of reciprocal action on both sides, or at any rate to the appearance of it. For instance, the British authorities are now desperately anxious to get release (commercially) on *Prelude to War*. They think it is an important film to show to the British people. They have applied continually to Mr. Robert Riskin's agency [Overseas Branch, Motion Picture Bureau, OWI] for permission to show this film and to date they have received no reply. Therefore, they are inclined to be somewhat sceptical of the good will of the people on this side and I think very naturally so.

The interchange of material between the US and British film departments has been pretty much of a one way street. While this may be of no concern — and no fault — of Special Service, it will nevertheless reflect in the British Ministry's attitude on any subject. I do not suggest that this atmosphere permeates the relationship between the British Ministry and the OWI, but I do suggest that it has something to do with our present problem.

Capra must have been well pleased with Wilcox's report and efforts. She had secured the promise of Archibald's invaluable help over such matters as the provision of advance notice of British production, and the viewing of all official films. The prospect for first hand footage, to be shot in Britain on Capra's behalf, looked reasonable enough. And, for good measure, Archibald threw in a word or two about the urgent need for direct liaison between Special Service and the MoI, and on how best to achieve it. 'The only practical way to work with the Ministry on all problems pertaining to the procurement of film material, shooting projects and general information', he elaborated, was for Capra to cable or write to Jack Beddington, head of the MoI's Film Division. 'For the purpose of maintaining workable communications', Capra should suggest that someone like Arthur Elton take over 'all the requirements and requests made by this unit' and should ensure that 'in future all negotiations with the Film Division will be channelled directly from this unit to Mr. Elton in London'. It was pretty straightforward and sensible advice — avoid as many intermediaries and middle men as possible, and deal directly with one person close to the top — but it seemed to work all the same.[35]

Subsequently, Capra found that his problems over the British shooting of material for his *Know Your Ally* film were soon overcome and on 8 April 1943 Wilcox reported that Dalrymple's footage had arrived.[36] Furthermore, a steady supply of information and MoI films was forthcoming to the Special Service Film Production Section in New York City. The British Army Film Unit's *Desert Victory* was among them. Wilcox had already intimated that 'according to reports [it] contains the finest material ever shot on British troops in action'.[37] And, after a viewing, Robert Heller of the New York detachment agreed. He informed Capra:

this is the finest documentary that has come out of the war. Its virtues are too many to describe. If we in America can evolve a use of combat film as effective as this, we shall have done more than rendered our best services. I think every maker of information films should be forced to see it and understand its techniques.[38]

Wilcox thanked Archibald for his services. He replied, in turn:

I can assure you that any service I may have rendered to Colonel Capra's unit has been of mutual benefit to all of us. I only wish I had known about the true state of affairs sooner. In conclusion, let me say that if the Film Division here did nothing more than provide a service to the unit which produced *Prelude to War*, *The Battle of Britain* and *The Nazis Strike*, it would have justified itself. The further fine films to come would be a bonus.[39]

Archibald was nothing if not diplomatic. In one very obvious respect, of course, there had been little in the way of 'mutual benefit'. For the British were still trying to acquire the films he praised so much. In fact, the MoI had first sought *Prelude to War* in January 1943. Due to OWI intransigence, in the main, they were denied public exhibition in Britain of any of the films in the *Why We Fight* series until the autumn of 1943.[40] The fault was not Capra's. But, as Pamela Wilcox feared, it certainly 'reflected' upon him. Moreover, the issue she had raised of 'one way' trafficking in film materials, and the continued failure on the part of the American authorities to 'reciprocate', undoubtedly (albeit unfairly) cast Capra in a bad light as far as some people were concerned. Much of the resultant animosity would be revealed when Capra began work on *Tunisian Victory* in England a few months later.

The circumstances that led directly to Capra's involvement with *Tunisian Victory* have been traced to a private London showing, in mid-July 1943, of a rough cut of the film *Africa Freed*.[41] Made by Hugh Stewart and Roy Boulting, this was intended as the AFU's follow up to *Desert Victory*. Among the audience invited by the MoI's Films Division were Major General Lord Burnham, director of public relations at the War Office, Sam Spewack of the OWI's London branch, and Colonel Tristram Tupper of the public relations department of the US Army, European Theatre of Operations (ETO). Jack Beddington recounted the deep reservations they shared about the film in a note of 20 July 1943:

> General Burnham pointed out that not enough prominence was given to the American participation in the North African campaign and made at least two suggestions for remedying this. Lord Burnham's views were agreed by Colonel Tupper on behalf of the US Army. All present were in entire agreement. Since that showing, however, it has borne in on Mr. Spewack that Anglo-American friction is rising . . . He therefore feels it more necessary than ever to safeguard ourselves against attacks by American isolationist newspapers and even more by that section of the American community which has not made up its mind.
>
> He accepts the fact that we asked for American film and didn't get it, we asked for a joint film with Capra and didn't get it, and that there is no blame attached to anybody. His anxiety is the same as mine — this was a joint operation and to present a heavily loaded film can do an enormous amount of harm. He does not believe that an introduction by the American Ambassador or a high ranking general would prevent newspaper attacks.

Beddington and Spewack were agreed, finally, in considering it 'essential' that the Minister of Information, Brendan Bracken, and the Director of the Office of War Information, Elmer Davis, should see the film 'at an early opportunity'. Though Beddington felt personally that the potential conflict of interests should also 'be brought to the notice of the Secretary of War, Mr. Stimson'.[42]

The British had, indeed, sought American co-operation and film material on several occasions in the preceding months 'so that the part played by the Americans can be fully represented'. Apart from ascertaining that Capra was working upon a Tunisian campaign film of his own, however, they had met with little positive response.[43] Thus, the AFU was prompted to get on with production of *Africa Freed* as speedily as possible with the intention of making do with a foreword to the film which they hoped would explain the course of action that had been forced upon them. The idea of inserting a foreword was particularly important, as Stewart outlined in a memorandum dictated over the telephone on 20 July 1943, the same day that Beddington compiled his 'Notes of meeting with Mr. Spewack':

> We have all been aware for some time that there would be inadequate representation in *Africa Freed* of the part played by the Americans in the Tunisian campaign. This is due entirely to lack of satisfactory film material of American troops in action . . . In order to clear ourselves of the unavoidable charge of intentional bias, I feel we must say somewhere that we were short of good American battle material. The appearance of Frank Capra's film will, I am aware, complicate the issue.

It is difficult to determine whether Stewart was alert to the fact that Spewack had already expressed reservations about including any introduction, let alone the one which Boulting and Hodson had prepared. But he clearly did not know that Capra, too, had been starved of decent American footage on the Tunisian campaign and had been compelled to reconstruct it for himself in the Mojave Desert. Stewart, plainly, feared the worst and the worst would be Capra popping up at any moment with a film filled with all the American material which, Stewart suspected, the British AFU had been denied. Given the reputation the AFU had established that would be acutely embarrassing. And the only way to obviate such danger, he believed, was by means of a foreword hinting, at least, of their problems. Stewart was certain of one thing, however, and here he found himself in complete accord with Beddington and Spewack: 'This matter is one to be dealt with on a high level'.[44] So, indeed, it was. Since, however, the chronology of key events thereafter has sometimes become confused, it would be as well to establish it precisely at the outset.[45] The Public Record Office files, Hodson's published diary and Capra's private account of the time he spent in London, allow us to do just that and to spotlight many of the concerns which preoccupied all parties.[46]

The Minister of Information, Brendan Bracken, saw *Africa Freed* on Friday 30 July 1943. The day after, Hodson noted:

> Whatever folk say of *Africa Freed* we, working on it, have had a lot of fun despite our frustrations and torments. I suggested we should put a sign outside the theatres: 'This picture is not only long, but seems it'. In fact, those who've seen it, like it. Arthur Calder Marshall found it more 'human' than *Desert Victory* and I think that's so. Pictorially some of it is quite beautiful.[47]

On 2 August, Tupper and Spewack cabled Major General Alexander D. Surles, Director of the Bureau of Public Relations in Washington. They wished to 'strongly advise' that Frank Capra be sent to London 'this week' and 'with all available footage American troops in North Africa, and animations and any re-enactments already filmed'. Their cable continued:

> Have seen final cut British War Office film *Africa Freed*. Impressive production commentary favourable to American forces but due to lack of American scenes film gives inadequate impression of joint operation. Release of this film and of separate American film will undoubtedly create bad impression in Britain, America and other countries. British most anxious to release this month and will do so unless Capra appears soonest.[48]

Matters moved pretty quickly thereafter. Capra received a cable on 7 August stating that Surles was sending him to London. By August 10, he was in Washington being briefed by Surles and assembling a team which included John Huston and Anthony Veiller. On 11 August it was reported:

> General Surles and Mr. Brendan Bracken had agreed that Colonel Frank Capra and some technicians would proceed immediately to London, taking with them the US footage on the Tunisian campaign, and that Colonel Capra would then look at the British material and decide whether to make a joint film from the combined material or to let two separate films be made. Colonel Capra's decision in this matter is to be final and if he decides to make a combined film he will be the director.[49]

On the morning of 12 August, Roy Boulting was informed by telephone of Capra's imminent arrival and General Surles's request that no further work be done on their film 'until Capra has seen it'. Capra and his team left Washington on a 10.30 am flight the same day. He arrived in London on 13 August, with a script though none of the promised US film material.[50] The 'fiasco' which followed is perhaps best told in a distillation

Colonel Frank Capra confers with Captain Roy Boulting on the editing of the film.

of some of the participants own words. Given the sheer weight of anti-Capra feeling generally manifested regarding his role in the affair, it is especially useful to be able to privilege his personal version of events. The following entries are largely from the manuscript diary of Frank Capra and the published diary of James Hodson.

16 August: Frank Capra: Saw British film *Africa Freed*. Very good but American representation nil. Said so. British loath to joint venture now their picture finished. All Americans present up in arms because of inadequate American participation. British claim we gave them no film. Very true. We claim British gave us no film. They said it was all available. Something screwy here (pp. 1—2).

16 August: James Hodson: Frank Capra, the film director, and his comrades including John Huston, a son of Walter Huston, have now arrived. They saw our film of *Africa Freed* . . . said it was a swell picture and I think they were sincere in that. But they think we ought to have a joint film, an Anglo-American picture. So do we. Our Army Film Unit men said so 3 or 4 months ago, but could get no further.[51]

17-18 August: Capra: Dialectics with British. They want to talk of future instead of this picture. We threaten to leave. Finally British have big meeting with MoI and all services. Joint picture on. MoI and some American agency to have final approval. Film boys heartbroken as they feel they have fine picture which will now be delayed and taken over by Americans. Send cables to Surles and [Colonel Kirke B.] Lawton about sending over boys and film. Spewack big help. He has everything in hand (p. 2).

18 August: Cyril Radcliffe, MoI Director General, to Bracken: I have agreed with Burnham and the other Service departments to offer Capra the following conditions for a joint film on the Tunisian campaign. (1) He must produce a new commentary to be approved by us and the Service departments. His present commentary is all American. (2) He will bring over his film for us to see this week and he will not use in the joint film any material to which we object as make-up or fake. (3) He and Stewart (of the AFU) will be joint producers and the final film is to be subject to our approval. (4) The film to be completed in 4 weeks (though we all doubt this). If the final film does not satisfy these conditions, each will complete and produce separate films with explanatory openings. Capra has accepted these conditions thankfully and is bringing over film and cutters here.[52]

18 August: Capra: Talked to General Devers [ETO]. Very enthusiastic and alive as to picture needs. Job very badly done by Signal Corps so far . . . No public relations pictures. Own orientation pictures big hit. Praise by Devers. Radio from PM [Winston Churchill] from Quebec saying he will record sound track to introduce [*The Battle of Britain*] picture to British (pp. 2—3).

20 August: Capra: Out to Pinewood to see British picture again . . . The fights between Americans and British hard to understand (p. 4).

23 August: Capra: No boys yet (p. 5).

24 August: Capra: Called on Lord Burnham to talk over script. He turned us over to Major Woolley and Major De Beers, historians (p. 5).

L

25 August: *Capra*: White, Dunning and Beetly [editors] arrive with film. To Pinewood. Run first 8 reels . . . Stewart and Boulting like what they saw (p. 5).

29 August: *Capra*: Party at John Mills' house. Bob Hope, Frances Langford and others there. Much food and vodka. I got claustrophobic and walked home in blackout. Got lost and fell down. Impossible to get cabs after 9 pm. Black market cars. Terrific charges . . . Just realizing how far I am away from home. Never cease marvelling at British people. They are like golf balls. Soft cover and hard cores — each layer getting harder and harder (p. 6).

30 August: *Capra*: Shock of my life. The British haven't decided on joint picture yet. Some bloke called Tritton [public relations section, War Office] demands to see the film. I ask Stewart why and he says that was the deal. We bring over film, show it, then they decide on joint film. I blew up. I had turned this proposition down flat. So called J. L. [Beddington] and Sam [Spewack]. Great arguments. I stand put. I will show no film to anyone until I know joint picture was on or off. Stick to principle (pp. 7—8).[53]

31 August: *Capra*: Standing put. I think it wiser if everything cancelled. Now even hope they do so. British annoyed at not being able to have their way. Their idea of co-operation is to do it their way. I'm the wrong man for that stuff (p. 8).

1 September: *Capra*: More arguments. Spewack wonderful. Now convinced we're right. Our point is co-operation whether either side has any film or not, not only when it suits. Refuse to show film until this principle settled. At night Spewack and J. L. come in and say it's all settled. Lord Burnham will give the boys order to go to work with us. We have lost much time. We are disappointed as now we would rather pull out (pp. 8—9).

2 September: *Capra*: Looks like another crisis. I think they are making it so tough we will pull out (p. 9).

3 September: *Capra*: Everything all set again. We will be given excerpts to make rough cut. Then all services see it and decide whether to change, stop or go on. We won out of principle. All we want is to be an ally and not a stooge (p. 9).

4 September: *Capra*: First meeting with Stewart and Hodson on script. Not too far apart. Maybe it'll be alright after all (p. 9).

4-10 September: *Capra*: Working at Pinewood (p. 10).

15 September: *Hodson*: This film on Tunisia has been getting in the way of the diary. We are in the middle of an Anglo-American effort and we're enjoying it. The American script is so long that I said if we took *War and Peace* and *Gone with the Wind* and this script, we should have a great trilogy . . . The Yanks have a character in their script, Joe McAdams, the universal USA soldier. So in the joint one we've shoved an English soldier George Metcalfe. George was a greengrocer in civvy street but I've made him say: 'But we're a military family really — Dad was in the Boer War and I was at Dunkirk'. The generosity of the Americans when we write something that tickles them is unbounded. We had some blunt talk over who did the fighting in Tunisia and a day or two later Frank Capra came down to Pinewood with the suggestion that we ought not to be worrying who did the fighting, but we should make a film whose real theme is the unity of the Allies and the need for carrying on that unity into the days of peace. He wasn't sure we should agree, but we're 100% for that. I suggested that towards the end of the film we should show close ups of all the types of our soldiers fighting together and then say, 'But there's only one soldier'. We could almost call the picture 'One Soldier'.[54]

21 September: *Hodson*: I have been doing a little fighting to prevent our picture on the Tunisian campaign becoming disbalanced in favour of America. After all, we did most of the dirty work and had twice as many casualties. Only this week Henry Morganthau has had to point out to the American nation that America did not entirely win the war in Africa and that we British played an equal or perhaps rather more than an equal part. The Americans are going to have to bear more and more of the burden of this war. I want them to have the credit for that, but similarly I want us to have the credit for what we have done so far.[55]

26 September: *Capra*: Living at Pinewood and working night and day . . . I can't help believing we can work under any and all circumstances (p. 10).

27 September: *Capra*: Tony [Veiller] unhappy as to picture. I am unmoved and not very excited about anything. Seems to me we've done our work well so what the hell (p. 12).

29 September: *Capra*: Photograph the PM in his cabinet room. He gives series [*Why We Fight*] a marvellous send-off. Talked for half an hour. He even sends for me after, in his room alone. He is most grateful and appreciative of our work. Truly it has all been worthwhile if only because of that. He has brilliant mind and very easy to talk to. I'll never forget this day . . . The others and I working night and day on film. Don't hold out too much hope for successful showing (pp. 12—13).[56]

8 October: *Capra*: Had showing of rough cut for British big wigs . . . All frozen faced and tight assed gents who try to make you feel like a burglar. What keeps me from telling them all to go to hell I don't know (p. 16).

9 October: *Capra*: No news from the War Office. I hope they decide against the venture. Then I'll have a first class picture which we can release as the American version. Spewack keeps urging me to keep cool. But why all the co-operation should be on our side I don't know. The British seem to have such an inferiority complex about Americans, they are afraid to give any credit (p. 16).

10 October: *Capra*: Dinner with Bracken, Korda and Beddington. Bracken very charming and talked about joint coverage and joint pictures. I said it was a matter for the two governments. He wanted a plan but to me any plan was impertinent coming from me. No hint of how anybody liked the rough

Capra, with Major Hugh Stewart and Private Daphne Hudson.

cut. After Bracken left had big argument with Beddington who said I couldn't leave for America with rough cut but must finish it here. I told him I took no orders from the British. The fight for supremacy is obviously bitter but I must assert myself as I represent the USA (p. 17).

17 October: Capra: No word from British War Office although they saw picture 8 days ago. Very impolite of them (p. 17).

4 November: Hodson: We were at a farewell party to Frank Capra who today goes back to America, taking our Tunisian film with him. Yesterday he was presented with the American Legion of Merit. He deserves it, for he's done fine work for America and for us, too.[57]

4 November: Capra: Left London, 6.30 pm (p. 19).

Capra left for America, then, taking the joint film of *Tunisian Victory* with him. The official line was that 'The Anglo-American version had to be finished in Hollywood because the negative of Capra's material was there'.[58] But it smacked more of diplomacy than anything else. Hugh Stewart followed Capra to America supposedly to safeguard British interests. James Hodson caught up with them both, in February 1944, at a dinner hosted by Capra and attended by R. C. Sherriff, Victor Saville and James Hilton. A week later, he noted in his diary: 'Word from London that they finally approve of our film *Tunisian Victory*. This is good news'.[59] *Tunisian Victory* was shown to the press in London and New York on 16 March 1944 — a year after the end of the campaign it purported to cover. Capra must have been well pleased to leave England at the last. Certainly, he had got his film. In addition, he took the opportunity while stationed in London to secure an agreement with General Jacob Devers, in charge of ETO, to include his film teams in plans for the future invasion of Europe. That way he would be assured of a continual supply of first hand combat footage. His disillusion with the US sources of film material, born of his experiences back home, and his increasing awareness that the American film agencies in London were just as badly organised, convinced him that he would do better to centralise matters under his own control. This he did, while in London in August 1943. He communicated often with Devers and regularly cabled Surles, in Washington. By 3 September, the new PRO Section was approved so that 'All film that has the public in mind in ETO comes under this new set up'. And he was subsequently confirmed as the CO of the new PRO Special Coverage Section.[60]

But for all that, the interminable arguments with the British plainly took their toll. Capra contracted pneumonia in England. The emotional impact of the wider events he witnessed there undoubtedly had an effect. To judge from two entries in his diary, Frank Capra was profoundly disturbed by his experiences of the blitz in London:

16 September: An air raid alarm. 10 pm. The guns start to go off. This is the real thing. Bombs drop in the distance. Hyde Park guns shake the building. Tony and John and I go outside like most newcomers. Old ladies and children cower in the hallways. Maids and valets talk reassuring to them. These old ladies suddenly make war silly, stupid and brutal. I was scared but I was more sick at the thought of these dear old ladies and little girls being mangled. How far has man suddenly gone mad? Will we never learn to get along better than to drop bombs on each other? Surely God didn't mean that to happen? Please God put understanding and love into the hearts of men . . . Overhead drones of British planes headed for Germany, where other old ladies and children cower in hallways. Surely this must all be madness? (pp. 10—11).

7 October: Big raid on London . . . War is certainly silly, stupid and inefficient . . . I wonder how much longer the common people of the world are going to stand for this. I suppose not till the German people realise the futility of war. If they take the bombings much longer, then we are in for a real long war or a stalemate. If their fanaticism can make them stand up to such punishment then they really must believe in something. We believe just the opposite and so the destruction goes on. The flower of the nations wiping each other out. What a crime. Surely God didn't mean us to do all this to each other. It may be all part of suffering for that original sin but then God can't be merciful. Why must the noblest elements get destroyed and not the wicked? The whole thing doesn't make sense. I sincerely believe the common people will someday declare war on war itself. Until that happens we will fight each other for power, commerce or material interests. What a catastrophe Hitler has turned loose upon the world. What fools men be to follow men (pp. 13—15).

Commentators have often noted that Frank Capra was much changed at war's end and, in fact, it has even been suggested that 'World War II destroyed Capra as an effective film-maker'.[61] If that was the case then, perhaps, one might trace the beginning of Capra's demise and his disintegration as a film-maker of the first rank through the events and tensions he encountered in England during 1943. Perhaps, there again, Capra's London experiences and their emotional impact help explain the increased measure of sentimentality and illusion — the 'Capra-corn', so it was called — purveyed in his 1946 'fantasy of good will', *It's a Wonderful Life.* The title alone was redolent of the heady optimism inherent in most of Capra's classic 1930s successes and the film consciously espoused his pre-war values, his belief in positive thinking, the eternal values and the people. But it proved inappropriate to postwar circumstances and audiences found it immediately less appealing. Clearly, Capra had indeed lost some of his magic touch.[62]

NOTES

1   See, for example, William T. Murphy, 'The method of *Why We Fight*', *Journal of Popular Film*, 1, Summer 1972, pp. 185—96; David Culbert, '*Why We Fight*: Social Engineering for a Democratic Society at War', in K. R. M. Short (ed.), *Film and Radio Propaganda in World War II*, London, 1983, pp. 173—91; and Karsten Fledelius et al., *Why We Fight — An American Example of Wartime Orientation*, Copenhagen, 1974.

2   Thomas Cripps and David Culbert, '*The Negro Soldier*: film propaganda in black and white', *American Quarterly*, 31, Winter 1979, pp. 616—41; and William J. Blakefield, 'A war within: the making of *Know Your Enemy — Japan*', *Sight and Sound*, 52, 1983, pp. 128—33.
3   Anthony Aldgate, 'Creative Tensions: *Desert Victory*, the Army Film Unit and Anglo-American Rivalry, 1943—45', in Philip M. Taylor (ed.), *Britain and the Cinema in the Second World War*, London, 1988, pp. 144—67; Clive Coultass, '*Tunisian Victory* — a film too late?', *Imperial War Museum Review*, 1, 1986, pp. 64—73; and Ian Jarvie, 'The Burma Campaign on Film: *Objective Burma* (1945), *The Stilwell Road* (1945) and *Burma Victory* (1945)', *Historical Journal of Film, Radio and Television*, 8, 1988, pp. 55—73.
4   Frank Capra, *The Name Above the Title. An Autobiography*, London, 1972, p. 352. He is speaking there of his experiences in regard to *Tunisian Victory* though his words might just as well serve for his experiences over the Burma campaign film, upon which matter Capra has nothing directly to say in his autobiography.
5   The saga is well documented in Jarvie, 'The Burma Campaign on Film'.
6   Bosley Crowther, 'Element of Time. Observations on war documentaries as inspired by *Tunisian Victory*', *New York Times*, 2 April 1944, in AFU 41, Imperial War Museum, London.
7   Campbell Dixon, 'War films contrast', *Daily Telegraph*, 20 March 1944, microfiche on *Tunisian Victory*, British Film Institute, London.
8   *Documentary News Letter*, 5, 1944, p. 20.
9   See Aldgate, 'Creative Tensions', for a detailed discussion of the same and examination of the critical acclaim afforded *Desert Victory* in both Britain and America. Further materials assembled since the publication of that article testify, yet again, to the considerable amount of top level political approval which greeted this film.

Churchill, for instance, wrote to Roosevelt on 5 March 1943 as follows: 'My dear Mr. President, I hope you will accept the accompanying copy of the new film *Desert Victory* which I saw last night and thought very good. It gives a vivid and realistic picture of the battles and I know that you will be interested in the photographs of the Sherman tanks in action. I am having the film sent to you by air so that you may see it as soon as possible . . .'. Roosevelt replied on 17 March 1943: 'Dear Winston, That new film *Desert Victory* is about the best thing that has been done about the war on either side. Everyone here is enthusiastic. I gave a special showing for the White House staff and tonight the Interior Department employees are having a special showing because everybody in town is talking about it; and I understand that within ten days it will be in the picture houses. Great good will be done . . .'. (Both quoted in Warren F. Kimball (ed.), *Churchill and Roosevelt: The Complete Correspondence, vol. II*, Princeton, 1984, pp. 155—6.)

Churchill also wrote to Stalin, on 11 March 1943: 'I have just seen and enjoyed an excellent film of the Red Army victories at Stalingrad and of the capture of Paulus. The front line cameramen attached to our Eighth Army have produced a record of their victory in the desert. I have had the commentary translated into Russian and am sending you a copy in the hope you will find time to see it. The officers and men of the Eighth Army will, I am sure, be proud to know that the record of their victorious struggle will be seen by their Allies, the armies and people of the Soviet Union'. Stalin replied on 29 March 1943: 'Last night I saw, with my colleagues, the film *Desert Victory* you have sent us and was greatly impressed. It splendidly shows how Britain is fighting, and skilfully exposes those scoundrels — we have them in our country too — who allege that Britain is not fighting but merely looking on. I eagerly look forward to another film of the same kind, showing your victory in Tunisia. *Desert Victory* will be circulated to all our armies at the front and shown to the public'. (Both quoted in *Correspondence between the Chairman of the Council of Ministers of the USSR and the Presidents of the USA and the Prime Ministers of Great Britain during the Great Patriotic War of 1941–45, vol. I*, Moscow, 1957, pp. 103 and 110. My thanks to Professor Geoffrey Warner for providing me with details of the same.)

10   James Lansdale Hodson, *The Sea and the Land*, London, 1945, p. 117 (diary entry for 21 September 1943).

11   Hodson, *The Sea and the Land*, p. 105 (diary entry for 20 August 1943).

12   James Lansdale Hodson, *And Yet I Like America*, London, 1945, p. 8 (diary entry for December 1943, 'out at sea').

13   Transcript of interview with Roy Boulting, *British Service Cameramen 1939–45*, Department of Sound Records, IWM, accession no. 004627/06, pp. 46 and 48. Since granting me a first interview to discuss this subject, on 21 March 1986, Roy Boulting (now retired to Oxfordshire while writing his autobiography) has repeated his comments in many neighbourly, informal conversations regarding the matter.

14   Transcript of interview with Hugh Stewart, *Army Film Unit Cameramen 1939–45*, Dept of Sound Records, IWM, accession no. 004579/06, p. 20.

15   'The Courage of the Men', an interview with John Huston (21 June 1980), in Robert Hughes (ed.), *Film: Book 2. Films of Peace and War*, New York, 1962, pp. 23–4. By the time of my own interview with John Huston on 18 August 1972, in Edinburgh, his use of the word 'coony' had changed to 'canny' — perhaps to accord with the Scottish context, perhaps also born of his personal experience of living in Ireland, and his obvious delight in the overall Celtic 'fluence'. (My interview with Huston on that occasion proved the inspiration for much of my subsequent research into the Victory trilogy.) By the time of writing his autobiography, *An Open Book*, London, 1981, it is noticeable that Huston resorted to his typically straightforward vein when describing *Tunisian Victory* in terms such as 'trash', 'manufacture', 'the worst kind of fabrication', 'transparently false' and the like. With characteristic candour, he maintained there that 'it became immediately apparent that we, and not the English, stood to benefit by the collaboration. They had excellent footage as against our counterfeit material. Nevertheless the English film-makers agreed to abandon their project and proceed with us', pp. 102–4. Though sometimes unreliable, his autobiography would appear to be accurate in this instance. If nothing else, it certainly displays Huston's desire to distance himself from the *Tunisian Victory* fiasco.

16   See Capra, *The Name Above the Title*, pp. 341 and 355, especially, where he takes pride in quoting a favourable *Today's Cinema* review of *Tunisian*

Victory to press home the point that the 'reconstructed' scenes were done 'under supervision of men actually on the spot at the time' and, anyway, 'The major portion of the action is actual shots from the battlefields'. By such means, he believed, 'the "recreators" of the capture of the Mojave Desert's Hill 609 kept faith with our critics and audiences'.

17 Capra's autobiography will be employed initially. But reference will be made increasingly to the *Frank Capra Papers* (hereafter *FCP*) held in the Cinema Archives of Wesleyan University, Connecticut. My thanks go to Jeanine Basinger, Curator of the Cinema Archives, for allowing me access to the papers and for granting permission to quote from them. And to her staff for their help and assistance during the course of my visit there in April 1987.

18 See Capra, *The Name Above the Title*, pp. 334–5 and 349. And, especially, K. R. M. Short, '*Prelude to War* and "The Great Celluloid War" between the Office of War Information, the War Activities Committee, and the US Army, 1942–3', an invaluable paper delivered to the 9th International IAMHIST Congress, Vienna, September 1981. Also, Richard Dyer MacCann, *The People's Films*, New York, 1973, pp. 130–1.

19 Culbert, '*Why We Fight*: Social Engineering for a Democratic Society at War', p. 178. On p. 183, Culbert reaches the highly significant conclusion that 'As a general proposition, for American soldiers, audiovisual instruction existed mostly on paper until the autumn of 1943. Not only were films not ready, but distribution and effective utilisation remained acute problem areas until that time'.

20 Capra, *The Name Above the Title*, pp. 328–34. Though, crucially, Culbert, 'Social Engineering', p. 180 and pp. 190–1, questions some of the more 'unreliable' aspects of Capra's account of these matters.

21 Capra, *The Name Above the Title*, pp. 329 and 335. For background to the reorganisation resulting in APS see David Culbert (ed.), *Film and Propaganda in America: A Documentary History; World War II, Part 1*, Westport, 1990.

22 Aldgate, 'Creative Tensions', p. 153.

23 Capra, *The Name Above the Title*, pp. 327–8.

24 Capra to Munson, 12 November 1942, *Frank Capra Papers*, Wesleyan University, folder 6, box 6.

25 Lieutenant Colonel John B. Stanley to Capra, 18 November 1942, *FCP*, folder 6, box 6.

26 The minutes of the *Newsreel Association of Great Britain* held at British Movietonews, Denham, England, bear important witness to the difficulties continually experienced by the British newsreels in obtaining American stories, and the efforts they were compelled to exert in order to acquire them. See, *inter alia*, the following meetings: 13 August 1942 (minute 1154); 1 October 1942 (1185); 5 November 1942 (1227); 3 December 1942 (1237); 28 January 1943 (1273); 15 February 1943 (1282); 11 March 1943 (1301); 15 April 1943 (1326); 19 April 1943 (1329); 29 April 1943 (1332); 12 August 1943 (1398); 14 October 1943 (1449); and 10 May 1944 (1608).

27 See, for example, Brigadier General F. H. Osborn to Capra, 14 December 1942, where he states: 'This business with Mellett makes me so angry I don't trust myself any more. But I want you to know that the people in the Army — and that goes for everyone in it — have about you a very unique feeling of

appreciation and respect', *FCP*, folder 7, box 6. Also, Colonel S. Grogan to Major General Alexander D. Surles, 22 April 1943, which reads in part: 'Torrid conference today in which General Osborn and General Harrison assisted. Industry took stand pictures are not worthwhile showing and will not draw audiences, lacking entertainment value etc. . . . Elmer Davis very helpful, Lowell Mellett not at all helpful . . . Army is to use *Prelude to War* as a test picture . . . Music Hall, NY, will be furnished with one print by OWI for showing one week in May . . . only way out of an impasse since industry and War Department plus Lowell Mellett cannot agree', *FCP*, folder 9, box 6. For background concerning the fight over public distribution of *Prelude to War* see David Culbert (ed.), *Film and Propaganda in America: A Documentary History; World War II, Part 2*, Westport, 1990.

28   See C. F. Woit, War Films Co-ordinator, Walt Disney Productions, to Capra, 10 December 1942, *FCP*; and Carl Nater, Production Co-ordinator, Walt Disney Productions, to Capra, 5 January 1943, *FCP*, folder 8, box 6.

29   Capra, *The Name Above the Title*, p. 341. Also, Capra to Donovan, 11 December 1942, and Donovan to Capra, 18 December 1942, both *FCP*, folder 7, box 6.

30   Spiegelgass to Capra, 9 December 1942, *FCP*, folder 7, box 6.

31   Cohen to Capra, 13 February 1943, *FCP*, folder 8, box 6.

32   Zanuck to Capra, 14 January 1943, *FCP*, folder 8, box 6.

33   MacCann, *The People's Films*, p. 168. See, also, Aldgate, 'Creative Tensions', for an outline of Zanuck's considerable respect for the British army films, as formed on his trip to London in May 1942. *Documentary News Letter*, 4, 1943, p. 202, reprinted the *Time* magazine review (15 March 1943) of Zanuck's film. In his self-serving memoir, *Tunis Expedition*, New York, 1943, which was rushed into print to accompany the film's release, Zanuck remarked: 'I don't suppose our war scenes will look as savage or realistic as those we usually make on the back lot, but you can't have everything'.

34   See Wilcox to Capra, 8 December 1942, *FCP*, folder 7, box 6, for an outline of her career to that point, including work with the National Film Board of Canada. And, in particular, Ross McLean, Assistant Film Commissioner, National Film Board of Canada, to Major R. S. Williams, Assistant British Military Attaché, British Embassy, Washington, 27 March 1943, *FCP*, folder 9, box 6, for an outline of the key reasons given to secure an extension of her exit permit from the UK authorities — 'Our information is that Miss Wilcox has been a most useful member of Lieut. Col. Capra's unit'.

Elizabeth Sussex in *The Rise and Fall of British Documentary*, Berkeley, 1975, p. 116, quotes Edgar Anstey's recollections of her as follows: 'When he [Grierson] appeared, I remember, from Canada during the war with Pamela Wilcox, a young woman who was working closely with him at the time, and Herbert Spencer, I think it was, who is now looking after the Film Finance Corporation in Canada, who was also a young trainee of his, we felt that these two youngsters, aided, abetted, encouraged by Grierson, were looking rather askance at the old gentlemen sort of plodding along in the middle of the war, as we felt we were. Grierson was very inclined, for the morale no doubt, of his own youngsters, to try and inject a sort of greater drive and urgency and so on into their attitude, as compared with what they found amongst the plodders here. This didn't make him awfully popular, or at least we were so devoted to him that we tended to turn our criticism against these two poor young people, who really had a rough passage, but it was probably very healthy for everybody. I think he was also very anxious that they shouldn't feel any inferiority because they'd come to where the war was from a place where really it wasn't'. Pamela Wilcox's own account of her experiences with Grierson and Capra during the war is told in *Between Hell and Charing Cross*, London, 1977, pp. 41—55.

35 Wilcox to Capra, 'Report of my conversation with Mr. George Archibald', undated (but internal evidence suggests February 1943), *FCP*, folder 8, box 6. Much of the documentation cited in Aldgate, 'Creative Tensions', not least the monthly progress reports for the Army Council (Directorate of Army Kinematography, War Office 165/96, Public Record Office, Kew, London), echoes the British concern highlighted by Wilcox over such matters as the likely availability of *Prelude to War* and the *Why We Fight* series generally, which were keenly awaited in British 'official' circles.

36 Wilcox to Capra, 8 April 1943, *FCP*, folder 9, box 6.

37 Wilcox to Capra, 10 March 1943, *FCP*, folder 9, box 6.

38 Heller to Capra, 1 April 1943, *FCP*, folder 9, box 6.

39 Archibald to Wilcox, 9 March 1943, *FCP*, folder 9, box 6. Archibald's genuine willingness to help sooned turned to feelings of pique then outright anger, of course, when he learned that US distributors were dragging their feet over the number of showings afforded British 'official' films like *Desert Victory*. For which see the details outlined in Aldgate, 'Creative Tensions'.

40 See Riskin to Capra, 6 January 1943, *FCP*, folder 9, box 6, where he mentioned a request from Tom Baird of BIS, New York, for the MoI in London to receive a copy of *Prelude to War*. Also, 25th Monthly Progress Report for the Army Council, November 1943, Directorate of Army Kinematography, WO 165/96, which recorded that 'The first three subjects of the US Army *Why We Fight* series are now being distributed on a wide scale both in the UK and overseas'. In the event, they still did not include *Prelude to War* but comprised *The Nazis Strike, Divide and Conquer* and *The Battle of Britain*, with *The Battle of Russia* promised as the next one in the offering.

41 See Aldgate, 'Creative Tensions', p. 156, and Coultass, 'A film too late?', p. 68. In fact, Coultass believes the initial source of disquiet arose slightly earlier, on 23 June, at a luncheon meeting between Spewack and Ronald Tritton of the Public Relations Section (PR2) of the War Office.

42 Beddington, 'Notes of meeting with Mr. Spewack', 20 July 1943, INF 1/223, PRO.

43 Minutes of the Inter-Services Film Publicity Committee, 6 April 1943; M. Gordon to S. Gates, 30 April 1943; and Beddington to Major A. Newman, all INF 1/223.

44 Stewart to Beddington and Bernstein, 20 July 1943, 'dictated over the phone', and followed on 21 July by a memorandum of the same, INF 1/223, including the text of the proposed foreword to the film (written by Boulting and Hodson) which read: 'The conquest of Tunisia was a triumph for the United Nations who on sea, land and in the air worked as one. This film tells

of the part played by British arms during the shaping and achievement of the victory as recorded by the cameramen who marched alongside. It is firstly a tribute to the fighting men, seamen and workers of the British Empire but it salutes in pride the forces of America, Free France and other Allies whose part was equally vital and whose story is yet to be told'. The completed print of *Africa Freed* held at the Imperial War Museum, London, bears this foreword ever so slightly revised to read: 'This film, together with another made by our American allies, shows how victory was shaped and achieved'.

45 For example, Caroline Moorehead in *Sidney Bernstein. A biography*, London, 1984, pp. 156–7, distinctly muddles several key issues and seems blithely unaware that Capra's autobiography, at least, was already in print at the time of writing her own account, when she states: 'What Capra thought is not known'.

46 Capra's handwritten 'diary' for his wartime months spent in London, with the makeshift title 'Itenerary' [*sic*], can be found in one of 10 unnumbered folders in box 7 of the Frank Capra Papers, catalogued under 'World War Films Correspondence'. Though by no means a full account and inevitably much given to shorthand, it amply repays careful scrutiny. Capra's mis-spelling of British surnames, notably Stewart, Boulting, Hodson and Tritton, has been corrected throughout my text with both abbreviations and people's roles elaborated accordingly. Since, finally, there is little more information to impart by way of reference to the Capra manuscript diary (hereafter *FCD*), except for basic repetition of page numbers, these too will generally be provided in the main body of my text.

47 Beddington to Stewart, 27 July 1943, INF 1/223, and Hodson, *The Sea and the Land*, p. 100 (diary entry for 1 August 1943).

48 Tupper and Spewack to Surles, 2 August 1943, INF 1/223.

49 *FCD*, p. 1; Archibald to Beddington, 11 August 1943, INF 1/223.

50 Boulting to Beddington, 12 August 1943, INF 1/223.

51 Hodson, *The Sea and the Land*, p. 104 (entry for 20 August 1943).

52 Radcliffe to Bracken, 18 August 1943, INF 1/223.

53 Compare Huston, in Hughes (ed.), *Film: Book 2*, p. 23: 'They [the English] asked to see our film before it was decided that it should be presented jointly, and Frank, being very coony, refused to show it to them; he was rather insulted at the request'.

54 Hodson, *The Sea and the Land*, p. 115 (entry for 15 September 1943). For comment on the ending of the film see Coultass, 'A film too late?', pp. 70–72.

55 Hodson, *The Sea and the Land*, p. 117 (entry for 21 September 1943).

56 Churchill's speech was used as a foreword to *The Battle of Britain* which was plainly intended to herald the introduction of the films from the *Why We Fight* series that were exhibited in Britain from November 1943. The Capra Papers include a copy of Churchill's foreword to the film and the series, which is bound together with a speech (dated 20 February 1948) given by Capra to the British Consul in Los Angeles, thanking the British government for the award of the Order of the British Empire, *FCP*, folder 4, box 6. In a brief review of the film, however, the *Documentary News Letter* makes no reference to Churchill's speech. See *DNL*, 4, 1943, p. 227.

57   Hodson, *The Sea and the Land*, p. 129 (entry for 4 November 1943). Charles
     Wolfe, *Frank Capra. A guide to references and sources*, Boston, 1987, p. 6,
     states that Winston Churchill awarded Capra the Order of the British
     Empire in 1943. This is incorrect. According to the records of the Central
     Chancery of the Orders of Knighthood, Capra was appointed to be an
     Honorary Officer in the Military Division of the Order of the British Empire
     on 17 December 1946. Although these records give no details of a
     presentation ceremony, it is clear it must have been some time between
     17 January 1947 when the insignia was sent to the War Office for dispatch
     and 16 March 1948 when a warrant details form issued to Capra was
     returned to their office (letter to the author of 29 September 1988). Plainly,
     as the Capra speech to the British Consul (cited above) indicates, the award
     ceremony took place in Los Angeles on 20 February 1948.
58   See, for example, the two page summary account of the film's evolution,
     Tunisian Victory, 3 September 1947, AFU 41, IWM. Coultass, 'A film too
     late?', p. 70, neatly surveys the major problems that beset the film in
     America.
59   Hodson, *And Yet I Like America*, p. 165 (entry for 18 February 1944), and
     p. 173 (entry for 23 February 1944). Hodson's magnanimity, at least, was
     further demonstrated with his diary entry for 15 March: '*Desert Victory* won
     the Academy Award for the best documentary film of the year. This decision
     is a tribute to American fairness for Frank Capra's *The Battle of Russia* must
     have run it very close', p. 220.
60   See *FCD*, box 7, entries for 18 August (pp. 2–3: 'Job done very badly by
     Signal Corps so far'); 22 August (p. 5); 26 August (p. 6); 3 September (p. 9:
     'APS has not done very good job here'); 4 September (p. 10); 27 September
     (pp. 11–12). Capra's autobiography is not very helpful on this score since it
     seems to suggest he was made CO of the new PRO Special Coverage Section
     before he left America for Britain to embark upon the joint production, *The
     Name Above the Title*, p. 352.
61   See Culbert, 'Social Engineering', p. 187, where he quotes from a 1981
     Esquire interview with Capra: 'The war was a terrible shock for me. I hated
     the unnecessary brutality. Women and children being killed, terrified,
     huddling in fear. Going around dropping bombs on women and children.
     What the hell is wrong with us? I thought that perhaps I had put too much
     faith in the human race — you know, in the pictures I made. Maybe they
     were too much as things should be'. Also, Wolfe, *Frank Capra: A guide*, p. 6:
     'the carnage he witnessed during 1943 and 1944 led him to question the
     unambiguous argument for war he had so willingly and forcefully presented
     in the *Why We Fight* series. No longer, he claims, could he argue for social
     causes with the same conviction or handle the pressures of film production
     with the same confidence'.
62   The critical and public reception afforded the film is explored in Jeanine
     Basinger, *The 'It's a Wonderful Life' Book*, London, 1987, an excellent
     account which reveals more of the rich documentation now housed in the
     Cinema Archives of Wesleyan University.

14
Class and Nation

Ships With Wings

It is a commonplace of film history that the two major changes in British cinema during the war were 'democratization' and 'documentarization', the pursuit of reality and realism in subject matter and visual style.

Michael Balcon's Ealing Studios was in the vanguard of this movement and their sober, earnest and authentic wartime films, like *San Demetrio London* (1943), *Went the Day Well?* (1942), *Nine Men* (1943) and *For Those in Peril* (1944) have earned the plaudits of film historians for being in tune with the mood of the times.

The received view of British wartime cinema was established as early as 1947 when Roger Manvell wrote that 'the war film discovered the common denominator of the British people'. Because everyone knew of the war at first hand, film producers were dealing with a 'psychologically aware audience'. They could not afford, even if they had wished to, to continue to use the war as material for melodrama. He pointed to 1942 as the turning-point in the emergence of a new populist documentary-style British cinema, to replace the outdated and class-bound melodrama of the early war years. The keynote of films between 1942 and 1945 was seen to be strict accuracy in the depiction of warfare, the highlighting of personal issues of 'comradeship, bravery, fear, tension, endurance, skill, boredom and hard work', the absence of blatant heroics, jingoistic self display, and the projection of a national image of reticence, wry humour and stolid determination.[1]

Manvell proposed a canon of quality British films which in pursuit of this ideal had succeeded in creating a peculiarly British cinematic poetry. Among war films, he singled out *In Which We Serve* (Two Cities, 1943), *The First of the Few* (GFD–British Aviation, 1942), *The Gentle Sex* (Two Cities, 1943), *Millions Like Us* (Gainsborough, 1943), *San Demetrio London*, *The Way Ahead* (Two Cities, 1944) and *The Way to the Stars* (Two Cities, 1945) and among non-war films, *The Stars Look Down*

(Grand National, 1939), *The Proud Valley* (Ealing, 1940), *Love on the Dole* (British National, 1941), *This Happy Breed* (Cineguild, 1944), *I Know Where I'm Going* (GFD Archers, 1945) and *Brief Encounter* (Cineguild, 1945). The common features of these films were realistic contemporary settings, ordinary people and emotional restraint.

Manvell's pantheon constituted just the sort of film productions that the Ministry of Information, overseer of British wartime cinema, required for propaganda purposes both at home and abroad. It was the Ministry which formulated and promoted the concept of the 'People's War' and encouraged the production of films dramatizing the role of the fighting and support services.[2] Even when the public were tiring of war films and the British Film Producers' Association made urgent representations to the Ministry, new instructions were issued which continued to stress realism and democracy:

> Realistic films about everyday life dealing with matters not directly about the war, but featuring events in various phases of life in factory, mines, on the land etc., are advocated by the Films Division of the M.o.I. Special support will be given to the production of such films. A balance between war and non-war propaganda is desirable, emphasis should be given to the positive virtues of British national characteristics and the democratic way of life.[3]

The pivotal film in effecting the transition at Ealing from 'outdated and class-bound' melodrama to the new democratic docu-drama was *Ships With Wings*, which was premiered in November 1941 and went on general release in January 1942. It has earned retrospective notoriety as the symbol of all that was wrong with British cinema in the early war years.

Charles Barr, in his seminal study on Ealing films, followed Manvell in pointing to 1942 as a watershed year.

> Most of the British war films which are now remembered date from 1942 or later.

He saw this change as reflecting a process which was going on at many levels in the official conduct of the war, in the place found for the commercial cinema within this, in the whole war experience of the nation — as well as in the workings of Ealing itself. For Barr, Ealing war films represent a 'broad congruency' between Ealing and the 'national community'.[4]

Writing specifically about *Ships With Wings*, he pointed to the notorious early wartime slogan: 'Your Courage, Your Cheerfulness, Your Resolution, Will Bring Us Victory':

The distinction between leaders and led is inscribed into the syntax, as it is into the dramatic syntax of *Convoy* and *Ships With Wings*. The latter, and later, film, acts as a *reductio ad absurdum* of this desire for unity, showing that if there is no deeper structural change, it means simply accepting *these* officers, these conventions of behaviour (as of drama) — the whole package which in the earlier films has been perceived as moribund. All the embarrassing elements in *Convoy* are doubled: the heroics are more unlikely, the men more deferential, the enemy more caricatured. By the time of its release things had changed too much, both outside the studio and inside, for it to be seen as anything but anachronistic. One can't separate the content of *Ships With Wings* — the picture it offers of England at war — from its dramatic form and the orientation of those who made it. The whole effort is a theatrical one, belonging to the West End theatre and to a national cinema which had never decisively broken with it: this tradition encompasses its acting style, its dramatic conventions, its class assumptions and its implicit audience.[5]

Viewed today *Ships With Wings*, directed by Sergei Nolbandov from a script by Nolbandov, Patrick Kirwan, Austin Melford and Diana Morgan, does indeed look a romanticized and highly artificial tribute to the Fleet Air Arm, which despite documentary sequences shot aboard HMS *Ark Royal*, tells a story in the full-blooded imperial melodrama tradition of A. E. W. Mason's pre-First World War classic, *The Four Feathers* (United Artists, 1939). A reckless, daredevil pilot (John Clements) is cashiered from the Fleet Air Arm for causing the death of the heroine's younger brother in a crash. He goes into exile, flying charter planes in the Mediterranean. When the war breaks out, he redeems himself by flying a suicide mission and destroying a dam on an Italian-held island. The heroine Celia (Jane Baxter), daughter of the Admiral, chooses as her mate the airman who knows the meaning of discipline, quiet, pipe-smoking Michael Wilding. Their curly-haired son is trained to say 'aye, aye, sir' in anticipation of the time when he will follow his father and grandfather into the service. With John Clements reprising his *Four Feathers* role and knocking out a German with the line, 'Get up you filthy Hun, I want to hit you again', with Leslie Banks (the erstwhile *Sanders of the River*) playing the Admiral, with phlegmatic officers, stiff-upper lip ladies and foreigners who are either comic (Italians, Greeks) or sinister (Germans), it is four square in the heroic tradition mastered by Korda in the 1930s. Quite apart from this, it is replete with a host of the most obvious model shots of ships, planes, even the island, which create an indelible aura of phoniness.

But the question that Barr does not address is how did *Ships With Wings* look in 1942 and what did audiences make of it. In general, reviews were highly favourable: '*Ships With Wings* I think the greatest propaganda and recruiting film produced since *Target for Tonight* (Crown Film Unit, 1941). It is a real inspiration to every fit man with an ounce of spirit in his

The officer corps court the Admiral's daughter (Leslie Banks, Jane Baxter, Michael Wilding, John Clements and Michael Rennie).

make-up' (*Empire News*); 'Full marks to Michael Balcon and the Ealing Studio for a patriotic spectacle, guaranteed to provide a thrill wherever the English tongue is spoken' (*Daily Mirror*); 'These graphic scenes are a valuable contribution to national self-pride' (*Daily Express*); 'as a thriller this more than makes the grade' (*Reynolds' News*); 'an aerial thriller of titanic size' (*Sunday Express*); 'a thrilling, brilliantly effected presentation of a British aircraft carrier on her job — a credit to British film production' (*Daily Telegraph*). Many of them pointed to the *Ark Royal* as 'the real heroine of the film' and expressed admiration for the documentary sequences.[6] Indeed the film was given added topicality and poignancy by the sinking of the *Ark Royal*, which made headline news on 15 November 1941.

But it was the reception of the film in certain influential quarters that caused Michael Balcon to re-think his production policy. The first problem the film encountered was from no less a figure than the Prime Minister. Winston Churchill intervened in film matters several times during the war.[7] On this occasion, having had the film run for him privately, he decided that the climactic action sequence was a disaster for the Fleet Air Arm and would cause alarm and despondency. He wanted the picture withdrawn. 'This was not only a terrible blow to our pride but also to our pockets, as the film represented a substantial investment', recalled Balcon in his autobiography.[8] Ealing interceded with the Prime Minister who agreed to leave the final decision to the First Sea Lord, Admiral Sir Dudley Pound. Pound viewed the film and passed it for release, and Vice-Admiral Sir William Whitworth was reported as saying that 'it made me feel I wanted to jump into an aeroplane and have a go at the Hun'.[9] The film was released but Churchill's opposition had shaken Balcon:

> Although I was personally convinced that the approach must be realistic, I am afraid that in this instance, there was some departure from that principle, and the story was too heavily fictionalized . . . Looking back on this incident now, I can understand the Prime Minister's attitude. It was, I am sure, not only the climactic disaster to which he objected; he had detected in the subject matter a certain lack of authenticity.[10]

It is in fact unlikely that Churchill was concerned about the lack of authenticity. Notoriously sentimental, his favourite film was Korda's Hollywood production of *Lady Hamilton* (United Artists-Korda, 1940), which he ran frequently during the war, always ending up in tears. His concern was almost certainly just what he said it was, anxiety about the scale of the Fleet Air Arm losses in the climax. He was similarly concerned later about the excessive number of English dead shown in *The Next of Kin* (Ealing, 1942). The naval officers who viewed the film seem also to have been unaffected by any apparent lack of authenticity.

Balcon seems to be attributing to Churchill the hostile views about *Ships With Wings* that appeared in the high brow press, which was distinctly less enthusiastic about the film than the popular papers. *The Times*, while admiring the *Ark Royal* sequences, thought that 'in the callow stages of the story there is a good deal of dialogue that is so self-consciously the dialogue of admiral's daughters and dashing lieutenants of the Fleet Air Arm that it recalls the ecstatic chorus of the undergraduates in *Old Heidelberg*: "It's May; we are young; and this is Heidelberg"'.[11] C. A. Lejeune in *The Observer*, sending the whole thing up, suggested it should be set to music with the subtitle 'All for an Admiral's daughter'.[12] William Whitebait excoriated it in *The New Statesman* as 'a throwback in English films':

The characters in this drama . . . are beautifully stage-English, so much so that after a while not only their gestures and accents but the words they utter can be anticipated . . . We don't believe in any of the characters . . . Even the thrills don't thrill us to the point that we can forget that we are looking at well constructed miniatures in a studio. The only genuine part, as far as I was concerned, was the aircraft carrier (life-size and actual) . . . I am not, let me add, scornful of Boys Own Paper stories about the war as such (*Pimpernel Smith* came off) but *Ships With Wings* seems to me bad Boys Own.[13]

What stung Balcon was the full frontal assault on the film in *The Daily Mail*. Film critic Seton Margrave had reviewed the picture favourably on 7 November 1941, but following the sinking of the *Ark Royal*, *The Daily Mail* published a longer piece by battle-hardened war correspondent Noel Monks, newly returned from the Middle East. It was headed 'This film should be scrapped'.

You would imagine that, with a ship of such world renown as HMS Ark Royal as the central 'character', the British film industry would have sailed in and produced an epic worthy of the ship, the film industry and the Gallant Service represented, the Air Arm of the Royal Navy. Instead all three have been well and truly scuppered.[14]

He went on to criticize the depiction of naval procedure, to denounce the story ('slush') and to compare the film unfavourably with *Target for Tonight*, 'one of the best war pictures produced in Britain. That was real. The men in it were real. The story was real'. Balcon recalled:

I was so upset by this review that I asked Monks to come and lunch with me at the studio and after a set-to lasting an hour or so I saw the validity of his view and reconciled myself to it — up to a point.[15]

Balcon was also upset by a highly critical editorial in *Documentary News Letter*, which expressed mystification at 'the hysterical praise' accorded to the film by 'certain sections of the press', with one national daily finding room, at a time of paper shortage, to serialize the story, and the editor of another suggesting that high-ranking naval officers be released from their normal duties to speak in cinemas showing the film and so assist naval recruiting.

This is a film which on no conceivable basis of criticism can be accepted as anything better than a very ordinary little screen novelette with topical references . . . The propaganda line of the film would be more appropriate to a Ruritanian campaign than to the Second World War . . . It was a pity that the 'Ark Royal' was allowed to become involved in what seems to be a pretty cheap business. Films of this kind should not be made in war time.[16]

HMS Ark Royal, *the 'hero' of* Ships With Wings.

He may also have seen a fourth leader in *The Times*, expressing disquiet about the image of England conveyed in films, in terms which suggested that the writer had *Ships With Wings* in mind. It suggested that the image was likely to irritate or mislead our allies, while in no way deceiving our enemies:

> The portrait in the making promises to be thoroughly unsatisfactory . . . The characters who compose its features . . . belong to the kind of romance which may fitly culminate in the Flag Lieutenant marrying the Admiral's pretty daughter; the Admiral marrying the midshipman's amusing mother; and the harum scarum airman contenting himself with the glory of having saved all their lives at the last possible moment . . . They are in fact out of the puppet box marked 'service romance' which stands in every film studio . . . It cannot work well now that real ships, real tanks and real bombing planes, manned not by actors but by serving sailors, soldiers and airmen, have entered upon the scene to carry whatever romantic story has been started to a thrilling, realistic conclusion.[17]

It went on to compare such films unfavourably with *Target for Tonight* and *Forty-Ninth Parallel* (GFD-Ortus, 1941). The recurrent refrain in all the criticism was the need for greater realism.

The criticism was strong enough to prompt Balcon to commission Tom Harrisson of Mass-Observation to report on the showings of *Ships With Wings* and ascertain its propaganda value.[18] Harrisson was also working for Admiral John Godfrey, Director of Naval Intelligence, and decided to do special samples of the reaction of naval wives to the film, as the Admiralty was worried about their morale.[19] Mass-Observation prepared no less than four detailed reports, giving us a valuable record of the immediate reactions of audiences to this key wartime film.[20] The questions that the observers asked were first, what the individual audience member thought of the film, then, what they specifically liked or disliked about it, and finally, what the film made them feel about the navy.

The final Mass-Observation report, dated 21 April 1942, summarised the results of the investigations made in London, Edinburgh, Glasgow, Cardiff, Birmingham, Cheltenham, Bournemouth, Rochester, Chatham and Portsmouth. Their conclusion was unequivocal:

> In all the areas investigated, with both sexes and all classes and ages, this film has had an overwhelmingly good reception, and aroused a large amount of interest. Of the total sample, just under nine people in ten expressed some liking for the film, and six people out of ten stated that they liked the film particularly much, or used other very praising terms. A slightly larger proportion of women than men liked this film, and women were decidedly more praising in their comment on the film than men.

M-O concluded that 84 per cent of men, 90 per cent of women, 87 per cent of both sexes, were favourable to the film. There was a slight difference in reaction noted between the four different areas studied. Eighty-two per cent were favourable to the film in London, 85 per cent favourable in the merchant ports, 88 per cent in inland areas and 93 per cent in naval ports. The greatest approval then came from those areas which had the closest links with the Navy and the most intimate knowledge of naval personnel, affairs and procedures.

Indeed, in Harrisson's special area of interest, the naval wives, there was an even more affirmative return. Ninety-nine per cent of women in naval ports liked the film.

Mass-Observation found a 'small but definite and consistent class difference' as regards liking the film. The better-off were not quite as impressed by the film as the less-well-off.

Thus, 81 per cent of class AB liked the film, 89 per cent of class C and 90 per cent of class D. They also found that the younger age group approved of the film slightly more than the older generation: 89 per cent of under 35s liked it, 85 per cent of over 40s. It is interesting then that the greatest approval came from women, the young and the working class, the most committed and regular cinemagoers, those likely to have been most conditioned to the generic conventions of naval melodrama. Even so, the differences in approval are small and Mass-Observation justly concluded: 'From the above figures it will be seen how very widely the film appealed, and though there are small differences in sex, class and age, it can be stated that the film appealed to all to a very large extent'.

The report broke down the audience approval into three distinct kinds: those wo approved of the film generally, those who approved very much and those who qualified their approval. They found that there was a definite geographical split when it came to enthusiasm. Forty-nine per cent of London people liked the film very much, 53 per cent of merchant port people, 70 per cent of inland people and 73 per cent of naval port people. The most often mentioned points were the good photography, the good acting and the production of the picture. Mass-Observation concluded:

> The great mass of approval was emotional and not at all deeply thought out. The film appealed directly to people's feelings, the men were presented in a heroic setting and were made to perform heroic feats, and this went straight to the public's heart. People especially who had relations or friends in the Navy or in the Fleet Air Arm were interested and touched by the film.

Compared with this overwhelming sense of approval, Mass-Observation uncovered little unfavourable comment on the film. Only slightly over one person in ten of the whole sample was critical in any way. Men were more critical than women 'as is usual in this type of investigation'. The better off were rather more critical than the less well off: 19 per cent of class AB, 11 per cent of class C, 8 per cent of class D. The older age group were slightly more critical than the younger. Points of criticism included the length of the film, the acting, the love story, the model work, the obviousness of the propaganda. The film was several times compared to its disadvantage with *The Lion Has Wings* (United Artists-London Films, 1939), *Convoy* (Ealing, 1940) and *Target for Tonight*. But Mass-Observation concluded:

> There was really little tangible dislike of the film. Those people who seriously thought about the film when coming out of the cinema mostly felt vaguely that there was something wrong with the picture, but often found it difficult to express themselves in so many words . . . It thus seems that the major feeling of dislike and criticism was one concerned with the unreality of the way the film treated the Navy, and some who had gone for the purpose of finding out what the Navy was doing came away, feeling that they had seen just another fairy-tale.

Turning to the film's role as naval propaganda, Mass-Observation found that the film was shown against a background of general approval for the Navy, again slightly less in the AB classes (73 per cent) than the D classes (79 per cent).

> In a large number of people emotions and feeling were evoked *by seeing this film*. Pride in the Navy is mentioned by several; some people said the film made them more thoughtful than they had hitherto been about the Navy . . . Men and particularly young men, after seeing the film *felt that they would like to join the Navy*.

They found very little criticism of the Navy or the treatment of the Navy in the film.

The overwhelming evidence then is of approval of the film. Mass-Observation concluded:

> After studying the reactions of the people all over the country in all sorts of cinemas, after interviewing people who know nothing about the Navy, have brothers or husbands or sons in the Navy, and after interviewing men who are sailors themselves or have spent a lifetime on the seas, we come to the conclusion that the film has been a great success among all sections and classes of people. Nearly nine people in ten liked this film in some way. When we compare this figure to other figures obtained at previous investigation, this is an exceptional standard. The film appealed to a wide public and only the minority of 'sophisticated sections' of the population approved of it slightly less or criticised it.

Despite this conclusion, Mass-Observation went into some detail in their conclusion into the objections of the film's critics, which it saw as lack of realism. But having rounded up the points of criticism, it concluded:

> People did not notice them very much . . . They go to the cinema to be entertained, not to be educated. *Ships With Wings* entertained; it did not apparently educate. The film, therefore, was able to carry people along with it, over the logical bumps.

It did not educate, they thought, because,

> Many of the people who came to see this film, came *because* they liked the Navy and had an interest in it. The film, therefore, preached mostly to the already converted, and though it is likely that it succeeded in increasing people's admiration for the Senior Service, this tendency was not strong.

Kinematograph Weekly's record of the year's cinema success confirms the Mass-Observation survey analysis. *Ships With Wings* was the second most popular national attraction during the first month of its general release, outgrossed only by the Deanna Durbin musical *It Started with Eve* (Universal, 1943). It is also worth noting in this context that the public had also flocked to *The Lion Has Wings* in 1939 and *Convoy* in 1940, films with the same or similar 'faults' as *Ships With Wings*. *The Lion Has Wings* was one of the three top British box office successes of

1939 (the others being *The Citadel* (MGM, 1939) and *Pygmalion* (GFD, 1939). This may be explained in part by its novelty as the first film of the war. But the top British box office success of 1940 was *Convoy*, which had a story not dissimilar to *Ships With Wings*, with Clive Brook taking his ship into action against fearful odds and raffish cad (John Clements), who had previously run off with the captain's wife, redeeming himself in a heroic death. The 'other ranks' were cheerful 'gorblimey' cockney stereotypes.

What is striking about this evidence and the Mass-Observation report is not the criticism, which came from an educated minority, but the overwhelming approval accorded to the film. This suggests that the popular press was mirroring audience opinion far better than the high brow press. Conspicuously absent from the audience's comments are those criticisms which have attached to the film retrospectively, that it was the quintessence of outdated class-bound heroics and that it was full of fakery and unreality. The first Mass-Observation report on the film, based on a showing at the Gaumont Cinema, Haymarket, in London, included a technical note:

> The authors of this report have visited a great many films in the course of their film studies, and never remember seeing one so technically crude as *Ships With Wings*. The island in the middle of the Mediterranean was so obviously model, and all the sequences of the bombing of the town and blowing up of a dam were blatantly crude models.

This is exactly what strikes one when viewing the film today. Yet the final report noted: 'The alleged *faking* of some of the scenes was occasionally commented upon, though only people "in the know" seemed to have noticed this to any great extent'. Where *Ships With Wings* was criticized, it was compared unfavourably with *The Lion Has Wings* and *Convoy*, which contained sequences in exactly the same idiom of 'outdated, class-bound heroics'.

The Mass-Observation evidence suggests first that audiences accepted studio fakery, model-work and backdrops, on the one hand, and conventional class-based heroics, on the other, with much greater acquiescence than Charles Barr has allowed. Far from seeming anachronistic, it appeared urgent, timely and patriotic. It was after all what audiences were used to and what to an extent they had become conditioned to expect. Secondly, it suggests that there was no great audience demand for increased realism and particularly not during the darkest days of the war.

Yet despite this clear evidence of popular success, Balcon initiated a decisive shift away from melodrama and towards documentary realism. He recorded proudly in his autobiography: '*Ships With Wings* was our

The Italian-occupied cardboard island which is the target of the suicide mission.

last film that could attract this particular type of criticism because from then on we learned to snatch our stories from the headlines and they had the ring of truth'.[21] The evidence suggests that Balcon made this shift not on the basis of box-office returns but perhaps for three principal reasons. First, his strongly held and deeply felt patriotism was wounded by criticism from Winston Churchill, Noel Monks and *The Times*. The idea that unrealistic melodrama was damaging to the British cause would have carried great weight with him. Secondly, he desired artistic respectability and this was defined by such opinion leaders as *The Times, The Observer, The Documentary News Letter* and *The New Statesman* as lying in the realist aesthetic. Thirdly, the change may also betoken the radicalization of Ealing's personnel. Balcon recalled in 1974 of the Ealing staff:

> We were middle class people, brought up with middle class backgrounds and rather conventional educations. Though we were radical in our points of view, we did not want to tear down institutions . . . We were people of the immediate post-war generation and we voted Labour for the first time after the war; this was our mild revolution.[22]

This radicalism took the form of placing ordinary people at the forefront of film action rather than the officers and gentlemen of *Convoy* and *Ships With Wings*. It also saw the filming of J. B. Priestley's Utopian stage fantasy, *They Came to a City* (1944), which looked towards the post-war Socialist Jerusalem.

It is a singular fact, however, that after Balcon's change of direction, no Ealing film with the sole exception of the supernatural drama *Dead of Night* featured in *Kine Weekly*'s yearly round-up of top box-office successes. Few of the highly praised Launder and Gilliat films did well either, *Waterloo Road* (Gainsborough, 1944) being their most successful wartime film in box-office terms. There is in fact a clear disjuncture between what post-war and particularly post-1960s critics have seen as the key films of the Second World War and what audiences were going to see.

If you look at the British cinema solely from the viewpoint of box-office popularity, you get a rather different picture than the one provided by historians and critics. The popular successes are sometimes strikingly different from the retrospectively recalled critical successes. The top British box-office attractions during the war years were *Convoy* (1940), *Forty-Ninth Parallel* (1941), *The First of the Few* (1942), *In Which We Serve* (1943), *This Happy Breed* (1944), and *The Seventh Veil* (GFD-Ortus, 1945), with *The Wicked Lady* topping the poll in 1946. The top American attractions at the box-office during the war, with their British release dates, were *Rebecca* (United Artists-Selznick, 1940), *The Great Dictator* (United Artists, 1941), *Mrs Miniver* (MGM, 1942), *Random Harvest* (MGM, 1943), *For Whom the Bell Tolls* (Paramount, 1944). The 1945 winner is difficult to calculate because *Kine Weekly* changed its method of listing the titles. But *The Seventh Veil* in fact out-drew all the American films of the year. The evidence of star popularity confirms this pattern with the top British female star from 1943 to 1946 being Margaret Lockwood and the top male star from 1944 to 1947 being James Mason. This signals the triumph after 1943 not of Ealing realism but of Gainsborough melodrama and the desire to escape from the reality of the war in colourful sensationalism.

For audiences *then* the most memorable war films are not on the whole those which came after 1942 but those which came before. The British lists testify to the importance of both Leslie Howard and Noël Coward to the wartime cinema and to their popularity with the mass cinemagoing public. *Motion Picture Herald* records Leslie Howard rising from nineteenth most popular British star in 1940 to second most popular in 1942. *Kinematograph Weekly* puts him first in 1941 and 1942. The film he directed in 1941, *Pimpernel Smith* (British National, 1941), was runner up to *Forty-Ninth Parallel*, in which he also starred, as the top British box-office success of the year. *The First of the Few*, which he

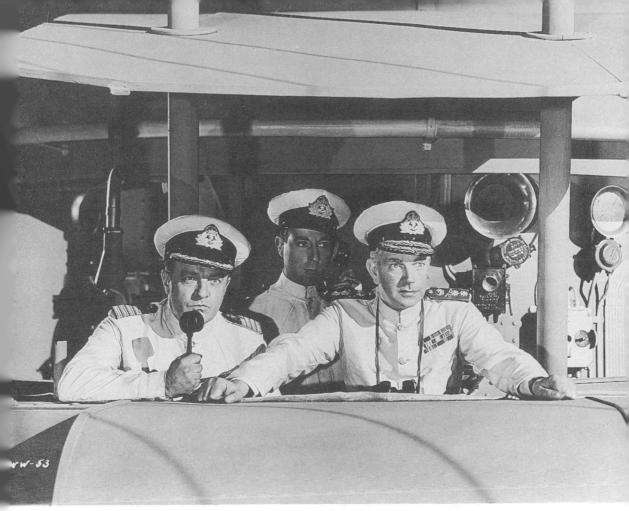

Heroic British officers on the bridge (Basil Sydney and Leslie Banks).

directed and starred in, was the top British film of 1942. This all suggests that the gentlemanly idealist which Howard incarnated on screen was an image with which the British audiences willingly identified in the early part of the war. There is certainly no evidence of audience dissatisfaction with gentleman heroes.

This acceptance of the gentleman hero links with the success of *Convoy* and *Ships With Wings*. When audiences do turn to a film about ordinary people at war, it is to Noël Coward's *In Which We Serve*, a film with a gentleman hero but one depicted within the context of a sympathetically evoked cross-class consensual effort. Latter-day disparagement of the film as patronizing and class-ridden should not blind us to its contemporary impact. Dilys Powell wrote of it:

The emotional impact of *In Which We Serve* was immense. The experiences of civilian and fighting men were presented as essentially one, bound together by ties of human love and devotion; but nobody felt that he had a stake in this drama . . . Noel Coward in *In Which We Serve* took a handful of typically British men and women and made from their stories, ordinary enough in themselves a distillation of national character.[23]

Even *The Documentary News Letter*, scourge of the inauthentic, declared: 'This is an exceptionally sincere and deeply moving film . . . And it is one of the best war films ever made'.[24] The success of *In Which We Serve* was followed by that of *This Happy Breed*, Coward's play about a lower-middle-class family in Clapham between the wars, filmed in Technicolor by David Lean. It is clear that Coward touched a chord in audiences, which latter-day commentators have been unable to appreciate.

Equally interesting is the success of *Mrs Miniver* and *Random Harvest*, set in Britain but made in Hollywood. Dismissed by some critics as false and artificial romances, they were clearly much appreciated by wartime audiences. The critic of *The Documentary News Letter* wrote with scarcely concealed disbelief of the reception of *Mrs Miniver*: 'You can sit at the Empire and hear practically the whole house weeping — a British audience with three years of war behind it, crying at one of the phoniest war films that has ever been made'.[25] But the combination of Greer Garson and Walter Pidgeon, an idealized middle-class England, an essentially noble picture of genteel suffering and patriotic endeavour was genuinely uplifting and 'a good cry' has always been therapeutic.

So if we leave on one side artistic and critical criteria and go on what the public wanted as manifested by paying its money at the box-office, certain trends are discernible in wartime cinema. First, there is continuity between the pre-war cinema and the wartime cinema. In the darkest days of the war, the people flocked to see comedy films starring George Formby, top British male box-office attraction from 1937 to 1943 according to *Motion Picture Herald*, and serious dramas starring gentlemen heroes like Leslie Howard, very much as they had done before the war. They were keen to see films about the war, hence the success of *Convoy, Forty-Ninth Parallel, Mrs Miniver, In Which We Serve*. But after 1942 to 1943, they were much less interested in seeing films about the war, realistic or otherwise. W. J. Speakman, former president of the Cinematograph Exhibitors Association, told a BFI conference in 1944 that war films were definitely on the way out:

The early ones, *The Foreman Went to France, Mr. Pimpernel Smith* (sic) etc. were in most cases completely successful, but the later ones, *One of Our Aircraft is Missing* etc., were a more doubtful proposition, and the latest ones still, *San Demetrio-London* etc. were definite failures. It is of course quite obvious that the public are war-weary, and in reaction from the war itself infinitely prefer to see something escapist.[26]

The public, however, was also willing to accept films like *Convoy, Ships With Wings, Mrs Miniver, Random Harvest* and *In Which We Serve*, which celebrate the class system, perpetuate the division between officers and other ranks and are by the standards of progressives backward looking. What critics dismissive of these films have failed to appreciate about them is the context in which they were shown: a country fighting for its existence against a monstrous evil, a time of heightened national consciousness and of increased sympathies between classes and individuals. Films like these succeeded because they were patriotic, like the people, but unlike the intelligentsia, as Orwell was fond of pointing out. They have dramatic stories and they have stars, two of the public's most cherished requirements in their films. The role of stars is crucial. Michael Balcon was complaining in 1941 about star-starvation in the British cinema.[27] He reckoned that there were only 5 top-flight leading British actors (Leslie Banks, Robert Donat, Leslie Howard, John Clements and Clive Brook), and companies were fighting each other to gain their services. In this context, it is worth noting that *Ships With Wings* starred both Clements and Banks. Gainsborough's success was partly due to the fact that they launched a whole new raft of British stars, headed by James Mason, Stewart Granger, Margaret Lockwood, Phyllis Calvert and Patricia Roc. Ealing, however, in their later films prided themselves on doing without stars and the results can be seen at the box-office.

The successful films from *Convoy* to *In Which We Serve* showed the British character at its best, decent, gallant, restrained, good-humoured. They showed people pulling together, regardless of class, both at home and in the services. They employed dramatic conventions and studio-settings that were accepted and understood. Whatever the falseness and artificiality that later commentators observed and whatever perceptions and attitudes to class and the class system they imported and imposed, the public felt these films to be emotionally true and that is more important with a mass audience than intellectual or academic truth.

There is no doubt that films came increasingly to use realistic settings and to spotlight ordinary people as the war went on. But this is not the whole picture of wartime cinema and needs to be modified. Realism in setting and character was a deliberate policy prescribed for the industry by the Ministry of Information, encouraged by the influential critics and opinion-formers of the high brow press, the documentary movement and the native film culture and willingly introduced by patriotic film-makers like Balcon. But realism was not an automatic guarantee of box-office success. Documentaries like *Target for Tonight* and *Desert Victory* were nationwide successes, and so were Noël Coward's films about ordinary people, *In Which We Serve* and *This Happy Breed*, though it is worth noting that the latter film also boasted Technicolor and a full complement

German tyranny (Edward Chapman and Frank Pettingell).

of stars. *Love on the Dole*, on the other hand, was not a box-office success and Ealing's realistic films never attained either the popularity of Gainsborough's melodramas or Ealing's own early wartime films, particularly their George Formby comedies and service dramas *Convoy* and *Ships With Wings*.[28] It is interesting to note that Julian Poole's study of audience preference in one Macclesfield cinema during the war confirms many of these national trends at a local level.[29]

To restore perspective to the analysis of British wartime cinema, it is important to acknowledge that many of the critically most prized films were often box-office failures and that the audiences cherished still Hollywood's roseate view of Britain and British society. The key to understanding the success of films, during the war may well lie in George Orwell's perception that England resembled 'a family, a rather stuffy Victorian family, with not many black sheep in it but with all its cupboards bursting with skeletons . . . It has its private language and its common memories and at the approach of an enemy it closes its ranks'.[30] It is this feeling which perhaps explains the success of *Ships With Wings*, with its black sheep making good, and of *In Which We Serve*, perfect exemplar of the nation as family. It also suggests a greater degree of underlying conservatism than is sometimes given credit for.

The nature of the change effected in Britain by the Second World War is much debated. On the one hand, Arthur Marwick and Paul Addison argue for substantial change; on the other, Angus Calder and Henry Pelling for comparatively little.[31] The problem should perhaps be viewed on two levels, which we can loosely call political and social. There certainly emerged a new political consensus based on plans for a welfare state; the circle of power was widened to include left wing intellectuals and trade unions. Greater dignity was bestowed on ordinary folk and the end of the war saw a Labour victory. There was substantial political change: the radicalization of important sections of the working and middle classes who voted Labour for the first time in 1945, the introduction of the welfare state, independence for India, the nationalization of staple industries. But there was considerably less social and cultural change. The House of Lords, the public schools and the monarchy survived. Society continued to be to a large degree deferential. The class system remained intact. As James E. Cronin noted:

> The political triumph of Labour was . . . accompanied by a consolidation of working class culture and ways of life. The war, such a powerful solvent of political allegiances, disturbed merely the surface of social relations and allowed the enduring structures of society to reassert themselves powerfully after the war.[32]

Perhaps what the war did was to create a greater degree of sympathy between the classes, more social mixing, the desire to recognize and fulfill the legitimate aspirations of ordinary people. This is what Orwell saw happening in 1944:

> We are not justified in assuming that class distinctions are actually disappearing. The essential structure of England is still almost what it was in the nineteenth century. But real differences between man and man are obviously diminishing and this fact is grasped and even welcomed by people who only a few years ago were clinging desperately to their social prestige.[33]

But for real social and cultural change we have to wait until the 1960s when British society and British cultural values underwent the sort of sea change they did not experience in the 1940s.[34] It is this distinction between political change and social conservatism that Anthony Howard evidently had in mind when he observed: '1945 saw the greatest restoration of traditional social values since 1660'.[35] This, I suggest, is what the audience preference in films tells us, that for all the very real desire for the implementation of the Beveridge Report and for full employment and better housing after the war, there was also an acceptance of the class system, traditional social structures and long established cultural values. 'Tell me what you like,' said John Ruskin, 'And I'll tell you what you are.' British wartime cinema audiences liked *Mrs Miniver, In Which We Serve* and *Ships With Wings*.

NOTES

1   Roger Manvell, *Twenty Five Years of British Films 1925—45*, London, 1947, pp. 84—5.
2   On the Ministry of Information and its wartime policies and campaigns, see Ian McLaine, *Ministry of Morale*, London, 1979.
3   The actual instructions have not survived in the MoI records in the Public Record Office but are summarized in *Kinematograph Weekly*, 30 July 1942.
4   Charles Barr, *Ealing Studios*, London, 1977, p. 13.
5   Barr, *Ealing Studios*, p. 26.
6   These reviews are collected in Mass-Observation File Report 967, 17 November 1941.
7   For Churchill's intervention in *The Life and Death of Colonel Blimp* see Ian Christie (ed.), *Powell, Pressburger and Others*, London, 1978, pp. 105—20 and Jeffrey Richards and Anthony Aldgate, *Best of British: cinema and society 1930—70*, Oxford, 1983, pp. 61—74; for his intervention in *The Next of Kin* see Jeffrey Richards, *Thorold Dickinson: the man and his films*, London, 1986, p. 101.
8   Michael Balcon, *A Lifetime of Films*, London, 1969, p. 133.
9   *Daily Mail*, 7 November 1941.
10 Balcon, *A Lifetime of Films*, p. 133.
11 *The Times*, 10 November 1941.
12 *The Observer*, 9 November 1941.
13 *New Statesman*, 15 November 1941.
14 *Daily Mail*, 20 November 1941.
15 Balcon, *A Lifetime of Films*, p. 134.
16 *Documentary News Letter* 2, December 1941, p. 221. It was the *News Chronicle* which serialized the story and the *Daily Express* which called for naval officers to speak in cinemas showing the film. Balcon refers to the DNL in his article, 'Propaganda and the Feature Producer', *The Ciné-Technician* 8, February—March 1942, pp. 4—5.
17 *The Times*, 18 May 1942.
18 Balcon, 'Propaganda and the Feature Producer', pp. 4—5.
19 Nicholas Pronay and D. W. Spring (eds), *Propaganda, Politics and Film 1918—45*, London, 1982, p. 242.
20 Mass-Observation File Reports 967, 17 November 1941; 1059, 28 January 1942; 1204, 12 April 1942; and 1218, 21 April 1942. The final M-O report, summarizing the previous three, is printed in Jeffrey Richards and Dorothy Sheridan (eds), *Mass-Observation at the Movies*, London, 1987, pp. 364—80.

21 Balcon, *A Lifetime of Films*, p. 134.
22 John Ellis, 'Made in Ealing', *Screen* 16, Spring 1975, p. 119.
23 Dilys Powell, *Films since 1939*, London, 1947, pp. 25—8.
24 *Documentary News Letter* 3, October 1942, pp. 143—4.
25 *Documentary News Letter* 3, August 1942, p. 112.
26 British Film Institute, *Film Appreciation and Visual Education*, London, 1944, p. 43.
27 *Daily Express*, 15 September 1941.
28 On *Love on the Dole* see BFI, *Film Appreciation and Visual Education*.
29 Julian Poole, 'British Cinema Attendance in Wartime: audience preference in a Macclesfield cinema 1939—46', *Historical Journal of Film, Radio and Television*, 7, 1987, pp. 15—34.
30 George Orwell, *Collected Essays, Journalism and Letters* 2, Harmondsworth, 1971, p. 88.
31 Arthur Marwick, *Britain in a century of Total War*, London, 1968, *War and Social Change in the 20th Century*, London, 1974, 'People's War and Top People's Peace?: British society and the Second World War', in Alan Sked and Chris Cook (eds), *Crisis and Controversy*, London, 1976, pp. 148—64; Paul Addison, *The Road to 1945*, London, 1977; Angus Calder, *The People's War*, London, 1971 and Henry Pelling, *Britain and the Second World War*, London, 1970.
32 James E. Cronin, *Labour and Society in Britain 1918—1979*, London, 1984, p. 137.
33 Orwell, *Collected Essays* 3, p. 39.
34 Jeremy Seabrook and Trevor Blackwell, *A World still to Win: the reconstruction of the post-war working class*, London, 1985; Arthur Marwick, *British Society since 1945*, London, 1982; Jeffrey Richards, 'The Hooligan Culture', *Encounter* 379, November 1985, pp. 15—23.
35 Michael Sissons and Philip French (eds), *The Age of Austerity*, London, 1983, p. 31.

Filmography

Let George Do It (1940)

Production company: Ealing Studios
Distributors: ABFD
Director: Marcel Varnel
Producer: Michael Balcon
Screenplay: John Dighton, Austin Melford, Angus MacPhail and Basil Dearden
Photographer: Ronald Neame
Editor: Ray Pitt
Art director: Wilfred Shingleton
Musical director: Ernest Irving
Songs: Harry Gifford, Fred Cliffe, Eddie Latta and George Formby
Cast: George Formby (George Hepplewhite), Phyllis Calvert (Mary Wilson), Garry Marsh (Mark Mendez), Romney Brent (Slim Selwyn), Bernard Lee (Oscar Nelson), Coral Browne (Iris), Diana Beaumont (Greta), Hal Gordon (Alf Arbuckle), Donald Calthrop (Frederick Strickland), Ian Fleming (Colonel Harcourt), Torin Thatcher (U Boat Commander), Bill Shine (Steward), Ian Wilson (Ted), Ronald Shiner (Musician)
Running time: 82 minutes

49th Parallel (1941)

US release title: The Invaders
Production company: Ortus
Distributors: GFD
Director: Michael Powell
Producer: Michael Powell and John Sutro
Screenplay: Emeric Pressburger
Dialogue: Rodney Ackland

Photographer: Frederick Young
Editor: David Lean
Art director: David Rawnsley
Music: Ralph Vaughan Williams
Cast: Laurence Olivier (Johnnie Barras), Anton Walbrook (Peter), Leslie
  Howard (Philip Armstrong Scott), Eric Portman (Lt Hirth), Raymond
  Massey (Andy Brock), Glynis Johns (Anna), Finlay Currie (Factor),
  Richard George (Commandant Bernstorff), Raymond Lovell (Lt
  Kuhnecke), Niall NacGinnis (Vogel), Peter Moore (Krantz), John
  Chandos (Lohrmann), Basil Appleby (Jahner), Charles Victor (Andreas),
  Frederick Piper (David), Eric Clavering (Art), Ley On (Nick), Charles
  Rolfe (Bob), Tawera Moana (George), Theodore Salt (US customs
  officer), O. W. Fonger (US customs officer)
Running time: 123 minutes

Pimpernel Smith (1941)

US release title: Mister V
Production company: British National
Distributors: Anglo-American Film Corporation
Director—producer: Leslie Howard
Screenplay: Anatole de Grunwald and Roland Pertwee (from a story by
  A. G. Macdonell and Wolfgang Wilhelm)
Photographer: Mutz Greenbaum
Supervising editor: Sidney Cole
Art director: Duncan Sutherland
Music: John Greenwood
Cast: Leslie Howard (Professor Horatio Smith), Mary Morris (Ludmilla
  Koslowski), Francis L. Sullivan (General von Graum), Hugh McDermott
  (David Maxwell), Raymond Huntley (Marx), Manning Whiley (Bertie
  Gregson), David Tomlinson (Steve), Peter Gawthorne (Sidimir
  Koslowski), Allan Jeayes (Dr Benckendorf), Denis Arundell (Hoffman),
  Philip Friend (Spencer), Joan Kemp-Welch (Schoolteacher), Lawrence
  Kitchin (Clarence Elstead), Basil Appleby (Jock McIntyre), Percy Walsh
  (Dvorak), Roland Pertwee (Sir George Smith), Charles Paton (Steinhof),
  Aubrey Mallalieu (The Dean), George Street (Schmidt), A. E. Matthews
  (Earl of Meadowbrook), Brian Herbert (Jaromir), Arthur Hambling
  (Jordan)
Running time: 121 minutes

Ships With Wings (1941)

Production company: Ealing Studios
Distributors: United Artists
Director: Sergei Nolbandov
Producer: Michael Balcon

Screenplay: Patrick Kirwan, Austin Melford, Diana Morgan and Sergei Nolbandov

Photographers: Mutz Greenbaum and Wilkie Cooper (interiors); Roy Kellino and Eric Cross (exteriors)

Editor: Robert Hamer

Art director: Wilfred Shingleton

Music: Geoffrey Wright

Cast: John Clements (Lt Dick Stacey), Leslie Banks (Vice-Admiral Wetherby), Michael Wilding (Lt David Grant), Michael Rennie (Lt Peter Maxwell), Jane Baxter (Celia Wetherby), Ann Todd (Kay Gordon), Hugh Burden (Lt Mickey Wetherby), Basil Sydney (Captain Fairfax), Hugh Williams (Oberleutnant Wagner), Edward Chapman (Papadopoulos), Betty Marsden (Jean), Frank Pettingell (Fields), Frank Cellier (General Scarappa), John Laurie (Lt Cmdr Reid), Cecil Parker (German Air Marshal), John Stuart (Commander Hood), Charles Victor (MacDermott), Morland Graham (CPO Marsden), Charles Stuart (Von Rittau)

Running time: 103 minutes

The Next of Kin (1942)

Production company: Ealing Studios

Distributors: United Artists

Director: Thorold Dickinson

Producer: Michael Balcon

Screenplay: Thorold Dickinson, Sir Basil Bartlett, Angus MacPhail and John Dighton

Photographer: Ernest Palmer

Editor: Ray Pitt

Art director: Tom Morahan

Music: William Walton

Cast: Mervyn Johns (Arthur Davis), Nova Pilbeam (Beppie Leemans), Stephen Murray (Ned Barratt), Reginald Tate (Major Richards), Geoffrey Hibbert (John), Philip Friend (Lt Cummings), Phyllis Stanley (Miss Clare), Mary Clare (Ma Webster, Joss Ambler (Mr Vernon), Basil Sydney (Naval Captain), Brefni O'Rourke (Brigadier), Alexander Field (Durnford), Jack Hawkins (Major Harcourt), Torin Thatcher (German General), David Hutcheson (Security Officer), Frederick Leister (Colonel), Charles Victor (Seaman), Frank Allenby (Wing Commander Kenton), Thora Hird (ATS Girl), John Williams (British Officer), Basil Radford and Naunton Wayne

Running time: 102 minutes

The Young Mr Pitt (1942)

Production company: Gainsborough Films
Distributors: 20th Century—Fox
Director: Carol Reed
Producer: Edward Black
Screenplay: Frank Launder and Sidney Gilliat (from a story by Viscount Castlerosse)
Photographer: Frederick Young
Art director: A. Vetchinsky
Music: Charles Williams
Dress designs and decor: Cecil Beaton
Cast: Robert Donat (William Pitt the Younger/the Earl of Chatham), Robert Morley (Charles James Fox), Phyllis Calvert (Eleanor Eden), John Mills (William Wilberforce), Raymond Lovell (King George III), Herbert Lom (Napoleon Bonaparte), Max Adrian (Richard Brinsley Sheridan), Felix Aylmer (Lord North), Albert Lieven (Talleyrand), Stephen Heggard (Lord Nelson), Geoffrey Atkins (Pitt as a boy), Jean Cadell (Mrs Sparry), Agnes Lauchlan (Queen Charlotte), Ian MacLean (Dundas), A. Bromley Davenport (Sir Evan Nepean), John Salew (Smith), Stuart Lindsell (Earl Spencer), Henry Hewitt (Henry Addington), Frederick Culley (Sir William Farquhar), Frank Pettingell (Coachman), Leslie Bradley (Gentleman Jackson), Hugh McDermott (Melvill), Roy Emerton (Dan Mendoza), Alfred Sangster (Lord Grenville), Margaret Vyner (Duchess of Devonshire), Austin Trevor (Registrar)
Running time: 118 minutes

Went the Day Well? (1942)

US release title: 48 Hours
Production company: Ealing Studios
Distributors: United Artists
Director: Alberto Cavalcanti
Producer: Michael Balcon
Screenplay: John Dighton, Diana Morgan and Angus MacPhail (from a story by Graham Greene)
Photographer: Wilkie Cooper
Editor: Sidney Cole
Art director: Tom Morahan
Music: William Walton
Cast: Leslie Banks (Oliver Wilsford), Basil Sydney (Major Ortler), Marie Lohr (Mrs Frazer), Frank Lawton (Tom Sturry), Elizabeth Allan (Peggy), Valerie Taylor (Nora), C. V. France (Vicar), Mervyn Johns (Sims), David Farrar (Jung), Harry Fowler (George Truscott), Norman Pierce

(Jim Sturry), Muriel George (Mrs Collins), Hilda Bayley (Cousin Maude), Johnny Schofield (PC Joe Garbett), Edward Rigby (Bill Purves), Thora Hird (Ivy Dorking), Patricia Hayes (Daisy), John Slater (Sergeant)
Running time: 92 minutes

In Which We Serve (1942)

Production company: Two Cities
Distributors: British Lion
Directors: Noël Coward and David Lean
Producer: Noël Coward
Screenplay and music: Noël Coward
Photographer: Ronald Neame
Editors: David Lean and Thelma Myers
Art director: David Rawnsley and Gladys Calthrop
Cast: Noël Coward (Captain Edward Kinross [Captain D]), Celia Johnson (Alix Kinross), John Mills (Shorty Blake), Bernard Miles (CPO Walter Hardy), Joyce Carey (Kath Hardy), Kay Walsh (Freda Lewis), Derek Elphinstone (Number One), Michael Wilding ('Flags'), Robert Sansom ('Guns'), Philip Friend ('Torps'), James Donald (Doctor), Ballard Berkeley (Engineer Commander), Chimmo Branson ('Snotty'), Kenneth Carten (Sub-Lieutenant), George Carney (Mr Blake), Kathleen Harrison (Mrs Blake), Wally Patch (Uncle Fred), Richard Attenborough (Young Stoker), Penelope Didley Ward (Maureen Fenwick), Hubert Gregg (Pilot), Frederick Piper (Edgecombe), Geoffrey Hibbert (AB Joey Mackridge), John Boxer (AB Hollett), Leslie Dwyer (Parkinson), Walter Fitzgerald (Colonel Lumsden), Gerald Case (Captain Jasper Fry), Dora Gregory (Mrs Lemmon), Daniel Massey (Bobby Kinross), Ann Stephens (Lavinia Kinross)
Running times: 115 minutes

Thunder Rock (1942)

Production company: Charter Films
Distributors: M-G-M
Director—editor: Roy Boulting
Producer: John Boulting
Screenplay: Jeffrey Dell and Bernard Miles (from the play by Robert Ardrey)
Photographer: Mutz Greenbaum
Art director: Duncan Sutherland
Music: Hans May
Cast: Michael Redgrave (David Charleston), Barbara Mullen (Ellen Kirby), James Mason (Streeter), Lilli Palmer (Melanie Kurtz), Finlay Currie (Captain Joshua Stuart), Frederick Valk (Dr Stefan Kurtz), Sybilla Binder (Anne-Marie Kurtz), Frederick Cooper (Ted Briggs), Barry Morse

(Robert), Jean Shephard (Milly Briggs), George Carney (Harry), Miles Malleson (Chairman), A. E. Matthews (Kirby), Olive Sloane (Newspaper Director), Brian Herbert (Flanning), James Pirrie (Pilot), Tommy Duggan (Clerk), Tony Quinn (Clerk), Harold Anstruther (British Consul), Victor Beaumont (Hans), Alfred Sangster (Director)
Running time: 111 minutes

Fires Were Started (1943)

Alternative title: I Was a Fireman
Production company: Crown Film Unit
Distributors: Ministry of Information/GFD
Director—screenplay: Humphrey Jennings
Story collaboration: Maurice Richardson
Producer: Ian Dalrymple
Photographer: C. M. Pennington-Richards
Editor: Stewart McAllister
Art director: Edward Carrick
Music: William Alwyn
Cast: Chief Officer George Gravett (Sub-Officer Dykes), Lt Fireman Philip Wilson-Dickson (Fireman Walters), Lt Fireman Fred Griffiths (Johnny Daniels), Lt Fireman Loris Rey ('Colonel' Rumbold), Fireman Johnny Houghton (Sidney 'Jacko' Jackson), Fireman T. P. Smith (B. A. Brown), Fireman John Barker (Joe Vallance), Fireman William Sansom (Bill Barrett), Assistant Group Officer Green (Mrs Townsend), Firewoman Betty Martin (Betty), Firewoman Eileen White (Eileen)
Running time: 75 minutes

Western Approaches (1944)

US release title: The Raider
Production company: Crown Film Unit
Distributors: Ministry of Information/British Lion
Director—screenplay: Pat Jackson
Producer: Ian Dalrymple
Photographer: Jack Cardiff
Editor: Pat Jackson
Music: Clifton Parker
Art direction: Edward Carrick
Colour: Technicolor
Colour control: Natalie Kalmus
Naval supervision: Captain Packenham, RN
Naval liaison: Lieutenant Lupino, RNVR, and Owen Rutter
Cast: Officers and men of the Allied navies and the merchant fleets.
Running time: 82 minutes

Tunisian Victory (1944)

Production company: British and American Service Film Units
Distributors: Ministry of Information/US Office of War Information
Director—producers: Lt Colonel Hugh Stewart, British Army Film Unit, and Col. Frank Capra, US Army Signal Corps
Commentary: J. L. Hodson and Captain Anthony Veiller
Original music: William Alwyn
Additional music: Dimitri Tiomkin
Narrators: Lt Colonel Leo Genn, British Army Film Unit, and Captain Anthony Veiller, US Army Signal Corps
Soldiers' voices: 'British Tommy' — Bernard Miles, 'American Doughboy' — Burgess Meredith
Production personnel:
   British Army Film Unit: Lt Col. Hugh Stewart; Captain Roy Boulting; Sgt Clark; Sgt Best; Sgt Anderson; Private Brown, ATS.
   US Army Signal Corps: Col. Frank Capra; Capt. John Huston; Lt William F. Claxton; Lt Merrill G. White; Captain Anthony Veiller; Sgt. Dunning.
   British Cameramen in Tunisia: Capt. H. W. Ringold; Capt. A. Black; Sgt J. A. West; Sgt H. M. Wilson; Sgt J. Radford; Sgt H. French; Sgt J. Huggett; Sgt D. Courtney; Sgts Penman and Colman.
Running time: 78 minutes

The Way to the Stars (1945)

US release title: Johnny in the Clouds
Production company: Two Cities Films
Distributors: United Artists
Director: Anthony Asquith
Producer: Anatole de Grunwald
Screenplay: Terence Rattigan (from a story by Terence Rattigan and Anatole de Grunwald based on a scenario by Terence Rattigan and Richard Sherman)
Photographer: Derek Williams
Art director: Paul Sheriff and Carmen Dillon
Editor: Fergus McDonnell
Music: Nicholas Brodsky
Cast: Michael Redgrave (David Archdale), John Mills (Peter Penrose), Rosamund John ('Toddy' Todd), Douglass Montgomery (Johnny Hollis), Renee Asherson (Iris Winterton), Stanley Holloway (Mr Palmer), Basil Radford ('Tiny' Williams), Felix Aylmer (Rev. Charles Moss), Bonar Colleano Jr (Joe Frizelli), Joyce Carey (Miss Winterton), Trevor Howard (Squadron Leader Carter), Tryon Nichol (Colonel Rogers), Bill Owen (Sgt 'Nobby' Clarke), Grant Miller (Wally Becker), Jean Simmons

(Singer), Johnnie Schofield (Jones), Charles Victor (Corporal Fitter), David Tomlinson ('Prune' Parsons), Hartley Power (Colonel Page), Vida Hope (Elsie), Hugh Dempster ('Tinker' Bell), Anthony Dawson (Bertie Steen), Murray Matheson (Joe Lawson), Charles Farrell (American Orderly)

Running time: 109 minutes

Index